WORLD WAR II
IN THE AIR

EUROPE

WORLD WAR II
IN THE AIR
EUROPE

EDITED BY

Colonel James F. Sunderman, U.S.A.F.

VNR VAN NOSTRAND REINHOLD COMPANY
NEW YORK   CINCINNATI   TORONTO   LONDON   MELBOURNE

First published in paperback in 1981
Copyright © 1963 by Litton Educational Publishing, Inc.
Library of Congress Catalog Card Number 80-13027
ISBN 0-442-20045-5

Van Nostrand Reinhold Company
A division of Litton Educational Publishing, Inc.
135 West 50th Street, New York, NY 10020

Van Nostrand Reinhold Ltd.
1410 Birchmount Road, Scarborough, Ontario M1P 2E7

Van Nostrand Reinhold Australia Pty. Ltd.
17 Queen Street, Mitcham, Victoria 3132

Van Nostrand Reinhold Company Ltd.
Molly Millars Lane, Wokingham, Berkshire, England RG11 2PY

Cloth edition published 1963 by Franklin Watts, Inc.

16 15 14 13 12 11 10 9 8 7 6 5 4 3 2 1

Library of Congress Cataloging in Publication Data

Sunderman, James F   ed.
    World War II in the air.

    Reprint of the 1962-63 ed. published by F. Watts,
New York, in series: The Watts aerospace library.
    Includes indexes.
    CONTENTS: [1] The Pacific.—[2] Europe.
    1. World War, 1939-1945—Aerial operations—
Addresses, essays, lectures. I. Title.
[D785.S9 1981]   940.54′49   80-13027
ISBN 0-442-20044-7 (v. 1)
ISBN 0-442-20045-5 (v. 2)

ACKNOWLEDGMENTS

The selections in this book are used by permission and special arrangements with the proprietors of their respective copyrights who are listed below. The editor's and publisher's thanks to all who made this collection possible.

The editor and publisher have made every effort to trace the ownership of all material contained herein. It is their belief that the necessary permissions from publishers, authors, and authorized agents have been obtained in all cases. In the event of any questions arising as to the use of any material, the editor and publisher express regret for any error unconsciously made and will be pleased to make the necessary correction in future editions of this book.

Putnam and Co., Ltd., for "Twilight in Norway: The RAF At Bay" by Peter Wykeham. This selection is from the book FIGHTER COMMAND by Peter Wykeham. Copyright 1960 by the author. Reprinted by permission of the publishers.

Souvenir Press for "Dunkirk: Victory within Deliverance" by Alexander McKee. This selection is from the book STRIKE FROM THE SKY by Alexander McKee. Copyright 1960 by the author. Reprinted by permission of the publishers.

E. P. Dutton & Co. for "War Over Britain" by Ivor Halstead. This selection is from the book WINGS OF VICTORY by Ivor Halstead. Copyright 1941 by the publishers. Reprinted by permission of the publishers.

Reynal and Hitchcock, Inc. for "Of Death in the Sky" by Richard Hillary. This selection is from the book FALLING THROUGH SPACE by Richard Hillary. Copyright 1942 by Reynal and Hitchcock. Reprinted by permission of Harcourt, Brace & World, Inc.

Random House, Inc. for "Fighting Talk: Tactics of Aerial Warfare" by Group Capt. J. E. Johnson. This selection is from the book

WING LEADER by Group Capt. J. E. Johnson, RAF. Copyright 1956 by the publishers. Reprinted by permission.

Holt, Rinehart and Winston, Inc. for "Dawn Attack on Russia" by Heinz Knoke. This selection is from the book I FLEW FOR THE FÜHRER by Heinz Knoke. Translated by John Ewing. Copyright 1953, 1954 by Heinz Knoke. Reprinted by permission of the publishers.

Simon and Schuster, Inc. for "Rule Books Are Paper" by Ernest K. Gann. This selection is from the book FATE IS THE HUNTER by Ernest K. Gann. Copyright 1961 by the author. Reprinted by permission.

E. P. Dutton & Co., Inc. for "Bluie West Eight: Arctic Saga" by Bernt Balchen. This selection is from the book COME NORTH WITH ME by Bernt Balchen. Copyright 1958 by the publishers. Reprinted by permission.

Murray Green for "Counterattack Europe: The First 18 Months" by Murray Green. Written especially for this volume by the author.

Grover C. Hall, Jr. for "First Fighter to Big B" by Grover C. Hall, Jr. This selection is from the book 1000 DESTROYED by Grover C. Hall, Jr. Copyright 1946 by the author and reprinted by his permission.

W. W. Norton & Co. for "Abortion" by Bert Stiles. This selection is from the book SERENADE TO THE BIG BIRD by Bert Stiles. Copyright 1947 by Mrs. Bert W. Stiles. Reprinted by permission of the publishers.

The authors for "The Amazing Michael Gladych" by Robert S. Johnson and Martin Caidin. This selection is from the book THUNDERBOLT! by Robert S. Johnson with Martin Caidin. Copyright 1958 by the authors. Reprinted by permission of the authors.

Air Force Magazine for "Scandinavian Carpetbagger" by Capt. Eric Friedheim. This selection is from the August 1945 issue. Reprinted by permission.

Air Force Magazine for "Air Power in the Invasion" from the July 1944 issue. Reprinted by permission.

Air Force Magazine for "Pacing the Attack" by Maj. Arthur Gordon. This selection is from the September 1944 issue. Reprinted by permission.

Air Force Magazine for "Patton's Air Cavalry" by S/Sgt. Mark Murphy. This selection is from the November 1944 issue. Reprinted by permission.

Air Force Magazine for "Special Delivery to No Man's Land" by 1st. Lt. Joseph D. Guess. This selection is from the January 1945 issue. Reprinted by permission.

Random House, Inc. for "Last Encounter with the Luftwaffe" by John T. Godfrey. This selection is from the book THE LOOK OF EAGLES by John T. Godfrey. Copyright 1958 by the publishers. Reprinted by permission.

Random House, Inc. for "Dogsbody" by Group Capt. J. E. Johnson. This selection is from the book WING LEADER by Group Capt. J. E. Johnson, RAF. Copyright 1956 by the publishers. Reprinted by permission.

Air Force Magazine for "Striking Oil" by Air Force Overseas Correspondents. Reprinted by permission.

Random House, Inc. for "Walter Nowotny" by Pierre Clostermann. This selection is from the book THE BIG SHOW by Pierre Clostermann. Copyright 1951 by Random House, Inc. Reprinted by permission.

Random House, Inc. for "The Closing Ring" by Hans Ulrich Rudel. This selection is from the book STUKA PILOT by Hans Ulrich Rudel. Reprinted by permission of the publishers.

Holt, Rinehart and Winston, Inc. for "ME-262 Jet Fighter: The Luftwaffe's Last Stand" by Adolph Galland. This selection is from the book THE FIRST AND THE LAST by Adolf Galland. Translated from the German by Mervyn Savill. Copyright 1954 by Holt, Rinehart and Winston, Inc. Reprinted by permission of the publishers.

Joseph Warner Angell for "Guided Missiles Could Have Won" by Joseph Warner Angell. This selection was first published in the December 1951 and January 1952 issues of Atlantic Monthly. Reprinted by permission of the author.

Editor's and publisher's grateful thanks are due the United States Air Force and the National Archives who generously supplied the photographs included in this volume.

Prologue

Arthur Gordon

WHEN the Nazis surrendered uncon-ditionally at one minute past midnight on May 9, 1945, the gods who love irony must have laughed. The nation that had first counted on airpower to bridge the perilous gap between its aspirations and its capabilities, then used the air in revolutionary ways to conquer a continent — there was this nation, shorn of its air strength by superior airpower, its cities beaten into dust and ashes, its industry crip-pled and driven underground, its ar-mies rendered powerless to halt the march of the invaders.

The Germans themselves were more than willing to admit that airpower had boomeranged on them with ter-rible impact. In the weeks after VE Day one top Nazi general after another added his voice to the almost unani-mous chorus: "We failed primarily because your airpower robbed our skies of protective wings, our armies of mobility, our tanks of oil and our factories of raw materials." This from the men who had counted on air weap-ons to lead them to world domina-tion. Irony indeed.

For the laughing gods, however, the irony must have been the sharper for the narrowness of the margin of fail-ure. More than once, even after Ameri-can strength was thrown into the balance, the Germans nearly won the air war. Given a little more foresight, they might have created a single-engine fighter force that would have halted our air invasion of Europe. Given a little more time, a little more luck, they might have brought their V-weap-ons and their jet planes to a point where they could have forced a stale-mate. But as one of their airmen re-marked bitterly after his capture, their timing was consistently bad, their critical decisions on how to apply their strength were usually made too soon or too late.

This was most unfortunate for the Germans. It is the application of power, not power itself, that decides battles. Thinking, not sheer mass of planes or tanks or guns, is what wins wars. In the air, where there were few precedents to follow, few textbooks to study, the side with the best brains was bound to win.

It did.

Contents

PART FIVE: THE STRATEGIC AIR OFFENSIVE: A FLAMING YEAR

PART SIX: D-DAY TO V-E DAY

WORLD WAR II
IN THE AIR

EUROPE

PART ONE

GLORY IN DEFEAT: THE NAZI ONSLAUGHT

September, 1939– December, 1941

The time will come, when thou shalt lift thine eyes
To watch a long-drawn battle in the skies,
While aged peasants, too amazed for words,
Stare at the flying fleets of wondrous birds.
England, so long the mistress of the sea,
Where winds and waves confess her sovereignty,
Her ancient triumphs yet on high shall bear,
And reign, the sovereign of the conquered air.
                Translated from GRAN's *Luna Habitabilis* (1737)

Clouds of smoke rise as German bombers fly over the outskirts of Warsaw. The Luftwaffe, with 3,750 first-line combat aircraft, met no opposition from the Polish Air Force, which had only 500 planes, many of them obsolete.

Introduction

THE GREATEST WAR in all of history struck like lightning at dawn on September 1, 1939, when the 3rd, 4th, 8th, 10th and 14th Armies of Nazi Germany poured across the German-Polish borders. Swiftly and without warning formations of modern combat fighters, bombers, and dive bombers streamed out of the skies to strike the 450-plane Polish Air Force on its airfields at Cracow, Grodno, Kattowitz, Lwow, Lublin, Lida and a dozen other places. Spearheading the rolling columns of Nazi armor and infantry were nearly 1600 aircraft of the Luftwaffe's Air Fleets I and IV. Within two days the Polish Air Force had been wiped out.

Protected by complete air superiority, the German Panzer Divisions moved forward behind a screen of horrendous destruction from the air and swept through the archaic Polish horse cavalry with precision and skill.

Dive bombers took out transportation facilities, demolished bridges, railroad stations and communications, immobilizing and paralyzing Polish ground forces. The JU-87D "Stuka" dive bomber, star of the campaign with its terror-making siren, left cities, towns, hamlets, and farms in rubble and death. It strafed and bombed refugee-cluttered highways and in general brought to the land of Poland a degree of frightfulness and horror from the skies that had no comparison in history.

So was World War II born, with a Nazi blitz from the air that portended the shape of things to come. As it had begun, so would the war be fought through the long years ahead and so would it be ended, with a measure of aerial destruction upon the perpetrators that even the madman Hitler could not have concocted in his wildest tantrums.

The German invasion of Poland invoked a string of national alliances which spread the war like grassfire. On September 3, 1940, France and England declared war on Germany, honoring their defense pact with the Polish government. Thus in three days the war had become world-wide, for now involved were all the possessions, colonies, dependencies, territories, and dominions of two great world powers.

At the outset, on September 1, 1939, German overall air strength stood at 3750 first line combat aircraft with between 500 and 1000 in reserve. Main types in the Luftwaffe were the Messerschmitt ME-109 and ME-110 fighters; Junkers JU-87; "Stuka" dive bombers; Heinkel HE-111, Dornier DO-17, and JU-88 heavy bombers; and JU-52 transports. By the spring of 1940, Luftwaffe first line operational aircraft numbered well over 4500. In addition

3

the Luftwaffe possessed nearly 6000 training craft.

In contrast the French Air Force comprised some 1540 planes, of which 314 were based in French North Africa. The majority were no match for the modern, high performance Luftwaffe equipment. French fighters numbered 700 of various types: Morane Sauliner 406s, Hawk 75As, Block MB 151s and 152s, Dewoitine D. 520s and the twin engine Potez 631s. Among the 260 French bombers were Leo 451s, Armot 351s and 354s, Douglas DB-7s and Martin 167s. An additional 180 reconnaissance and 400 close support fighter bombers completed the French Air Arm. No one type played a distinguishing role in the entire war.

For the British the figures were higher and the equipment somewhat better. Total Royal Air Force inventory was 1911 aircraft of which 500 were the eight-gun Hurricane Is, and 13 squadrons of Gloster Gladiator biplane fighters which were obsolescent but curiously effective at first. RAF Bomber Command had 480 first line bombers with ten squadrons in Fairey Battles and 23 Squadrons with Bristol Blenheim IVs, Vickers Wellington Is and IIs, Armstrong Whitworth Whitley IIIs and IVs and Handley Page Hampdens. The 171 Reconnaissance aircraft in RAF Coastal Command included units of Avro Ansons, Lockheed Hudsons, Short Sunderland flying boats and a limited number of the completely obsolete Saro Londons, Supermarine Stranraers, and Vickers Vilde-

beest biplanes. At overseas stations throughout the world RAF aircraft totaled only 435 fighters and bombers.

Following the quick conquest of Poland and throughout the winter of 1939-40, the German Luftwaffe repaired the minor losses it suffered in its first blitz campaign through Poland (approximately 275 aircraft were destroyed) and it made preparations for the spring 1940 offensive. Little air activity took place during this period except reconnaissance on both sides, occasional Luftwaffe bombing of British ports, and rare encounters over France with British and French air patrols. The three great European powers, in a declared state of war, spent the dull cold months preparing what air, sea, and land forces they had for action when the spring thaws set in. Dubbed the winter of the "Phony War," it was a period of the most hectic preparations, especially for Britain and France. Their air forces were largely obsolescent and their aircraft industry and air training programs were geared to small peacetime schedules. British aircraft production could not exceed 700 planes per month while the French was pitifully small. In desperation they turned to the United States and by the close of 1939 the two countries had ordered 2500 American combat aircraft. Before spring of 1940 their orders to American industry had risen to 8200 combat planes of the latest and most modern design, including P-39s, P-40s, A-20s, B-26s, B-25s, B-17s, and C-47s. Arrangements

4

The French Air Force with a limited number of first-line fighter aircraft was no match for the Luftwaffe. Here a group of German soldiers examines a burned French airplane.

During the "Phony War" the Royal Air Force used its forward positions in France to perform extremely valuable photo reconnaissance flights over all of Germany. This RAF crew is being briefed for a "recce" mission over a German airfield.

were also hastily made with British Dominions overseas — Australia, New Zealand, and Canada — for a high priority joint aircrew training on a mass scale.

But time ran out for all this preparation to do any immediate good.

On April 9, 1940 the German blitzkrieg struck again. This time Hitler's air and ground legions rolled out of Western Germany across little Denmark without opposition and within 24 hours that small country had fallen.

On the same morning 500 Luftwaffe transports (mostly JU-52 tri-motors), supported by 500 combat fighters and bombers descended on Norway. Large formations of transports flew over key airfields and cities disgorging paratroopers on Oslo, Bergen, Trondheim, Stavanger, and Narvik. Trojan-horse merchant ships, tied up in Norwegian harbors, opened their hatches and belched combat ready troops. Within

Tri-motored Junkers 52s carrying 17 German paratroopers each, disgorged them over Norwegian cities and in a matter of hours Norway was in German hands.

Two pretty skiers watch a German pilot and ground crew ready a bomb load on a Stuka JU-87 bomber at an airfield in occupied Norway.

hours every airfield, harbor, and key military headquarters in the country was in German hands. Overhead the fighters and bombers of the Luftwaffe patrolled the coastlines in tight aerial blockade. By the evening of the 9th the well-planned maneuver had succeeded and the government lay in the hands of the Norwegian Nazi puppet, Major Vidkun Quisling, who had collaborated in advance with the Nazis.

There was little doubt that Hitler would next turn his powerful Wehrmacht (armed forces) loose on the rest of Western Europe. All but a few combat elements of Luftflotten (air fleet) V in Norway were quickly transferred to Luftflotten II and III in Western Germany. By early May the Luftwaffe there numbered 3500 combat aircraft and 500 transports.

The expected blow fell in the early morning hours of May 10. Swarms of German transports (475 total) unloaded parachutists onto airfields and strategic points in Holland. At the same time the dive-bombing techniques so effective in Poland were repeated. Dutch highways, railroads, bridges, and military fortifications were swiftly attacked and destroyed. The air assault was followed up by highly mobile armor and infantry divisions which linked up with the parachutists. On May 14, the open city of Rotterdam was bombed mercilessly with over

30,000 civilian casualties. Five days later it was all over. The small Dutch Air Force was wiped out and the army obliterated. Without pausing the Nazi juggernaut rolled on into neutral Belgium.

The Luftwaffe was now at peak effectiveness. Nearly 3000 German bombers and fighters ranged over Belgium and France attacking the French Air Force and the RAF on 70 airfields. The 600 French and British fighters stationed there were no match for the overpowering Luftwaffe and although they did take a heavy toll of German fighters and bombers, their losses were frightening. 195 precious Hurricane fighters were destroyed, nearly one-fourth of all RAF fighter strength. What was left moved farther south into France or returned to England to continue the fight from British bases. RAF bombers suffered equally staggering losses. Diversionary RAF strikes on industrial targets deep in Germany did not take the heat off the Luftwaffe's front line attack. By May 21, Allied airpower in France was almost non-existent. In ten days the German ground forces broke through Belgium to the English Channel, cutting off the 400,000 man British Expeditionary Force (BEF) from the main French armies and the RAF and French air squadrons supporting them. When the Belgian forces surrendered to the Germans the gallant BEF was pinned against the Channel at Dunkirk, facing extermination.

Operating now from English bases, the battered RAF gained temporary air superiority over their beleaguered forces at Dunkirk and between May 26 and June 5 nearly 340,000 English and French troops were evacuated to England in one of the most incredible operations of the war.

Following the Dunkirk deliverance the German Wehrmacht turned toward France proper. The Luftwaffe, unopposed in the skies, swept down on the French troops throwing the demoralized armies into panic and confusion. On June 3, the Luftwaffe struck Paris in the first air attack on that magnificent city. This strike was followed by a massive attack on the ground by 100 German divisions with more than 2000 tanks. From positions in Belgium, German armies struck south at four places, outflanking the famed Maginot Line with a speed that precluded any counterattack by the French. Amid hysteria, panic, and confusion the French fled in headlong retreat. Overhead the young Luftwaffe pilots had a field day strafing and bombing roads cluttered with soldiers and the citizenry of the country fleeing for their lives on foot, in autos, on bicycles, and in animal drawn carts. "The carnage was beyond description," wrote a newsman observer. There was precious little French or British airpower left to counter the slaughter.

On June 10, with the Nazi armies a few miles outside Paris, the Italians stabbed France in the back. Elements of Mussolini's 400,000-man Fascist

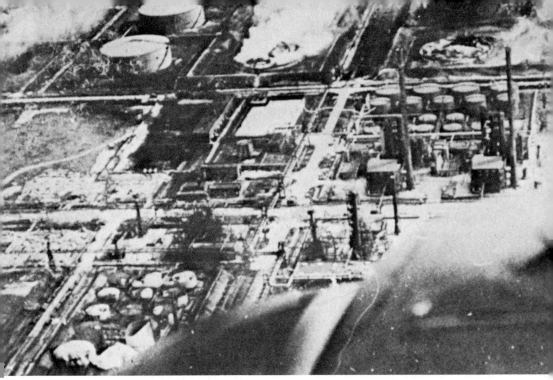

The Luftwaffe sets oil tanks ablaze at Le Havre, France.

Long lines of British troops wait on the beaches at Dunkirk, France, for the boats that will take them to England.

9

Army poured across the Alps and through the Riviera into Southern France. Bomber squadrons of his 4000-plane air force, unopposed in the air, struck viciously at undefended French cities and ports. Caught between the giant pincers of two armies and two air forces, the French Government fled Paris. Four days later, on June 14, the Germans entered the ghost-like city — triumphant, cocky. During the next week French resistance cracked completely and on June 22, the French capitulated and signed the armistice at Compiegne. In one month the great French nation had been overwhelmed. Hitler was ecstatic. It had taken him less than two months of the spring campaign to conquer all of Western Europe, all that is, except England. Only the tiny island remained outside his grasp and the Fuehrer himself stood on the lonely Cap Gris Nez staring across the narrow English Channel.

"There are no more islands," he raved. "The English Channel is nothing but a river." Loudly he predicted he would dictate peace from London before the end of the summer.

His plan was simple and it was called "Operation Sea Lion." First phase was elimination of the RAF. Second phase, water-borne invasion and defeat of the British on their own territory. To Hermann Goering's Luftwaffe fell the first task — elimination of the RAF — for Hitler knew

A Lockheed Hudson of the Royal Air Force approaches Dunkirk on a patrol flight. The smoke is from burning oil tanks. During the nine days of evacuation from the Dunkirk area, the RAF mounted 3,561 sorties over the beaches. A "sortie" is one mission by one airplane.

that unless the Germans held complete control of the air overhead, there was little chance the invasion of England could succeed.

The date for *"Alder Tag"* (Eagle Day) — beginning of the all-out air offensive against the RAF — was set at August 10, with invasion planned for September 15. The pompous Goering had estimated four days to defeat the RAF Fighter Command and thirty days to clean up the remainder of British airpower.

On airfields spread from Brest across the Low Countries to Hamburg in Western Germany, Reichmarshal Goering regrouped and prepared his Luftwaffe for the coming clash over Britain. By the middle of July the Luftwaffe's Luftflotten II and III were ready. These two air fleets, reinforced and well stocked with combat supplies, comprised nearly 4000 first-line fighters and bombers. The eve of the Battle of Britain was at hand.

Across the channel on British airfields the RAF could count 2591 aircraft of all types. Only 620 were Hurricane and Spitfire fighters — the handful of planes which would write history in the three months ahead — and a small reserve of around 300. Flying with the RAF now were several new squadrons of Polish and Czech pilots who had fled the Nazi controlled continent of Europe. Soon French and Belgian pilots would join the RAF's growing ranks.

Preliminary Luftwaffe attacks began in the middle of July on channel shipping. Luftwaffe planes undertook mine-laying in the English Channel along with irregular night raids on cities.

The crescendo of Nazi air attack built up rapidly in late July and early August. RAF Bomber Command struck back in night sorties on airfields and targets in Germany and on fleets of invasion barges seen gathering on the French and Belgian coastlines.

By early August air battles over England had risen to a high pitch. It was already obvious to Luftwaffe chiefs that something had gone wrong with their plans to eradicate the RAF quickly. Luftwaffe losses were running high. In one August week alone they lost 256 aircraft to 130 for the RAF. Between August 8 and 23 German air losses reached 403. On *"Alder Tag"* Day, August 15, the Luftwaffe mounted a 1500-sortie effort which met furious opposition indicating the RAF was in no way weakening. For the rest of August and into September heavy continuous day and night aerial battles filled English skies. The famed JU-87 Stuka dive bomber, the scourge of Poland, Holland, Belgium, and France, proved a dismal failure when confronted by the faster, more maneuverable British Hurricane and Spitfire fighters. The Luftwaffe soon found need to provide escort fighters to escort fighters, so dogged were the RAF defenders. Armament on German bombers was found inadequate to deal with RAF fighters and the Luftwaffe bomber's short range did not

The famed JU-87 Stuka dive bomber, the scourge of Poland, Holland, Belgium and France, proved a dismal failure when confronted by the faster, more maneuverable British Hurricane and Spitfire fighters.

permit their pilots the luxury of evasive action enroute to or return from target.

When September 15 arrived (the scheduled date for seaborne invasion) the RAF was stronger than at the beginning of the battle, and the British people were nowhere near giving up. On this date the Luftwaffe flew against England in a mass grudge operation which the RAF met in an historic encounter. Luftwaffe formations were thrown into such confusion by RAF fighters that few reached their targets. Many dropped their bombs indiscriminately before fleeing back to their airfields on the Continent. This day marked the peak of the Battle of Britain, and although only 56 Luftwaffe aircraft were shot down, the ferocity of aerial engagement was at its height. From then on there was absolutely no doubt as to the final outcome, though bitter fighting continued unabated throughout the month, costing the Luftwaffe 435 more aircraft.

In early September the primary mission of the Luftwaffe — to destroy the RAF — was all but forgotten as Hitler ordered the hate bombing of London in retaliation for RAF Bomber Command raids on German targets around Berlin. If the RAF could not be destroyed, reasoned the Fuehrer, the British people would be hammered into submission.

In early October, Luftwaffe strategy switched from daylight to night bombing, an admission that their original plan had failed. The end of this month marked the end of the Battle of Britain. The Luftwaffe had lost nearly 60 per cent of the original force of 3500 aircraft, while RAF losses totaled 915.

As to the Battle of Britain, it was one of history's great events, and the world shall never forget Winston Churchill's tribute to the RAF: "Never in the field of human conflict was so much owed by so many to so few." While nothing can ever degrade the individual heroism of RAF Fighter

A Heinkel HE-111 over the Thames River in a daylight attack on London.

Command pilots, German High Command errors in strategy and tactics contributed much to the final outcome. Instead of concentrating on the destruction of the RAF in the sky, on their aerodromes, and on wiping out the British radar installations which played so vital a role in spotting incoming German formations and vectoring British fighters to the attack, the Luftwaffe chief diluted his air forces over a wide variety of targets: English Channel shipping, British anti-invasion forces, harbors and ports, British industries and cities at large. These bomber attacks contributed little to the gaining of German aerial supremacy over England, a condition which Hitler needed before he could cross the Channel with his invasion barges. German misuse of its numerically superior airpower was fatal, and the errors committed led the mighty Third Reich into its first major defeat of World War II.

Victorious British airpower had given the war a completely new look. Within two years the island of England would be converted into a gigantic aerial springboard against Germany.

However, the end of the Battle of Britain was little cause for joy in the island kingdom. The Luftwaffe continued to hammer populated cities from November, 1940 until May, 1941 and the period became known as the "Blitz" — the revenge bombing of London and major British industrial areas for failure to defeat the RAF and in retaliation for RAF Bomber Command night attacks on Germany.

Throughout the terrible winter of the night Blitz, German bombs rained on England. The obliteration of Coventry on November 14-15 and the savage incendiary raid on London of December 29-30, 1941, left deep scars on the brave English people. There were nearly half a million casualties during the "Blitz." The night attacks continued throughout the winter but on a gradually reducing scale. The three Luftwaffe air fleets in Western Europe showed the effects of aircraft and pilot attrition from British anti-aircraft and night fighters. The introduction of the RAF's new twin engine, radar-equipped interceptor, the Bristol Beaufighter (replacing the Hurricane, Defiant, and Blenheim night fighters) gave the German pilots a brand new problem they never did successfully solve.

Then too, by late 1940 the air war emphasis began to shift away from English skies to other parts of Europe. The Luftwaffe's "johnny-came-lately" partner, the Italian Air Force (*Regia Aeronautica*), was in serious trouble in the Mediterranean area.

After Mussolini entered the war, the *Regia Aeronautica* contributed little to the German campaign in Western Europe. Proudly the Italian "Il Duce" had sent 75 BR. 20 bombers, 100 Fiat CR. 42 and G-50 fighters to Belgian air fields in October, 1940. Within two months they were withdrawn, having been completely ineffective against the RAF. Their combat

London fires burn into the next morning after a "night Blitz" raid by Hitler's bombers. This picture was taken from one of the bridges across the Thames.

The introduction of the RAF's new twin engine, radar-equipped interceptor, the Bristol Beaufighter, gave the German pilots a brand new problem they never did successfully solve.

15

record proved typical of the entire *Regia Aeronautica* which looked good on paper with a total of nearly 5000 aircraft. But in first-line strength, the story was different. Nearly two-thirds of the Italian fighters were the obsolete Fiat CR 32 and CR 42 biplanes while the two mainstays, the Fiat G.50 and the Macchi C.200 Saettas were underarmed and no match for the British and French. About one-half of the 1000-plane Italian bomber force was the effective three-engine medium craft, the S.M. 79 Sparviero, and the remainder consisted of torpedo carrying S.M. 79s, BR. 20s, S.M. 81s and Z.1007s. An additional force included 700 reconnaissance type aircraft and 76 transports of the S.M. 75 and S.M. 82 variety.

Initial combat for the *Regia Aeronautica* were bombardment strikes on Southern French cities, the British-held island of Malta, and on British forces stationed in the Egypt and Suez Canal area. While they were bothersome, these attacks were never critical.

The first major reversal for Mussolini's airmen came in November, 1940 with the Italian assault on Greece. The small Royal Hellenic Air Force prevented the numerically greater *Regia Aeronautica* from gaining air superiority over that country. On the heels of this came a second setback in North Africa. Here Italian ground forces, supported by 500 aircraft, launched an assault east out of Libya along the coastline to capture Egypt and the Suez Canal. It was turned back decisively by counterattacking British ground forces and RAF units, with less than 300 aircraft of obsolescent types (Lysanders, Gladiators, Blenheim I's, Fairey Battles, Hawker Harts). A complete Italian fighter group was captured by the British on the ground at Martuba, and by January, 1941, Mussolini's African venture was facing complete disaster.

Thus the Axis situation in the Mediterranean called for quick German help and Luftwaffe units were hastily dispatched from France and the Low Countries to pull Mussolini's chestnuts out of the fire. By the end of January, 1941, Luftwaffe reinforcements in Sicily numbered 150 JU-87 Stuka dive bombers, 40 ME-119 fighters, 120 JU-88 and HE-111 bombers, 40 ME-110 fighters, and 20 reconnaissance fighters. Malta and the vital Sicilian straits now came under German air control. A month later additional Luftwaffe units were sent to North Africa to help forestall a major British drive into Italian Libya from Egypt.

Simultaneously strong Luftwaffe units from Western Europe moved into the Balkan states bordering Russia and by March, 1941, over 1100 German combat aircraft in Rumania and Bulgaria were poised for the spring 1941 offensive.

In the traditional "blitzkrieg" pattern of previous offensives, the German invasion of Greece got underway in early April. Within three weeks that country had fallen to the Panzer

16

divisions supported in the air by 400 Luftwaffe fighters and bombers. The Royal Hellenic Air Force, which had held the Italians at bay, was quickly destroyed by Goering's planes, and the royal road to the Middle and Far East was now open to Hitler's legions.

Flushed with success by the new spring offensive, the German High Command turned their attention to the island of Crete, a strategic piece of real estate off the coast of Greece held by the British. On May 20, after strong air bombardment, swarms of German JU-52 transports disgorged thousands of paratroopers onto the island while troop-laden gliders swiftly descended into dry river beds and flat fields. The airborne invasion, supported by 650 combat fighters, bombers, and fighter bombers, overwhelmed the gallant defenders at a high cost. Nearly 5000 paratroopers and glider men, along with 170 JU-52s, were lost.

But the operation was a success for the Germans, a boldly conceived plan and strictly a Luftwaffe show. It gained for Hitler a strategic foothold in the Eastern Mediterranean, directly north of Egypt and the vital Suez Canal waterway.

The tide of Nazi conquest was again running high. All of Western and Eastern Europe, except Britain, lay under Nazi control. From the Arctic Circle and out in the North Atlantic to the shores of North Africa, the Luftwaffe ruled the skies. Hitler could now dream of conquering the Middle East and pour his forces into India.

Turning his back on unconquered England, Hitler made the greatest strategic error of the war. With more than 3000 first-line aircraft (one-half of his total Luftwaffe) grouped along the 1000 mile Russian border in East Prussia, Poland, Rumania, and Bulgaria, the Fuehrer suddenly attacked the Soviet Union with whom he had a non-aggression pact. The campaign at first was a repetition of the highly successful "blitzkrieg" used in Poland, France, and Greece. The mobile, mechanized ground forces rolled into Russia at many points, led by the experienced, morale-high Luftwaffe paving the way with fighters and dive bombers.

The Russians fell back from the Baltic to the Black Sea. Though the Russian Air Force was numerically superior to the German (12,000 to 15,000 first-line aircraft), its organization was poor and the planes themselves far inferior to those of the Luftwaffe. Most fighters were the obsolescent I-15s and L-16s. Assault aircraft were ancient R-Z biplanes. Russian bombers (TB-3s, DB-3s, SB-2s and 3s) could not live in the air against German fighters.

In the first few days of the Russian campaign, the Luftwaffe gained air superiority. Hundreds of Russian aircraft were destroyed in the air and on the ground while many were captured on airfields by the swiftly moving German ground forces. Estimates of Russian aircraft losses range between 8000 and 9000 during the first five months. Nevertheless, the Soviet Air Force failed to disintegrate and in July alone it made over 73,000 sorties while the Luftwaffe averaged 1500 to 2000 per day.

For the Russians the early stage of the war was a rear guard action. Heroic and suicidal missions by Russian pilots were normal. Glider-borne agents were landed behind German lines to harass the advancing Nazi legions. Formations of Russian bombers flew boldly into superior Luftwaffe attackers to deliver their bombs. Aerial ramming tactics were not uncommon. Losses in both aircraft and pilots were phenomenal.

So rapid was the German advance that by July, 1941 Smolensk was surrounded and the Luftwaffe was bombing Moscow. In the next three months, the Luftwaffe carried the German front to Leningrad and Estonia was conquered. Spreading south, tactical successes were many on the central front and south in the Black Sea area.

With the onset of winter, however, things began to change for the Germans. The Russian enemy had actually melted into the vastness of their country and while victory after victory went to the Luftwaffe, decisive strategic action was impossible. Soon time, distance, weather, losses, and over-commitment of forces began to show on the Luftwaffe. The stubborn Russian defense of Kiev set back the Nazi timetable and by early October, with the Germans pinned down outside Leningrad, the Russian Air Force be-

gan to reappear in strength. Other foreboding things were happening. Unseasonable wet weather turned Luftwaffe airfields into seas of mud and soon an early and unusually severe winter set in, freezing aircraft lubricants, and cementing aircraft in hub-deep frozen ground. All along the Russian front Luftwaffe losses began to mount. More than 300 aircraft were shot down near Moscow by Soviet fighters. Many more were lost in accidents and aerial resupply of units along the vast front. Out of 3000 aircraft at the start of the offensive, the Luftwaffe was down now to around 1700 and reinforcements could not be brought in without weakening other combat theatres in Western Europe and the Mediterranean. Only 500 remained on the Moscow front out of an original 1500.

The high tide of conquest had been reached. While the Luftwaffe would temporarily gain air superiority in sections along the endless Russian front, never again would it be able to enjoy the dominance it had during the summer and fall of 1941.

On December 6, the day before Pearl Harbor, a Russian counterattack at Moscow threw the Germans back and made improbable the capture of the Soviet capital.

Elsewhere around Europe, 100 Luftwaffe fighters and dive bombers were hastily dispatched to North Africa to reinforce the Italian Air Force pitted against the advancing British. In the west, British Bomber Command night

A German photograph showing a Russian railway station burning after an attack by the Luftwaffe.

Royal Air Force and Russian crewmen prepare a Hurricane for take-off at a field in North Russia. Two RAF squadrons of 39 Hurricanes were sent to aid in the defense of Murmansk.

19

raids on industrial targets on the Continent and in Germany were growing in number and effectiveness. Hitler could not afford to draw on his fighters on this front to replenish the dwindling forces in Russia.

Thus was the state of the air war in Europe when the Japanese warlords leveled a surprise attack on Pearl Harbor — an attack which brought the United States into the war in Europe.

Though the German air forces were over-extended on all fronts surrounding the Fatherland, the Luftwaffe of December 7, 1941 was still the most powerful air force in the world. Its strength stood at more than 5000 combat aircraft spread from Moscow to the English Channel, from Norway to North Africa. This force was backed up by an aircraft production capability of more than 12,500 per year. Luftwaffe combat equipment was superior to 95 per cent of that possessed by the enemies it faced. Two years of continuous combat had given German flyers and air leaders a high level of skill and seasoned experience. So strong was the Luftwaffe, so firmly backed up by a solid industrial base, so entrenched in tactical and strategic positions throughout Europe, it would take three and one-half years for the Allies to destroy it.

With the spring thaws of 1940 Hitler moved quickly against Denmark and Norway by sea and by air. Within two days the Luftwaffe had occupied all key airfields and the Nazi ground forces all key positions in Norway. The falling Chamberlain Government in Britain quickly assembled forces to capture Trondheim, in northern Norway, and on April 14 the British expedition landed at Namsos, north of Trondheim and at Aandalanes to the south, with the objective to surround and capture the key Norwegian town. Harassed by Luftwaffe aircraft, the British ground forces needed fighter protection but no bases existed for such support.

It was then an RAF intelligence officer borrowed a Tiger Moth from the Norwegians, surveyed the surrounding country and found a frozen lake covered by three feet of snow, 32 miles southeast of Aandalanes. With the aid of 200 Norwegians a strip 800 yards long, 75 yards wide, was cleared in the middle of the lake. Meanwhile No. 263 RAF Squadron with Gladiator biplanes was loaded on the aircraft carrier HMS Glorious and by April 24 the ship was ploughing through the cold heavy seas near Norway. On a signal from the lake, the 18 pilots and their CO, Squadron Leader J. W. Donaldson, (none had ever flown off a carrier before) left the flight deck and headed out into the low mist for a destination in enemy-held country that was not on the maps, that none had ever seen before.

*Miraculously all 18 landed safely on the ice runway of Lake Lesjeskog.
Spring thaws had already melted the ice around the edges. Gasoline supplies had to be dog-sledded to the squadron in four-gallon tins. Unknown
to the pilots the Luftwaffe had been curiously and secretly watching every
move. Despite the odds, the RAF pilots' spirits were up and their courage
unfathomable and their orders were to patrol Dombaas early the next
morning. The plan was the first of several attempts to get an air foothold
in Norway and rescue that country from the Germans. It was a desperate
venture, the men brave who carried it out, but all were doomed from the
start. This was obvious even to the strongest of heart in the early morning
hours following their arrival on the frozen surface of Lake Lesjeskog.*

Twilight In Norway:
The RAF at Bay

Peter Wykeham

IN THE SEMI-ARCTIC TWILIGHT of the
next day their first serious troubles
began. The Gladiators were frozen up,
engines would not start, controls were
rigid with ice, landing wheels stuck to
the surface of the lake. But by five
o'clock two aircraft got off and patroled
Dombaas, where their appearance
cheered the soldiers in the way that
the actual sight of our own aircraft was
always to cheer them. Seeing aeroplanes, however ineffective, they were
comforted. Air action unseen, however
effective, left them cold. While this
first party was airborne, the German
reconnaissance aircraft were already
brooding over the lake, while frantic
attempts went on to start the remain-

ing Gladiators. At last the Luftwaffe
began leisurely bombing and machine-
gunning the grounded fighters, and
should certainly have eliminated the
whole base in the first thirty minutes.
Somehow two more Gladiators got into
the air and drove off the bombers,
while a naval light A.A. detachment
gallantly fired their Oerlikon guns
from the lake's edge.

This day, April 25, was an agony at
Lake Lesjeskog. As soon as the few
Gladiators flying landed, they were
set upon by the German aircraft overhead, while the lake began to break up
under the bombing. It is almost past
crediting that, in this hopeless situation, 263 managed to fly 30 sorties

21

during the day, and shot down five enemy aircraft. By noon ten of their fighters were destroyed on the lake, and by the end of the day only five were left serviceable. But no pilots were lost, for no aircraft had been shot down in air fighting. In the evening, Squadron Leader Donaldson took his surviving Gladiators to a small clearing at Setnesmoen, slightly to the south, and set them down on a strip 400 yards long by 80 yards wide. By superhuman efforts some of the ground equipment was forced through to join them, and on the 26th the five flew patrols and reconnaissances once more. Their oxygen was exhausted, and they could not reach the heights which the prudent Luftwaffe now maintained.

At the end of the day they were reduced to one Gladiator and no fuel. The gallant efforts of the naval aircraft from *Glorious* and *Ark Royal* to preserve Namsos and Aandalanes had been equally fruitless, and without air support the whole campaign in Central Norway began to collapse. No. 263 were safely evacuated in a merchant ship, arriving at Scapa Flow on May 1. Their smashed aircraft and wrecked equipment still lie in Norway as a sad monument to a gallant but utterly hopeless attempt at air defense of an area, and as a proof that the weapon itself is only a component in the air defense system.

In the meantime, the operations against the far more isolated Narvik

At the end of the day they were reduced to one Gladiator and no fuel. Their smashed aircraft and wrecked equipment still lie in Norway as a sad monument to a gallant but utterly hopeless attempt at air defense of an area, and as a proof that the weapon itself is only a component in the air defense system.

showed some possibility of success. An Anglo-French force was ashore nearby, and were building up for an assault on the town. As our forces withdrew from the Trondheim area Wing Commander R. L. R. Atcherley arrived at the British H.Q. near Narvik to arrange the air support for the next move. The Luftwaffe were now operating from Trondheim, and bombing had already begun. Atcherley, whose dynamism attained almost frightening proportions, borrowed a Walrus amphibian from the navy, sought for and found two possible sites at Bardufoss and Skaanland, enrolled civilian volunteers by the hundred, and blasted a series of landing-grounds out of the snow, ice, and rocks. The work went on for 20 hours a day under conditions of appalling difficulty. Mindful of the lessons of Lake Lesjeskog, Atcherley and his engineers built taxiways and protection pens, camouflaged positions for aircraft, and air-raid shelters for ground crew. Melting snow flooded the works and was repelled again, and when the transport lorries proved inadequate 200 mules were drafted to help out. In three weeks the landing grounds were ready.

Back at Fighter Command yet another Air Component H.Q. had been assembled at Uxbridge, and sailed for Norway on May 7. Four days after Hitler's main European offensive opened, the carrier *Furious* left for the Narvik area, carrying on board the undaunted crews of 263 Squadron, now furnished with a fresh batch of

Gladiators, and 46 Squadron with Hurricanes, commanded by Squadron Leader K. B. Cross. Early on May 21, the first flight of 263 took off from the flight deck, in villainous weather, and the guiding Swordfish led it straight into a mountainside. The naval aircraft and two of the Gladiators crashed, but the rest managed to turn back and find the carrier, and what is more to make their first landing on a flightdeck. Next day they got safely to Bardufoss and immediately began operations.

The 46 Squadron Hurricanes were still aboard *Furious*, which had withdrawn farther out into the North Sea. Their destined base of Skaanland was flooded by the thaw, and until they arrived the assault on Narvik was not to begin. *Furious* returned to Scapa Flow and transferred 46 Squadron to *Glorious*. In the meantime, the Germans were pushing north from Trondheim. On the 26th, *Glorious* was back in Norwegian waters and 46 flew off, but after the first three aircraft had nosed over in the soft ground at Skaanland the rest were diverted to Bardufoss and operated from there.

Both squadrons now began working together. Yet again they were without radar, and had little or no warning of enemy raids. Moreover, they were some 50 miles north of the bases and anchorages of the expeditionary force, while the Germans were coming up from the south. Thus they had to fly the wasteful system of standing patrols until another tiny strip was prepared at Bodo, south of Narvik. Three Gladiators under Flight Lt. Caesar Hull put into this little glue-pot, refueled from tins, took off and shot down two German aircraft over the heads of the Allied troops. Next morning Me 110s and Stukas descended on the landing-ground and began systematically destroying everything in sight. Hull got off the ground minus his flying helmet and shot up a number of Ju 87s before his aircraft was so badly damaged that he crashed attempting to land.

On May 28, the Allies finally took Narvik. But events in France and the Low Countries had now made a farce of the whole operation, and there was nothing left but to withdraw. The soldiers themselves, with their usual grim humor, were now maintaining that the initials BEF stood for "Back Every Friday." 263 and 46 flew patrol after patrol to guard Narvik and the fleet of evacuation. It was arranged that the RAF should maintain this defense until all had left but the demolition engineers, when the Gladiators were to land on *Glorious*, and the Hurricanes, which had never landed on a carrier and supposedly could not, were to be destroyed on their landing ground. 263 duly took off from Bardufoss for the last time and landed their Gladiators safely on *Glorious*. Squadron Leader Cross, knowing that Fighter Command was desperate for Hurricanes, begged for permission to try to fly his aircraft on, and this was granted. Every pilot volunteered, and

on June 7 in the bright light of the Arctic midnight, 46 followed 263. As *Glorious* quivered and shook with the utmost speed that could be beaten out of her engines, they came in one by one to a safe landing and were made fast on her flight deck.

Nos. 263 and 46 flew 638 sorties during their period at Narvik; they had engaged the Germans in 95 combats and shot down 27 of them for the loss of seven aircraft in the air and five on the ground. Their conquest over conditions past describing was worthy of the hard-used word epic. The organization that supported them had achieved the impossible every hour of every day. The curtain that now fell on their display of skill and courage was swift and brutal.

On the afternoon of June 8 the *Scharnhorst* and *Gneisenau*, hunting for ships coming from Norway, fell in with *Glorious* as she steamed for Scapa. Her escorting destroyers turned and flew at the German battlecruisers with selfless heroism, but after two hours' unequal gunfire, helpless and burning from end to end, she slipped below the waves of the North Sea. With her went all the pilots but Squadron Leader Cross and Flight Lt. Jameson, who somehow gained a Carley float with 30 sailors. For five days they survived bitter cold and terrible privations, watching 25 of their companions die one by one. They were still alive when they were picked up by a fishing boat and brought to England.

Naval aircraft on the deck of one of His Majesty's Ships, an aircraft carrier, awaiting orders to take off for air action against Norway.

There were many bitter, dark days in the early part of the war. May 26, 1940 was one, for on this day the 400,000-man British Expeditionary Force (BEF) on the Continent was driven to the sea by the overwhelming "blitzkrieg" of German land forces spearheaded by thousands of Luftwaffe fighters and bombers.

It all happened in a brief 16 days during which Hitler's legions burst across the flat plains of Flanders (the traditional invasion route), and over-ran Holland and Belgium. By May 20, 10 days after the "blitzkrieg" started, Nazi armored columns had reached the channel coast at Abbeville. The valiant British were pinned against the water at Dunkirk.

For the RAF, whose meager forces were split defending the homeland and assisting the BEF in the Battle of France, it had been a grim two weeks. Losses had cut their fighter strength by 25 per cent and nearly 1000 precious planes had been destroyed. Their bases in France were gone.

Faced with extermination of their major land army, the British mounted the most dramatic withdrawal operation of the war — officially called "Operation Dynamo," but known to the world as the "Nine Days of Dunkirk." It began on May 26, 1940.

Everything British that could float or fly was thrown into evacuating the BEF across the channel to England. The pompous Hermann Goering promised to crush the effort by air assault of his powerful Luftwaffe. He had more than 3500 first-line fighters and bombers with which to do it.

On the sea a fantastic armada of 848 British ships from destroyers to private sloops, fishing smacks and dinghies of amateur sailors put out for the French coast to retrieve the troops.

Overhead the small RAF, battered and weary, flew cover as best they could with a portion of the 600 Hurricane, Spitfire, and Defiant fighters that remained. To commit the entire force would have left the British Isles defenseless against the Luftwaffe.

And so it was that aircraft of all vintages were resurrected, hastily jerry-rigged with machine guns and flown against the Luftwaffe over Dunkirk in the most desperate combined operation in the history of British arms. It was another defeat for the Luftwaffe.

Dunkirk: Victory Within Deliverance

Alexander McKee

THE REAL VICTORY of Dunkirk was won by the navy, but desperate efforts were made both by the RAF and the Fleet Air Arm, with totally unsuitable — and therefore expendable — aircraft, to aid the evacuation. At Detling an amazing collection of long-forgotten machines was assembled. Pilot Officer D. H. Clarke reported there for duty on May 31, flying a target-towing Skua of No. 2 Anti-Aircraft Co-operation Unit, Gosport. He was told that he was to patrol each night west of Dunkirk, dropping powerful flares to light up any attempt by the German Navy to interfere with the evacuation; he had precisely two hours night-flying experience. During the morning of June 1, as his operation was not timed until after nightfall, he assisted the ground crews who were working on about 50 Fleet Air Arm Swordfish, which were shortly due to take off on a fighter patrol over Dunkirk. The Swordfish was an obsolete biplane torpedo-bomber and it was hoped that the German bombers would mistake them for equally obsolete Gladiator biplane fighters, and be frightened off. They had already done one such patrol without being attacked, but the Germans were not fooled a second time.

Clarke noticed some Blenheim IVs which never left the ground, asked why, and was told: "Gas! We're fitted with tanks for spraying gas, just in case the Jerries start using it." There was also an Anson with what appeared to be an enormous rod sticking out of its nose. "What on earth have you got there?" he inquired of the pilot.

"Cannon, old boy — like it?" He almost purred. "Got a 110 and a 109 on the last trip, plus a 109 damaged."

"But where did you nick it from?" asked Clarke, whose own aircraft was unarmed.

"Ah, now there's a thing . . . plenty of guns if you know where to go to, old boy." The pilot was evasive. "Got some Vickers gas-operated, too — look." He pointed to the bullet-splashed side of the Anson, where a twin-barrel was poking out of a side window.

"Another one on the starboard side, a Lewis in the turret — and we cut a hole in the floor to fire at the silly clots who try to sneak in underneath. No mounting, we just hold a Vickers, and spray — works like a charm!"

The second "fighter-patrol" of the morning was flown by Fleet Air Arm dive-bombers and two-seater fighters. "The 37 Skuas and Rocs were a splendid sight as they took off in mass formation," recalled Clarke. "They looked a bit more operational than some of the others, even if their maximum speed was only 225 m.p.h. They came back just before lunchtime, so I stayed to watch them land. There were not many — I counted six; where were the others? One belly-flopped and I went across to see what had happened, the blood-wagon passing me on the way. That aircraft was a complete write-off. Bullets and cannon shells had ripped the fuselage from end to end; the after cockpit was sprayed liberally with blood, the inside of the glass-house reddened throughout by the forward draught. The front cockpit, if anything, was worse. Two bullet holes through the back of the pilot's seat showed where he had been hit, and his parachute, still in position, was saturated with blood. The instrument panel was shattered wreckage, and on the floor was a boot — and the remains of a foot.

"I was nearly sick with the horror of it. How that pilot flew home will never be known, for I found out that he was dead when they dragged him out. Of those 37 Skuas and Rocs, nine came back; of the nine, only four were serviceable."

The morning was not quite over yet. A shot-up fighter-Blenheim came in and landed; the pilot, Reg Peacock, was a friend of Clarke's. His lean face was grimy and sweat-stained, his black hair plastered down from the pressure of his helmet. "I think I'm the last of the squadron, Nobby," he said. "We were attacking a crowd of Dorniers when a whole swarm of 109s jumped us . . ."

"He went along to the mess with his crew for a beer," recalled Clarke. "An hour and a half later they were airborne once more. The starboard wheel was not fully retracted and they disappeared at low level with a decided list to port — too much rudder bias countering the drag of the wheel, I thought. They looked very pathetic limping back to Dunkirk all alone . . ."

EDITOR'S NOTE

The boast of Hermann Goering that his Luftwaffe would prevent the evacuation did not come true. In the nine days the motley armada of 848 ships, criss-crossing the channel, brought back 338,226 of the 400,000 men of the BEF. The BEF had been saved by a combination of Nazi bungling, disorganized, unpremeditated bravery, bad weather which hung over Luftwaffe airdromes for about half the period, and the valiant defense the RAF put up over the evacuation beaches and returning ships. The British Army lost 68,000 killed, missing, wounded, or prisoner; 2472 guns; 63,879 motor vehicles; half a million tons of ammo; and 226 ships of all classes. The RAF lost 106 fighters (80 pilots), and several score bombers. Luftwaffe losses ranged between 156 and 262 planes.

During the nine days and nights 820 bomber and recce sorties had been flown over the beaches. Fighter Command made 2739 fighter sorties — for an average of 300 a day.

Dunkirk was a military defeat. "But," said Winston Churchill in a speech to Parliament, "there was a victory inside this deliverance which should be noted. It was gained by the Air Force . . . We got the Army away . . . and all our pilots have been vindicated as superior to what they (the Germans) have . . ."

In the days following Dunkirk, RAF Fighter Command licked its wounds and counted numbers — 466 serviceable fighters were left, including 331 Hurricanes and Spitfires. Though badly mauled, British airpower was far from defeated and the British air chiefs set about in haste to rebuild and re-equip their units.

Aided by priority aircraft production and flight training, Fighter Command grew to 587 planes and 1200 pilots by June 30, and by August 3 it had 708 aircraft and 1434 pilots.

Facing the RAF across the narrow English Channel were two massive Luftwaffe air fleets, Luftflotten II and III on fields from Brest to Holland. Ready to fly from Southern Norwegian bases against north England was Luftflotten V. Total first-line aircraft for the three fleets numbered 2790 planes, including more than 1200 bombers, 280 Stuka dive bombers and 980 fighters, mostly ME-109s and 110s.

Thus were the forces lined up for the next great move in the European air war — the Battle of Britain.

Hitler's grand strategy for defeat of Great Britain rested on "Operation Sea Lion" — Nazi code name for the invasion of England. First step of the plan called for the elimination of the Royal Air Force. Next, air-sea landings on British soil and defeat of British armies on their own land.

Fortunately for the RAF, Hitler's hope that England would sue for peace without further bloodshed bought precious time to rearm. The summer days of June and July slid by with no serious air action from the powerful Luftwaffe. Despite the open invitation from Hitler, Britain refused to surrender.

Finally on August 10, two months after Dunkirk, Goering announced the beginning of the campaign to reduce the RAF, and the Battle of Britain got under way in earnest. The valiant RAF defense of the British Isles is a story well known. Instead of being defeated in four days, as Goering predicted, the small handful of RAF pilots aggressively met the overwhelming numbers hurled at them and in the first 30 days shot down 781 German aircraft, damaged 242.

Day and night the Luftwaffe attacked England, and day and night the courageous lads of Fighter Command in their Spitfires, Hurricanes, and night fighters rose to challenge the incoming formations. German chiefs on French airfields watched in dismay their bedraggled squadrons return carrying grim signs of bitter combat and telling grim tales of what wrath they encountered over England.

The order of priority of English targets (radar stations, airfields, industry) was soon discarded as the fanatic Hitler directed indiscriminate bombing of cities in retaliation for the stubborn resistance of RAF Fighter Command and the night raids on German cities of Bomber Command.

Sunday, September 15 — the original "Sea Lion" date for Hitler's armies to pour ashore in England — dawned quiet, clear, and full of sunshine. The mighty Luftwaffe had failed to achieve the first step. The RAF, instead of disintegrating, was growing stronger and on this day Goering would throw his forces at England in a fury hitherto unknown. It was a day that would live in the annals of air war — the climax of the Battle of Britain. And here is that story, told by a British writer.

War Over Britain

Ivor Halstead

IT WAS CLEAR in these early days of September that invasion plans were developing swiftly. There were small assemblies of men and materials on September 1, but as the days went by our reconnaissance planes told of intensifying activity. Before long hundreds of barges, ships, and other war equipment were reported to be assembled at Antwerp, Calais, Dunkirk, Ostend, Nieuport, and Le Havre. Our airmen saw them daily, hugging the coast and moving from one canal or port to another. Small warships were also moved near the self-propelled barges — over 150 feet long, and each built to carry about two trainloads of men and materials. Secret information revealed at this time, too, that Germany had commandeered every available barge of over 500 tons and that armies of workmen were employed in the shipyards altering the bows of the vessels so that tanks and guns could be more easily carried and disembarked. Added to these concentrations of barges were submarines in many of the harbors, some of the ocean-going type, large motor-vessels, tugs, and merchant ships. One report told of 45 large mer-

A formation of JU-87 dive-bombers with their top fighter cover of ME-109s over the English countryside. The JU-87s are in the first stage of a let-down for a bombing attack on an RAF airfield.

chant ships at Le Havre. New aircraft shelters were being built inland on the numerous aerodromes from which it was expected enemy aircraft would play their part in the invasion.

The German Air Force continued its daily attacks on Southeast Britain and London to prepare the way for a great invasion follow-up. Hitler was throwing in heavy air stakes because he knew deep in his heart of hearts that not one of the world-conquest schemes fermenting in his cunning brain could hope to succeed unless a fatal arrow could be plunged into the heart of Britain first.

He did what he could with his superior air weapon, wielded by the enthusiast Goering. The ugly conspirators were working to a new date. They were to be in the country of their dreams on September 15.

Every September day and every September night was a day and night of

A rare German combat photograph, taken over England, shows an air battle between a Dornier DO-17 and a Spitfire.

air-fighting, and Hitler's desperate need to dominate our RAF fighters could be measured by his almost drunkenly reckless expenditure of valuable bombers and fighters and much more of valuable pilots. Gaining in a sense of superiority and sureness of striking power every day, our own fighter pilots continued to take their heavy toll from the enemy. They brought down 52 on September 9 and 89 on the 11th. One of the longest continuous attacks on London came on the day and night of September 13/14, and this concentration is now known to have been an early rumbling of the gathering storm of a planned attack by land, sea and air, that was to put, London first, and then the whole of Britain, under Hitler's control. In this period, relays of German bombers came over and just let their bombs go blindly through the low lying clouds. One fell on the Chapel at Buckingham Palace. The King and Queen were in residence. Neither was hurt, but three members of the staff were injured. Another bomb fell on the House of Lords. Big stores in Oxford Street were hit, and high explosives and incendiaries fell in Mayfair. Many shoppers were killed as they walked in the busy streets.

Now dawned Sunday, September 15,

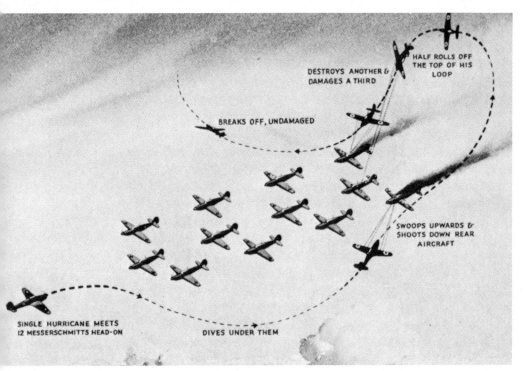

One Hurricane against twelve Messerschmitt ME-109s and that leaves nine. A drawing of the actual fighter attack tactic used against the German air formations.

A close-up of a Hurricane fighter on patrol.

With the towering St. Paul's Cathedral in the background, this London home guard spotter scans the sky for approaching German bombers.

the great invasion day, the peak of the blitz, and a day that will be remembered in the annals of the Royal Air Force with pride, even in coming centuries when new achievements have erased the memory of many of the old. It was a day of air fury, a day when Nazi bombers hurled themselves in waves against London and Southeast England in a series of the most desperate mass raids Germany had ever delivered.

During the day there were magnificent aerial battles six miles up in the shimmering blue over London. Flashes, rolling detonations, the crack of anti-aircraft guns, the zooming of diving machines, German aircraft cut in two by the knife-edge bullets from Spitfire wings, and falling in a trail of smoke and flame, bombs whistling and crashing, fires starting up, firebells clanging — surely Jules Verne and H. G. Wells, dreaming of the coming wars in the air, had conceived nothing more fantastic, thrilling, and wonderful than this reality unfolding before the fascinated eyes of those of us who were in London and saw it.

Here was the dream of the super film-producer developing to a magnificent dramatic intensity without rehearsal, and with stately St. Paul's and Buckingham Palace as part of the setting. And through all this day of almost continuous fighting our battle squadrons of the air not only held the enemy but out-maneuvered him, out-gunned him, and confirmed a qualitative superiority of man and machine that will never now be challenged or questioned. Here was the supreme test in the air for which the world had waited, and our boys, to the immense gratification and profound relief of all men and women of good will, were producing an indefinable spiritual something that defies and rises serenely above the effects of material onslaught, and against which poor Adolf Hitler battered his impotent fists, hurled his frenzied curses and exploded his bombs in vain.

The boys won new laurels on this supreme day, for they brought down a record catch of 185 enemy machines.* No need to wait for the evidence of the intelligence officer. The shattered Dorniers and Messerschmitts and Junkers were lying splintered and charred in Kensington, at Victoria Station, in the Thames meadows, at Rich-

* Official recount later put Luftwaffe losses at 56 destroyed.

mond, Dover, Esher, Tunbridge Wells, Dorking, Orpington, Chislehurts, Biggin Hill, Weymouth Bay, Porlock, Eastbourne, and baling out Nazi pilots descended on the English countryside like showers of summer snow. It had been history's biggest battle in the air, and the boys of the RAF had won it.

EDITOR'S NOTE
This day "had been the ultimate clash of human wills." The score was not imposing: 26 RAF planes lost, 56 Luftwaffe shot down. The story was written in the intensity of the fighting, the fury of desperation which both sides sensed. Massive fleets of Luftwaffe bombers and hordes of fighters streamed over England and were met by the entire force of Fighter Command. During the height of the battle Churchill asked the RAF Commander "How many fighters do you have left?" The answer was "None." All were committed. The air was congested with struggling aircraft, mid-air collisions, smoke trails, anti-aircraft shells bursting with bits of wreckage falling like rain. Pilots landed with blood on their cowling, parcels of human flesh in the air scoops — so close, so deadly had it been. Radio channels were swamped, air controllers were unable to cope with reports and orders.

The greatest effort of the Luftwaffe was turned into a rout. Only a few Luftwaffe bombers got through to their targets, so great was the confusion and chaos into which their formations were thrown. By nightfall a feeling of victory ran throughout England. On the Continent, Goering's Luftwaffe squadrons were licking their wounds from the worst defeat since the offensive began. And on the

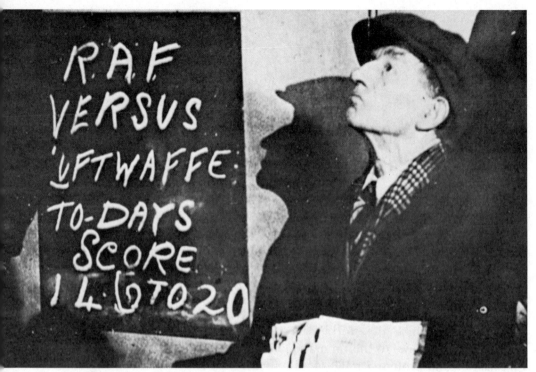

A London news vendor kept a daily box score of the dogfights between the RAF and the Luftwaffe.

17th of September Hitler postponed "Sea Lion" indefinitely.

While the Battle of Britain continued to the end of October, some days with intense ferocity, there was never any doubt that the RAF could turn back whatever the Germans put in the sky over England. By the end of September the great daylight armadas stopped coming. And the dreaded night attacks grew.

Targets were the big cities and the purpose for the deadly night raids was no longer to defeat the RAF but to retaliate for British bombing of German cities. To the very last day of the Battle of Britain — October 31, 1940 — the Luftwaffe kept the pressure on, despite continued high losses (325 in October).

Total box score for the Battle of Britain: July 10 to October 31, 1733 German aircraft destroyed to 915 for the RAF.

Most serious was the loss to both sides of irreplaceable men. Britain lost 415 pilots while 451 flew the entire Battle. It was estimated the life expectancy of a RAF pilot during these months was 87 flying hours, not long as time goes in combat.

By the end of October, convinced of the futility in trying to hammer the English people into submission from the air, Hitler called off his air legions and turned his forces toward the Eastern Front for the coming campaign against Russia and the Mediterranean.

England was saved by a handful of flyers.

Britain's Prime Minister Winston Churchill watches one of his Sterling heavy bombers take off for a mission over Berlin.

Of Death in the Sky

Richard Hillary

MY FIRST EMOTION was one of satisfaction, satisfaction at a job adequately done, at the final logical conclusion of months of specialized training. And then I had a feeling of the essential rightness of it all. He was dead and I was alive; it could so easily have been the other way round; and that would somehow have been right too. I realized in that moment just how lucky a fighter pilot is. He has none of the personalized emotions of the soldier, handed a rifle and bayonet and told to charge. He does not even have to share the dangerous emotions of the bomber pilot who night after night must experience that childhood longing for smashing things. The fighter pilot's emotions are those of the duelist — cool, precise, impersonal. He is privileged to kill well. For if one must either kill or be killed, as now one must, it should, I feel, be done with dignity. Death should be given the setting it deserves; it should never be a pettiness; and for the fighter pilot it never can be.

37

*One of the great contributions of the Battle of Britain was the develop-
ment of air combat tactics, both fighter and bomber that were used
throughout the war.*

*The basic rules of fighter combat, handed down from the great aces
of World War I, remained unchanged: use of sun and cloud, the surprise
bounce, team fighting rather than lone wolfing, aerial marksmanship,
determination and aggression, guarding against "blind spots." The cri-
teria for judging aircraft in World War II were the same as in World
War I: speed, rate of climb, maneuverability, and firepower. But the later
aircraft characteristics themselves had vastly changed. The Hurricane and
Spitfire, the ME-109 and 110, the P-47 and P-51 bore little resemblance
to the Sopwith Camel, the Fokker DR-4, or the French Spad. While
much of the old had to be relearned, a whole area of new air war techniques unfolded in the skies over Europe in the early 1940s.*

*Top British ace, Group Capt. J. E. "Johnny" Johnson, RAF, who
fought the Battle of Britain, here analyzes what was learned in that engagement about air weapons and their employment.*

Fighting Talk: Tactics of Aerial Warfare

Group Capt. J. E. Johnson, RAF

To us FIGHTER PILOTS this period, the
Battle of Britain, is full of interest
from a tactical point of view because
the tactics developed by both sides
formed the basis upon which our air
battles were fought for the remainder
of the war. It is worth examining these
tactics and some of the differing opinions held by those in authority at the
time.

The Luftwaffe possessed some excellent aeroplanes, and the Messerschmitt 109E had a higher ceiling and
better guns than either the Spitfire or
the Hurricane. The enemy fighter carried either four machine guns or two
machine guns and two cannon; the
latter compared very favorably with
our eight Browning machine guns.
The 109F, which was soon to make its
appearance over England, had one
cannon which was centrally mounted
and fired through the hub of the propeller, and later versions of this splendid fighter had three cannon.

During the fighting over Dunkirk,
our pilots found that their Spitfires
had slight margins of speed and climb

38

over the 109E. But most of these fights took place below 20,000 feet, and later, when we had to fight well above this height, it was soon discovered that the enemy fighter was decidedly superior because its supercharger was designed to operate more efficiently at the higher altitudes. When the Messerschmitt took evasive action by half-rolling and diving vertically for the deck, we found that we couldn't stay with it in this maneuver. Certainly the Spitfire was more maneuverable, but maneuvering does not win air battles, and tight turns are more of a defensive than an offensive tactic. The Spitfire's rate of turn would get you out of trouble if you saw your attacker in time, but only superior height would save you from the "bounce."

Group Captain J. E. Johnson, Royal Air Force top fighter pilot ace, in a relaxed moment during the Battle of Britain.

The Luftwaffe pinned great hopes on the stable companion of the 109, the twin-engined Messerschmitt 110D "destroyer" fighter. It had a greater range than the 109 and was accordingly often employed as a close escort to the bomber formation. It carried a formidable number of cannon, but it could not hold its own against either Spitfire or Hurricane. On more than one occasion the 109 had to help the twin-engined fighters out of a tight spot.

The Junkers 87 dive bomber, the Stuka, had enjoyed great success as a close-support weapon in the recent campaigns. It was little more than a piece of flying artillery and it could dive very steeply at a low forward speed. This meant that the pilot could line up his diving aircraft against a ground target with great accuracy and release his bombs when he pulled out at low level. But one of the basic principles of the employment of close-support aircraft is that they must be capable of holding their own against contemporary fighters. The Stuka contradicted this simple truth and paid the price in full when it met our Spitfires.

Of the three types of enemy bombers, the Heinkel 111, the Dornier 17, and the Junkers 88, the last named was superior to the other two and quite the most difficult to bring down. It had a high top speed, and when it dived with wide-open throttles our Spitfires couldn't catch it.

Morale was high in the Luftwaffe.

39

Their young fighter leaders had fought in the Spanish Civil War and had then blazed their way across half of Europe. Their fighter tactics were more advanced than ours and they were highly critical of our tight fighter formations.

Before the war our own fighter squadrons, together with those of other countries, flew in compact formations built up from tight elements of three aeroplanes. Such formations were ideal for spectacular fly-pasts, and although every fighter pilot must be able to "formate" closely on his leader to climb through cloud, this close style was to be of little value in the great air battles.

In Spain, the German fighter pilots soon realized that the speed of their 109s made close formations impracticable for combat. The large turning circle of the curving fighters dictated that a loose pattern was the only method in which individual pilots could hold their position in the turn and keep a sharp lookout at the same time. The high closing speeds, especially from head-on positions, made it essential to pick out and identify enemy aircraft as soon as possible, so that the leader could work his way into a good attacking position. The simple requirement was for a loose, open type of combat formation with the various aeroplanes flying at separated heights which would permit individual pilots to cover each other and search a greater area of sky than before.

Credit must be given to the Germans for devising the perfect fighter forma-tion. It was based on what they called the *rotte,* that is the element of two fighters. Some 200 yards separated a pair of fighters and the main responsibility of the number two, or wingman, was to guard his leader from a quarter or an astern attack. Meanwhile the leader navigated his small force and covered his wingman. The *schwarme,* four fighters, simply consisted of two pairs, and when we eventually copied the Luftwaffe and adopted this pattern we called it the "finger-four" because the relative positions of the fighters are similar to a plan view of one's four fingertips.

Let us examine the oustretched fingertips of the right hand and assume that the sun is shining from well above on the left side. The longest finger represents the leader and the index finger is the leader's number two, whose task it is to search the down-sun area of the sky. The wingman flies lower than his leader so that the pilots can see him well below the direct glare of the sun. An attack will usually develop from the sun, so we must have a constant search maintained in this direction. This is why numbers three and four fly on the right side of the leader, but slightly higher, so that we have two pairs of eyes always scanning the danger area.

When you fly your Spitfire five miles above the earth you will find that your wings hide a good deal of the ground and sky below. Suppose you are crossing the coast and Margate is just disappearing under your nose. The port

A formation of Spitfires, the single seater, day and night fighter, over Margate, England.

wingtip is over Clacton, the starboard wingtip slides across Gungeness, and Maidstone is just reappearing from the trailing edge of the wing. In other words, an area of about 1000 square miles is always hidden from your view at this height. But the finger-four, if properly flown in varying height intervals, is the best means of covering these blind spots below individual aircraft. The formation is loose and maneuver-able. The three pilots following the leader can search their respective areas of sky and keep him in sight without a great deal of uncomfortable neck twisting. The finger-four is easy to fly and far less tiring than the line-astern style. It permits an excellent all-round view, and the two wingmen, numbers two and four, separated by a distance of 500 or 600 yards, can guard the vital area above and behind.

It is easily split up into its basic elements of two aircraft, the smallest fighting unit in the air, since a lone pilot cannot protect himself from all quarters at the same time. It is a simple matter to build it into a squadron or wing formation. It is a great boost to morale, for the number four in a line-astern formation, tail-end Charlie, knows full well that if his section is bounced he will be the first to take a beating. But his equivalent in the breast formation is well up with his comrades and stands an equal chance of survival.

Some critics of the finger-four claimed that frequent turns made it difficult for the two wingmen to hold their flanking positions, but our pilots simply slipped into line-astern positions behind their leaders during tight turn and combat maneuvers. We found this criticism to be unjustified, and it is an interesting fact that towards the end of the war the finger-four was flown by fighter aircraft throughout the world. It has survived the test of time and the jet age, for it was used by both Sabre-jets and Mig 15s during the near-sonic fighting over Korea. Today, supersonic fighters carry out their operational training at speeds of over 1000 m.p.h. in this well-proven fashion.

Upon his return to Germany after a tour of operations in Spain, that great fighter pilot Werner Molder advocated that the open formation should be standard throughout their fighter arm. Tactically, the German fighter squadrons were ahead of us, for our two types of formation were either built up from a tight vic of three aircraft or four in line astern. The vic of three had little to recommend it and was an unfortunate legacy of peace-time flying, for the two wingmen had all their work cut out to stay near their leader and little time to search the sky. The high casualty rate of the wretched tail-end Charlies was a grim measure of the vulnerability of the line-astern formations. A further disadvantage of both these patterns was that the tightly packed aircraft were far more conspicuous in a clear sky than the widely spaced fighters of the finger-four.

Some of our squadrons provided two weavers in an attempt to guard themselves from the bounce. The weavers flew above the squadron and continually weaved and crisscrossed. They were usually the first to be picked off by the Messerschmitts, and the practice was stopped.

The fighter is simply a flying gun, and its basic qualities of speed and surprise could always be used to the greatest advantage. The outstanding pilots of an earlier generation than ours soon found that the leader with the height advantage controls the battle. With height the fighter leader can use the sun or cloud cover to the best tactical advantage. Those fighter pilots of earlier days had coined an apt phrase, "Beware of the Hun in the sun," and its warning was no less potent today.

In the 'thirties there was a growing body of opinion that maneuvers at high speeds were impossible because of the effects of "g" on the pilot. Dogfighting at speeds over 400 m.p.h., said the critics, is no longer possible. And so we had to learn, the hard way, that fighter tactics must be simple in character because elaborate techniques are not possible within the critical time available. A leader cannot retain control of even a small formation through a lot of complicated maneuvers, because the force is soon split up into individual, ineffective packets. Tactics must be simple, and the leader's task is to bring all the guns of his fighters to bear against the enemy in the shortest time. Leadership in the air consists not in scoring a personal kill but in the achievement of a decisive success with the whole force.

During his interrogation by the Allies at the end of the war and subsequently in his book,* Adolf Galland, one of Germany's greatest fighter pilots, accused his commander-in-chief of faulty direction and tactical misemployment of their fighter forces during the Battle of Britain. Galland asserts that Goering cut down the offensive power of his fighter squadrons by ordering them to act in an escort role and not permitting them to leave the bombers even when they could see Spitfires or Hurricanes maneuvering for attack. Before examining the validity of Galland's claims it is necessary

* *The First and the Last,* Holt, paperback reprint, Ballantine Books.

to know something of the theory of bomber support and escort by fighters.

The bomber is the true instrument of air power, and the fighter, when used offensively to assist the bomber, is merely a means to an end. In any fight for domination of the air it is the bombers, assisted by the fighters, which will decide the issue. When used alone, fighters can challenge the defenders to combat but the number of aeroplanes shot down in such clashes will rarely decide the main issue.

There are two methods by which fighters can assist bomber operations. Ranging formations of fighters can sweep ahead on the flanks, and behind the bombers. Usually they are well out of sight of the bombers, for they may be 50 or 100 miles away. Their leaders should have complete freedom of action to vary their planned flights so that they can take full advantage of the local tactical conditions. This type of fighter operation usually pays good dividends and is known as "bomber support by fighters."

Bomber "escort" by fighters is quite different from support, for here the fighters provide protection within sight of the bombers, and the nearest fighters, those of the close escort squadrons, are never allowed to break away and chase the enemy. The escort-cover squadrons guard both the close escort and the bombers, and we later found that to get the best results two of the usual three squadrons of the escort-cover wings should be free to leave the bombers. Against stiff opposition

43

high cover and top cover wings were used, but two-thirds of these forces were always free to break away.

It is not possible to lay down hard and fast rules about the proportion of fighters to be used in the support and escort roles. The allocation of fighters to these two tasks will depend upon the efficiency of the enemy's defense system and the type and number of his defending fighters. If the enemy chooses to ignore the free-lance fighter sweeps, which he should, and concentrates his fighters against the bomber formations, then it would be a mistake merely to increase the number of escorting fighters. The most effective remedy would be to plan the fighter sweeps to patrol the enemy airfields and from their superior height bounce the defenders when they climbed up. During 1941, our bomber pilots were greatly encouraged by the sight of masses of wheeling Spitfires, but there is no doubt that we tied far too many fighters to the bomber.

Fighters should always be used as offensively as possible and there is no doubt that Goering realized this, for after a conference with his air commanders before the Battle of Britain he issued clear instructions about their employment. Only part of the fighter arm, the Reichmarshal instructed, was to be employed as escort to the bombers; the remainder must be employed on free-lance operations in which they could come to grips with RAF fighters and indirectly protect the bombers.

No student of air warfare can find fault with the broad directive issued by Goering. Indeed, the Americans adopted the same tactics when they developed daylight operations to a high standard with their ranging fighter sweeps, which covered the length and breadth of Germany. But we know that the Luftwaffe fighter squadrons were by no means used in the tactically correct and flexible manner decreed at the time.

During the vital phase of the Battle of Britain when the bombing attacks were aimed at our airfields and aircraft factories, the Luftwaffe assembled massed formations of bombers with a close escort of 110s and large formations of 109s in the escort cover, high cover, and top cover roles. The timing of these heavy attacks was such that they usually followed a diversionary raid 30 or 40 minutes earlier against a coastal target. Although these tactics made life difficult for our controllers, who had to distinguish between the feint and the main thrust, we found that the 109s flew too high above the bombers and so gave them little protection.

During late August and early September, it was obvious that Goering's doctrine about the freedom of action of the 109s was not being followed, for the fighters were rarely seen unless they accompanied the bombers. Formations of fighters flew above, on the flanks and behind the bombers, and sometimes the 109s were seen weaving well below. Great gaggles of 109s were stepped up behind the bombers, and some idea of the size of these escorts can be judged from a great New Zealand fighter pilot, Al Deere, who reported that when the bombs from the leading Heinkels were falling on North Weald the rising screen of 109s stretched to Gravesend, a distance of more than 20 miles. These were poor tactics, for the lengthy assemblies of these unwieldy formations over the Pas de Calais often gave our radar ample warning of the approach of large raids. These large gaggles could be seen by our pilots from a great distance, and the high proportion of fighters tied to the bombers denied to the Messerschmitt squadrons that flexibility and freedom so essential to fighter operations.

Apart from the high altitude superiority of the 109 over our Spitfires, which only the introduction of a more powerful engine could redress, our squadrons had largely resolved the tactical inferiority which had marked the beginning of the fighting. We had recognized the principle that two fighters constitute the smallest element which can fight, and survive, in the air. The vulnerable vic of three was fast disappearing, and pilots who found themselves alone knew that there was no future in a hostile sky.

Although some of our squadrons still clung to the line-astern formation, the individual sections of four aircraft were separated by greater horizontal distances and we were evolving a more flexible abreast style of fighting. Our leaders had re-learned the value of height in the air battle, and even on the few occasions when they possessed an apparent height advantage over the 109s they now rarely failed to leave covering Spitfires high in the sun.

Time is one of the most important factors in air fighting. During the Battle of Britain the requirement in terms of time was to intercept with our fighters before the bombs fell. Far better to have one squadron above the Huns than half a dozen below!

There are other strong reasons for not committing fighters in too large formations. The vital element of surprise was often lost because the tight formations of Hurricanes and Spitfires could be seen from a great distance by the Luftwaffe's escort fighters. In addition, the leaders soon found that the larger the formation the more unwieldy it is in the air and the more difficult to control. My own later experience on both offensive and defensive operations confirmed that two squadrons of fighters was the ideal number to lead in the air. On some subsequent operations, when large numbers of enemy fighters opposed our fighter sweeps over France, I led a Balbo of five squadrons, but we got in each other's way in a fight and only the leaders were able to bring their guns to bear. Our common radio frequency was insufficient to control the activities of 60 pilots, especially in a fight. Finally there was the weather to contend with, for when we climbed our Balbo through layers of cloud we

45

sometimes spent more time searching for each other than looking for the enemy.

It is interesting to note that the pattern of the great daylight air battles fought over Germany between the United States Army Air Forces and the Luftwaffe vindicated the tactics used by Park* during the Battle of Britain. The German problem in 1944 was the same as ours four years previously: to stop large bomber formations, escorted by fighters, from reaching their targets in daylight. The Germans fell into the trap of trying to operate their fighters in formations of up to 60 strong, the same size as one of our Balbos of five squadrons. These cumbersome gaggles denied to the enemy fighter pilots those essential and inherent qualities of their aircraft — speed, surprise, and maneuverability — and they fell easy prey to the ranging and aggressive American fighters.

* Air Vice Marshall K. R. Park, Commander-in-Chief, R.A.F.

Throughout the winter and spring of 1941 Luftwaffe pressure on Britain decreased as units moved from Western Europe onto airfields in the Balkan States of Bulgaria and Rumania and to Poland and East Prussia along the 1000 mile Russian Front.

Russian-German relations had been balanced on the delicate edge of a non-aggression pact that was worth little more than the paper upon which it was printed. The treaty merely assured Hitler temporary immunity from attack in the rear while his legions gobbled up Europe, country by country.

Now that his West European ventures were over (except a badly battered Britain which he feared no more), he turned arrogantly toward the Kremlin.

His plan, called "Operation Barbarossa" envisioned the application of the "blitzkrieg" technique against massive, but weak, Russia. In a summer-fall campaign of six weeks he estimated he could slash the Soviet armies to pieces. Then, with the Communist nemesis out of the picture he could turn West once more and deal with England at his leisure.

On Sunday morning, June 22, 1941, his troops struck out suddenly into the endless plains of the Soviet Union. The 135 divisions he threw across the Russian frontiers were commanded by some of the best professional soldiers on earth — von Runstedt, von Brauchitsch, Halder, Guderian, van Kleist, Kesselring, and others. The forces made a frontal assault in three major directions — Leningrad in the north, Moscow in the center, and Stalingrad in the south.

*Again spearheading this massive attack were four Luftwaffe Air Fleets,
I, II, IV, and V, comprising 2000 aircraft and including 1000 twin-engine
bombers, 350 dive bombers, 600 fighters, 700 tactical and strategic reconnaissance aircraft, 300 transports, and around 75 twin-engine fighters.*

*Opposing the Luftwaffe on this June morning were approximately 7500
front-line aircraft of the Soviet Air Force consisting of 3000 fighters, 2500
medium and light bombers, 1500 transport/bombers, and 500 liaison aircraft.*

*The ill-fated venture got off to a good start. The initial offensive, rem-
iniscent of the successes in Western Europe, plunged the well-oiled German land-air machine quickly and deeply into the great enigma of Russia.
Soviet land and air forces disintegrated before the powerful drive and fell
back, disappearing beyond the horizon.*

*Here, from the diary of a Luftwaffe fighter pilot is a word picture of
how it was ... at first ...*

Dawn Attack on Russia

Sr. Lt. Heinz Knoke, Luftwaffe

JUNE 21, 1941: Three weeks have passed since the squadron was last on operations.

We are now based at Suwalki, a former Polish Air Force station near the Russian border. Stukas and fighter-bombers use the field also.

For the past two weeks our armies have been massing in increasing strength, all along the Eastern frontier. No one knows what is happening. One rumor has it that the Russians will permit us to cross the Caucasus in a thrust to occupy the oil fields of the Middle East and the Dardanelles and seize the Suez Canal.

We shall see.

In the evening orders came through that the airliner on the scheduled Berlin-Moscow run is to be shot down. The commanding officer takes off with his headquarters section; but they fail to intercept the Douglas.

We spend the night sitting in the mess. The guesswork continues.

What is the significance of "Operation Barbarossa"? That is the code name for all the vast military activity in the east of the Reich. The order for shooting down the Russian Douglas airliner has convinced me that there is to be war against Bolshevism.

JUNE 22, 1941: 0400 hours. General alert for all squadrons. Every unit on

47

the airfield is buzzing with life. All night long I hear the distant rumbles of tanks and vehicles. We are only a few miles from the border.

0430 hours: All crews report to the squadron operations room for briefing. The Commanding Officer, Capt. Woitke, reads out the special order for the day to all the armed forces from the Führer.

Germany is to attack the Soviet Union!

0500 hours. The squadron takes off and goes into action.

In our flight, four aircraft, including mine, have been equipped with a bomb-release mechanism, and I have done considerable bombing practice in recent weeks. Now there is a rack slung along the belly of my good "Emil," carrying 100 five-pound fragmentation bombs. It will be a pleasure for me to drop them on Ivan's dirty feet.

Flying low over the broad plains, we notice endless German columns rolling eastward. The bomber formations overhead and the dreaded Stuka dive-bombers alongside us are all heading in the same direction. We are to carry out a low-level attack on one of the Russian headquarters, situated in the woods to the west of Druskininkai.

On Russian territory, by contrast, everything appears to be asleep. We locate the headquarters and fly low over the wooden buildings, but there is not a Russian soldier in sight. Swooping at one of the huts, I press the bomb-release button on the control stick. I distinctly feel the aircraft lift as it gets rid of the load.

The others drop theirs at the same time. Great masses of dirt fountain up into the air, and for a time we are unable to see because of all the smoke and dust.

One of the huts is blazing fiercely. Vehicles have been stripped of their camouflage and overturned by the blast. The Ivans at last come to life. The scene below is like an overturned ant heap, as they scurry about in confusion. Men in their underwear flee for cover in the woods. Light flak guns appear visible. I set my sights on one of them, and open up with machine guns and both cannon. An Ivan at the gun falls to the ground, still in underwear.

And now for the next one!

Round again, and I let them have it. The Russians stand fast and begin firing back at me. "Just wait till I take the fun out of your shooting, you *Schwein!*"

Round yet again for another attack.

I never shot as well as this before. I come down to sixty feet, almost brushing the treetops in the process and then pull up sharply in a climbing turn. My Ivans lie flat on the ground beside their gun. One of them leaps to his feet and dashes into the trees.

I carry out five or six more attacks. We buzz round the camp like a swarm of hornets. Nearly all the huts are in flames. I fire at a truck. It also burns after the first burst of fire.

0556 hours. Flight landing in formation.

The chief sees smiling faces all round when the pilots report

Aircraft are refueled and rearmed at top speed. The field is in a state of feverish activity. The Stukas return from their mission in support of our armored units advancing on the ground. Their crews are jubilant, too.

0630 hours. Only 40 minutes after landing we are off again. Our objective is the same headquarters as before, and from a great distance we are guided to our destination by the smoke rising from the burning buildings.

This time considerable quantities of light flak come up to welcome us. It is just like that time near Canterbury. Once again I give special attention to the Ivans at their flak guns. This time I put down my bombs on one of the emplacements. Dirt and dust, the gun-site burst! And that takes care of the Ivans.

The Russians appear to have taken cover and hidden their vehicles in the forest round the camp. We work over the forest systematically with our machine guns. Fires break out in different places. That must be where they have their fuel dumps. I fire at every target which presents itself to me, until the magazines are all empty.

We land at 0720 hours. Once again the flight is prepared for action at lightning speed. Ground crews work with swift precision. We pilots help them and have to give them a full account of the operations. This time we set up a record by being completely ready in 22 minutes. We take off again immediately.

There is not much left of the Russian camp by now. Every target which we spot in the surrounding woodland is thoroughly strafed. I place my bombs on the last building which is still standing. Krupinsky does the same, which takes care of anything remaining. The camp is totally destroyed.

After 48 minutes in the air we land again and taxi over to the dispersal area. We now take a short breather and enjoy our first meal of the day.

New operation orders have arrived. Russian transport columns have been observed by our reconnaissance aircraft retreating eastward along the Grodno-Zytomia-Skidel-Szczuczyn highway, with our tanks in hot pursuit. We are to support them by bombing and strafing the Russians as they retreat.

Take-off at 1007 hours, accompanied by the Stukas. They are to dive-bomb the Russian artillery emplacements in the same area.

We soon reach Grodno. The roads are clogged with Russian armies everywhere. The reason gradually dawns on us why the sudden surprise attack was ordered by our High Command. We begin to appreciate the full extent of the Russian preparations to attack us. We have just forestalled the Russian timetable for an all-out attack against Germany for the mastery of Europe.

This is one day I shall never forget. Our armies move forward everywhere, the spearhead units thrusting ahead. The Russians are taken completely by surprise. Soldiers on the roads on our side wave as we pass low overhead. The congested roads and lanes on the Russian side are subjected to concentrated bombing and machine-gun fire.

Thousands of Ivans are in full retreat, which becomes an utter rout when we open up on them, stumbling and bleeding as they flee from the highway in an attempt to take cover in the nearby woods. Vehicles lie burning by the roadside after we pass. Once I drop my bombs on a column of heavy artillery drawn by horses. I am thankful not to be down there myself.

We take off at 2000 hours for our sixth mission on this first day. There has been no sign of the Russian Air Force the entire day, and we are able to do our work without encountering opposition.

EDITOR'S NOTE
While the Soviet Air Force was numerically superior to the Luftwaffe, it had little else in its favor except the courage and tenacity of its airmen.

The disparity in fighters was especially marked. The obsolescent I-15 and I-16 (which made up the bulk of the fighter force) were no match for the Luftwaffe's ME-109 and 110s. Even the MIG-1s, Lagg-3s, and Yak-1s, just coming in service in 1941 were inferior in speed and firepower. The IL-2 Stormovik dive bomber could not compare with the JU-87 Stuka. Soviet PE-2 and DB-3 twin-engine light bombers were underarmed and their performance and capabilities far short of the JU-88 and HE-111 Luftwaffe counterparts. German air technology of the 1930s had definitely far outclassed that of the Soviet Union.

Neither the German nor the Russian Air Forces possessed a strategic long-range bomber force able to strike the enemy's resources far behind the battlefront. Both nations had designed and built their air forces for support of ground armies alone. This proved fatal for both nations.

What gave the numerically inferior Luftwaffe the great advantage was its surprise mass attacks on Soviet airfields and the superior performance of its combat aircraft and its pilots.

By the end of the summer of 1941, the Luftwaffe had complete control of the air above the battle areas. In the fall, things began to change. Strong reinforcement of Soviet fighters poured from the factories which the Russians had moved beyond the Ural Mountains. With aircraft production capacity estimated at 5000 per month, the Russians came back with vengeance and by the end of the autumn of 1941 forced the Luftwaffe onto the defensive. Weather, accidents, and combat had taken a terrific toll of German aircraft and men. The demands for aircraft in North Africa and Western Europe precluded reinforcements being sent to the Russian Front.

The Russian I-16, used successfully in the earlier Manchurian war against Japan, was considered to be an obsolete airplane on the Eastern front.

PART TWO

STRIKEBACK OVER EUROPE: BUILDUP AND SHAKEDOWN

January, 1941 – June, 1943

Introduction

HITLER'S MILITARY CONQUEST of Europe rolled at high crest when the Japanese carrier task force struck suddenly at Pearl Harbor on December 7, 1941 — an act that brought the U.S. into the war against Germany.

England alone had defeated the mighty Luftwaffe and remained a free political entity in Western Europe. In Eastern Europe, Soviet Air Forces all but disintegrated before the Luftwaffe air offensive and her ground forces had fallen back with cruel losses into the amorphous vastness of Russia, defeated on the field, but unconquered in spirit and in fact.

To the south, Nazi Panzer Divisions with strong Luftwaffe support had crossed the Mediterranean into North Africa. Here under Gen. Erwin Rommel, "The Desert Fox," the German offensive was striking eastward along the African coast toward Egypt and the Suez Canal.

In the Atlantic Ocean, German submarines in "wolfpacks" stalked the sea lanes preying on merchant shipping while overhead Luftwaffe patrol bombers ranged far out to strike individual merchantmen and convoys bound for the beleaguered British Isles. The air-sea blockade of Europe was an effective thing.

Long before Pearl Harbor, Russia and England had turned for help to the industrial arsenal of the world, the U.S., which up to December 7, 1941, was precariously maintaining neutrality on the one hand while on the other supplying the Allies with weapons and materials for war.

As early as 1938, President Roosevelt foresaw the coming conflict and U.S. involvement in it, and further, that airpower would play a key role in winning it. The Naval Expansion Act of May, 1938 authorized a 3000 plane program to modernize our carrier striking forces. In January, 1939 the President called for a $300,000,000 Army Air Corps expansion to include 6000 aircraft. As important as were these measures in building up U.S. air forces, equally significant was the stimulus these appropriations gave to building a U.S. industrial base to produce air weapons for all countries fighting Germany. Money cannot be translated into production-line combat aircraft in weeks, or months, but in years. Fortunately the war did not begin for the U.S. in 1938, 1939 or 1940, the years during which our aircraft industry began shifting out of low peace-time gear. In the winter of 1939-40 large British and French orders for nearly 11,000 first-line American combat aircraft poured into U.S. aircraft industries, adding further stimulus to their mushroom-growth.

In 1938, American industrial output was 100 military aircraft per month. By April, 1940 it had reached 402 per month and was tooling up for double that amount. This phenomenal growth was but a trickle compared to production set into motion by the Pearl Harbor attack.

In January, 1942 President Roosevelt reorganized the machinery for industrial mobilization. The giant automobile industry and all of its tremendous resources were wholly committed to the production of aircraft and war material by June, 1942. Labor organizations promised not to strike for the duration of the war. Factories went on a 24-hour basis, six and seven day weeks. Aircraft production received high national priority as the President called for 45,000 combat planes in 1942 and 100,000 in 1943 (85,000 were actually produced that year). By the end of 1943, the aircraft industry labor force reached a peak of 2,100,000 men and women. Mass production became a fine art. In early 1944, the Ford Willow Run factory alone equaled the production of the entire Japanese aircraft industry and half that turned out by Germany. Total monthly U.S. output shot up from 2464 aircraft in December, 1941, to a top of 9113 in March, 1944, and an annual output that year of 110,000.

American warplanes in demand by the Allies reflected the U.S. military air concepts of the 1930s — emphasis on the heavy bomber which could be flown as fast as pursuits and could defend itself against fighters, and the degradation of the fighter concept and its design development.

Thus only three fighter models, designed in the middle 1930s, were immediately available to carry the U.S. brunt of the early years of the war: the Bell P-39 "Aircobra," and the North American P-40 "Warhawk," (both of which were inferior to the German ME-109 and 110) and the Lockheed twin-engine P-38 "Lightning" — which first saw action in late 1942 and could hold its own against the Luftwaffe. It would be a full year later, 1943, with the appearance of the Republic P-47 "Thunderbolt" and the North American P-51 "Mustang," that U.S. fighters could match and surpass the best in combat fighters German technology could put into the air.

American medium bombers were much better: the Douglas A-20 "Havoc" (called the "Boston" by the British), the North American B-25 "Mitchell" and the Martin B-26 "Marauder" (the "flying coffin" to most crewmen) served well throughout the war.

Lone star in the first-line heavy bomber class was the Boeing B-17 "Flying Fortress" and of these the U.S. had only 23 on hand when Hitler attacked Poland. The B-17 had been a controversial piece of equipment in the budget-lean peacetime years, both in political and military circles. It was a superlative bomber, advanced for its time, and by Pearl Harbor the "Fort" stood ready for mass production. The Consolidated B-24 "Liberator" which teamed up with the B-17 in the strategic campaign from late 1942 onward was still a drawing board design in September, 1939. Within two years it would be appearing in small numbers.

Thus was the colossal task cut out for the U.S.: gear up the entire national effort, provide the Allies with combat air weapons and at the same time build up and modernize the Army Air Forces and the Naval Air Arm into large, strong and effective forces, deployed for action and combat ready. Fortunately, the industrial base to do this was there. Congressional appropriations were forthcoming, military leadership was prepared for the herculean job, and eager young men by the tens of thousands streamed into the air arm to fight the war from the cockpit and flight deck.

Prior to Pearl Harbor, aircraft purchased in the U.S. by friendly foreign nations with cash or under Lend-Lease went overseas by shipboard or by aerial delivery. British and Canadian pilots in 1939 and 1940 ferried 2400 American warplanes to England from fields in Canada and on the Atlantic seaboard. Between June 6, 1941 and Pearl Harbor British airmen ferried 1350 aircraft to England. Meanwhile the U.S. Army Air Corps Ferrying Command pioneered air routes across the North Atlantic via Scotland, and the South Atlantic via Brazil, to Cairo and points north and east. In August, 1941 civilian crews of Pan American Air

Ferries (a subsidiary of Pan Am Airways) began delivery of C-47s and B-25s on the southern route to Africa for British and Russian forces. By the end of 1942, 102 B-25s were turned over to Russia. A third route via Alaska to Siberia became a major traffic-way for air delivery of U.S. warcraft to the Soviet Union — by the end of the war more than 1000 Lend-Lease P-63s, P-39s, A-20s, and B-25s were delivered via "Alsib" route.

Plane delivery by Army Air Force crews began in November, 1941, when several B-24 Liberators were flown to Cairo for the British North African Forces. This flight was the beginning of what later became a massive aerial delivery and supply force, reorganized in June, 1942 as the Air Transport Command (ATC). From June, 1942 to the end of the war ATC made 268,000 ferry deliveries; of which 219,000 were to domestic U.S. bases and 45,000 to overseas destinations. It lost 594 planes on overseas runs and 419 in the U.S. ATC crew deliveries to overseas countries were supplemented by foreign aircrew deliveries. Russian airmen picked up planes in Alaska, in Cairo, Teheran, and other points, while British crews took delivery on American and Canadian bases for the flight to England.

U.S. supply of combat aircraft to its foreign Allies rose to mountainous proportions. Allocation of aircraft through June 30, 1942 included 6634 to England, 1835 to Russia, 407 to China, and 104 to other Allies. Total to Great Britain for 1942 numbered around 10,000. The build-up continued into 1943 with Russia receiving 3431 (94 per cent of our commitment), and Britain 9262 for that year, exclusive of transports. Total U.S. delivery to the Soviet Union from June 22, 1941 to September 20, 1945 was 15,000 aircraft, 80 per cent of which were A-20 medium bombers, P-39, P-40, and P-63 fighters.

American supply and delivery of aircraft was only part of the overall Allied air force build-up. Throughout the Battle of Britain and the long winter of the "Night Blitz" British production rose, with emphasis on the defensive fighters — the Hurricane (hero of the Battle of Britain) and its superior partner the famed Spitfire. As these fighters rolled off British assembly lines and into RAF combat squadrons, the tough, fast, versatile little twin-engine "Beaufighter" made its appearance in night combat and on daylight sweeps into Europe. It was followed by the all-wooden "Mosquito" which became one of the most versatile fighter/bombers of the war.

At the beginning of 1942, British four-engine heavy bombers were coming into service. Three models were put into production from the drawing boards, and before flight test, saving two to three years development-test time and proving to be one of the great visionary decisions of the war. They were the "Stirling," the "Halifax," and the "Manchester" (which later in redesign became the "Lan-caster," outstanding British heavy of the entire war). By February, 1942 RAF Bomber Command averaged a daily combat serviceable rate of 374 bombers. By late spring, Bomber Command was ready to carry out a 1000-plane night mission to Cologne, Germany, officially called "Operation Millennium." Actually 1046 aircraft were dispatched on the night of May 30-31, 1942. Photo reconnaissance showed unprecedented damage. Colossal fires from the bombs swept through the city, uncontrolled. Churchill promised Germany would receive "city by city, from now on" an equal taste of British airpower. It was Cologne which firmly gave the British concept of night strategic area bombing its strongest support and endorsement.

Meanwhile, and concurrent with supplying aircraft to Britain, Russia and other Allies, the U.S. set about to expand its Army and Naval Air Forces at a schedule that staggers the imagination.

In September, 1939, on the eve of the war, the total U.S. Naval and Marine Corps Air Arms measured only 7 large and 1 small aircraft carriers, 5 patrol wings, 2 marine aircraft wings, 5900 pilots and 21,678 enlisted men, 5233 aircraft of all types, including trainers, and only a few bases outside the U.S. The Army Air Corps consisted of 26,000 officers, cadets, and enlisted men on 17 air bases and four depots. 2000 were pilots. The force was equipped with 800 first-line combat aircraft of which three standard models were the obsolete Douglas B-18s, Douglas A-17 attack bombers, and the P-36 fighter. The Naval Expansion Act of May, 1938 was the first of a series of air rearmament actions during the next two years. Appropriations were heaped on top of each other in frantic effort to catch up with the one-half million-man German Air Force, the 50,000 to 75,000 trained aircrews it had on hand, and the Luftwaffe's 4100 first-line combat planes that could be matched only by U.S. models on drawing boards. By July, 1941 authorization for army and navy aircraft had reached 50,000 planes.

By December, 1941 major Army air installations had grown to 114 with 28 more authorized. Combat groups had expanded to 67, with 18 overseas, 28 1/2 in reserve and 20 1/2 in training. Thanks to stepped-up flight and technical training programs, officer and enlisted man force levels had risen to 354,000, pilots to 9000, mechanics to 59,000. First-line combat plane inventory numbered 2846. In December, 1940 the peace-time Air Corps had been reorganized and renamed the Army Air Forces, with Gen. H. H. Arnold as its chief, gaining for all practical purposes autonomy of operations and management needed for war footing. Six months later four brilliant young air force officers (Lt. Cols. Harold L. George and Kenneth N. Walker and Majs. Laurence S. Kuter and Haywood S. Hansell, Jr.) drew up a plan called AWPD/1 which forecast air strategy and requirements for the air war against Germany and Japan. The plan called for the AAF's major contribution to be strategic bombing offensive featured by daylight precision bombing. It set down as the requirement for the defeat of Germany and Japan, an air force of 239 combat groups and 108 separate squadrons, 63,467 planes of all types and 2,164,916 men. The air offensive against Germany, these officers predicted, would reach its maximum power in April, 1944. With almost uncanny accuracy and vision they were proved right. AWPD/1 became a book of air prophecy. Peak strength of the AAF reached 2,400,000 men, 243 combat groups, and approximately 80,000 aircraft. Offensive power of the AAF was at its height in the spring of 1944 in Europe.

Along with the build-up of its own and its Allied Air Forces, the U.S. constructed air bases in Newfoundland, on British possessions in the Caribbean, in Dutch Guiana, in South America, in the Panama Canal, Puerto Rico, Iceland, and Greenland, with the Azores coming about mid-war. These bases provided excellent outposts for hemispheric defense and springboards for air patrol against enemy submarine operations. Through them, particularly those in Newfoundland, Greenland, and Iceland, poured the planes and equipment bound for England and the build-up under a code name "Operation Bolero."

Under "Bolero" American forces streamed by sea and by air to scores of bases being carved out of the pleasant

English countryside. During the summer and fall of 1942, B-17s, C-47s, and the twin-engine P-38s airspanned the North Atlantic to begin the formation of the American Eighth Air Force in England. Before the 1942 winter set in, 882 aircraft, mostly B-17s and C-47s arrived in England. On June 18, Maj. Gen. Carl A. Spaatz set up Eighth AF Headquarters in Bushy Park, outside of London, and on July 4, 1942 the first U.S. air combat took place when 6 A-20 medium bombers attacked German airfields in Holland. A month later Gen. Ira Eaker led the first heavy (B-17) attack of the war in a mission to the marshaling yards at Rouen-Sotteville, France. With RAF fighter escort, the daylight sweep was successful. During the next three weeks ten more small missions were flown by the Flying Fortresses of Eighth Air Force in a test of the American theory of daylight bombardment and the equipment to carry it out. Of the 11 missions only two B-17s were lost. American air leaders were jubilant.

Meanwhile the invasion of French North Africa, "Operation Torch," was being prepared to take the pressure off the British Eighth Army which Field Marshal Erwin Rommel's Afrika Korps had driven to El Alemein, the last defense before the Suez Canal. Much of the growing strength of the U.S. Eighth Air Force in England was

Three of the Eighth Air Force's World War II leaders are pictured in this "standup" staff briefing in England at the height of the Command's strategic aerial bombardment of Nazi Europe. In the middle of the photo facing the camera are: General Carl A. Spaatz, Lt. Gen. James Doolittle, and Maj. Gen. William Kepner.

transferred to Twelfth Air Force (the African Invasion Air Force) commanded by Brig. Gen. Jimmy Doolittle.

Eighth Air Force Bomber Command missions were thus subordinated to the training and preparations for "Torch" and only three more operations were flown over Europe before October, 1942. Biggest was the 107-plane heavy bomber sortie on Lille, on October 9. By this time the German fighter defense had felt out the Fortresses and attacked with vengeance. Eleven B-17s were shot down and the formation was thrown into confusion. The U.S. daylight strategic bombardment concept had yet to prove itself in deadly combat.

The shift of U.S. air emphasis to the Mediterranean in the fall of 1942 left the RAF Bomber Command with its radar-equipped night bombers as the principal air offensive until the spring and summer of 1943 when the African invasion was successfully completed and the combined U.S.-British daylight and night bomber offensive against German-held Europe could get underway in earnest from England.

Eighth Air Force, with only two to six groups, hampered by bad weather, supply shortages, inexperienced crews, and maintenance problems that cut down its forces to 50 per cent operational aircraft, conducted only occasional missions during the winter of 1942-43. Rarely 100 B-17s could be put in the air at one time. Main targets were submarine bases and yards in France and the Low Countries that could not be damaged with normal bombs because of their rugged construction. Then, too, Luftwaffe opposition stiffened and 10 per cent losses on a 106-plane mission to Bremen, Germany on April 17, 1943 were unacceptable. These losses indicated a tremendous build-up of German defense fighters (500 to 700) in Western Europe. Confronted by an efficient enemy warning and control system and increased effectiveness of German anti-aircraft fire around major targets, the American daylight precision bombing concept still faced the ominous task of proving itself equal to or better than the British night concept.

By late spring, 1943, Eighth Air Force and British Bomber Command were ready for the coming air offensive. American air leaders were firm in their strategic air convictions based on daylight precision bombing. The combat aircraft, the units, and personnel build-up were in high gear, the shakedown missions of the past year had blazed the trail, hardened crews, hammered out bitter lessons on the anvil of desperate aerial combat.

In the East, Russian Air Forces began to rise out of the ashes of destruction. When the Germans attacked Russia, the Soviets wisely dismantled aircraft factories in Kiev, Leningrad, Kharkov, and Moscow and moved them beyond the Ural Mountains, outside the range of German bombers. Now these factories were pouring out more effective fighters like the MIG-1,

Yak-1, and Lagg-3 and total aircraft output was up to nearly 5000 per month.

Hitler's directive to destroy the Russian aircraft industry had not accounted for the short range of his twin-engine bombers. For the second time since the war began, the Luftwaffe's shortcomings (lack of a long-range strategic bomber force) proved a weak link in German armor and strategy.

By December, 1941 Soviet fighter strength on the Moscow front built up to 1000 fighters, as against a depleted Luftwaffe of 500, of which about one-half were serviceable at all times. The bitter winter brought sub-zero temperatures and poor visibility, all but immobilizing the Germans. Ill-equipped for a Russian winter, the German government appealed to the public to donate furs and woolens for the men on the Russian Front, but it was of little avail. On the other hand, the Soviets thrived on the cold; they were equipped and trained to operate in the most bitter winter weather.

In early 1942, Hitler was forced to withdraw one of the three Luftwaffe Air Fleets from Russia to build up air defenses in Western Europe against the growing Anglo-American bomber offensive, and to meet the needs of his forces in the Mediterranean area where Allied air build-up was in progress. By spring of 1942, Soviet and German Air Forces were on equal numerical footing and later that year the Soviets received nearly 2000 fighters from

England and the U.S. These Hurricanes, P-40 Tomahawks and P-39 Aircobras added to the expanding numbers of new Russian Lagg-3, Lav-5, and Yak-9 fighters equipped with 12.7mm machine guns and 20mm cannons. New designs of the twin engine IL-2 Stormovik and PE-2 light bombers with improved operational characteristics and armor added strength to the Soviet air capabilities.

While Soviet air strength was building up numerically it still had many operational lessons to learn. During the summer and autumn of 1942, the tempo of air fighting on all fronts rose to high crescendo. In May, despite numerical inferiority, German Air Forces played a large role in evicting the Red Army from the Crimea and in autumn spearheaded a strong drive toward Stalingrad and the Caucasus. Soviet airmen did little to stop this offensive. By early winter, however, Soviet air reaction stiffened. The newly-created ADD Long Range Air Command with bombers and transports ferried tens of thousands of ground troops to Stalingrad from other fronts. Nearly 1000 new Russian fighters and bombers were brought in to work over German airfields in the Stalingrad area.

The second bitter Russian winter (1942-43) hit the Luftwaffe a deadly blow. Ice, fog, snow, and paralyzing sub-zero temperatures cut their operations to 25 per cent. Soviet fighters played havoc with German troop transports which did get into the air. The

German aerial resupply of Gen. von Paulus' Sixth Army before Stalingrad was able to deliver only one-third of the daily 300 tons of supplies the Sixth Army needed to exist. This deficiency led directly to the surrender of von Paulus at Stalingrad in February, 1943, marking a virtual end of German airpower as a decisive force along the 1000-mile Russian Front.

Throughout Russia, German air power began a rapid decline from which it would never recover. At Leningrad, for example, two Soviet Air Armies comprised nearly 2000 aircraft against 300 for the Luftwaffe standing against them.

Large credit must go to the British-American Combined bomber offensive planned at the Casablanca Conference in early 1942. This offensive drew two-thirds of all German fighter strength back into Western Europe to defend the "Fatherland" against mounting day and night raids from British bases. Then, too, German aircraft losses on the Russian Front measured in the thousands. Nearly 1000 elite experienced Luftwaffe pilots had been killed in Russia, while a large share of the experienced pilots left were transferred to Western Europe. From 1942 onward the caliber of Luftwaffe flyers on the Russian Front would be low.

By mid-1943, with the help of U.S. combat aircraft reinforcements, P-39s, P-40s, A-20s, and B-25s, the Russian Air Force had reappeared in the skies as a major factor in the war, and held the decided edge over the Luftwaffe.

The air initiative of the war now passed to the Allies in a vast circle surrounding Nazi-conquered Europe. Germany was about to experience a year of horror and destruction unprecedented in the history of warfare.

Before the smoke had drifted from the debris at Pearl Harbor, the commercial airlines of America, through the Air Transport Association, had offered their complete resources to the U.S. Government. Assimilation into the military got underway immediately. Pilots, executives, ground personnel, and above all the commercial airlines, were brought into the Air Corps Ferrying Command. These were hectic days, responding to the critical need for large scale air delivery overseas to Europe and the Pacific of men, material, and combat aircraft.

The new organization soon took shape in the birth of the Air Transport Command in June, 1942. By the end of the war this "greatest airline in history" would spiderweb the world with eight air routes (South Pacific, South West Pacific, Central Pacific, South Atlantic, African, North Atlantic, China-Burma-India, and Alaska) and would consist of 200,000 personnel. It would fly nearly 8 billion passenger miles, 1-1/3 billion ton miles, 1/2 billion plane miles, log nearly 2-1/3 million hours in the air supplying our far-flung combat theatres and our Allies world-wide.

The chaotic beginning of ATC was not without reason. Even as hundreds of airline crews and scores of commercial airliners reported into ATC bases to fly for the Army the bases themselves were still being scraped out of the earth. Items from crew quarters to aircraft servicing facilities to navigational aids were under construction or non-existent. Most pilots had only domestic-route flight experience. Long distance, overseas flying was something entirely different and new. Some trans-ocean routes had been pioneered in the pre-war days by commercial airlines and the Air Corps Ferrying Command. Others were completely new.

Incredible dramas took place in the cockpits of ATC aircraft along the primitive trans-ocean aerial routes in early 1942, drawing on the skills and the courage of airmen as flight had never done before. If some flights and crews would disappear from the face of the earth, others would return with stories of heroic and tragic propositions.

One such happened to Ernest K. Gann, one of many airline pilots flying army cargo out of Presque Isle, Maine. This newly-established U.S. terminal of the North Atlantic route suddenly had become important because of the critical need for combat aircraft and supplies in Europe.

Airbase sites on the treacherous fiord-cut coast of Greenland had been selected and radio-navigational equipment was badly needed to guide the coming flow of combat aircraft over the North Atlantic to England. Gann's job was to deliver the steel beams of a radio tower to the Greenland site in his twin-engine C-47. Dead reckoning navigation, in a part of the world where compasses play tricks on pilots, where aerial maps were yet to be chartered, where narrow deep fiords offered a one-time approach — these were the major problems facing Ernie Gann. There was another, which he could not know about until it was almost too late. Here is that intriguing story . . .

The Rule Books Are Paper

Ernest K. Gann

THIS WAS the very beginning of what later became the world-girdling Air Transport Command.

And it was very much of a beginning: hesitant, tangled in cross purposes, and at times nearly chaotic. The army personnel at Presque Isle, which proved to be on the northern border of Maine, were beside themselves with chagrin and confusion. They were sud-

The Air Transport Command's Douglas C-47 workhorse saw duty all over the world. This one is flying cargo over the Pyramids in Egypt.

Some of the transport C-47s were loaded with "almost any type of cargo."

denly invaded from the skies by a force of civilian air crews which jammed every facility. Our ten crews were relatively easy to assimilate since somehow our impending arrival had been duly announced through channels, but a much larger group of TWA planes and crews arrived wearing white caps and thin white shirts as if they were still flying through the heat of Kansas. While we were sent off to billets in a nearby tourist camp and advised to look after our own feeding, no one had the faintest idea what should be done about the hapless TWA crews, much less why they had been ordered to come in the first place. As the teletypes sought an answer from Washington, some recklessly inspired officer ordered their airplanes loaded with the contents of a freight train which had been standing alongside the field. Nothing was weighed. The airplanes were simply loaded until they were full. No one bothered to inform the TWA crews where they were supposed to fly their cargoes. Just as the loading neared completion an order came down to unload the planes again. The weary curses of the G.I.s had barely subsided when all of the TWA crews were ordered back where they had come from. They flew away to the south, quite empty and as thoroughly bewildered as those who had called forth these logistic phantoms.

The citizens of Presque Isle, hitherto mostly dependent upon the price and quality of potatoes for gossip, found new zest in the presence of our men. It was a lovely little town surrounded by undulating hills of trim potato fields, each delivered of drabness by bordering pine trees. A swift and clear river meandered down from the hills and paralleled the main street. The long early-summer evenings at this latitude allowed the sun to linger affectionately upon the tree-shaded streets and erased the look of stolid respectability from the houses, lending them instead an air of enchantment. There were delicious fresh lobsters to be had cheaply in the hotel, and on Tuesday nights the same establishment featured a New England boiled dinner which thoroughly converted the most skeptical of our company.

And since Presque Isle had so long hungered for new events, and because it was the sort of small American town where nothing untoward would escape discussion, we were soon subject to both direct and indirect examination.

Why had we come? Were we in the Army? Then if we were not in the Army what were we doing flying Army airplanes?

Anxious to make friends, we did our best to answer such questions, but it was difficult, for the only truth was that we did not know the answers ourselves. Nor could we explain why it was that if indeed we were pilots, none of us wore any emblem which might support our claims. We could not seem to convince our listeners, either male or female, that the wearing of symbolical wings elsewhere than on a uniform was frowned upon. It was a hoary axiom of flying that young neophytes were possessed of several things in lieu of actual air experience — among which were large ornamental wings and a large and complicated wrist watch. In time a few of our more romantically ambitious crew members sent away to a mail-order house for the largest wings they could buy. They reported immediate and thrilling social progress.

We were assigned four airplanes which in normal utilization of crews would leave one as a part-time spare or permit its substitution for others under repair. These airplanes were a patchwork collection of our standard airline DC-3s. Where the brown army paint had already begun to peel, we could see portions of faded lettering which had once identified the proprietor airline. Two of the airplanes were haggard with age and one which had survived a crash on United soon became known as "No-go" because of its tendency to take forever to reach flying speed. It also displayed a remarkable habit of flying a trifle sideways once it was coaxed into the air. The most diligent and clever manipulations of controls and trim tabs could not correct this exasperating fault. One of our pilots remarked that while he appreciated its strength of character he would prefer an airplane with a lesser passion for the earth. Its disinclination to fly became more vicious with heavy use, and finally it led one of our company to his death.

The other airplanes were new military versions of the DC-3, a type soon to become much trusted and beloved. These were C-47s equipped with two Pratt & Whitney engines and furnished with metal bucket seats. They flew splendidly through a variety of nearly impossible conditions and never betrayed us.

Our long-inbred caution received a severe shock when we learned of the weights we were expected to fly. In the same airplane we had been held to the law of 25,346 pounds. Now we should lift a presumed 31,000, an increase which left us dubious because it canceled our ability to fly on one engine until long after take-off. Moreover, the loads were not accurately weighed but merely estimated. This led to some interesting surprises. Distribution of the loads in the airplane was purely a matter of convenience. We were rarely in proper trim and at length became quite accustomed to flying either nose or tail heavy.

There were other innovations to remind us that the conservative days of airline flying were no more. We were assigned radio operators, who squeezed themselves into a cubbyhole behind the captain. In spite of this confinement, their horizons were limitless, for their wireless telegraph keys had a vast communicative range; and so it was the pilots, restricted to human speech, who became the isolated ones. These skilled operators had been hastily recruited from the security of their airline radio rooms and were generally of such a peculiar nature that we despaired of ever fully understanding them. They kept much to themselves, lost in esoteric electrical discussions. These were the men, so long unseen, with whom we had talked on our regular schedules. For years they had been only voices, and now we were not quite sure they were real.

We were also assigned a flight mechanic, and most of these men we had known before. They flew with the airplane, curing its various ills only after we had landed. They were all thorough professionals of long experience and we trusted them implicitly. We could only hope the reverse held true.

Additional fuel tanks had been improvised in the cabins of the planes. These were of composition rubber and were connected to the regular fuel system by a makeshift and rather fragile series of pipes and valves. Yet they must have been efficient, for we smoked near them often and suffered no harm.

A plywood table had been erected directly over the tanks on one side of the cabin, and upon this we applied ourselves to the business of long-range navigation. We soon discovered the table also made a tolerable bunk. When so employed, it occasionally caused a certain lack of harmony among the crews. Since none of the airplanes had automatic pilots, the co-pilot was held captive in the cockpit while the captain fulfilled his secondary function as navigator. After a prolonged session with McIntosh's

still unfamiliar azimuths and declinations, the captain would sometimes be quite overcome with ennui. He would stretch out upon the table to consider his findings more comfortably. This frequently took a considerable time, and the anguished cries of the co-pilot demanding relief were lost in the drumming of the engines.

So it was that in only a few days we threw off our cloaks of conservatism. We were almost totally independent. The army told us where the cargo was destined. How, and when it arrived, became our individual responsibility.

None of us believed this pleasant and relaxed situation could endure for long. But we underestimated both the perception of our military masters and also the formidable task to be done. It did not occur to us that the Army Air Force, preoccupied with training for actual combat, lacked experienced men for such an endeavor or that they also recognized the values of a tight professional group which would be operating free of elephantine officialdom. Using us without danger of interference or superior restriction, a general could accomplish far more than he could with his own personnel. The last thing they wanted us to do was join the army.

At first we flew cargo and army technical personnel to a place called Goose Bay in Labrador, returned to Presque Isle, and repeated the flights on a 24-hour-a-day basis. Because they are not of flesh and blood, airplanes presumably cannot tire; hence the leather cockpit seats were often still warm as one flight crew replaced another.

The actual flying proved to be simple enough. I was amused to find that once again we were flying with charts much given to the word *"Unexplored."*

Northward beyond the St. Lawrence River, the land seemed stunned into silence, still waiting for first breath, as if not yet sure of its liberation from glacial ice. And the pattern past all the horizons was monotonously the same — a seemingly endless repetition of deep and quiet lakes cupped in primeval forests. It was nearly impossible for a stranger to distinguish one lake from another, and in these skies everyone was a stranger. There were no radio aids of any kind except at Goose Bay, where a feeble and notoriously unreliable range station had recently been installed. Thus we were obliged to rely upon the primitive dead reckoning of our open-cockpit days and often found it expedient to hold firmly north until we picked up the wild Hamilton River. We would thence follow its twisting course eastward until at last we stumbled upon the flat projection of land which contained the airport.

In good weather the flight was child's play. But occasionally the season abandoned its assigned character and gave us the back of its hand. Then a solid overcast would descend upon the granite outcroppings and hang graceful stalactites of vapor between the higher trees. The rain replaced all useful sounds in our earphones with the whining and screeching of tormented animals. Yet all this was done facetiously, with more teasing than violence. The worst days never produced the ugly thunderstorms . . . nor was there even mildly rough air. Instead, the impression of any real threat was withheld, the weapons dulled, as if we were being persuaded to remain hereabouts for the winter — and then, if we had the nerve, to match cunning.

Our heavily loaded airplanes were so soggy in spirit they responded like ailing whales and could not be urged above the overcast where we might have a chance for a sunsight. Thus we were often compelled to creep like furtive thieves along the very treetops, skimming the lakes so low we could sometimes see fish jumping, stealing our progress bit by bit through gloomy caverns of cloud.

My co-pilot Johnson had the nose for such flying, for it was a small, saucy, turned-up nose, ideally suited for pressing against the windshield as he sought the quick loom of hazards and opportunities ahead. His eyes were doll-like, deceptively innocent, and his pink and nearly beardless face was that of a healthy baby. His hair was a cropped mass of golden ringlets, and as he peered thoughtfully ahead, he became a hopeful child yearning before the window of a candy store.

In truth, Johnson was a flying leprechaun capable of astounding mischief.

He was resolute, absolutely fearless, and so utterly devoid of nerves that he could fall instantly into a deep sleep though all hell's noises might be vying for his attention inside and outside the airplane. Even the loss of an engine or a ticklish fuel predicament could not stay him from his slumbers. Perhaps this was why, at the age of 25, he carried a special folder of identity cards to prove he could buy a drink.

Our radio operator was Summers, a man of pungent vocabulary and fiercely independent spirit. He wore glasses which he seldom bothered to clean even though he was nearly helpless without them. Yet for what he lacked in keenness of sight he compensated for with the most delicate auditive powers. He could wrest a signal from the silence of a tomb, hearing it long before our detection, or he could separate and identify a puny, fleeting dit-dah from roaring pandemonium. His sending "fist" danced lightly upon his key and was much admired by his colleagues.

Tetterton, our flight mechanic, was a genial bull of a man who had forsaken a career as a racing driver so that he might more completely realize his love for fine machinery. Engines were not mere assemblies of metal, gears, oil, and cylinders to Tetterton. He cared for engines as living creatures, speaking to them softly as he worked, cursing and cajoling in accordance with the particular behavior of each.

These men, wrapped for indefinite periods in an aluminum cocoon, were typical of all the others. Their faith in me as we proceeded into the relatively unknown was difficult to justify. I was embarrassed by its completeness, and touched by the thought of their volunteer status. They could, in distrust or disaffection, have left me at their will and sought more prudent commanders. I led them quite helplessly into many questionable situations. Some of these were entirely of my own doing, and others occurred as natural developments in our new existence.

All of us had much to learn and there were no instructors save ourselves.

Thus we were often obliged to throw large portions of the rule book away and fly by our wits. No one, for example, except Lowell Yerex's colorful airline in Honduras, knew much about flying cargo by air. We learned one night that there was more to it than just heaving assorted material into the cabin and closing the door.

Our first cargo for the north proved to be portions of a radio station which would one day serve to guide bombers and fighters toward the European theatres of war. The pieces were mostly long steel girders, pre-cut, for later assembly into an antenna tower. We hardly glanced at the piles of metal as we passed through the cabin on our way to the cockpit. It was a provocative night and we were intrigued with the subtle pleasures of making a takeoff we should never have attempted on our regular line.

The field at Presque Isle was officially closed to operations because of fog. It lay with deadening serenity upon the ground and there was not even a suggestion of wind to brush it away. The visibility was less than fifty yards. Yet we had practiced blind take-offs many times and were confident of our ability to make one under genuine conditions. The technique was simple enough — a matter of lining up precisely with the desired runway, carefully setting the gyrocompass, concentrating on it, then taking special care to hold course within a degree or two. It was customary to make such take-offs every time a chief pilot held an instrument flying check, but then, of course, he had perfect visibility from his side of the cockpit. Here, there would be none for either Johnson or myself.

We followed the tail-lights of a jeep to the end of the runway and swung around until our magnetic compass matched its direction. We set gyros, altimeters, and carefully completed the cockpit check list of instruments, engines, and controls. This we carried out from memory, our voices chanting the sacrament as priests before an altar.

We were ready. Johnson turned our radio to the range station so we could climb out on the proper leg. Summers was in his crypt behind me. Tetterton stood waiting in the dark passageway which led back to the cabin. Past the moisture-laden windshields we could see a single pair of lights on each side of the runway. Beyond, only a void.

"All set?"

A moment of anticipation. Then a common urge silently to bless the engines.

I did not switch on the landing lights because the fog would only reflect their brilliance and annoy us.

I shoved the throttles forward, jockeying the rudder pedals slightly to compensate for the initial surge of power, and devoted myself to the instruments before me. We gathered speed.

Normally we allowed the tail of these airplanes to rise of itself until a satisfactory angle of wing attack had been achieved. The change of attitude occurred at approximately 50 miles per hour and the airplane was held on the ground until flying speed, or better, was acquired.

I sensed nothing wrong until we had passed 60 miles an hour. The tail had not left the ground. I shoved forward on the controls, spun a few turns on the stabilizer wheel. The tail rose very slowly. I considered it unimportant, concentrating my entire attention on holding a perfect gyro course. I thought I could still slam on the brakes and stop if we drifted off the runway. The runway lights were looming swiftly out of the fog and sliding past like rocket balls. Then, to my astonishment, precious seconds before I had intended, the airplane left the ground.

We had bare flying speed and I heard Johnson cry out. His warning of

68

a stall was superfluous for I was shoving forward on the controls with all the strength within me. And I could not move the controls! I spun the stabilizer as far forward as it would go. We were shuddering into an uncontrollable climb which could only end in a blind spin. My altimeter read less than 100 feet.

I yelled for help from Johnson. He threw himself on the controls. The nose had to go down.

Tetterton, alert to our dilemma, yanked up the landing gear.

We shoved forward on the control yokes until our muscles locked. Our blood pounded up to our faces in stinging pin pricks and our breathing became grunts of desperation.

Yet we could not move the controls an inch forward. If we relaxed only an instant the yokes would fly back in our laps. We might hang for one second before we fell off in a final dive through the fog.

"Tetterton! Go back! See what —"

He had already gone.

We dared not ease off the throttles. If we were to climb so against our will, then we must maintain all possible speed and power. This was the most basic law of flight. To consider the strain on the engines was useless anyway. We had not a hand to spare from our frantic pressure on the controls.

The air speed lingered. It refused to pass 90 miles per hour.

"Tetterton!"

There was no answer.

But Summers swung out of his niche and asked what I wanted. His complete unawareness of our predicament was almost a relief. Even watching us, breathless, and held rigidly in our positions like grotesquely posed statues, he failed to show fear.

"He's back in the cabin. See what the hell . . ."

Summers dodged into the darkness and we waited, hypnotized by the quivering needle of the air speed.

The engines remained howling at full emergency take-off power.

Gradually, hardly daring to believe the instrument, we watched the air speed needle creep past 95.

We saw it at 96.

We saw it at 97.

Then the air speed held, and slid to 100. We wanted to cheer. At last we had an airplane in hand. For now we could feel the controls; there was give — as sudden and wonderful a feeling as can be imagined. We breathed. We luxuriated in the sensuous feeling of command and control. During those awful moments we had been little boys, although we struggled like men. Our need had been speed.

It was again like an introduction to dying, without quite passing the barrier. And I thought, this is not like the ice with Hughen, or the cold mental remains of instant danger with Beattie, or the visual shock of spewing oil over the jungle.

This was a quick revelation smashed at our senses while we were blinded, and my heart would not cease its throbbing.

But the airspeed crept past 105 and then 110. We could even ease our pressure on the controls although the stabilizer was still rolled all the way forward.

At last we broke out above the fog into a glorious parade of stars. I wanted to hear a band.

Johnson, the nerveless, wonderful Johnson, said, "Jesus . . ."

Then he wiped the beads of sweat from his pink forehead and said once more, "Jesus . . ." There was no hint of an oath in his voice. Nor was his word a prayer of gratitude. He was simply expressing as best he knew, in the most formidable phrase he could then muster, an indirect appreciation of his escape. "Jesus." He savored this name softly and shook his head in wonder.

We found that one man could hold the controls, so I asked Johnson to reduce the power carefully. Each succeeding moment brought more sensitivity to the controls. We were approaching 700 feet, a safe altitude. Our air speed was steadily climbing, and we could see.

There was now time, as we climbed toward the stars, to consider our near-catastrophe. It had obviously nothing to do with our blind take-off. Each minute the airplane was beginning to fly as it should, so surely and with such comparative ease that I could now roll back the stabilizer to a decent position.

Finally, Tetterton came forward and leaned between us, panting. His shirt was splotched black with his sweat and the veins on his hands stood out like heavy worms. And he at first also found himself wanting for some means properly to express his woe. So he bowed his head in weariness and lit a cigarette. Then, staring vacantly at the floor, he hoarsely and reverently repeated Johnson's exact verbal refuge. "Jesus . . ."

"What?"

"Those damned steel radio towers! They should have been tied down. When you jammed on take-off power, they all just naturally slid to the tail! Must have been a couple of tons of 'em. I dragged the pieces forward fast as I could. Summers helped."

Then Summers, glasses steamed with his own heat, said resentfully, "A thing like that might kill a man."

I could easily visualize their struggles in the dimly lighted cabin as they fought to drag the heavy girders up a floor inclined at least 20°. And, far worse, they could not have known at what instant the floor might violently reverse its angle and tumble them into eternity.

We had nothing further to say on the incident, for in fact Summers had said it all. So we remained silent, each man wrapped in his thought, trying to behave as if nothing had happened.

Summers went back to his radio cubicle and switched on his light. He pushed it down close to his tiny desk so that its glow would not spread forward to the cockpit. In a few moments I heard him clicking away at his key, a thin, delicate sound which inexplic-

70

ably prevailed above the engines; and I wondered with whom in the world he could be conversing at such a time and whether he would mention that his fortune had so recently demonstrated its perfect match to our own.

Tetterton remained in the dark passageway behind us smoking. And I sensed, more from his observant silence than anything else, that he was still troubled. Finally he leaned forward between us so that he could look out at the stars, though his true interest was almost at once revealed to be elsewhere.

"How long did you leave the engines at full power?" he asked so casually that it was as if he were speaking of a time weeks before. He said it as primly as a spinster inquiring the length of a sermon unattended, and I thought, Good God, how can he care for the time when the engines have just spared his life? Yet I knew the reason for his question, and took a moment to delight in it. And I wondered at how fixed a man could become upon his special pursuit. The dentist attacks an ailing tooth not seeing the whitening knuckles of his patient squeezing the chair. The prin-

ter discovers a typographical error and is wounded, though the error may be infinitely less damaging than the words. Now Tetterton suspected me of abusing his engines and he wanted an accounting in spite of his deliverance.

"I haven't the faintest idea. I wasn't exactly watching the clock."

"How high did the head temperatures go?"

"I wasn't watching them either."

Tetterton made no attempt to conceal his frown of disapproval. The parallel wrinkles across his forehead became deeper in the subdued cockpit light and he turned his head owlishly several times, directing his amazement first at Johnson and then at me. We had, his eyes accused us, been grievously delinquent.

"We're supposed to fill out the log book. What am I going to put in the spaces for engine take-off and climb?"

"How about . . . I love you."

The forehead wrinkles became gashes and his lips compressed until they were nearly invisible.

"Thanks," he said with the heavy mockery of a man betrayed.

What Lindbergh did in 1927 in his Ryan monoplane, young American kids of the Army Air Forces were doing in 1942 by the hundreds. In their P-38 fighters, C-47 transports, B-26, B-25, A-20 light and medium bombers and B-17 heavies, these neophyte airmen equipped with only a lot of courage and little navigation knowledge, spanned the dangerous North Atlantic by the hundreds.

It was all a part of "Operation Bolero," joint U.S.-British effort to build up Air Forces in England for the reconquest of Hitler's Europe. Eventually nearly 15,000 U.S. combat aircraft would be flown this route to bases in England and Europe, with the peak load of 8400 in 1944.

But in 1942 the route was new and beset with many unknowns. It traversed through some of the worst weather on the face of the globe. Navigational aids were few and unreliable. Bases along the route were being cut out of the rock and ice of Greenland. Yet in that year 882 aircraft out of 950 which started, arrived in England via the North Atlantic, including 366 heavy bombers, 150 mediums, 183 transports, and 183 fighters. No one flight across the North Atlantic at that time could be termed routine.

There were tragic accidents, and strange disappearances of aircraft. Sometimes crews were brought back from the dead as Arctic air pioneer Bernt Balchen relates here.

Bluie West Eight: Arctic Saga

Bernt Balchen

ALL THIS SUMMER of 1942 the "Bolero" movement — code word for the prelude to the Allied invasion of Western Europe — has been in full swing. Aircraft in an endless stream have been pouring across Greenland, most of them refueling at Narsasuak, called Bluie West One (BW-1), but a number of them coming in here at BW-8. It is a tribute to Yankee training and skill that these young air force pilots, fresh from civilian life and inexperienced in long-range flying, have so few accidents and forced landings — less than one in a thousand. But now the summer phase is coming to an end, and we are getting into the fall, with its storms, darkness, heavy icing, high winds, and must be prepared for bad luck to strike any day.

It strikes early in November when a B-17 Flying Fortress, engaged in a routine search mission for a missing transport plane, makes a wheels-up landing on a heavily crevassed section of the Cap, in one of the roughest and most inaccessible parts of Greenland. The ensuing rescue effort, the biggest ever attempted in the north, goes on for half a year and involves a number of aircraft as well as Coast Guard and Navy vessels and dog teams and motor sledges. A total of five men are killed before the evacuation is completed, and one of the crewmen, Lt. O'Hara, loses both legs. I make three belly landings in the snow with a PBY, the only ones ever accomplished, to bring out the last survivors. The whole operation is called by the air force one of the great sagas of the Arctic, an unparalleled story of suffering and sacrifice and human endurance during almost six heart-breaking months on the Greenland Icecap.

The missing C-53 transport which set this chain of events in motion ran into engine trouble on a flight from Iceland and was forced down somewhere on the east coast of Greenland. The first word at BW-8 is confusing. They report by radio that they are at 9200 feet altitude, and give their position at Lat. 61° 30′ N. and Long. 42° 30′ W., which would place them out over the water. Three days later comes another message from the C-53 giving the same position but 2000 feet altitude. Atterbury Dome, one of our chain of weather stations on the east coast, reports seeing flares shot in the air to the north; but our search flights over several hundred miles of the area are without result. No further word ever comes from the downed plane; it vanishes forever.

Meantime 120 planes from the "Bolero" movement have been called on to intensify the search, combing the Cap in grid patterns whenever there is a break in the increasingly bad weather. We are nearing the winter solstice, and shall have no sun left at all in another three or four weeks. The crews take off before dawn and land after dark, with flare pots for runway demarcation, in order to utilize the few remaining hours of daylight.

On November 9 comes word that one of the "Bolero" planes, a Fortress with a crew of nine, has failed to return. The big bomber was assigned to the northern sector of the search pattern, which would place it somewhere on the west leg of the Curio Range, a radio range we had set up at Angmagssalik, and in the area of the Atterbury Dome weather station. Now with two planes down, and the sun sinking lower toward the horizon each day, we must redouble our efforts before darkness loses in. I commandeer a civilian C-54 from TWA, to extend the range of the search, and day after day we comb the Cap in vain.

The freezing winds are building to gale force, and always as we fly there is the threat of a sudden williwaw. Once I am at 12,000 feet over the Icecap when we hit a violent downdraft, the down-roll of a williwaw curling off the Cap, which drops us to 8000 feet with

A Douglas C-54 four-engine transport taking off from an Air Transport Command base in Greenland during "Operation Bolero."

our plane still in climbing attitude, throwing us on our side with the rudders full out opposite in an effort to counteract. Then we hit the reverse draft, and shoot upward again to 15,500 feet, in descending attitude. I estimate the wind velocity at about 175 miles at this time, and with an indicated air speed of 215 m.p.h. our ground speed is only 37 m.p.h. For 20 minutes our four-engine ship is tossed like a leaf in a cyclone. It's the severest turbulence I have ever encountered in an airplane, and I think in all my flying this is the narrowest escape of my life.

On November 24, after two weeks of futile search, I follow a hunch and make a long sweep to the southward.

Ahead I see a little red star climbing the dark sky, and then another flare and another, and I alter course and drop down. The wrecked Fortress is lying in a valley of a glacier, at an altitude of about 4000 feet, like a crushed dragonfly on the ice. It has hit in the worst possible area of the Cap — an active part of the glacier, scored with crevasses and bottomless canyons in the ice. I see from the air that the impact has broken the fuselage behind the wing, and the tail end of the plane is hanging down into an abyss. Held on the level ice only by the weight of its front end, the bomber is obviously in a precarious position.

It is a miracle that any of the crew

74

are alive. They were flying low over the Icecap in heavy overcast, we learn later, and suddenly one wing tip struck the ice, and the plane flipped and then leveled again, skidding and cartwheeling to a halt at the very rim of the crevasse. Lt. Monteverde, the pilot, was unhurt, but one crewman, Sgt. Spina, had broken his right wrist, and another was badly cut by safety glass when he was thrown through the nose. The navigator, Lt. O'Hara, helped carry Spina back into the plane, and some snow sifted into his boots, but he gave it no thought at the time.

The crew lashed canvas over the shattered nose, and huddled inside the unheated plane, with icy gusts blasting through the cracks in the twisted fuselage. The blizzard let up after three days, but when they crept out they discovered that the ice around them was so badly fissured it was dangerous to move in any direction. They needed medical help for the two crewmen, and their radio was not operative, so O'Hara and Spencer, the co-pilot, volunteered to make a try for the coast. They were still within sight of the plane when a snow bridge gave way, and Spencer plunged out of sight. He slid a hundred feet down a hidden crack in the glacier and, by one chance in a million, landed on a block of ice wedged in the fissure. His crew-mates lowered a parachute shroud line to him, and inch by inch he worked his way back up the slippery wall, only to be stopped by an overhang at the surface. They passed down a machete to

him, and he clung to the shroud line with one hand as he chopped his way over the protruding rim.

Now O'Hara noticed for the first time that he had no feeling in his toes, and realized that the snow inside his boots had frozen both his feet. Monteverde tried to thaw them with the heat of his own body, holding them against his bare stomach, while the other crewmen redoubled their efforts to get the radio going. At last they managed to pick up signals, but the transmitter still could not give out their position. The glacier was active, the ice fissures around them widened, and bit by bit the sagging tail of the plane settled deeper into the crevasse. They had almost given up hope when on the 24th they heard the faraway drone of my engines.

I take one look at the crumbling glacier, and instruct them not to leave the plane unless roped together. I have on board emergency supplies — stoves and sleeping bags and clothing and first-aid equipment — and my first couple of drops are made with cargo parachutes. The howling wind whips them past the plane before the crew can grab them, and the bundles slip over the rim of the abyss. I decide to try free-dropping without chutes, and warn the men to stay under cover inside the wreck. I come down to about 50 feet over the glacial valley, bucking the violent air that boils off the Icecap, and kick out the remaining bundles, actually hitting the fuselage several times. The wind is so strong that the drifting snow streams from the B-17's wingtips as I pull up after the drops and head for the auxiliary stations at Atterbury Dome, 80 miles away.

I rip out a page from my diary and make a sketch as I fly, showing the location of the wreck and distances and routes, and weight it and drop the instructions to the station. Here they have dog teams and motor sledges, and in command is Lt. Max Demarest, one of the best young glaciologists in the States. He is experienced in Arctic travel, and I feel certain that the crew will be evacuated without further difficulty.

I am back four days later, as soon as there is another break in the storm, to drop additional medical supplies for O'Hara. While I am circling the wreck, I pick up a radio call from an approaching Grumman, a Coast Guard amphibian piloted by Lt. Pritchard, who was with me last year at BW-8. I tell him he can make a wheels-up landing with his little amphibian on a level area near the downed Fortress, and I will drop him rope and bamboo poles and snowshoes for crossing the crevasses to the wreck. An hour later Pritchard reaches the stranded party. O'Hara's feet have started to become gangrenous, and he cannot be moved back to the Grumman without a sled, so Pritchard guides the two other injured crewmen across the glacier to his rescue-plane and flies them out safely. From the air as I circled I have already spotted two motor sledges from Atterbury Dome, with Lt. Demarest and

Sgt. Tetley, only 20 miles from the wreck, making good time across the Cap. They should reach the Fortress by late tonight, and take out O'Hara, and Pritchard will return in the morning for the rest of the crew. I head back to BW-8, confident that our troubles are almost over.

The Arctic is an unscrupulous enemy. It fights with any weapon that comes to hand, it strikes without warning, and it hits hardest just when you think the fight is won. The following morning, November 29, it strikes a double blow. First comes a report that Demarest's motor sledge has broken through a snow bridge, only 100 yards from the Fortress, and he has fallen to his death in a crevasse. Less than an hour later I hear that Pritchard and another Coast Guard crewman have taken off on their second evacuation flight with the B-71 radio operator, Howard, and failed to return to base. It is not until the following March that the remains of the Grumman are discovered, flattened against a mountainside in the blinding snow. All three men were killed instantly.

Now begins the long wait. The Arctic winter has closed in, and the violent storms have reached their peak. Every day when the weather allows us to fly, our planes make supply drops over the wreck, despite severe icing conditions and intense gales. O'Hara's gangrenous legs are getting worse, and he must have medical attention. Sgt. Tetley with the second motor sledge has remained with the Fortress crew

76

since Demarest's death, and Monteverde decides that the only chance to save O'Hara's legs is to make a desperate gamble for the coast. Tetley estimates that he can make the trip in two days. He wraps O'Hara in his sleeping bag and puts him on the sledge, taking along a tent and emergency rations for three days. With him go the two strongest members of the B-17 crew, Spencer and Wedel, the flight engineer. Spencer knows only too well the danger of hidden crevasses, and he walks ahead on snowshoes to test the trail, and Wedel follows behind.

About two miles from the wreck they come to a smooth slope on the glacier, and Tetley decides they can all get on the sled and ride to make better time. As Wedel comes alongside to climb aboard, a concealed snow bridge collapses beneath him, right beside the sledge. He makes one desperate grasp, his fingertips sliding off the sled runner, and vanishes from sight. Tetley guns the motor, and they hurtle the gaping hole just in time. There is no chance of ever finding Wedel's body, they know, and they push on across the Cap with O'Hara. A couple of miles farther, the oil line to the motor congeals and breaks, and without Wedel's engineering ability they cannot repair it. Tetley and Spencer set up the tent and carry O'Hara inside, just as another heavy blizzard strikes.

There they are discovered three days later by Capt. Pappy Turner, flying out of the 6000-foot landing strip at Ikatek (Bluie East-2) only a short hour by air from the wreck. He drops food and medical equipment and also a walkie-talkie, so we can keep in touch with the survivors at the sledge camp as well as the three crewmen at the wrecked Fort six miles away. Another rescue caravan sets out from Atterbury Dome with 35 dogs. They are within 10 miles of the sledge camp when bad weather forces them to retreat, and they struggle back to the Dome with only eight dogs left. Two months have gone by, and hope is beginning to fade that any of the survivors will be alive by spring.

Late in December I am called to BW-1 for a conference with Col. Wimsatt, commanding officer of the Greenland Base Command, and Adm. Smith, commander of the Greenland Naval Patrol, to discuss whether anything else is left to try. I have one last trick to outwit the Arctic. Back in 1925, when Amundsen and Ellsworth were forced down on their first attempt to fly to the North Pole, I remember that Riiser-Larsen and Dietrichson took off the heavily loaded Dornier Wal flying boats by skidding them on their bellies across the floe ice, and I propose a belly landing on the Cap with a PBY.

But the Navy, disposing of the PBYs, doesn't see it my way. I'm given a glacier-cold shoulder. No planes for me for such a lunatic purpose.

I tell them if I'm to crawl in on my hands and knees, I'll get the boys off the Icecap. I'm boiling hot under the collar, and Wimsatt and I go out for fresh air. Soon afterward we have a wire on the way to Gen. Devers, our commanding general stationed in England, in which we request a plane. He cables right back that I may have the plane, but it must be manned with volunteers.

And now, at long last, the Navy wakes up and gives me two of their PBYs.

I poll the crew members of the planes to see who will volunteer for this mission. Every man steps forward. I select a skeleton crew consisting of Lt. Dunlap, the pilot of one PBY, and his radio operator and crew chief, and also Dr. Sweetzer, the medical officer at BW-2. We strip the armor plating and all machine guns from the plane to make it as light as possible, and wait for the first available weather. Just as I am about to start, on February 5, a message is handed to me:

"Factory indicates forward bulkhead of PBY too weak for landing on snow. What are your plans?
COMMANDING GENERAL,
ARMY AIR FORCES"

I scribble my answer and hand it to the messenger: "Going ahead as contemplated.

5 February, 1943."

I have sent a couple of B-17s ahead to the rescue area, to scout conditions, and at eight o'clock this morning they report the weather fair and calm, the ground temperature about 10° below zero. I have decided to evacuate the group at the sledge camp first, because of O'Hara's critical condition. We have had no time to make a test landing, but I figure that if anything is going to happen it will happen anyway, test landing or not.

The area at the sledge camp has a slight upslope of about 2 per cent only. I tell Dunlap to bring the plane in at normal landing speed, like a power stall letdown on a glassy sea. We set the air speed at a fixed 80 knots, sinking about 200 feet a minute, and hold the plane in this position until the hull grazes the snow. Dunlap cuts the throttles, and the PBY slides smoothly right up to the camp. Spencer is standing in front of the snow hut they have built over the tent, and Tetley scrambles out as we halt. Dr. Sweetzer and I crawl inside.

O'Hara is lying in his sleeping bag, his face a waxy yellow, emaciated and weak, but he forces a little grin. I carry him to the plane in my arms, as light as a bundle of rags. He weighed 180 pounds when he landed on the Cap three months ago, and now he is only about 80 pounds. Spencer and Tetley crawl aboard the PBY, and I give it the gun. The hull of the flying boat has already frozen to the snow, and it will not budge.

The men scramble out onto the wings and rock the plane back and forth until it is free, but before they can climb back inside it has frozen tight again. I order the crew to get out and stand at either wingtip float, wiggling the plane up and down until it breaks loose, and I start sliding. I taxi

78

slowly in a wide circle, and the men line up on the snow outside this circle, and wait for me to come around. As soon as the right outboard engine has passed over their heads, they dive for the blister one by one, like jumping aboard a merry-go-round, and the radio operator and Dr. Sweetzer grab each man in turn by the scruff of his neck and the seat of his pants, and haul him inside. I shove the throttles forward, and after a few seconds of eternity the hull breaks the snow's grip and we are airborne.

Throughout the winter, spring, and summer of 1942 American aircraft and units arrived in England by air and by sea under "Operation Bolero" to form the U.S. Eighth Air Force and unite with the RAF in the air build-up for the coming destruction of Nazi Germany and the reconquest of Europe.

"Bolero" originally called for invasion of France in fall, 1942 or spring, 1943. It was to be delayed a year by a second front in Africa, hastily planned for November, 1942 to take pressure off the defeated British Eighth Army pinned down at El Alamein in Egypt and relieve the Russian retreat in the Ukraine by drawing German forces to the Mediterranean.

With the shift of British-American emphasis to the Mediterranean the AAF's Eighth Air Force in England was directed to give large part of its growing strength to a newly-organized African invasion air force — the Twelfth, commanded by James H. Doolittle, recently returned from the historic Tokyo Raid. Eighth Air Force strategic operations were to be subordinated to the North African venture.

Nevertheless, beginning in the summer of 1942 the depleted Eighth initiated small scale combat strikes over Europe in a test of U.S. air concepts, equipment, training, and command leadership.

The British were frankly skeptical of the American daylight bombardment plans. They had tried the earlier, lighter-armed B-17E "Flying Fortress" over Germany and found it wanting in defensive firepower. Besides, the "Fort's" small bomb bay could not carry the massive two-ton blockbusters required for night mass area bombing missions which the British were pursuing. British air leaders were openly doubtful of the American concept to the point of being hostile. And in the British press it was chided as "foolish, wasteful plans and efforts of U.S. air leaders." British logic reasoned: day bombardment had proven failure for the Germans at Dunkirk, in the Battle of Britain, over Malta, and at Stalingrad. It had been prohibitively costly for the British over Europe in the first two years. Up to the advent of the Eighth Air Force in England it simply had not worked. The day fighter had the edge over the day bomber every time.

But by 1942 American bombers — the B-17F and the slab-sided B-24 — had two new contributions not previously available. These were the famed Norden bombsight which could pickle-barrel a bomb from high altitude beyond effective enemy anti-aircraft artillery, and heavy defensive armor to protect itself against any enemy air fighters patrolling the skies of Europe. American airpower had developed long-range bombers as a defensive weapon in the 1930s and American industry was geared to produce the B-17 and B-24 in large numbers. Moreover, American military airmen were loud exponents of the daylight strategic bombardment concept, having developed, taught and practiced it in the U.S. during the 1930s. There would be no turning back the clock of military air concept; no argument would deter American airmen from carrying out their plans.

Thus was the first year over Europe a year of trial and error for the Eighth Air Force, a year of build-up and shakedown missions. It was a year which hammered out in the ordeal of combat the refinements of American day bombardment techniques; a year that set the pattern for the great daylight sweeps of 1943-44 which ripped open the heart of Europe.

And it was during this time the "Combined Bomber Offensive" — the U.S. by day, the British by night — took form and substance.

Counterattack Europe:
The First 18 Months

Dr. Murray Green

THIS IS THE STORY of an experiment which began, appropriately enough, on July 4, 1942. On the morning of the 166th anniversary of our independence, six A-20 Boston bombers borrowed from the Royal Air Force by the fledgling Eighth Air Force took off on the first mission of a three-year campaign that was to help preserve that independence for ourselves and our posterity.

As a mission, this sweep of Luft-waffe airdromes in Holland flown in the company of 6 other twin-engine A-20s manned by their regular RAF crews, was less than a tactical success. The low-flying Bostons were spotted by "squealer" ships that radioed a warning ahead. The Germans had a reception committee waiting. One American pilot made his normal turn and allowed the flak tower gunners to anticipate his course. He was shot down. Another, Capt. Charles Kegel-

The Douglas A-20 was used very successfully by the British in the tactical support of troops. The A-20s pictured here have D-Day markings, black and white stripes.

man, had his right propeller shot off. He searched the sand dunes for a place to belly land, when he heard his tail gunner exhort him to "Give 'em hell, Captain." "Why not?" he asked defiantly, and swung his nose toward a harassing flak tower, squeezed the trigger until he silenced it, then wrenched his crippled ship around at water level and made it back to the field.

The Theatre Commander was so impressed by the report of Kegelman's feat that he wrote in pencil across it: "This officer is hereby awarded the Distinguished Service Cross." Three other crew members who flew that day also received the Distinguished Flying Cross.

America hailed this heroic beginning and at Headquarters Eighth Bomber Command that day, the following notation appeared in the official log: "Arrival of aircraft; 1 B-17E — Total: 1."

The B-17 Flying Fortress, with an able assist by the B-24 Liberator, gave meaning to an American concept of high altitude daylight precision bombing. But before they could conduct it, the Fort and Lib aircrews had to penetrate the political fog of doubt and question, just as they had to prove themselves in combat against the fiercest aerial opposition in the world.

The Eighth Air Force was established on paper in January, 1942 in the winter of our discontent following the Pearl Harbor disaster. In February, Gen. Henry "Hap" Arnold, Commanding the Army Air Forces, sent Brig. Gen. Ira C. Eaker to England to establish a bomber command headquarters and to prepare for the arrival of the fighting men and planes.

In May, 1942 Maj. Gen. Carl "Tooey" Spaatz took command of Eighth Air Force at Bolling AFB, in Washington, D.C. One month later, he opened his headquarters at Bushy Park, on the outskirts of London, after which the aforementioned token raid in borrowed A-20s took place.

But Eighth Air Force was to put its faith in daylight precision bombing. Spaatz and Eaker counted on a combination: the quality of their crews, the firepower of the B-17, and the accuracy of the secret Norden bombsight to attain their goal.

By mid-August, 1942, enough B-17s had crossed the Atlantic to permit the planning of the first high-level mission. After the weather "scrubbed" some starts, 18 B-17s impatiently took off on Monday, August 17. Twelve headed for the Rouen-Sotteville railroad marshaling yards, the other six on a diversionary sweep. The mission got off none too soon. The day before,

in the *London Sunday Times*, a leading article fairly bristled with "plain speaking" as to how the B-17s and the B-24s were not cut out for the job of flying over heavily defended enemy territory. Perhaps these planes were more suitable for patrol missions over the Atlantic submarine and shipping lanes, the air correspondent suggested.

The trans-Atlantic telephones burned as Washington demanded to know what it was all about. Fortunately, Gen. Spaatz was spared the necessity for apologies. The Fortresses, with Gen. Eaker, Eighth Bomber Commander, riding in the "Yankee Doodle," one of the lead planes, plastered the target and returned unscathed.

The first climax of the modest offensive against *Festung Europa* came on October 9, 1942. A mission, including for the first time, the slab-sided B-24 Liberators, was dispatched against the French industrial city of Lille where the great Fives-Lille steel plant was made to order for high-altitude precision attack. The term "air raid" was for the first time inadequate. At Lille, it was an air battle pitting 108 formation-flying American bombers, protected along the way by a total of 500 escorting fighters vs. 242 German interceptors. The "green" bomber crews made mistakes. Aborts ran high and traffic control over the target looked like a conjuncture of freeways in downtown Los Angeles. Some bombardiers had jettisoned their loads in mid-English Channel and were derisively christened "chandeliers." But 69 bombers made it to the targets, at a cost of 1 Lib and 3 Forts. Final claims by our side distilled to 21 fighters shot down, 21 probables, and 15 damaged.

A dramatic victory of sorts, Lille represented a sharp reversal of the traditional bomber vulnerability to aggressive fighter interception. If the public applauded the Libs and Forts as destroyers of the Luftwaffe, the professionals regarded this prowess strictly as a valuable by-product. The primary objective was to destroy ground targets by precision attack.

The men who flew to Lille did not realize it, but that mission was the largest one mounted by the Eighth Air Force for the next six months. In the dynamic, quick-changing war picture, strategic air took a back seat. Temporarily ahead of it were placed the requirements to mount "Operation Torch," our maiden amphibious landing in North Africa, scheduled for November. Programming account was also taken of an urgent appeal to President Roosevelt by Prime Minister Churchill for air support of his Eighth Army in Egypt which had finally turned on Rommel at El Alamein in the summer of 1942 and pushed for a decisive breakthrough.

As the weather turned bad and the nights grew long, control of the U-boat menace in the Atlantic suddenly took a turn for the worse in October, 1942. In November, the blackest single month of World War II, sinkings rose to a terrifying level.

Fledgling Eighth Air Force was now invited to take a crack at the uninviting submarine pens which the Nazis had sited all around the Bay of Biscay — at Lorient, at St. Nazaire, and La Pallice. The prospects for distinctive service in this mission were not bright. The vastly more experienced RAF had in 1941 dropped 400 tons on Lorient alone, causing damage to the port area and to the town itself. But the U-boat shelters, built with 12 feet of reinforced concrete overhead, reflected simultaneously the Teutonic fondness for massive construction and for boasting to match. Certainly, the sub-pens were as bombproof as the technology of that era could make them. Goebbels crowed that "Britain's RAF holds Germany by the wrist, but Germany's U-boats hold Britain by the throat." Late in 1942, few would gainsay that Nazi boast.

Indeed, there was a strong and growing belief that the U-boat wolfpacks could bring Britain to her knees before the U.S. could intervene in sufficient strength to tip the balance back. The failure of a similar U-boat campaign in 1917-18 was dismissed by German strategists because the Kaiser had failed to establish U-boat bases on Atlantic ports. This shortcoming Hitler had quickly rectified in 1940.

Against the formidable submarine bases which resembled tiny cardboard shoe-boxes from four miles up, was pitted the Eighth Air Force whose plans for precision bombing were so large and whose means to accomplish

The Boeing B-17, a four-engined bomber, was the early mainstay of the Eighth Air Force in Europe. This B-17, photographed from another Flying Fortress in the same formation, is flying through a sea of flak.

it were yet so modest. Three important missions were sent in against the sub-pens. Fighter opposition was ferocious and skillful. Yellow-nosed FW-190s attacked from the rear in such a way that the high sweeping tail fin of the Fortresses screened them from the fire of the radio hatch and top turret. The Germans brought in fresh concentrations of flak, including 100 big guns sited around St. Nazaire — now known as "Flak City."

Several bomb hits were recorded directly on the submarine installations. The B-17s claimed 10 enemy fighters destroyed, plus four probables and three damaged. But they limped back exhausted and depressed by their own losses and the lack of replacements which seemed to reflect that no one cared much one way or another.

There were encouraging letters from the RAF and the British Admiralty which attested to the destruction caused and the lengthening of the U-boats' turn around time. But the principal depressant was the knowledge born of combat experience. The AAF learned the hard way that the destructive power of a single bomb, or even a few bombs, was less devastating than expected. What they needed was a concentration of bombers whose cumulative effect could cause the Germans to despair of repairing heavy damage. But this called for more bombers and more crews — neither immediately available.

Another side effect of marking time was reflected in a certain impatience that showed up on the home front. People in the United States had acquired the notion that an air force, to be effective, could or should fight a major engagement every day. Doubtlessly, this illusion was fostered a bit (like the pickle-barrel bombing accuracy myth) by overzealous salesmen of airpower and blindness generally distributed at all levels of understanding to the realities of air warfare. No one expected a naval task force — or a ground army, for that matter — to fight several big-scale battles each month, repair their damage, and replace casualties overnight. Yet, the Eighth Air Force was expected to do so.

Some critics recalled that the RAF on May 31 and June 2, 1942, had sent out 1000-plane raids against Cologne and the Ruhr, respectively, and emerged with only a few casualties. Still other critics believed that ships or tanks, or perhaps machine guns, should warrant higher production priorities than bombers. And in the other services, one school of military strategy felt that if bombers were to come first, they could serve our national interest better in the Pacific or in the Mediterranean.

Carping criticism of the AAF did not extend to the men of the RAF. After 2½ years of trial and error, the RAF could appreciate what the Eighth Air Force was trying to accomplish, even though British leaders believed that this objective could better be attained by night area bombing. The RAF had taken the initiative away from the Germans who had initiated the concept of mass bombing and even coined the word "Blitz" for it.

By mid-1942, the RAF had begun to spread ruin and terror throughout Germany. In the face of Hitler's increasing obligations on the Eastern and Western fronts, the Luftwaffe strove to maintain peak strength everywhere, with the result that it was unable to dominate the air anywhere. In a surprise foray, late in October, 1942, about 100 Lancasters penetrated 400 miles (deeply for that time) with escort and plastered the Schneider armament works at Le Creusot. They knocked out the plant for eight months at a cost of only one plane.

Some influential voices were raised on either side of the Atlantic suggesting that the best way to use the comparatively small American bomber force was to incorporate it into the RAF's night bombing pattern. But the AAF would not accept assimilation — for reasons which went beyond the need for separate identification, just as the AEF in World War I insisted on retaining its separate identity.

It was more than a matter of patriotic pride. It was a means of testing a theory of war deeply felt. Daylight precision bombing was not only grounded in logic but had dug roots into the substructure of our psychology. Americans traditionally respect marksmanship. This goes back to the squirrel rifle of the frontier days when the scarcity of powder and shot put a premium on accuracy. Secondly, precision-bombing was our best answer to real or feigned antipathy for area bombing of "civilian" objectives which the RAF favored. Thirdly, pinpointed accuracy was essential to participation in the Pacific war — primarily a naval engagement. Its beginnings could be traced to Billy Mitchell and his intrepid flyers. In the early 1920s they justified the air service by blasting a succession of obsolete U.S. and Ger-

man warships out of the water off Hampton Roads. Last, but certainly not least, the Norden bombsight, a Navy-assisted research and development project of the 1930s, showed great promise as an instrument of precision bombing.

The growing controversy over daylight bombing came to a head at the Casablanca Conference. In mid-January, 1943, President Roosevelt and Churchill came together, in company with their leading political and military advisers, to lay the basis for future strategy. In the absence of Gen. Spaatz, who was in North Africa, Gen. Eaker flew to Casablanca. He was handed a

Allied leaders at the Casablanca Conference. From left, seated: President Franklin D. Roosevelt of the United States and Prime Minister Winston Churchill of Great Britain. Standing: Lt. Gen. H. H. Arnold, Admiral Ernest J. King, General George C. Marshall, Admiral Sir Dudley Pound, General Sir Alan Brooke, and Air Chief Marshal Sir Charles Portal.

series of questions by Gen. Arnold. On the answers to those questions depended the future of Eighth Bomber Command. Gen. Eaker presented these reasoned arguments:

1. Day bombing permitted destruction of relatively small targets that could not be found or seen at night;

2. Day bombing, being much more accurate than night bombing, permitted a smaller force to be employed against a given target. This economy would permit simultaneous attacks on several targets, splitting enemy defenses and reducing losses;

3. Day bombing, or the threat of it, kept enemy defenses alerted round-the-clock, caused him to lose production, sleep and effectiveness;

4. Day bombing would reduce airdrome, air space and communications congestion in the U.K. This problem would intensify as the U.S. and British bomber forces increased.

5. And finally, consecutive day and night bombing would complement each other, offering unparalleled opportunities to sustain the attack.

The Allied leaders accepted these arguments. One day, two weeks later, the word went out for the first time to the Eighth Bomber Command — "Target — Germany." A new air of optimism filled air staff briefing rooms as for the first time mission briefers swung their pointers to targets on Ger-

man soil. Fifty-three bombers attacked the U-boat production yards at Wilhelmshaven on January 27, 1943. The drop was made through a smoke screen and some rather attentive, but not too accurate, flak. The results attained at a cost of three ships were only fair, but it was only a beginning.

While Eighth Air Force was getting untracked, the RAF went into high gear as the weather improved. They went into Cologne and hit the U-boat equipment plants in several heavy raids. In a series of coordinated attacks on submarine yards, repair shops and Diesel engine works, the RAF hit Lorient, whose great concrete pens could house 30 U-boats. There was one raid of 1000 tons on the night of February 13, 1943. St. Nazaire felt the weight of a deluge of 1000 tons in 30 minutes on the night of February 28. This bombardment penetrated only an occasional heavy concrete shelter, but the successive battering destroyed nearby electric power sources, machine shops, and other supporting facilities. Simultaneously, industrial centers in Western Germany and the Ruhr began to feel the weight of successive 1000-ton raids. One in mid-March battered the famous Krupp works in the Ruhr.

Of particularly grim satisfaction was the resumption of raids against Berlin which — with the exception of a few sporadic Russian raids — had been spared of Allied air attacks since December, 1941. Some precision timing on January 30, 1943, gave unique cause for delight in the West and proved a real tonic to Allied morale. Anniversaries of the Nazi accession to power were customary occasions for a spate of party oratory in Berlin. Both Goering and Goebbels were scheduled to address the party meeting at the *Sportspalast*. The first raid by RAF "Mosquitos" struck at 11 A.M. just as Goering stepped to the podium. The *Reichsmarschall* and his hearers hastily repaired to the nearest air raid shelter. At 4 P.M., Goebbels was about to take the rostrum for his offering as to how well things were going, but another well-timed air raid unceremoniously broke up the meeting for the rest of the day.

Perhaps the effect of the prank raids was more psychological than physical, but the Germans took very seriously the fact that daylight bombers for the first time had been able to penetrate to the capital. Their presence was a fresh reminder of the emptiness of Goering's boast that Berlin would be spared of attack. To Germans there was revelation of the vulnerability of Germany's vitals to the mounting air assault.

The March 1 raid on Berlin was no prank as 900 tons showered down and left 20,000 people homeless and fires that burned for three days. On the 27th and 29th equally heavy and even more concentrated raids made clear the pattern of destruction which the Allies, principally the RAF in this period, methodically visited upon the homeland of the enemy.

The contribution of Eighth Air Force in this period was still modest, but of growing proportions.

Wilhelmshaven became a regular "customer" for its attention. In mid-March a daylight attack by U.S. bombers on Vegesack near Bremen did heavy damage to submarine building and repair ships. It cost the Germans seven severely damaged U-boats out of 15 in the stocks.

On April 4, 1943, 133 Forts — the largest AAF raid up to that time — hit the Renault plant in France. On April 17, the Eighth Bomber Command went into Bremen. They lost 16 bombers out of 106, but really plastered the target. The sustained and unremitting character of these operations was without precedent. By April, 1943, there was hardly a day when Allied planes were not over enemy territory during the 24 hours.

Sir Archibald Sinclair, British Secretary of State for Air, estimated the air offensive had by March, 1943 wrecked 2000 German factories, cut steel production by 1½ million tons annually, and reduced Saar and Ruhr coal production by 80,000 tons a day.

As the warm weather approached, the prospects for a decisive bomber campaign brightened. There was a spectacular rise in American production as the "Arsenal of Democracy" went into high gear. In May, 1943, the U.S. produced 7200 planes, including 5000 combat types. Among them was an increased proportion of bombers. The Eighth Air Force doubled its

A Royal Air Force twin-engined Mosquito, the airplane that drove Luftwaffe chief Hermann Goering from the speaker's platform at the *Sportspalast* in Berlin, January, 1943.

strength by the addition of six heavy bomber groups and in May, just one year since Gen. Spaatz had taken command, the Eighth Air Force received high priority to conduct a Combined Bomber Offensive in concert with the RAF Bomber Command. The chief targets were to be the German aircraft, ball bearing and oil industries.

The task was formidable and the mission hazardous, for the bombers as yet had no nose turrets to protect them from frontal attack. The escorts provided them could not penetrate much beyond 200 miles inland. So the Eighth Bomber Command devised self-protection by packing 18 bombers into a tight combat box, and stacking two or three boxes into what was known as a combat wing.

Other significant changes in the character of strategic bombing occurred. Two-ton and four-ton "blockbusters" began to be used against main objectives. They were effective against structures that could withstand the impact of smaller bombs. The British Air Ministry asserted that the "blockbusters" were paying their way.

There was also a return to dispersal of the bombing effort. Since half the German fighter force was already tied down to the relief of the Mediterranean and Russian fronts, the strain on German defenses in the West could be increased by spreading the blows over a wider area. Thus, the 1000-ton raid became commonplace in 1943 as against the 1000 plane raids of 1942. Now, only 400-500 planes could drop 1000 tons, reflecting improvement in technology.

A significant shift in the respective burdens borne by the collaborators in this Combined Bomber Offensive is reflected in a few statistics culled from the files of the U.S. Strategic Bombing Survey which was later established by President Roosevelt to provide an authoritative and unbiased evaluation of air power in World War II. The figures showed that the USAAF "total bomb tonnage dropped" in 1942 was but 2003 tons as against 74,489 tons for the RAF. By September, 1943, however, the AAF had attained the same monthly level as the RAF at about 23,000. By the war's end the AAF total of 1,463,423 tons had surpassed the RAF's total tonnage of 1,307,117.

By the summer of 1943 only a small fraction of this tonnage had been delivered, but the shakedown of Eighth Air Force was virtually complete and its build-up proceeding at a geometric rate.

The Germans belatedly realized that disaster would overtake them if the Combined Bomber Offensive were not halted. Hitler ordered a switch of virtually all aircraft production facilities to fighters. At the same time, available interceptor groups were rushed westward as the Luftwaffe doubled its strength in June, 1943 over that of January, 1943.

The air battle was now joined. Both sides threw every available resource into the struggle for mastery of the air over Western Europe. The outcome would largely determine Allied plans for a second front, now deferred to 1944. The account of that air battle which lasted one full year is another exciting chapter in the story of air power and its decisive effect on the final victorious outcome of World War II.

EDITOR'S NOTE

From the start the Germans developed a healthy respect for the firepower of a Fortress formation. Ever since a crippled "Fort" took on a flight of ME-109s over Holland in autumn of 1942 and shot down two and damaged others, the word among Luftwaffe pilots was "lay off those *verdamnt* Forts."

It was not until later when Focke-Wolf-190s and ME-109s were equipped with heavier armament and the Germans had studied B-17s shot down over Europe, that the Luftwaffe devised improved tactics for attacking the Forts.

The appearance of the Forts over Europe also gave urgency to a re-gear of German aircraft production. In December, 1941 the German aircraft industry produced 510 bombers, 130 fighter bombers, and 360 fighters. By December, 1943 monthly production had shifted to 400 bombers, 255 fighter bombers, and 600 fighters. A year later, single-engine fighters had risen to 1425 per month, twin-engine fighters to 245, while only 15 bombers rolled off production lines.

Thus, by 1943 the pattern of German air effort, from production to combat air operations was changing rapidly from offense to defense.

Allied air leaders hopefully recalled that no nation in history had ever won a war by defense and looked to the year ahead with confidence and determination.

While the Eighth Air Force build-up and shakedown missions were underway, the RAF continued its daylight and night fighter and bomber sweeps over Europe. For two years the RAF had been ranging over the Western fringes of Europe, limited by short radius of action of their fighters. Spitfires, Hurricanes, Typhoons, Beaufighters, and U.S. A-20s would sweep the Low Countries and France hunting targets of opportunity and engaging the Luftwaffe in aerial battle.

Flying with the RAF were pilots of many nationalities — French, Poles, Czechs, Dutch, Belgiums, Norwegians, and others, who had fled their countries after defeat and joined the British to fight Hitler. In some cases, units were composed entirely of nationals of one country, using British and American equipment, as with the resurrected French Lafayette Escadrille Squadron flying P-40s in North Africa, the Ardennes Squadron in the Middle East, and the Lorraine and Bretagne bomber squadrons in the Mediterranean area. Others were integrated into RAF units and flew from British bases.

Deeply motivated to eliminate the Nazis and restore their nation to freedom, they were a group of resolute, daring, determined flyers. Here is a dramatic glimpse of a Spitfire fighter patrol sweep over France by Pierre Clostermann, French ace flying with the RAF in early 1943.

Ranger Over France

Pierre Clostermann

HALF-PAST SIX. The ringing of the alarm clock tore me out of bed. Lord, how cold it was! I peeped under the blackout curtain — low clouds, ceiling less than 2000 feet, and what a wind! It screamed through the telegraph wires outside and every gust shook the 20 doors in our quarters.

I lit a cigarette and put the light on. Tom and Danny, my roommates, had gone back to sleep. I hurriedly put on a couple of pullovers over my pajamas, a leather waistcoat, my battle-dress, two pairs of long woolen stockings and my flying boots, into which I slipped my map.

The dark concrete bulk of the Ops. Room loomed in the night. I could dimly hear the throb of the air-conditioning plant for the underground rooms. After the bitter cold outside, I felt as if I were plunging into a deliciously warm vapor bath as soon as I passed through the heavy metal doors. The room, lit by mercury vapor lamps, seemed like a scene from another world.

The sergeant on duty was kept on the go answering a dozen continuously ringing phones. Without even looking up he handed me the "Met" report and the area controller's instructions. Ten-tenths cloud at 4000 feet. Wind at sea-level 320°, 35 m.p.h.; 50 m.p.h. at 5000 feet. Visibility moderate, dropping to 500 yards in the showers. Twelve Typhoons were to carry out a sortie in the Chartres area from 0840 to –850 hours at zero feet. A piece of cake, if it weren't for the wind.

I woke up the rest of the gang. Ken and Bruce were O.K., but Jacques proceeded to bind like hell. I shook him up. Five minutes later we were on our way over to Flight. On our way we checked the fixing of our big 45-gallon auxiliary tanks, slung like bombs between the Spitfires' two radiators. The mechanics lay on the ground, working away by the light of their storm lanterns.

"Take-off at 8 o'clock sharp," Ken shouted to them.

It was 7:25, just time to get outside a cup of coffee and a few biscuits. Time for breakfast proper when we got back — if we did get back.

Huddling round the miserable stove, Jacques, Dumbrell and I listened while Ken, map in hand, gave us the gen.

"We'll cross the French coast, either on I.F. or above the clouds, then we'll go as far as Amiens flying low. We'll turn left and patrol the area Saint-Quentin, Noyon, Beauvais, and we'll come back at 13,000 feet. Like that we'll stand a decent chance of intercepting a low-flying transport. Roughly line-abreast formation, 100 yards between aircraft, crossing over from left to right when we alter course. Every man for himself if it comes to a scrap. The first one who spots a target tells the rest and leads the attack."

0750 hours. Strapped in our Mae Wests, cluttered up with our dinghy as well as the parachute, we climbed laboriously into our cockpits, helped by the mechanics. My breath immediately froze on the windshield. I switched on my radio, my cameragun, the carburetor, pilot head and gyro-intake heaters and the de-icing equipment. My fingers were numb under three layers of gloves — silk, wool, and leather — and it was quite a business messing about with all those tiny buttons crowded together on the instrument panel.

0755 hours. I got them to see the

mirror was properly adjusted. A glance at the sight, I set the safety-catch of the guns. All set. A glance toward Ken.

"All clear."

"Contact."

A whine from the starter. One cylinder fired, then two more. I pumped furiously and all at once the engine burst into life.

It was still very dark and the mauve flashes from the exhausts lit up the snow. It was two minutes past eight. Navigation lights on, wingtip to wingtip, we climbed through the black, threatening clouds.

We emerged at 13,000 feet above the thick layer of strato-cumulus, over the Channel. At once we took up the battle formation. Complete silence over the radio. In spite of icing we had switched over to our auxiliary tanks without anything going wrong. In the gathering dawn the clouds were edged with light.

The German spotters had probably picked us up. The usual irritating radar interference started up in our headphones, worse with each sweep of the beam. Suddenly Bruce Dumbrell waggled his wings and turned for home. The perfect ellipse of his wings was outlined against the pale sky for the space of an instant and I could make out a thin white stream flowing from his radiator. Glycol escaping. One aircraft less. In theory one of us ought to escort him over the sea but if we did that we should have to return to base without completing our job.

Ken said nothing and merely sig-naled to us to close up again for the dive through the cloud-layer. It was a tricky business. Ken had worked it out that if we didn't time it right there was a risk of coming out in the coastal flak belt. The "Met" forecast had to be right too as, if the cloud base was lower than expected, we wouldn't have enough margin to rectify any error in our I.F.

We plunged into the opaque mist. Ken had his eyes glued to his instruments. Jacques and I desperately clung to his wingtips. Suddenly we found ourselves in clear air again, at less than 1500 feet over a cluster of little wooded hillocks intersected by a narrow marshy valley. A fine rain was falling, shreds of mist dragged over the ground, the light was glaucous, like in an aquarium. That awful curdling of the stomach muscles as usual. We must watch out now.

"Hullo, Skittles, Red Leader calling. Combat formation, drop your babies."

Having got rid of our auxiliary tanks, we dived to get up speed. Ken was skimming the river in the middle of the valley; Jacques beyond him was following the road, keeping below the level of the telegraph wires. I was half-way up a slope, bothered by constant clumps of trees. I kept a cautious lookout for high-tension wires. One hundred and seventy-five yards a second. In that grisly visibility the fatal obstacle came on you in a flash. On the ground, apart from a glimpse through my hood of a couple of women sheltering under an umbrella, there wasn't a

93

solitary cart, nothing. A few roofs outlined against the horizon, a factory chimney or two. White smoke from a small marshaling yard approached rapidly. Doullens, probably. We veered toward the south, to leave the French town clear on our left. We had neither permission nor inclination to attack a train — no point in risking flak unnecessarily.

The rain started to come down in sheets. I must really watch out now. Amiens must be somewhere not far away in the murk.

"Look out, flak!"

A shout from Jacques over the radio. Instinctively, I turned. A fan-shaped cluster of white puffs spread in front of my windshield. Tracers started whipping through the trees. Then, under my wings, I saw roofs, allotments. In a rift the towers of the cathedral loomed up, too close. I roared over wet cobblestones, greasy macadam, dirty slates, clusters of gray houses. It was Amiens.

Skimming the chimneypots we veered to the left and emerged level with a station. A glimpse of a few railwaymen, rooted to the spot, caught between the trucks of a goods train, then flashes from the loco park as a battery of three automatic guns opened up, their stuttering barrels wreathed in smoke.

Each of us on his own, weaving, full throttle, we made off, pursued by orange tracer. It was only a few miles from the town that we formed up again. I discreetly checked on the course Ken was setting and studied the map as best I could. No doubt about it, Ken had boobed as we came out of Amiens, at the Langean fork. We were heading for Noyon and Compiegne instead of Saint-Quentin. The Canal du Nord passed beneath us, then the Oise. Sure enough, here was Compiegne forest, slashed by a bank of fog apparently anchored to the trees.

Suddenly we heard the controller's voice, very distantly as we were flying low!

"Hullo, Skittles, look out for Huns and Tiffe boys around."

I wedged myself against the seat and tried to pierce the murk into which we plunged, six feet above the denuded branches. Suddenly all hell was let loose — we roared into a fearful madhouse of planes. Yellow cowlings marked with black crosses cut through the tracer trails. At least 40 Focke-Wulfs, all apparently gone berserk. With my thumb I immediately released the safety catch of my guns. My earphones were screaming.

I just avoided colliding with a Focke-Wulf. Glued to the back of my seat by the centrifugal force I did a tight turn behind another and let fly with my machine guns as I passed. Then, my finger still on the button, I had to break away violently. I could see another hovering just behind in my mirror, his wings lit up by the flashes of his four cannon.

Having got rid of that one I drew a bead on another, who seemed to have lost his head and was waggling his wings. All of a sudden a Typhoon loomed up in my windshield, coming straight for me. I kicked the rudder bar desperately. I just about grazed him, and caught my wingtip a terrible crack in a branch. Sweating and holding my breath I righted my Spitfire, just as a Focke-Wulf in flames crashed in front of me, mowing down the trees in a fearful shower of sparks.

Stick right back I made vertically for the clouds, firing a burst of cannon on the way at a Focke-Wulf which was so close that the black crosses on his fuselage filled my gunsight. With his tail-plane half torn off, he went into a spin and crashed into a clearing.

Once I got into the shelter of the clouds I breathed more easily. That bunch of pirates, 609 Typhoon Squadron, commanded by my Belgian friend Demoulin, must have dropped unexpectedly on a wing of Focke-Wulfs taking off from Compiegne airfield. We had landed in the middle of the party by mistake!

Nerves tensed, I came down into the scrap again. I saw three flaming masses on the ground and three thick columns of black smoke rose above the forest. Visibility was getting worse and worse. I caught a glimpse of a couple of Focke-Wulfs vanishing into the mist. No one left in sight. I could vaguely hear Ken and Jacques over the radio, excitedly chasing after a Focke-Wulf. They ended by shooting it down somewhere or other and then the wireless went dead for a bit.

I called Ken to tell him my juice was getting low and that I was going back to Detling. Half an hour's I.F. through cumulus with flanks heavy with snow and I found myself over the sandy spit of Dungeness, in a fog you could cut with a knife. I asked for a homing and was brought back slap over base by the controller. As I made my approach, skimming the treetops I saw Ken and Jacques touching down. Ken caught a packet in his starboard wing from 20 mm, but he signaled that he had bagged a Jerry.

With the help of my mechanics I jumped down from my Spit, stiff and cold, only to hear that immediately after breakfast I had to return to Dispersal on stand-by readiness.

While allied airpower was building up in Western Europe the intensity of aerial fighting on the Russian Front mounted. Nowhere is this better illustrated than in the German drive to dislodge the Russian Army from the bastion of Sevastopol, in the Crimea. Despite the setbacks of the bitter winter of 1941-42, and the comeback of the Russian Air Force to numerical superiority by spring of 1942, the Luftwaffe was far from defeated.

Here Werner Baumbach, elite Luftwaffe dive-bomber pilot who ended the war as Hitler's Chief of Bombers, describes the Luftwaffe role in the terrible last days of Sevastopol.

Sevastopol-Ring of Death

Werner Baumbach, Luftwaffe

HERE I AM back in the Crimea.

The heaviest rocket bombs are all ready in case the Russian fleet tries to relieve the fortress of Sevastopol, now isolated.

My old Ju-88 has brought me nonstop straight across the Balkans from Italy. We came down from 16,000 feet to our destination, Eupatoria airfield. The heat was almost unbearable. It brought a return of the fever I have only just got over, and with it a sort of mental paralysis. I was glad enough of my thin khaki uniform. I took a Fieseler Storch to visit the headquarters of the divisional general commanding the Eighth Air Corps, whom Jeschonnek had informed of my coming. I came in low into the valley of the Ishuruk-su in which lie the town and Khan's palace of Baktshisarai, "the house of the gardens," then headquar-

ters of Col.-Gen. Baron von Richthofen.

I climbed again until I received a green light signal. There was a Volkswagen waiting. It was late afternoon and the air was like a hot bath.

We drove through the high walls of the Khan's palace in the center of the town. It had previously been a museum. An A.D.C. met me in the garden. We hurried through a whole series of halls and rooms and a pergola on the sunny side and after a short period of waiting I found myself in the presence of Col.-Gen. von Richthofen.

Seated at his desk, his back to the wide-open window, Richthofen almost looked a Khan himself, with his high cheekbones, small, narrow eyes, and weather-beaten features. Our talk was brief and military. He explained the attack on Sevastopol, which had just begun, and outlined what was required of the Luftwaffe, which was to smother the fortress with bombs. I was to visit the airstrips involved the same day.

Richthofen seemed to be in his element. It was a job after his own heart. He was one of the most striking figures among the Luftwaffe leaders in the war. His friendship with Jeschonnek, the Chief of Staff, must have made things easier for him.

Next morning I flew over Sevastopol myself. Bombs at the feet of the army — a *sine qua non* as it had been before. When the army wanted a decision in a battle there were loud shouts for "that whore, the Luftwaffe." But when it was a matter of deciding a whole campaign, such as the Moscow offensive in the summer of 1941, the idea was not carried through to its logical conclusion.

But was the taking of Sevastopol really of strategic importance? To the German leaders it seemed more a question of prestige and a political factor against Turkey. It was certainly to Russia's interest to hold it, though it is probable that they had "written off" the garrison. At that moment it must have suited them to tie down big German forces there so that they had to postpone the next part of their program. We may conclude that the Germans were led into a trap when they set out so late to capture the fortress.

In all we had assembled about 400 Stukas, bombers, and fighters on the airfields in the vicinity of Sevastopol. It meant that we had to keep 200 to 250 aircraft always ready for action every day.

From the air, Sevastopol looked like a painter's battle panorama. In the early morning the sky swarmed with aircraft hurrying to unload their bombs on the town. Thousands of bombs — more than 2400 tons of high explosive and 23,000 incendiaries — were dropped on the town and fortress. A single sortie took no more than twenty minutes. By the time you had gained the necessary altitude you were in the target area.

With all the smoke and dust, amid the roar of the detonations, the battle area is largely invisible to our troops on the ground, though they could see the bombers fly down into the wasps' nest which is the shrinking defense ring. The screaming descent of the Stukas and the whistling of falling bombs seemed to make even nature hold her breath. The storming troops, exposed to the pitiless heat of the burning sun, paused for the few seconds which must have seemed an eternity to the defenders.

The Russians clung to their mother earth with unparalleled obstinacy. If no other way lay open, they blew up their forts and defense works, often a long way underground, together with their assailants and themselves. The Russian A.A. was silenced in the first few days so the danger to aircraft was less than in attacks on the Caucasus harbors or Russian airfields. Yet our work at Sevastopol made the highest demands on men and material. 12, 14, and even up to 18 sorties were made daily by individual crews. A Ju 88 with fuel tanks full made three or four sorties without the crew stretching their legs. It meant tremendous wear and tear for the aircraft and the ground staff, those unknown soldiers who could not sleep a wink in those days and nights and were responsible for the safe condition of their machines.

Under the massive weight of the bomb carpets, the heavy artillery of the army and the "Thor" super-mortar, even the most desperate defense was bound to break down. Day by day the ring got smaller and smaller. Thousands of German and Russian soldiers died in fierce hand-to-hand fighting.

The earth drank in streams of blood and sweat while in the old palace of the Tsars at Yalta the army chiefs prepared to celebrate victory — incidentally a celebration which was to be rudely disturbed by a Russian air raid.

The only times when there was a short pause was when the sun sank behind the Black Sea, its last rays bathing the fortress and harbors in a blood-red glow. And only when the last Russian soldier had fallen in the Chersonese or surrendered in the lighthouse did the end come on July 4, 1942.

Such was Sevastopol, a name spelling something gruesome and horrific to all who were there. Attacker and defender alike fought with a fury which was quite exceptional even for this war.

PART THREE

NORTH AFRICA:
THE DESERT AIR WAR

June, 1942–June, 1943

Introduction

THROUGHOUT HISTORY the Mediterranean has been an open highway of conquest through which nations, kingdoms, and empires have marched to meet their rendezvous with fate.

In 1940, the Italian air-ground forces of empire-bent Benito Mussolini struck out for Egypt along the North African coast only to be hurled back by the British. The Italian debacle was retrieved by Hitler who sent to North Africa one of his top commanders, Gen. Erwin Rommel with elite, crack Panzer Divisions supported by strong Luftwaffe elements. This force became known as the Afrika Korps and by June, 1942 it had driven the British back across the desert to El Alamein, the last strongline before the Nile River. At stake now was Egypt and the Suez Canal, possession of which by the Third Reich could effectively choke to death an already gasping British Empire.

The critical situation stirred an articulate British Prime Minister Winston Churchill to appeal for American air reinforcements at once, and for substitution of the early planned ground invasion of Europe for one in Africa. The Churchill arguments had attractions: conquest of North Africa would provide a base for an attack on and invasion of the soft underbelly of Europe; it would eliminate the pro-Nazi Vichy-French government holding Algeria; it would free the vital Mediterranean sea lanes — lifeline of the free world to the Orient; it would relieve pressure on the British Eighth Army defending the Suez Canal and draw German air strength from the Russian Front where a Panzer drive was rolling toward the Caucasus. President Roosevelt bought the idea.

In response, small American air reinforcements of B-24s and B-17s began arriving in Egypt as early as June, 1942 and by mid-August a B-17 heavy and B-25 medium Bomb Group (the 98th and 12th) and the 57th Fighter Group with P-40 "Tomahawk" fighters were in action with the RAF Desert Air Force in support of Lt. Gen. Bernard L. Montgomery's hard-pressed Eighth Army.

Organized into Ninth Air Force, these American units played a significant part in the Battle of El Alamein (October 24 — November 5, 1942) which broke the back of the Afrika Korps, beginning for Gen. Rommel the great retreat out of Egypt back into Libya and Tunisia. Controlling the air and pounding the Afrika Korps as it pummeled backwards out of Egypt, the tactical Ninth and the RAF Desert Air Forces demonstrated for

100

Casualties of the El Alamein Line. An RAF repair depot convoy approaches the Gizeh Pyramids near Cairo.

the first time the power and effectiveness of coordinated air-ground effort in which the first job of air force is to reduce the enemy air forces to impotence, second to isolate the battlefield by attacks on supply and communication lines in the enemy's rear, and third to hammer directly at enemy ground forces. This new concept employed at El Alamein was to be further refined during the African campaign and used through the war in Europe. It was the birth of tactical airpower as we know it today.

Subjected to the full weight of Montgomery's coordinated air-ground offensive, Rommel fell back and by February, 1943 drew up to make a stand behind a string of fortifications in Tunisia called the "Mareth Line."

Meanwhile, on November 8, 1942, "Operation Torch" — the Allied invasion of North Africa — got underway under the command of Lt. Gen. Dwight D. Eisenhower with landings at some half-dozen places along the coast from Casablanca to Oran in Algeria.

The invasion fleet met little enemy air resistance as troops poured ashore. British and U.S. Navy Carrier forces stood offshore to counter enemy air if it appeared. U.S. Navy Task Force 34 Air Group, commanded by Rear Adm. Ernest D. McWhorter consisted of four aircraft carriers *(Ranger, Sangamon, Santee,* and *Swannee)* with 108 F4Fs, 36 SBDs, and 27 TBFs. Aboard the *Chenango* were 70 P-40s of the AAF's 33rd Fighter Group under Lt. Col. William Momeyer destined for Port Lyautey Field at Casablanca. Beginning on November 10, these Army Air Force land-based fighters were catapulted from the *Chenango* in one of the dramatic operations of the campaign and staged through Port Lyautey Field for combat duty out of a desert strip in Algeria.

Units of the Twelfth Air Force, staging out of airfields on Gibraltar, began arriving on secured airfields around Oran on the afternoon of D-Day.

"Operation Torch" met little resistance. The Vichy-French forces put up only token opposition. Algiers fell on D-Day, Oran on D plus 2 and by November 11 all French Forces in Morocco and Algeria surrendered on orders from the French Commander Adm. Jean Darlan, a prisoner of war. The single air opposition to the invasion was put up by four Vichy-French Dewoitine airplanes which attacked units of the 31st Fighter Group as it was landing at Oran on a flight from Gibraltar. The Luftwaffe was conspicuously absent.

Allied forces quickly drove eastward into Tunisia only to be stopped by Rommel within 20 miles of Tunis. Here the war bogged down as winter storms set in. Hectic airfield construction got underway to accommodate groups and squadrons pouring into North Africa with their P-40s, P-38s, B-25 and B-26 medium bombers, C-47 troop carriers, and B-24 and B-17 heavies.

At the same time Allied Air Forces underwent reorganization for the coming campaign. Anglo-American air units were merged into one operational force called the Northwest African Air Forces (NAAF) under Maj. Gen. Carl "Tooey" Spaatz with subordinate units called Northwest African Strategic Air Force under Gen. Doolittle and Northwest African Tactical Air Force commanded by Air Vice Marshall Sir Arthur Coningham, RAF. The NAAF was brought under the overall Mediterranean Air Command headed by the brilliant Air Chief Marshall Sir Arthur W. Tedder, British airpower pioneer.

The Afrika Korps was now caught between the giant pincers of the British Eighth Army supported by the RAF Desert Air Force and U.S. Ninth Air Force on the East, and the Anglo-British invasion forces supported by the Northwest African Air Forces on the west. Rommel's position was precarious. Resupply and troop reinforcement across the narrows of the Mediterranean through the ports of

While the Afrika Korps and the Luftwaffe were being beaten at El Alamein, British and American troops were landed in French North Africa. Here a Martlet takes off from its aircraft carrier during the landing operations.

Allied air attacks on German airfields in Tunisia continued through December 1942 and January 1943, creating the terrific loss of Axis aircraft which started Rommel on a retreat out of Africa. The planes shown here were found at Derna Aerodrome in Tunisia.

Bizerte and Tunis held the only hope of sustaining him, and this lifeline became a happy hunting ground for Allied flyers.

Allied air attacks on German Tunisian airfields, supply dumps, roads, bridges and troop positions continued through the months of December and January creating a terrible attrition of Axis air and ground forces, supplies and ammunition which Rommel could ill afford.

On February 14, the cagey "Desert Fox" struck back with a ground offensive westward through Tunisia's Kasserine Pass aimed at capturing a covey of new and important Allied airfields. It almost succeeded, but for Allied air which was quickly thrown into the breach. Fighters, mediums, and heavies laid down a barrage of firepower, halting the breakthrough and initiating a counter air attack which by the end of March had wrested control of the air over Tunisia from the Luftwaffe. It was here the North African Air Forces demonstrated the real meaning of planned, organized tactical airpower in a theatre of operations.

In the east, the British Eighth Army, spearheaded by devastating Ninth and Desert Air Force attacks, broke through Rommel's strong Mareth Line fortifications and pressed on into Tunisia driving the Afrika Korps before it.

By day and by night Allied heavy, medium, and fighter bombers pounded at Rommel's forces locked in the hills of the constricting Tunisian bridgehead. With the principal ports of Bizerte and Tunis ground into unusable ruins, Allied airmen concentrated on the beleaguered Afrika Korps with more than 2000 air sorties a day.

While the bulk of the combat tactical air missions in North Africa were direct support to ground forces, air-to-air combat at times reached high proportions, but never on the scale later experienced in Europe. This is indicated in the small number of aces, only 28 in all of Northwest African Air Forces. Top man of NAAF was Maj. Levi R. Chase who knocked down 12 Luftwaffe fighters during the campaign. He was tied by 2nd Lt. William J. Sloan of Twelfth Air Force, also with 12 victories. Ninth Air Force fighter pilots destroyed 610 enemy fighters in aerial combat, losing 227 for a ratio of 3 to 1.

On the night of April 18-19, 90 heavy bombers plastered German airdromes in Tunisia and by the 22nd the Luftwaffe was almost non-existent. What few planes were left evacuated to Sicilian airfields.

Rommel's plight was serious. His only resupply now was by air, and slow, lumbering six-engine JU-52 and ME-323 transports from Sicily and Italy had to run the Allied air blockade to allow a trickle of men and materiel to reach Africa. The most notable of such missions was a desperate effort by 100 JU-52s and ME-323s on April 18, 1943. Spotted by Allied fighter patrols as they skimmed low over the Mediterranean waters, the ill-fated formation was pounced upon by Air Force fight-

Mitchell B-25 bombers of the United States Army Air Force and Baltimore bombers of the South African Air Force flying together in formation on their way to attack Rommel's forces as they moved toward Tunisia from El Alamein.

A British bomb bursts among Junkers JU-88s at one of the Luftwaffe's Tunisian airfields.

A formation of B-25 bombers with an escort of P-38s engages an Axis air convoy of JU-52 planes over the Sicilian Straits. The German air transports are almost at water level and to the left can be seen a B-25 in the middle of his strafing run. Twenty-six of the JU-52s were shot down.

ers in an historic engagement known as the "Palm Sunday Massacre." More than 70 were blasted into the sea and onto the beaches.

By early May the once powerful Afrika Korps was dislodged from the Tunisian hills and driven out onto the coastal plain. Here, on May 6, Allied tactical air forces laid down, in devastating pattern, 2146 individual bomber, fighter/bomber, and fighter sorties along a 6000 yard front in advance of the U.S. First Army. This scythe of airpower cut a channel of death across the coastal plane to the city of Tunis.

Hopelessly split and penned against the sea, 270,000 Axis troops, who had been ordered to fight to the last man,

surrendered. Voluntarily, thousands from the elite Panzer Divisions marched in columns, without guards, to the Allied prisoner cages to the tune of German marching songs. Many drove up in their own motorized vehicles for admission to a POW camp. The timeless desert sands of North Africa had witnessed another conquering army meet its rendezvous with fate.

The "invincible Nazi," whose hob-nailed boots had trampled a Continent into submission had beheld the power of Allied tactical air warfare. Though the long, bitter road to final victory in Europe still lay ahead, North Africa had paced the course.

From the tactical and strategic air considerations of the desert air war to the flyer's diet of Spam and dehydrated cabbage, an official Air Force *correspondent gives this incisive look into the North African campaign.*

191 Days of Desert War

Maj. Arthur Gordon

"OPERATION TORCH," as the African invasion was called, was dictated by the activities of a man then known as the "Desert Fox" — Rommel. As his panzers clanked forward on the dusty coastal road that led to Alexandria, in 1941 the situation in the Mediterranean grew more critical. To those on the Allied side responsible for the conduct of the war, it became increasingly evident that he must be stopped. The worst thorn in Rommel's side was Malta. If Malta fell and Rommel's supply lines grew stronger, then there was every probability that Egypt would fall too. With Egypt would go the Suez Canal and the Middle East. The Germans would flank the Russians, win the Caucasian oil which they so desperately needed and possibly link up with the Japanese in the Indian Ocean. By July, 1942, the consequences of not stopping Rommel were so obvious and so grave that earlier plans had to be shelved. Our Britain-based air offensive would have to struggle along as best it could, without the services of some of its most experienced squad-

rons and, even more disheartening, without the P-38 Lightning fighter cover originally scheduled to escort the heavies to worthwhile targets in Germany.

At the time of "Torch," American air power was already represented in Egypt by the Ninth Air Force. At the start of the battle of El Alamein, October 23, 1942, it had 164 aircraft consisting of a squadron of Fortresses, a squadron of Liberators, two P-40 groups, and one B-25 group. These, plus British air strength of some 1100 planes, were opposed by about 2000 Axis planes of all types. The Luftwaffe had its hands full dealing with these guardians of Egypt. It was not equal to a heavy assault on its rear. The responsibility for that assault was given to the Twelfth Air Force which landed with the invasion forces on November 8.

"Torch" differed sharply from subsequent invasions in that it was directed against territory held by a power that was semi-friendly, or at worst only half hostile. Adequate air cover, it was thought, could be provided from carriers and nearby Gibraltar. There were two operational plans for the invaders, a war plan in case the Vichy French forces resisted, and a peace plan in case they did not. The uncertainty as to which plan would be followed persisted until a few hours before H-hour.

For the invasion, an American paratroop force was flown from Britain in C-47s in the first American airborne operation of the war. Their story is worth recalling because it indicates the growing pains incident to any new project, in peace or war, and because it was the small seed from which grew the great vertical envelopments later in Normandy, in Southern France, in Holland, and across the Rhine.

The planes took off on the night of November 7, expecting to receive a friendly welcome in daylight the next day. The flight down was a rough one. Most of the planes had been undergoing modification until a matter of hours before take-off. In some planes, wingtip lights burned out, making formation flying in the wretched weather almost impossible. When the C-47s finally reached Africa, they found severe fighting in progress. French fighters raked the defenseless transports with machine-gun fire, forcing several to crash-land in the desert. These were some of the difficulties, but even so the the operation had a measure of success inasmuch as the scattered arrival of the C-47s thoroughly confused the French air defenses and had them tilting at

shadows.

On the whole, air opposition was light. Spitfires from Gibraltar made short work of such Dewoitines as offered resistance. Carrier-ferried P-40s swooped onto captured airfields. Within a day or two some heavy bombers, including the "veteran" 97th Group from England, were moved in. Mediums and fighters also arrived to begin the long task of hacking at Rommel's rear guards and his supply lines.

Living conditions faced by these airmen were rugged, to put it mildly. Ground crews performed miracles of ingenuity in keeping aircraft operational in a climate that seemed to consist of dust storms and bottomless mud. Missions were flown on short notice, with organization improvised on the spot. Fighter pilots attended bomber briefings to get a picture of the type of mission they were being called on to escort. Troop Carrier dropped the paratroops that captured Bone airdrome, flew countless air supply missions, learned how to operate on a shoestring.

But even in those early days, the pattern of tactical support was emerging precisely as predicted by the logicians in the pre-war classrooms. First: gain air superiority. Second: isolate the battlefield. Third: provide direct cooperation with the ground forces in the liquidation of the enemy. The success of the second phase depended, obviously, on the first. Without air control there could be no interdiction of the battlefield. And

The weary B-24 crews who harassed the retreating Afrika Korps faced rugged living conditions on the desert.

until the battlefield was isolated, close cooperation could have no more than local effect. All this the air planners knew already. The African campaign was to teach them how to apply that knowledge successfully.

Air superiority was not gained in a week, or a month. At the time of the African landings, the embryonic Twelfth Air Force consisted of 551 aircraft. There were 1700 miles between it and the other jaw of the Anglo-American pincer. And the Luftwaffe fought hard. But the truth was that the GAF at this moment of its greatest territorial expansion was simply stretched beyond the limits of

its capacity adequately to supply itself. Committed to major efforts in both Russia and Africa, with the growing weight of the RAF's night assault oppressing its cities and the AAF's Britain-based day offensive already casting an ominous shadow, its doom in Africa was sealed from the moment our landings succeeded. The Germans must have wondered in bitter afterthought whether their African squadrons, pulled out in time, might not have tipped the scale at Stalingrad.

At the time, their faith in Rommel was so high, and stakes for which he fought so glittering, that any such admission of defeat was out of the question. So they fought on, until the harbors of Tunisia were choked with ships sunk by the AAF, and the desert battlefields littered with the skeletons of more than 1000 of their first-line aircraft.

While the North African ground campaign was slogging through the mud that marked the end of 1942, air power was slashing at Rommel's overextended supply line, blocking roads, strafing motor columns, sinking ships, and shooting down air transports.

Much of the doctrine of tactical air power was being reasserted in action: that to operate effectively in conjunction with the ground forces, you first must have control of the air, that when you do have such control, the primary role of tactical air power consists in attacking supply lines in the rear rather than close support in the immediate battle area. New lessons were learned every day about the value of softening up the enemy air force by bombing airdromes before launching a ground attack, about the importance of hand-in-glove coordination between air and ground commanders, about the necessity for integrated air forces that could act as a whole rather than scattered squadrons operationally tied to a particular army or navy unit.

This principle of unity of command was accepted at Casablanca in January, 1943. In the following month, the converging Twelfth and Desert Air Forces were merged in the Northwest African Air Forces under Gen. Spaatz, with a second air command in the Eastern Mediterranean, under Air Marshall Tedder. It was not until the end of the year that the solution of the joint command problem found clearest expression in the creation of the Mediterranean Allied Air Forces, in which the function of air units, not their nationality, determined where they were placed and how employed.

As the days lengthened and spring arrived, Gen. Spaatz's forces proceeded with the arduous and necessary task of whittling down the Luftwaffe. A constant problem in those early days was how to find enough fighters to protect the bombers against the still threatening Axis air power. The original heavy bomber group, the 97th, found revenge for the pasting it had taken from the GAF on its first night in Algiers by plastering Axis shipping and harbor facilities. In December, it had been joined by three squadrons of Liberators from the 92nd Group in England, who lived in the desert on Spam and dehydrated cabbage, harassed Rommel's rear guards, and struck across the Mediterranean at Naples and the Sicilian airdromes. Several groups of mediums, living under conditions just as rugged, gave the Nazis a foretaste of what B-24s and B-26s could do. There were some bad moments in the Tunisian campaign — as, for example, when Rommel flung his Panzers through Kasserine Pass. On that occasion everything with wings was thrown against him, even the heavies flying below medium altitude. But there were also red-letter days like the famous Palm Sunday engagement when P-40s of the 57th Group caught a swarm of JU-52s and ME-323s flying men and supplies to Rommel's hard-pressed forces and shot 79 into the sea in a slaughter reminiscent of the Battle of Britain.

In the Mediterranean Theatre of Operations (MTO) there was more variety of air combat — if not more heroism — than was dreamed of in Northern Europe at that time. High-, medium-, and low-level bombing, bridge-busting, strafing of armored columns and airdromes, skip bombing of Axis shipping — all these tactics and many others appeared in the 191 days between the landings in North Africa and the collapse of the Axis forces there.

It was in this period, too, that an aerial weapon whose potentialities had never been fully exploited began to be recognized as the indispensable aid to modern warfare. In 1939, one of Germany's best generals, Werner von Fritsch, had predicted that the side with the best aerial photo-reconnaissance would win the war. In Britain, the RAF had skilled photo-interpreters assessing bomb damage in making target selections based on high altitude photos brought back by unarmed Spitfires or Mosquitoes. A squadron of American Lightnings, profiting by RAF experience, was almost operational. But it was in Africa that tactical reconnaissance proved itself invaluable to the ground forces. At one point during the final stages of the drive on

Tunis, when weather grounded the recce boys, the ground commander flatly refused to move until his air photo coverage was obtained. Flying P-38s (F-versions) members of the 90th Photo Recon Wing experimented with night photography, and brought low-level photo-recon missions — dicing missions, as they were called — to a state of development which was invaluable later on in Italy and still later in the battles of France and Germany. They got little recognition for their work — photo recon was strictly hush-hush in those days — but they came to be acknowledged as the real eyes of the army. To the long-range planners, with an eventual D-day in mind, their work proved beyond question that complete photo-coverage of the invasion area and its defenses would be indispensable to successful landings.

With the final collapse of the Axis African forces on May 18, 1943, air power was free to turn its attention across the Mediterranean to what Mr. Churchill had once called the "soft underbelly" of the Axis. The Northwest African Air Forces was, by this time, a battle-hardened aggregation of nearly 4000 aircraft, with 2630 American airplanes, 1076 British, and 94 French. The first Axis target to feel the weight of its blows was Pantelleria. Between May 30 and June 11, this heavily-fortified Italian island rocked under more than 6000 tons of bombs and finally capitulated without a ground assault — the first territorial conquest to be achieved solely through air power. It was a great victory, and a relatively cheap one: we lost 63 aircraft and claimed 236 of the enemy's while gaining fighter fields indispensable for the invasion of Sicily. It was a great victory. . . .

Tobruk, key port on the North African Coast between Bengazi and the Nile River, was overwhelmed on June 20, 1942 by Rommel's Afrika Corps in the final all-out attempt to seize the Suez Canal. The British garrison of 25,000 soldiers were captured and imprisoned, and the Rommel forces rolled to a stop before El Alamein, high point of the German advance.

All the northern Mediterranean shore and all of the southern shore up to Alexandria, Egypt was now in enemy hands, and Rommel's supplies could flow straight across the Mediterranean without interruptions. Main bases for German supply ships were the Libyan ports of Tobruk and Bengazi. The fall of Egypt was imminent, in fact many of the hotels in Cairo already had their menus printed in German and Rommel had stated he would make his headquarters at the Shepherds Hotel.

Bengazi and Tobruk immediately became prime targets for RAF twin-engine Wellington bombers and American B-24s and B-17s which were hastily sent to the Middle East. The whole Western Mediterranean, from Greece to Crete and down to Africa now became hunting grounds for Allied flyers ranging out of Egypt and Palestine. In four months every single tanker trying to reinforce Rommel was sunk in those waters; 8 out of 10 ships bound for Tobruk and Bengazi were sent to the bottom, many in the port city's harbors.

Tobruk began to feel the weight of Allied air bombardment shortly after its capture by the Germans. So vital was it to the Germans that the heaviest possible anti-aircraft artillery and fighter plane defense was thrown up against the nightly British and American raids. So vital was it for the British to deny Tobruk's port facilities to Rommel that on the night of September 13-14, 1942, commandos were sent ashore in a vain effort to block the harbor and disrupt the city.

That night the port city and its harbor were turned into a ghastly inferno. Twenty to thirty British "Wimpys" (Wellingtons) wove into and out of the target area dropping flares while overhead U.S. heavies unloaded tons of TNT. The violent explosion of an ammunition dump was felt by American flyers five miles up. Offshore naval warships added heavy streams of shells into the city.

From the cockpit of a B-17 five miles above the holocaust of Tobruk that night a B-17 pilot describes this unearthly scene.

Midnight Raid on Tobruk

Capt. Rowan T. Thomas

OUR CREW looked like weird creatures from Mars or fictional characters out of the pages of Jules Verne or H. G. Wells trussed up in their oxygen masks, heavy fleece-lined leather jackets, and large flying boots. Maj. Fennell and I had only masks and safety belts on, as we needed freedom of movement to meet every emergency.

The stars seemed so close that we felt we could reach out and grasp them. This is a common illusion over the desert. The angular distance down to the city of Tobruk was only 5° or 10°, but we knew it was probably 40 miles — or 13 minutes — before we would be over it. Our only indication there was an earth beneath us was the brilliant bursts of bombs and gun fire.

Maj. Fennell spoke to Bombardier Taulbee over the interphone: "How's the visibility, Sergeant?" Taulbee, who had been with the major since he left the States, replied, "Visibility not good, sir. I cannot distinguish enough of the ground to bomb."

"Judge, take the controls," the major exclaimed, as we skirted to our right, east of the town. He checked his lighting and adjusted his panel light lower so enemy fighters above could not spot us from the glow. The top of the pilot's compartment is glass and from certain angles these lights may be seen by a fighter above us.

When I took the controls I recognized the high altitude feel that a plane gets flying at 25,000 feet. Our air speed indicated 140 and I knew that by adding two miles an hour for every 1000 feet of true altitude I could approximate my speed at 180, although more accurate computation is left to the navigator. We must rely on the navigator's instruments and take no chances. Nothing is what it seems to be to the naked eye. We cannot completely trust our mental and physical reactions in high altitudes.

Maj. Fennell again took the wheel and kept up a continuous conversation with Bombardier Taulbee as we neared the target. It certainly looked red-hot beneath us.

A furious battle was being waged down below where the peninsula of Tobruk jutted out into the Mediterranean. We could not tell water from land, but we could see terrific fire we knew was coming from British and American naval units at sea. From the intensity and regularity of the flashes we could determine about where our naval ships were. Seven or eight quick flashes a split-second apart ran down the line of the ships' guns.

The ships had closed in a few miles from shore and were pouring broadsides into the peninsula. On land, the German artillery fired from three sides, setting up a deadly raking crossfire. The whole area beneath us was a seething inferno.

God be with the commandos tonight, I thought. If those poor devils can live through this, we haven't any right to be afraid. We're much safer than the boys who are landing from those ships in marshy mud, in the face of steep cliffs blazing hellfire.

I wondered if the commandos had fought their way into the city. Would it be possible for them to take the heavily-fortified stronghold? Would they be able to reach the 20,000 Allied prisoners held by the Germans and give them arms according to plan?

Our Flying Fortress was now in the zone of intense AA fire. Something was wrong with our props; then I remembered we had desynchronized them to deceive detector devices. Bingo! here we were, hanging over the boiling cauldron. Seven or eight searchlights leaped into the black night, searching the skies near us. The fireworks we had been observing so calmly were now meant for us. Every second might bring a fighter, pouring cannon and machine-gun fire into our sides.

We jerked up our oxygen masks and talked quickly, instantly clamping them down again. The crew were at their battle stations, those unsung heroes of combat, the tough little tail and bottom gunners, freezing at their posts, where there is no engine heat.

Tonight we had been ordered to stay over the target at least 30 minutes. Thirty minutes hanging between life and death!

"Let's make the run," snorted Maj. Fennell. "And make it short."

I called Bombardier Taulbee. "Copilot to bombardier: prepare to make bombing run!"

Our aerial fleet was not in formation — it was every man for himself. We were flying singly but had instructions as to our direction of flight so we wouldn't collide in mid-air.

We spotted a red glow. Was it a fire or a searchlight? One mistake might mean our lives. We decided it was a flare dropped by English low-altitude "Wimpys" for us to bomb by. They were flitting below us like flies around a drop of molasses.

"Whew!" whistled the major. "Look! Look!"

"Thar she blows!" I shouted, as a ring of searchlights encompassed our entire zone.

Flaming onions left behind by the British filled the sky. Hundreds of guns thundered and blazed at the planes below us. Big balls of dazzling brilliancy came up in long, slightly arching courses and exploded a distance from us.

"Drop your bombs on that flare!" Maj. Fennell called to Bombardier Taulbee. "This is it!"

I glanced at the PDI — it was flicked

114

on. When the PDI (about the size of the hour hand on an ordinary clock) flicks on, you are in your greatest danger. If you can stay on that straight course for just a few seconds without being hit, you probably will make the raid okay. It is when you fly this straight course, which is necessary for bombing, that your life is at stake. This is the time when the enemy tries to hit you. He knows where you will have to be to make a bomb run on his most valuable positions, so here he concentrates his fire. Unless you live those few seconds safely the target is lost. This is the test and the pay-off. If the enemy doesn't do something he is a gone duck. This is the flier's most anxious moment — the moment before he drops his bombs.

Our target was a land area tonight. We could bomb the flare inside the AA ring and be sure of hitting the enemy area. I wondered if Taulbee would do as well tonight as he did in China when he had blown up Generalissimo Chiang Kai-shek's practice shacks so accurately that the Generalissimo sent a special messenger to plead with him to stop.

The PDI, instead of going to direct center, needled to the right and left as the bombardier got the range. Two or three cushioned puffs jarred us. Three searchlights cutting through us told us we were nearly hit. I hoped no shrapnel had lodged in the motors to force us down later.

"Settle down, Taulbee!" called Maj. Fennell. The PDI settled in the neutral or middle mark and at last we heard the voice of our bombardier.

"Bombs away, sir!"

We dropped three 500-pounders. Flashes came back to our eyes. Glancing down to my right I gazed, fascinated. Almost five miles below us I could see a pattern of red objects. They were about the size of red cannon balls coming up in a perfect square pattern. As they came higher each missile got hotter and farther apart. This was the enemy's answer to our bomb.

"Turn left," I said to the major, tapping him on the shoulder. He raised out of his seat to see what I was pointing at and then turned swiftly to the left. A barrage that looked like an acre of melting explosives zoomed right up where we were a few seconds ago. Molten steel in square patterns, each bullet the same space apart, jarred us violently. Powerful rays of a searchlight held us. We squirmed out of that hot bed.

Following a path southward for a short time, and then changing altitude 1000 feet higher, we made the turn which would place us on our second bombing run exactly 180° opposite. A few seconds elapsed before a lurid, pinkish glow emblazoned the entire sky.

I turned to Harry Schilling, who had now come out of his turret to stand behind us, and put my thumbs down. He did the same, smiling broadly. We both realized our bombs had hit something terrific. When bombs burst five miles beneath one, they ordinarily look like penny firecrackers through the night haze and clouds. But ours had burst like huge cannon crackers.

"Sir," called Radio Operator Mc-Junkins, "we must have hit an ammunition dump. Did you see that hell of an explosion?"

Maj. Fennell looked at me and smiled. We now made our last turn for the second bomb run. I motioned to the major to stay away from the north tip as our Intelligence had warned us. He nodded. I pointed at the clock, and then at the gas gauges, showing we had been over the target 25 minutes. He nodded again as we changed altitude to throw off the AA range finders.

Just as we got to the edge of the "hot circle," 29 searchlights swept into the skies. Behind them were radio-controlled guns. These 29 guns operated automatically with 29 lights, all situated in a circle around one master beam.

Simultaneously these rays caught a "Wimpy" about 400 feet up in the clearing — one of those stalwart pilots who flew delicate, fabric-covered airplanes with only one gun turret and a top speed of 140!

We saw that stubby, brave, little airplane scurrying to avoid that formidable avalanche of radio-controlled, beam-synchronized fire. He would be written off the books in less than five seconds.

The searchlights formed a beautiful geometrical pattern of blue rays, resembling two funnel spouts together. This cone of blinding light converged, one on the top and the other on the bottom of the hapless "Wimpy." The lights seemed to go right through the plane and make an inverted pattern in the sky. He was a white moth being caught and devoured by rays of flame. Suddenly the "Wimpy" burst into a ball of fire and plummeted to the earth.*

"God rest your soul," I muttered. Then I added, "I hope when you crash you'll take a hundred of the s.o.b.s who caused this war with you."

The ruthless rays now shifted onto another stray "Wimpy" who had come to the aid of his brother. He fell into the clutches of the beams and went tumbling down from the night skies to join him in death. British "Wimpy" pilots flew in low pattern against the greatest of odds. They did a heroic job this night. After what I saw then I never wanted to hear again criticism of the British as fighters.

The searchlight began probing around us. The ack-ack was coming entirely too close. We slipped away for a few minutes and then came back at a different altitude. Our given time had elapsed, and Maj. Fennell ordered a quick run at the target to drop all our remaining bombs in rapid succession. Explosions underneath our Fortress raised it ten feet in the air three successive times.

* It took sheer, raw guts to fly "Wimpy" missions and the RAF boys who did it drew highest admiration from friend and enemy alike. At one time a "Wimpy" outfit moved up front with 52 planes. In six weeks, it had 6 left. When asked how it was, the RAF commander replied in typical British phrase: "It was a bit sticky."

"The devils are giving us everything they've got tonight," I said to the major. He was too absorbed in his duty to reply.

Over the target again, we spied a flare just dropped by our boys in medium bombardment below us. As they scampered away we heard the familiar voice of Bombardier Taulbee again:

"Bombs away, sir!"

Our entire load hurtled down in a stream of destruction. Flames again showed that Taulbee had hit the target.

Our run had been straight across the target, some four minutes for the run and some six minutes to get out of the "hot circle." All we had to watch for now were fighters on our trail, cunningly scheming to follow us back to our landing field and pounce on us when we were nearly out of gas.

It was terrifically cold as we turned homeward. Every time I shut my jaws they would pop at the hinges. I had to blow air in my cheeks to keep from biting them when I closed my mouth. My eyes were streaming tears. Looking down on that 50-mile radius of fierce combat, which was to continue throughout the night, I knew these were the last moments of many brave men.

An RAF Halifax bomber is readied for a night raid on Rommel's positions.

By day the RAF Desert Air Force and the American Ninth scoured the barren desert with their light and medium bombers, dive bombers and fighter strafing sweeps.

Two air weapons in particular threw fear and terror into the Axis troops: the Hurricane "Tank Busters" — the famed Battle of Britain fighter specially modified as an anti-tank weapon, and the swift, versatile, deadly twin-engine British Beaufighter used on low-level air strikes deep into enemy territory.

Here American war correspondent Gordon Gaskill describes in vivid prose a "Beau" sweep across 600 miles of desert from Egypt to the Nazi airdrome at Derna, Libya. To the steel-nerved pilots of the Desert Air Force it was a routine mission, just another day's work which might draw a 25-word communique from headquarters.

To Gaskill, it was a ride at . . .

Fifteen Feet Above Hell

Gordon Gaskill

BERTIE WAS COMMANDING to-day's flight. But ten minutes before the zero hour we were still playing darts. He made two bull's-eyes in six throws; I barely hit the board. The radio was playing "The Land of Hope and Glory" from London, and most of the other pilots in the mess were humming and singing.

Five minutes before zero hour Bertie said, "We'd better fix you up with a parachute." Then he grinned and added, "Not that it will do you any good." For to-day I was doing what very few American correspondents have ever done before — I was flying into actual battle as the third and extra man aboard a Beaufighter mystery plane, one of the deadliest planes in the world. And a parachute does you no good, because a Beaufighter flies at an enormous speed only 15 feet above the ground. You never have a chance to bail out. The Italians call the Beaufighter the "Wrath of God," and the Italians should know, because, for them, it's been the curse of Libya.

I think it is the most beautiful but most murderous plane that ever flew the heavens. It is an all-metal monoplane with twin 1500-horsepower engines. It's the fastest in the Mideast — well over 300 miles an hour. Heavy armor plating turns the machine-gun bullets. Above all, the guns are unbelievably powerful. There's a small

Their low-level strafing mission "on," two Royal Air Force Beaufighter pilots run for their airplanes.

button on the wheel, just under the pilot's thumb. When you touch it, six machine guns and four cannons spit out a solid sheet of death — irresistible as lightning. The devil himself should pilot a Beaufighter.

We climbed into the plane. The observer squeezed past me and inched toward his plastic teardrop in the stern. Then Bertie climbed in. He wore shorts, socks, suede shoes, a short-sleeved shirt, and a blue pullover a girl in London had knitted for him. He also wore a flying helmet, but carried in his hand a battered old felt hat. That was for good luck; he always flew with it.

I stood directly behind the pilot, hanging on to two tubular pipes above me. I was to stand there nearly five hours. After a while I discovered that I could hunch my shoulders and wedge myself between the pipes, thus leaving my hands free to take notes.

It was a beautiful day, and hard to believe that our four planes were flying off to kill, burn, and destroy. The sky was splotched by small, drifting clouds, and their shadows mottled the desert. Over our own territory, we flew 1500 feet. Whenever we passed a body of troops Bertie pulled a lever to give the signal that identified us as a friend. This is important. Three days before, a Beaufighter had been shot down by British anti-aircraft ack-ack. The plane hit the ground at 250 miles an hour and was destroyed, but I had a drink that same night with the pilot. He had only a slight cut over his right eye. He wasn't a bit sore.

"They would have been ruddy fools not to shoot at me," he said. "I was a little late signaling."

At battle headquarters we got our final orders: We were to fly 300 miles into hostile Libya and shoot up an enemy airdrome next to Derna on the Mediterranean coast. This is the most dangerous work of all, because airdromes are well guarded. It was past lunchtime, but we were not hungry. Each of us ate four biscuits smeared with bully beef. A corporal brought us a thermos jug of hot tea. Then we were off again.

A dense tangle of barbed wire separates Egypt from Libya. Once across it, the Beaufighters went into their unique and terrible battle positions. Bertie looked back at the other three planes, waggled his wings, and edged the stick forward. The plane darted toward the earth. I could distinguish every pebble when we finally leveled off not more than 15 feet above the ground. We flew at that height, and often lower, the entire time we were in enemy territory.

When flying so low were almost invisible. An enemy plane above us probably would never see us. Our camouflage melted perfectly into the desert. We hugged the ground so closely that the rolling hills hid us from ground observers. Flying so low, no enemy fighters could get beneath us, and they were afraid to dive at us for fear of hitting the ground.

We flew at enormous speed, and still the throttles were not wide open. It was breath-taking and fantastically dangerous. To a pilot flying so fast and so low, the desert has a hypnotic effect that numbs his judgment. It is easy to drop lower and lower by inches, then by feet, until you fly into the ground. Several pilots have done that. Others have torn off their wingtips on telephone poles. The merest wrong touch means instant death. Now I understood what the other pilots meant last night when they told me: "Punch Bertie in the ribs every once in a while to wake him up."

Several times I thought I saw the sea, but the waters vanished as we winged toward them. The flat desert dropped away behind us. The ground became rougher and the wadies, desert ravines, deeper. As the land rolled, so we flew. We dipped down into each valley and lifted just in time to clear the next ridge and dip again. Always 15 feet up; I looked out the window and saw the three other "Beaus" winging along close behind. We were like the albatross I had once seen in the South Atlantic, almost dipping his wings in the sea. We were birds, too — birds of death.

Once we shot over a herd of camels grazing in the desert brush. They didn't even look up as we approached, because, by some devilish miracle of engineering, you can't hear a Beaufighter coming toward you. All the noise goes out the rear, and you don't hear a sound until it is directly on top of you. Then it's too late. Camels fled in terror only when we nearly sheared them.

We came at last to an arm of the sea. Our target was only ten minutes away. In the alleyway behind me, the sergeant had been fitting drums of shells into the cannons. He closed bulletproof steel doors at my back. Bertie turned the firing knob on the wheel, so that it now read "FIRE" instead of "SAFE."

He was just in time. Suddenly, on the left, we saw an Italian blockhouse, a sort of tiny fort. We had never meant to approach it, but it was too late now to hide. We couldn't risk having a warning telephoned ahead. Our slight error in navigation was fatal — but not for us.

The "Beaus" were four dark angels wheeling sharply toward the blockhouse. Bertie didn't look like a clerk now. Those blue eyes that a few months ago were scanning columns of figures were now pressed to sights. The hands that used to work an adding machine were ready at the firing button.

Puffs of smoke broke out from the blockhouse. They'd seen us, but we never saw their shells. All my instincts cried out for greater speed, but Bertie didn't touch the throttle. If we flew too fast our fire would be too widely spaced on the ground. It wouldn't do enough damage. Bertie

eased the stick back, and we shot up to 200 feet. Then he put the nose down gently, and we came diving in at the blockhouse. He touched the firing button. Beneath me a murderous giant began clearing his throat. A solid sheet of death spat from our four cannons and six guns. Our fire plowed up the earth. A cloud of choking powder smoke swept through the plane.

The royal flag of Italy was flying serenely from a staff. On the ground, a man was running for safety to the blockhouse. He never got there. I saw his white face turned up, and I could imagine how terror bubbled up within him as he saw for the last time in his life the "Wrath of God" upon him, swift and inexorable as doom. I saw our bullets march toward him and over him, and I saw him lying motionless on the ground like a discarded doll as we roared over him.

Our shells marched up to the blockhouse, where they were still firing at us. Sixteen cannon and 24 machine-guns of the four "Beaus" tore at the white walls. The firing ceased. Bertie gunned the engine. The plane leaped forward as we fled away. Barely in time, he jerked back the stick to clear the hill beyond the blockhouse. We were sure no one would give the alarm.

We sped on. We crossed two more ridges, and there, dead ahead, was the airdrome, with tents shining white in the sunlight. We banked sharply and stole away to the east, following a concealing valley up to the very edge of the drome. Once again we darted up to 200 feet. Once again we nosed down. Once again Bertie touched the firing button.

The Germans and the Italians on the ground never heard us coming. They never had a chance. I saw about eight of them lounging about the tent, and we left them still lounging — in death. Our shots fell just to the right of a large truckful of men. They began running, but the Beaufighter on our left cut them down. The truck burst into flames and overturned.

We were nearly past the drome now. We saw on the ground the bones of the planes already destroyed, for Beaufighters had been here before. Away from the drome, the four of us banked again sharply and beautifully to the left, like lazy birds, and headed back again. This time, they were better prepared for us. I saw a gunner on the side of a plateau with a machine-gun, and his tracer bullets spat at us. A bullet smashed against the windshield, 18 inches from my face. Thank God, it was bulletproof! The pilot tapped the button lightly, and the man with the machine-gun fell down. I do not think he saw our wings or heard our thunder as we flashed over him.

Now we were over the airdrome again, and again our guns belched out death irresistible. Bullets and incendiary shells, explosive and solid. Three grounded planes, two German and one Italian, were destroyed. The tents were cut to ribbons. A gasoline truck vanished in a spurt of flame. A column of black smoke spread and began rising.

We fled for home then, our throttles wide open, darting back into the valley for safety. They followed us with guns, and we saw tracers smoking over and under us. Some hit us, we found later, but did no damage. A Beaufighter can take it.

I looked out and back to see how the flight had fared. The other three were there, safe and beautiful, one on the right, two on the left. We skipped over rude Italian fortifications built into cliffs and wadies, all apparently untenanted. Once Bertie thought he saw a gunner aiming at us, and he touched the firing button for the last time that day. A spot on the ground burst into dust, but when we winged over we saw no one was there. In all the 600 miles of Libya, except for the blockhouse and airdrome, we never saw a soul. Only the desert — barren, cold, and lifeless, like the face of the moon.

There was none better loved by the fighting man of World War II than Ernie Pyle, war correspondent, friend of generals and privates.

Ernie traveled the war fronts of the world, always up where the fighting was. His stories expressed what most men could feel, see, and think, but could not say.

During the North African campaign Ernie Pyle did a stint with a B-17 squadron at an airbase somewhere in the desert. His moving description of a mission return has become a classic in the literature of air war.

Miracle at Sunset

Ernie Pyle

IT WAS late afternoon at our desert airdrome. The sun was lazy, the air was warm, and a faint haze of propeller dust hung over the field, giving it softness. It was time for the planes to start coming back from their mission, and one by one they did come — big Flying Fortresses and fiery little Lightnings. Nobody paid a great deal of attention, for this returning was a daily routine thing.

Finally, they were all in — all, that is, except one. Operations reported a Fortress missing. Returning pilots said it had lagged behind and lost altitude just after leaving the target. The last report said the Fortress couldn't stay in the air more than five minutes. Hours had passed since then. So it was gone.

Ten men were in that plane. The day's accomplishments had been great, but the thought of ten lost friends cast a pall over us. We had already seen death that afternoon. One of the returning Fortresses had released a red flare over the field, and I had stood with others beneath the great plane as they handed its dead pilot, head downward, through the escape hatch onto a stretcher.

The faces of his crew were grave, and nobody talked very loud. One man clutched a leather cap with blood on it. The pilot's hands were very white. Everybody knew the pilot. He was so young, a couple of hours before. The war came inside us then, and we felt it deeply.

After the last report, half a dozen of us went to the high control tower. We went there every evening, for two things — to watch the sunset, and to get word on the progress of the German

123

As described by Ernie Pyle, many B-17s returned to their bases in North Africa with engines out and otherwise badly damaged. The crew of this returning Flying Fortress was lucky. They had to feather only one engine — number three.

bombers that frequently came just after dusk to blast our airdrome.

The sunsets in the desert are truly things with souls. The violences of their color is incredible. They splatter the sky and the clouds with a surging beauty. The mountains stand dark against the horizon, and palm trees silhouette themselves dramatically against the fiery west.

As we stood on the tower looking down over this scene, the day began folding itself up. Fighter planes, which had patrolled the field all day, were coming in. All the soldiers in the tent camps had finished supper. That noiseless peace that sometimes comes just before dusk hung over the airdrome.

Men talked in low tones about the dead pilot and the lost Fortress. We thought we would wait a few minutes more to see if the Germans were coming over.

And then an electric thing happened. Far off in the dusk a red flare shot into the sky. It made an arc against the dark background of the mountains and fell to the earth. It couldn't be anything else. It had to be. The ten dead men were coming home!

"Where's the flare gun? Gimme a green flare!" yelled an officer.

He ran to the edge of the tower, shouted, "Look out below!" and fired a green rocket into the air. Then we saw the plane — just a tiny black speck.

It seemed almost on the ground, it was so low, and in the first glance we could sense that it was barely moving, barely staying in the air. Crippled and alone, two hours behind all the rest, it was dragging itself home.

I was a layman, and no longer of the fraternity that flies, but I could feel. And at that moment I felt something close to human love for that faithful, battered machine, that far dark speck struggling toward us with such pathetic slowness.

All of us stood tense, hardly remembering anyone else was there. With all our nerves we seemed to pull the plane toward us. I suspect a photograph would have shown us all leaning slightly to the left. Not one of us thought the plane would ever make the field, but on it came — so slowly that it was cruel to watch.

It reached the far end of the airdrome, still holding its pathetic little altitude. It skimmed over the tops of parked planes, and kept on, actually reaching out — it seemed to us — for the runway. A few hundred yards more now. Could it? Would it? Was it truly possible?

They cleared the last plane, they were over the runway. They settled slowly. The wheels touched softly. And as the plane rolled on down the runway the thousands of men around that vast field suddenly realized that they were weak and that they could hear their hearts pounding.

The last of the sunset died, and the sky turned into blackness, which would help the Germans if they came on schedule with their bombs. But nobody cared. Our ten dead men were miraculously back from the grave.

And what a story they had to tell! Nothing quite like it had happened before in this war.

The Tripoli airdrome, which was their target, was heavily defended, by both fighter planes and anti-aircraft guns. Flying into that hailstorm, as one pilot said, was like a mouse attacking a dozen cats.

The Thunderbird, for that was the name of their Fortress, was first hit just as it dropped its bomb load. One engine went out. Then a few moments later the other engine on the same side went. When both engines went out on the same side it was usually fatal. And therein lay the difference of that feat from other instances of bringing damaged bombers home.

The Thunderbird was forced to drop below the other Fortresses. And the moment a Fortress dropped down or lagged behind, German fighters were on it like vultures. The boys didn't know how many Germans were in the air, but they thought there must have been 30.

Our Lightning fighters, escorting the Fortresses, stuck by the Thunderbird and fought as long as they could, but finally they had to leave or they wouldn't have had enough fuel to make it home.

The last fighter left the crippled Fortress about 40 miles from Tripoli. Fortunately, the swarm of German fighters started home at the same time, for their gas was low too.

The Thunderbird flew on another 20 miles. Then a single German fighter appeared, and dived at them. Its guns did great damage to the already crippled plane, but simply couldn't knock it out of the air.

Finally the fighter ran out of ammunition and left. Our boys were alone with their grave troubles. Two engines were gone, most of the guns were out of commission, and they were still more than 400 miles from home. The radio was out. They were losing altitude, 500 feet a minute — and then they were down to 2000.

The pilot called up his crew and held a consultation. Did they want to jump? They all said they would ride the plane as long as it was in the air. He decided to keep going.

The ship was completely out of trim, cocked over at a terrible angle. But they gradually got it trimmed so that it stopped losing altitude.

By then they were down to 900 feet, and a solid wall of mountains ahead barred the way homeward. They flew along parallel to those mountains for a long time, but they were then miraculously gaining some altitude. Finally they got the thing to 1500 feet.

The lowest pass was 1600 feet, but they came across at 1500. Explain that if you can! Maybe it was as the pilot said: "We didn't come over the mountains, we came through them."

The co-pilot said, "I was blowing on the windshield trying to push her along. Once I almost wanted to reach a foot down and sort of walk us along over the pass."

And the navigator said, "If I had been on the wingtip, I could have touched the ground with my hand when we went through the pass."

The air currents were bad. One wing was cocked away down. It was hard to hold. The pilots had a horrible fear that the low wing would drop clear down and they'd roll over and go into a spin. But they didn't.

The navigator came into the cockpit, and he and the pilots navigated the plane home. Never for a second could they feel any real assurance of making it. They were practically rigid, but they talked a blue streak all the time, and cussed — as airmen do.

Everything seemed against them. The gas consumption doubled, squandering their precious supply. To top off their misery, they had a bad headwind. The gas gauge went down and down.

At last the navigator said they were only 40 miles from home, but those 40 miles passed as though they were driving a horse and buggy. Dusk, coming down on the sandy haze, made the vast flat desert an indefinite thing. One oasis looked exactly like another. But they knew when they were near home. Then they shot their red flare and waited for the green flare from our control tower. A minute later it came — the most beautiful sight that crew had ever seen.

When the plane touched the ground

they cut the switches and let it roll. For it had no brakes. At the end of the roll the big Fortress veered off the side of the runway. It climaxed its historic homecoming by spinning madly around five times and then running backwards for 50 yards before it stopped. When they checked the gas gauges, they found one tank dry and the other down to 20 gallons.

Deep dusk enveloped the field. Five more minutes and they never would have made it. The weary, crippled Fortress had flown for the incredible time of four and one-half hours on one pair of motors. Any pilot will tell you it's impossible.

Perhaps the real climax was that during the agonizing homeward crawl that one crippled plane shot down the fantastic total of six German fighters. The score was officially confirmed.

Adversity has produced some of the best humor of the air war. Such is the case with a B-24 crew who absorbed a giant share of flak over the German stronghold of Bizerte on the Tunisian coast in December, 1942. Bizerte was what U.S. flyers called a "dirty run." Its defenders were "flak happy" and well they should be for this key port was the main entry point for Axis troops and supplies which funneled down through the Italian peninsula and Sicily. On this occasion, the B-17 had already lost two engines and three feet of wing when a stray flak fragment shorted the electrical circuit of the bail-out buzzer, causing the buzzer to go off accidentally. Crew members in the rear compartments lost no time hitting the silk. There was one, however, whose posterior was so large he could not slip through the small escape hatch.

Have 'Chute, Can't Jump!

Lt. H. M. Locker

IT WAS the day after Christmas.

We took our regular place, number three in the last element of the formation, and off to Bizerte we went. We flew east past docks south of the town just far enough to miss the flak.

Swinging north and back west for our run on the target we could see the flak hopping all around the planes in the first element. I knew it would get worse as element after element of three ships came up to the bomb release line. And our B-24 was the last of the group.

Every plane was leaving a beautiful vapor trail to guide the flak and fighters to us. Now we were in the stuff. It was bursting all around in those greasy black puffs. Many times the ship bounced from an explosion. Someone in the rear called out, "We're hit," but we could feel no difference on the controls. It was time for the bombs to go. We were loaded with six 1000-pounders. I watched the bomb release light blink six times.

I turned then for a look at Tom Borders, flying number two in the "Birmingham Blitzkrieg," letting his bombs go. I've always had a mania for watching those beautiful golden eggs come sliding out. This time I wish I had curbed my curiosity, for just as my eyes found him there was a blinding flash and the loudest explosion I've ever heard. I saw the tail of Tom's ship fly backward, then down toward the ground five miles below. It was the only visible piece of the ten-man crew and airplane. A direct flak hit in his bomb bay had set off three tons of TNT. When the flash and smoke cleared there just wasn't anything left.

But right now we were having our own troubles. I remember saying, "Poor boys, God bless them," and, in the same instant I saw our right wingtip curl up. About three feet had been broken off by the explosion. Number-three and number-four engines were just starting to burn. The rest of the formation turned north to avoid the

flak, but we were too busy to turn and began to fall back fast.

Right down flak alley we flew. The constantly bursting shells and shrapnel hitting the plane reminded me of a sudden hail storm heard from the inside of a tin shed. I managed to get the fire out of number four, but number three was stubborn and burned more fiercely. I finally feathered it. Number four still was running, but it was not much use. The vibration shook the whole ship. The blaze coming out of the trailing edge of the wing grew larger and larger. I knew it was burning around the gas tank and would soon cause an explosion.

About that time all hell popped loose. All our guns were blazing at seven FW-190s that had just attacked right through the flak. Suddenly a hole about two feet square appeared in the wing where number-three gas tank is located, and flames shot out. It must have been a hit from the bottom because the fire in number three gradually dwindled to the burning of oil. We called for the P-38s to come up and help us, but the message probably never went through. Enemy fighters kept hitting us in the rear.

Harry Lawrence, our pilot, hadn't said a word so I told the crew to put on their chutes and then go back to their guns. Just then one fighter got our instrument panel and windshields with a 20mm shell. It exploded right in front of Harry, and for a second I thought his face was bleeding as he looked toward me. I knew I was hit too because blood was running into my eyes and oxygen mask. I jerked off my glasses and threw them to the floor. I thought my right eye had been knocked out.

The same shot had shorted the parachute bell so Fozzy bailed out.

After Fozzy . . . Buck was going to follow, but with his broad beam and seat-pack chute he couldn't quite squeeze through the escape hatch. He tried so desperately, however, that he . . . came crawling out of the nose with the seat of his breeches torn nearly out. Tapping me on the shoulder, he shouted, "You've got to land this thing because I'm too god-damn big to get out."

Someone called up and said we were afire in the bomb bay, radio compartment, and in the waist. I told them to fight the fire but keep an eye on the '190s. Suddenly our aileron controls went limp, and the tail dropped abruptly. I knew we had an elevator knocked off. Harry and I were shoving forward with all our might making for the clouds still below us. Though our guns were going constantly, we were almost helpless. The fighters kept coming in raking the ship from one end to the other. But the flak had stopped. At last the clouds closed around us, and the men cheered up.

But instrument flying without instruments is no fun when you have only two engines and a rudder to help you. Somehow we came out below the clouds and were in a valley, limping on and on toward the sun.

Finally she quit flying. A mountain was coming up in front, we were losing altitude, and we didn't know our speed. Suddenly a little patch of plowed ground came into view. I grabbed for throttles and switches and let her hit. We made it. . . .

One of the last dramatic chapters of the North African air war took place off the Tunisian coast in the latter days of the campaign.

The Germans had made use of air transport for resupply of their African forces. In fact JU-52 transports brought the first German troops into Africa in November, 1941.

Throughout the winter of that year the airlift to Africa increased as the Allied sea blockade of North African waters tightened. By late March, 1942 more than 500 air transports, JU-52s, SM-82s, ME-323s based in Italy and Sicily made twice daily runs across the narrow Sicilian straits to Tunisia, acompanied by strong fighter escort.

The Allied air leaders watched this growing traffic much like a cat would watch a mouse, and laid plans to eliminate it at the propitious moment. Most flights originated at Naples, Italy, staged through airdromes in Sicily. The main terminals were Sidi Ahmed and El Aouina in Tunisia. Flight routes, altitudes, speeds, operational patterns were studied.

By early April the time seemed ripe to "flush the game." The traffic had reached such heavy volume that crippling transport losses would be critical to Rommel now hard pressed by Allied air-ground offensives on two sides. To cut his one last resupply line would be fatal.

Code name for the Allied plan was "Operation Flax." It called for P-38 fighter sweeps over the Sicilian strait with bombers and fighters striking departure and terminal airdromes in Sicily and Tunisia.

"Flax" was kicked off at 0800 hours on April 5. Twenty-six P-38s intercepted a mixed formation of 7 JU-52s escorted by 20 ME-109s, 6 FW-190s, and one FW-187, a few miles northeast of Cape Bon. At the same time B-25s hit two ferry boats, sunk an escorting destroyer, and shot down 15 Luftwaffe fighters. Meanwhile Spitfire-escorted B-17s struck Tunisian airdromes of Sidi Ahmed and El Aouina while other B-25s and B-17s blasted airdromes in Sicily. German losses totalled 210 aircraft (26 JU-52s and ME-323s destroyed, 67 damaged) while the Allies lost only 8 planes.

In the days following, "Flax" continued hacking at the German air shuttle runs to Tunisia. On April 10, 25 transports were shot down. The following day Allied pilots got 31.

On the afternoon of Palm Sunday, April 18, 1942, the Axis Air Transport to North Africa received the coup de grace. At 1500 hours that day the Luftwaffe had run a large aerial convoy to Tunisia. On its return to Sicily it was jumped by four squadrons of the 57th Fighter Group (75 planes) patrolling off Tunisia with a top cover of Spitfires. The event has become known in history as . . .

The Palm Sunday Massacre

Maj. Richard Thruelsen
and
Lt. Elliott Arnold

WHEN A HARPY named (Axis) Sally called a group of American pilots, "the butchers of the 57th," during one of her regular propaganda broadcasts from Berlin, she endorsed, by a typical bit of Nazi vilification, one of the most astounding transactions of the Mediterranean air campaign. That transaction was, simply, the exchange of 75 airplanes for six. This piece of Yankee plane-trading required just ten minutes and broke the arch of the aerial bridge over which the Germans were attempting to supply their forces in Africa. Whatever its other repercussions, this fact alone makes the deal worth memorializing. Tunisia was won when an outmaneuvered army lost its supplies.

For the 57th American Fighter Group, which had fought its Warhawks across Africa from El Alamein as a part of the British Desert Air Force, Palm Sunday, 1943, promised to be just another day in a long campaign. The German line cutting off the northeastern tip of Tunisia from Enfidaville to Cap Serrat on the Mediterranean was a comfortable distance from the Group's South Tunisian landing strip

at El Djem, the day was April at its best and there were rumors of something special for Sunday dinner. And there was always the chance that they might hit the jackpot. It was known that the German Command was using large convoys of tri-motored transports — the dependable Junkers 52s — to bring essential supplies and personnel to the African battlefronts. These planes flew from supply bases in Sicily, crossed the narrow neck of the Mediterranean now denied their surface vessels by the vigilance of medium-bomber patrols and the Allied fleet and landed at one of several airdromes in the Tunis area. The cutting of these regular supply flights and the destruction of any considerable number of the transports would put the Germans squarely on the spot. This job was given to the fighters and a watchful, patient patrol was added to their daily sweeps over the enemy's lines.

Day after day went by, patrol after patrol. Occasionally, a small convoy of transports was sighted and chased and a few planes shot down. The bag of JU-52s grew slowly and surely. On April 10, a sea sweep of B-25 medium bombers and their P-38 fighter escort met a convoy of gasoline-laden Junkers flying low in the Sicilian channel, headed for Africa. Bombers and fighters went down to 50 feet to attack "on the deck." More than 20 of the JU-52s were shot down. But the real blow, the kill which would sever the service, continued to evade the Allied patrols. Somehow the convoys continued to slip in and out of the African airfields, bringing precious gas and ammunition and troop reinforcements. Somehow, the big one always got away.

They continued to get away during the early hours of Palm Sunday — if, indeed, they flew at all. The morning patrols, droning over the blue sea on their off-shore vigil, saw nothing. The 57th went out that morning. The 79th American Group went out. The 239 Wing RAF went out. And 7 Wing, South African Air Force. Several hundred Warhawks watched the Tunisian mouseholes and came back empty-handed. Early in the afternoon the 79th Group, the English and the South African Wings went out again and returned with nothing to report. It looked as though the trap was to remain unsprung for yet another day. At 4:30 the four squadrons of the 57th — the Black Scorpions, the Fighting Cocks, the Exterminators, and the Yellow Diamonds — prepared for the final patrol of the day.

The briefing was perfunctory — by this time the pilots could have recited their instructions from memory. Pick up Spitfire cover to be provided by 244 Wing RAF. They will meet you north of Sousse, over Hergla. Proceed to the Gulf of Tunis and patrol easterly and westerly off Cape Bon. Come back when gas supply dictates. Capt. Curl will lead the formation.

The order in which the squadrons would fly was given and the pilots walked out. There was a few minutes of aimless talk before the jeeps started for the dispersed planes. The sun was lowering, the tents were pleasantly warm and the Sunday feeling of detachment, which somehow pervades even the most active scenes of war, hung over the preparations for the mission. As usual, there was a little last-minute trading. Pilots who had chores or something better to do looked around for substitutes who wanted to build up their combat time. A veteran who had fought his way across Africa, found an eager newcomer to take his place. Six months later, the old hand still suffered when he recalled that decision:

"I was reading a book. I'd been out on the morning patrol. And now this do was going out. More of the same old stuff, I thought. Lots of sky and lots of water and no Jerries. I wanted to get along with that book. So I got this eager beaver who wanted to go. And I read my book. Think of it! Think of it — I should be back there reading a book when that happened!"

The group took off a little before five. 48 planes climbed out of the El Djem airfield for altitude. One turned back shortly after take-off, with engine trouble. The other 47 planes flew north, following the road to Sousse. There they slid over the shoreline and, somewhere around 8000 feet, they met the 12 graceful Spitfires which were to accompany them as top cover — the Spits being much better at altitude than the Warhawks. Turning north-westwards, the formation flew over the sea — a long column of planes flying four abreast, with the mothering Spits just a little higher than the rest. Across the Gulf of Hammamet they paraded, still climbing. At 16,000 feet, their beedrone must have come out of an apparently empty sky. The Cape Bon peninsula, splotched with evening shadow, slid up out of the sea and near Korba, where they crossed the coastline, there was a little flak. It spent itself below the 59 ships. From the middle of the peninsula more flak came up and then they crossed the shoreline on the other side, near Ras el Fortass. There was water beneath them again now. This time it was the Gulf of Tunis.

Everything had been quiet. The squadron and the flight leaders had watched the earth and the rest of the pilots had watched the sky around them. But there had been nothing said. Now Capt. Curl broke the radio silence: "Left turn, Exterminators, left turn."

They swung into the sun, losing altitude. Off the promontory upon which the cathedral and the ruins of Carthage stand they turned about and headed out toward the islands of Zembra and Zembretta. The formation was now spaced up into the sky like a flight of stairs, each line of four planes abreast making a step. The bottom of this flight of stairs was at 4000 feet; the Spits at the top were at 15,000.

Twenty minutes passed while the formation slid back and forth along its patrol line. The shadows of Zembra and Zembretta grew on the sea and the folds of the hills on Cape Bon were purple and the Tunis Gulf took on a dark and metallic sheen. Off the tip of Bon they turned into the sun again. Fifteen minutes of patrolling left. Gas for just one more run and then it was home and another uneventful patrol would be done.

No one, probably, will ever know who saw the enemy first. It is generally agreed, however, that the formation was six miles off the Cape Bon shoreline, midway between Ras el Ahmar and Ras el Fortass and heading southeast into the setting sun when the leading and lowest element sighted two German fighters 1000 feet below, coming straight at them. The two enemy planes apparently saw Curl and his element at the same time, for they both made steep diving turns. Watching them carefully, alert for a trap, Curl suddenly saw a sight which brought him up straight in his seat.

Off to the right, flying a parallel and opposite course in a perfect V formation, were 30 tri-motored transports. Behind them was another V of 30 and behind that still another. As one pilot described them later: "They were flying the most beautiful formation I've ever seen. It seemed like a shame to break it up. Reminded me of a beautiful propaganda film."

The Junkers were flying low, not more than a few hundred feet off the water. Painted in dark hues of gray and green and blue, they blended with the dark sea. Above and around them were weaving 25 or 30 single and twin-engined German fighters, acting as a protecting escort. Upstairs there might be more. Curl searched the sky. His own squadrons were stepped up above him. The watchful Spitfires were weaving specks. Every eye was on the quarry.

The last V of the transports, heading seawards, was opposite the first element of the Warhawks, flying east, when Capt. Curl intoned over the radio:

"Juicy, juicy. Let's go get them, boys. Watch for the fighters."

In the headphones, humming slightly with the carrier wave, you could almost hear the vast, collective excitement in those 59 American and English planes. A squadron leader somewhere in the formation said, in a matter-of-fact voice, "Stay in pairs, boys," and somebody gave a yelp and then there was a high-pitched howl as the first line of four Warhawks split into pairs and went down in a long, sweeping turn to the right. The second element followed. The German fighters, turning into the attack from all directions, came at the Warhawks. The Palm Sunday Massacre was on.

What followed was too confused, too concentrated in time and space, to be described from a single point of view. It is better to take a few of the parts and get from them an idea of the general whole.

The pilot flying on Capt. Curl's wing, in the first element of the Exterminators, the squadron which headed the formation, reported:

"After Curl gave the warning we went down, the two of us, full gun. The transports, meanwhile, must have seen us, for they went ahead wide open. This sudden spurt left 12 or 15 stragglers behind the last V. Curl and I hit those. I fired on the first plane which came into my sights. A short burst left his port engine burning. The flame trailed the whole length of the plane. The center or nose engine was also on fire. The Warhawks have three fifty-calibre guns in each wing and throw a lot of lead. I lost Curl during this pass. As I pulled up I saw the Junkers stall and hit the water with a big splash. I made a quick climbing turn and got on the tail of another transport — and then pulled away suddenly when I mistook another Warhawk for a Jerry.

"All three Vs of the transports were turning toward land by now. I got my second Junkers near the beach — it crashed into the surf and exploded. Another crashed near it at the same time and I saw a Warhawk hit the water. There weren't any chutes in the air. I don't think the transports carried any. I turned off the radio about that time. There was so much yelling and yammering that it didn't make any sense. I had an inconclusive scrap with a Me-109 before I ran out of ammunition and found myself low on gas. That ended my part of the scrap."

Capt. Roy Whittaker was leading an element of the Fighting Cocks, the second squadron to go down into the melee: "I attacked the JU-52s from astern at high speed and fired at two planes in the leading formation. The bursts were short and the only effect I saw was pieces flying off the cabin of the second ship. I pulled away and circled to the right and made my second attack. I fired two bursts into two more 52s — again in the leading formation. They both burst into flames. The second flew a little distance and then crashed into the water. I lost sight of the first and didn't see it hit. I then made a third pass and sent a good burst into the left of the formation, at another Junkers. As I pulled away it crashed into the water. By that time the Me-109s were among us. As I pulled up to the left I saw a 109 dive through an element of four Warhawks and I tagged on his underside and gave him a long burst in the belly. He crashed into the sea from 1000 feet.

"I then joined up with some Warhawks which were luffberrying with six Me-109s. I met one of these fighters with a quartering attack and hit him with a short burst. Pieces flew from the plane and he started smoking, but he climbed out of the fight." Capt. Whittaker claimed three JU-52s and one Me-109 destroyed; one JU-52 and one Me-109 damaged.

Lt. Richard Hunziker, another Fighting Cock Pilot, was on his second combat mission and had never seen an enemy aircraft when he spied what looked like ". . . a thousand black beetles crawling over the water. I was flying wing ship on Maj. Thomas, who was leading our squadron. On our first pass I was so excited I started firing early. I could see the shorts kicking up the water. Then they hit the tail of a JU-52 and crawled up the fuselage. This ship was near the front of the first V. As I went after it I realized I was being shot at from transports on both sides. It looked as though they were blinking red flashlights at me from the windows. Tommy-guns, probably. The ship I was firing at hit the water in a great sheet of spray and then exploded. As I pulled away I could see figures struggling away from what was left of the plane.

"I'd lost Maj. Thomas. There were so many Warhawks diving, climbing and attacking that it was difficult to keep out of the way of your own planes. I made a circle and then heard someone say, over the radio: 'There's Me-109s up here — come up and help us.' So I climbed to 5000 and flubbed around among the dog-fights, not knowing just what to do. Finally I got on the tail of a 109. As I was closing I noticed golf balls streaming past me on both sides. That meant there was another enemy fighter behind me, firing at me with his 20 millimetre cannon.

"So I took evasive action. That brought me over the shoreline, where I hooked on to another enemy fighter. My first squirt hit near the nose of the ship. Pieces flew off and he went into a steep dive. I followed him closely, still firing, until he crashed in a green field with a big splash of smoke and flame. Then I heard them giving instructions to reform."

From two score of these individual stories the pattern of the action can be assembled. The 90 or so transports, in their three arrowhead formations, turned for the beach in the vicinity of Ras el Ahmar after the first rushing attack by the Warhawks. Half of the convoy fell flaming into the sea and never reached the shoreline. Another score crash-landed on the beach itself or in the open fields nearby. Most of these planes burned when they hit. Another dozen Junkers made belly landings further inland. A few of the transports probably escaped in the general confusion. Meanwhile, the enemy fighters were flying madly around in what was later described as "a confused and inferior fashion, possibly due to the low altitude at which the engagement took place." Half of these fighters were shot down.

Ten minutes after the first shot was fired the air over that part of the Gulf of Tunis was cleared. Off Ras el Ahmar the sea burned red and a great circle of debris bobbed in an oil scum; from the beaches rose the tall black columns of a dozen funeral pyres.

Off the tip of the Cape, the Warhawks, ammunition gone and gas dangerously low, gathered for the homeward flight. Overhead the faithful Spits, after disdainfully shooting down one Italian fighter and chasing off several Me-109s which had ventured into the area, continued their vigil. The Spits, led by their 22-victories ace, Squadron Leader Neville Duke, could claim only one enemy destroyed that day, but they had played their part well in keeping a friendly umbrella over the Warhawks below.

Back at El Djem the news of the massacre began trickling in through the radioed reports of the homecoming planes. By the time the last stragglers had landed the station was a bedlam. The accepted greeting was: "How many did you get?" The returning pilots, deafened by the roar of their guns and engines, began shouting the minute they tumbled out of their ships. Everyone else, wildly excited, started shouting, too. Dinner was forgotten and a party laid on. The 57th will never forget that party.

It took the intelligence officers until midnight to sort out the claims of that epic ten minutes. The startling total was: 59 JU-52s (transports), 14 Me-109s (fighters), and two Me-110's (fighters) destroyed; one JU-52 and one Me-109 probably destroyed; 17 JU-52s, 9 me-109s, and two Me-110s damaged. Six Warhawks were lost.

Twenty-five days after the Palm Sunday Massacre the Axis gave up in Africa.

On the following day, a small fleet of ME 323s tried again to make the African coast: 12 out of 20 were shot down. Despite these high losses the Germans would not give up. Rommel's situation was becoming untenable. His dire need was fuel for his mechanized forces and air transport was his only source of supply. On April 22, the Germans made another attempt to run the air blockade, but their entire fleet of 21 ME-323s were shot down over the Gulf of Tunis by Spitfires and P-40s, along with 10 German fighter escorts. In desperation, meager flights were tried at night only to meet British night Beaufighters. By the end of April, Rommel's last line of supply had been cut off entirely. The great surrender of the Africa Korps began within several weeks.

Three Boobies to Cairo

Maj. Richard Thruelsen, A. C.
and
Lt. Elliott Arnold, A. C.

THE RAF MAN was short and dark and wore a small mustache. He sat on the terrace of the Hotel Continental-Savoy in Cairo and sipped a drink. Someone asked him about his most hair-raising experience and he thought for a while and said:

"You probably think it was in the air. Actually it was on the ground, in Tunisia."

He was flying a Spitfire out of an airfield at Souk el Khemis in April, 1943, serving as part of an escort for bombers. His plane was shot down east of Medjez el Bab. He bailed out and then started to walk back.

He walked for hours. Finally he reached a river and walked along the bank, tramping heavily in his weariness. Suddenly on the other side of the river, from behind a rock, a soldier appeared and pointed a tommy-gun at him.

"Halt," the soldier shouted across the 30 feet of water. "Who the hell are you?"

"I'm an RAF flier," the pilot said.

"RAF — my God! Don't take another step, sir. You're in the middle of a Jerry mine field!" the soldier shouted.

The pilot stood still. The soldier

thought for a few moments and then yelled, "See that boat in the water? Try to make your way down the river bank, get on the barge, and then paddle your way across."

The pilot walked gingerly down the bank. Carefully he placed one foot after another. Finally he reached the boat. He prepared to jump the three feet from the bank to the boat, when another soldier appeared on the other side of the river.

"Hey," he shouted. "Don't touch that boat. It's a booby-trap!"

The pilot, poised for the leap, pulled himself back. The soldier considered the situation and then called out:

"Better just dive in and swim across."

The pilot nodded and took off his shoes. He got ready to dive in.

"When you get to the middle, be careful," the soldier continued, leaning on his rifle and watching, quite interested. "There's a trip wire in the middle that sets off the entire mine field . . ."

The pilot finished his drink and got up and left.

PART FOUR

AIR ASSAULT
FROM THE SOUTH
Sicily and Italy
1943-1945

A German fighter, one of 85 shot down during the first three days of the invasion, burns near Gela, Sicily.

Introduction

WITH THE SURRENDER of the Africa Korps in Tunisia in May, 1943, British and American leaders turned their full attention to Hitler's Fortress Europe. Here the intensity of the air war had mounted during the past year. The offensively-designed Luftwaffe had been forced into fighting a defensive air war on all fronts.

At this point the combined Chiefs of Staff gave the British-based U.S. Eighth Air Force and the RAF Bomber Command the go-ahead to pursue the Combined Bomber Offensive against German war production resources with all possible vigor.

In the Mediterranean, plans got underway to invade Sicily, the steppingstone to the assault on the soft underbelly of Europe proper.

Thus the main Allied military spotlight of the coming year would be shared jointly by air-ground-sea invasion of Southern Europe and the strategic air offensive against Germany. For air forces the task ahead was the destruction of the Luftwaffe and its industrial base, capable of producing 17,500 planes per year.

Prelude to the Sicilian invasion was the destruction of the Luftwaffe based there and in southern Italy. During the month of June the Northwest Africa Air Forces destroyed most of the 31 Luftwaffe airfields on the island

wiping out nearly 1000 enemy planes in the process. Between July 1 and July 10 alone, Allied flyers flew over 3000 combat sorties forcing evacuation of the Luftwaffe to bases in Italy. So effective were these air operations that on Sicilian D-Day, July 10, 1943, the 3000 ship armada carrying the American Seventh and the British Eighth Army to the beaches encountered no serious air attack.

The airborne phase of the Sicilian invasion, the first such operation tried by the Allies in the war, was a different story. Transports of the Twelfth Air Force's 51st and 52nd African-based Troop Carrier Wings, were set up to drop paratroopers and troop-laden gliders behind the beaches during the night preceding the beach landings. Fate intervened. Smoke from pre-invasion bombing raids rose in great clouds a mile high, cutting visibility for the low-flying transports to zero. Strong winds carried the transports off course, scattered a paratroop regiment far and wide. Fully-loaded gliders, scheduled to release off shore and glide in the silent darkness to fields behind the enemy-held beach fortifications, were mercilessly dispersed. Some 50 gliders came down short and landed in the sea and on the beaches with many of their battle-garbed glider troops helplessly drowning before

Bound for Gela. Paratroops adjust their packs and parachutes before entering the C-47 that will take them across the Mediterranean for the air drop on Sicily.

rescue could be effected. Trigger happy gunners of our own sea invasion armada mistook the low flying Sicilian bound transports and gliders for Nazi planes as they passed in the darkness low over the fleet. They opened fire, increasing the mayhem of the night. Eight aircraft went down to friendly gunfire. While the Luftwaffe offered no resistance, German anti-aircraft fire was particularly heavy on the beach approaches and on July 11, 23 Allied transports were shot down. Again, two days later, gunners on an Allied convoy misidentified U.S. C-47s for German transports and shot down 7 more.

The Sicilian invasion succeeded but it added up to grand scale confusion. Nevertheless, valuable lessons were learned: the need for coordination of plans with all units involved, better aircraft "distinctive markings" and identification codes, more efficient navigational aids, larger drop zones, and proper release points for gliders. These bitter lessons were to make later large scale airborne operations in Normandy and Southern France successful ventures.

During the invasion, Allied Air Forces ranged the Italian peninsula and even up into France, striking enemy rail and road communications, marshaling yards, supply dumps, port facilities, and targets of opportunity. By July 13, Twelfth Air Force Fighters were operating out of Pachino, Sicily, and under cover of darkness the German forces slipped across the Straits of Messina to Italy in a move reminiscent of Dunkirk.

On July 25, with Allied forces a few miles from his shores, Dictator Mussolini resigned. The Italian government secretly sued for peace but the German armies took over the country.

On September 3, the British Eighth Army poured across the three-mile wide Straits of Messina onto the toe of Italy, preluded by a strong air attack on German airdromes, especially the massive complex of airfields at Foggia, Italy on the Adriatic Sea. On September 9, the U.S. Fifth Army under Lt. Gen. Mark Clark went ashore at Salerno on the east coast, bent on quick capture of Naples and link-up with the British forces driving northward.

When a vicious German counterattack, on September 12, threatened to

General Dwight D. Eisenhower and General Henry H. Arnold plan air strategy for the invasion of Italy.

drive the Salerno beachhead back into the sea, NAAF heavies, mediums, and fighter bombers were called in. In four days more than 3400 air sorties were thrown against the German ground forces around the beachhead with bomb concentrations averaging 760 tons per square mile.

On the night of the 13th and 14th, Twelfth AF Troop Carrier planes dumped two regiments of paratroopers accurately behind the German lines. Two days later the Fifth Army broke out and connected up with the British driving north along the Adriatic Sea. The combined forces moved northward up the peninsula.

Allied flyers now turned on the Luftwaffe airfields around Rome, destroying more than 300 aircraft in two days. Operating from Italian bases around Salerno, Twelfth Air Force wrested control of the air over all Italy and held it from then on.

On October 1, the Fifth Army moved into Naples and the British captured the vitally important complex of airbases at Foggia on the west coast, from which heavy U.S. strategic bombers could now hammer at targets in all of Central Europe.

Here the ground campaign bogged down as the bitter winter set in and the ground forces ran up against a string of fortifications across the peninsula called the Gustav Line.

It was about this time that air forces in the Mediterranean underwent another reorganization with the merger of the NAAF and the Mediterranean Air Command into the Mediterranean Air Forces (MAAF) under the command of Gen. Ira Eaker (formerly of Eighth Air Force in England). Major components were Twelfth Air Force (now a tactical air force) under Maj. Gen. John K. Cannon and Fifteenth Air Force under Maj. Gen. Nathan F. Twining (later to become Chairman of the JCS). Back to England went Generals Eisenhower, Spaatz, and Doolittle and Air Chief Marshall Tedder to begin the great job of preparing for the cross channel invasion to Normandy in spring, 1944.

By the end of December, 1943, the big Foggia airbase complex had been repaired in a herculean engineering feat, and onto the steel-matted runways moved the rapidly growing Fifteenth Air Force with its B-24s, B-17s and its P-38 and P-47 fighter units. From airfields around Naples and Salerno, the tactical Twelfth prepared for the coming offensive.

Several unsuccessful attempts had been made during January and February, 1944, to pierce the Gustav Line. Most dramatic was the January 22 attempt coordinated by a landing south of Rome at Anzio — aimed at capturing the Italian capital. Despite strong air support from Twelfth Air Force and five U.S. carriers off shore, the Germans were able to contain the Anzio beachhead. Through the bitter weeks ahead the Anzio foothold, backed up by continual air support, held out though it was continuously raked from end to end by German

The ruined abbey of Monte Cassino.

artillery fire. On March 15, a major effort was made to break through the Gustav Line at Cassino, the center anchor. In a spectacular series of raids, 483 heavies of Fifteenth Air Force pulverized the town of Cassino and the historic monastery overlooking it with 1205 tons of bombs. Unfortunately, the Fifth Army failed to follow up the attack immediately, giving the Germans time to recover from their stunned condition and regroup. When the Fifth Army did move, it was stopped cold.

Four days later, on March 19, the MAAF kicked off a coordinated air offensive called "Operation Strangle," aimed at choking off supplies reaching the German forces. "Strangle" targets were the limited number of north-south railroad lines and roads over which ammunition, food, and troop reinforcements funneled to the German front from North Italy. Bridges, tunnels, intersections, freight yards, even coastal shipping, became prime objects of Twelfth Air Force medium bombers, fighter-bombers, and fighters.

Between March 19 and May 13, Twelfth Air Force tactical planes flew more than 5000 sorties. Within the first few days rail lines were badly damaged and by May 8 rail traffic had practically ceased moving south, forcing the German logistics to the highways. But motor transport failed them too as the Twelfth turned the roadways of Italy into highways of death. In desperation the Germans tried coastal shipping. It shared the same fate. By early May only 400 tons of supplies a day were reaching 15 German divisions facing the Fifth and Eighth armies at the Gustav Line, most of it slipping through at night by truck. "Strangle," brilliantly conceived and executed, lived up to its name. The Germans could not sustain their positions and their strength without adequate supplies.

When the Allied Offensive of May 11 got underway, the Gustav Line quickly crumpled and the beleaguered defenders of Anzio were relieved. Where land offensive had failed, air interdiction had succeeded.

Rome fell on June 4 — two days before the Normandy invasion of France.

Supported by 50,000 tactical air sorties in June alone, elements of Allied ground forces swept north driving the Germans into the mountains south of the Po River where they were pinned to their positions, besieged and hammered from the air until they collapsed in April, 1945, victims of a terrible winter of starvation and attrition.

Long before their surrender, however, nine Allied divisions, numerous Twelfth and Fifteenth Air Force units, along with American and British aircraft carriers, had been withdrawn to prepare for the invasion of Southern France. When Allied forces poured ashore in Southern France, on August 15, 1944, proof of our complete mastery of the air in the Mediterranean was forcefully demonstrated. Only one Luftwaffe plane appeared to oppose nearly 3000 Allied air sorties on that day. It was a far cry from the beginning of the Sicilian campaign when the Mediterranean-based Luftwaffe comprised over 1500 fighters, bombers, and dive bombers and Allied combat air strength measured 856 bombers and 670 fighters, including carrier-borne aircraft. The air battle had been decisively won, and Italy confirmed the North African lesson that defeat of enemy air forces is the essential prerequisite to victory on the ground.

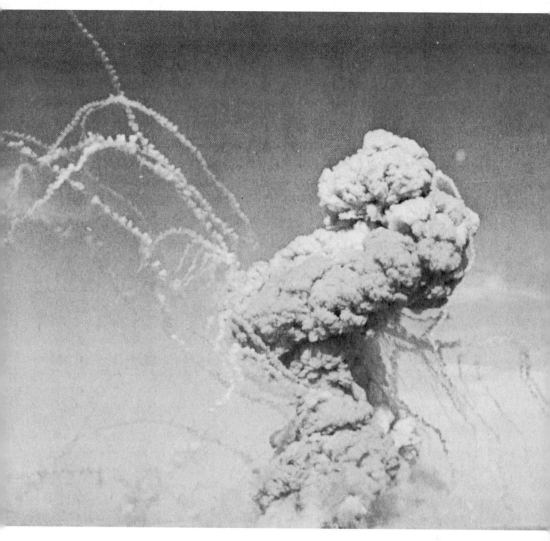

Nazi dive bombers blow up a munitions ship bound for Sicily.

"*Ladbroke*" is a word Troop Carrier pilots will not soon forget, the code name for one of four separate airborne operations in the invasion of the island of Sicily—a pleasant land a few miles across the Straits of Messina from the toe of Italy.

It was capture of this key island in the narrows of the Mediterranean that would open the Mediterranean to unrestricted sea commerce between Gibraltar and the Suez Canal, and provide the Allies their stepping-stone to the first assault on Fortress Europe.

The main forces planned for the capture of Sicily were the British Eighth Army and the American Seventh, both of which would be disgorged on the beaches by naval surface craft — the Eighth under Gen. Bernard L. Montgomery (the hero of El Alamein) on the east coast, and the Seventh led by Gen. George S. Patton, Jr. on the southern coast.

In order to neutralize the enemy beach defenses and prevent the Germans from pinning down these two major invasion forces, airborne attacks were scheduled to precede them on the night of July 9-10: "Husky I"—a parachute drop five miles northeast of Gela and "Ladbroke," a glider mission to a point south of Syracuse.

On July 9, 1943 the joint British-American force of 3000 ships steamed across the Mediterranean from North Africa carrying the invasion armies. On African bases airborne forces were preparing for an evening takeoff: 226 C-47s of the 52nd Troop Carrier Wing loaded 3405 paratroopers of Gen. Jim Gavin's 82nd Airborne Division for the "Husky I" drop, while the "Ladbroke" force of 144 C-47s and C-53s of the 51st Troop Carrier Wing attached their tow ropes to CG-4A gliders containing 1200 men of the British 1st Air Landing Brigade.

The unarmed "Ladbroke" force was to fly to Sicily from fields in the Enfidaville-Kairouan-Sousse area of Tunisia at altitudes less than 500 feet and approach the island from the south under cover of darkness. The glider troops had one mission, to capture the Ponte Grande bridge over which Highway 115 crossed two canals about 1½ miles southwest of Syracuse. Flight path of the formation was to be a "cleared corridor" between the converging British and American sea invasion armadas.

It was the first big airborne operation by the Allies in World War II and before it finished there would be terrible mistakes and casualties. But this evening, they were unforeseen.

Here is the story, told for the first time by one of the pilots who towed a glider to Sicily on this eventful night.

Ladbroke at Syracuse

Maj. Dennis E. McClendon, USAF

"LADBROKE IS TONIGHT," he said. "We will take off beginning at 7:30. I am going with you boys as a co-pilot."

Nods and applause met Col. Aubrey Hurren's opener.*

"We are to release our gliders 3000 yards offshore, south of Syracuse, so the gliders will have a chance to sneak in over the pillboxes and anti-aircraft fire before they are noticed. We will not cross the shoreline at any point."

The tow pilots were pleased, much preferring suicide in forms other than pulling loaded gliders at low altitudes and slow speeds over enemy beach defenses.

Then the mission briefing began in earnest. The intelligence and operations officers in turn uncovered a myriad of detail: routes, altitudes, winds, possible flak guns and searchlights, nearest enemy fighter fields, friendly fighter escort, clouds, landmarks identifiable in the quarter-moonlight. The homework seemed in apple-pie order.

Next Col. Hurren introduced Maj. Gen. G. F. Hopkinson, the commander of the British 1st Air Landing Brigade,

all dressed up in paratrooper battle gear capped by a silly maroon beret.

What Hopkinson told us in his dry, indirect British way, really amounted to a pre-game pep talk. First he ran through the long successes of British arms, including Wellington at Waterloo and battles we had never heard of before. About the time British successes were getting a little thick he announced that in his small way he intended to add a little bit to the history of British indomitability tonight: he was going with his men in one of the gliders. Then came his clincher: "This will be the first time in history that the Americans have had to pull the British into battle!" That remark sold him to the American pilots and he got a round of cheers.

Despite assurances to the contrary, some of us still had misgivings about the navy over which we would fly enroute to Sicily. Several times during the African campaign navy gunners fired on Air Force transports in broad daylight. The word had gotten around the Air Force that our seaborne brethren would fire first, check identity second. It was not a comfortable feeling.

After the briefing we were given a

* Col. Aubrey Hurren was commander of the 62nd Troop Carrier Group, 51st TC Wing, based at Goubrine in North Africa.

hot meal and driven to our aircraft on the line. There our crewmen, Minnie and Herb,[1] joined Grad[2] and me and and we all lovingly inspected our C-53. "Old 381" wore a big "88" in white chalk on the fuselage. Further down the strip, a 15-passenger CG-4A glider was branded "88." A long, snaked nylon tow rope connected the two. The numbering system used for "Ladbroke" started in the 60th Group, the first to go. They ran from "1 through 54." Our Group, the 62nd, picked up with "55" and continued through "109." This meant Grad and I would be in the middle of the second group of aircraft and gliders.

Our glider crew came high-stepping over to 381 soon after our arrival on the line. Someone had arranged for the tow plane crews and the glider pilots to convene a few minutes before takeoff. This was our only contact with them. The glider pilot, Sgt. Evans, was a British soldier surprisingly cheerful and literally breaking out with "jolly good show," "old chap," and all that. We took an immediate liking to him. His co-pilot, also a sergeant, and the 15 men who were to ride the glider were English enough to have stepped out of a movie lot. After introductions all around, we sat down on the hot dirt and ran through the mission's details.

When the business end of our pre-takeoff meeting finished, we ran out of things to say to each other. Still a few minutes remained and everyone's mind turned inward. There's a lot to think about in the few minutes before going into battle. I looked up and down the runway choked with airplanes and people and a quick shiver of anticipation ran through me. Even the least imaginative among us felt some sort of fatalistic identification with the making of history.

It was impossible to note all the last-minute turmoil on the deceptively quiet, sun-drenched, dry dusty runway and not project oneself ahead a few hours. As a tow pilot, with luck I could expect to be back in a relatively short time, have a hot meal, and tell big war stories to the ground crews and staff officers. But the spectacle of what would happen to the glider crews bothered me. The thought of those frail tube-wood-fabric-and-glue craft hissing softly into the dark strange land with the pilots peering below at the faintly visible ground, trying to pick out their small landing areas, was not at all pleasant. We had studied aerial reconnaissance photos of the glider landing areas on Sicily. The terrain, well broken up and laced with tiny Sicilian farms, divides itself with loose-rock fences. The prospects of landing in those postage-stamp patches in the dark didn't seem as cheerful to me as it did to Sgt. Evans and his men. They took it all with typical British stoicism. If they reserved any fear it didn't show through.

"We do expect to get rid of this

1 Tech. Sgt. Clarence Minneman, crew chief, and Staff Sgt. Herbert Glass, radio operator.
2 Second Lt. Burgess Gradwell, co-pilot.

great beast of a glider you've given us," said Sgt. Evans, "right into the trees or fences. But you won't mind it will you, with your great busy production lines and all?"

Luckily, just then someone down the line gave the wind-up signal. We shook hands all the way around again. The British trooped off to their squatty-looking gliders while we climbed into our scalding-hot C-53 and took up our crew positions. Old Doc Bagley, our squadron flight surgeon promised us a double shot of "combat crew" bourbon when we got back from Sicily. Right about now the idea began to sound real good.

The sun was slanting low in the west as our lead ship began to roll. When the last one left the ground, all but those standing by as spares were headed toward Sicily. The field behind blended into the empty desert. Grad and I were flying Number 12 position in the 51st Squadron, which in turn was Number 4 of a four-ship echelon led by our Squadron Operations officer, Capt. Johnny B. Blalock.

Assembling the large, slow, unwieldy formation of the 62nd's 50-plus tow ships with gliders took time and much juggling. The four-ship echelons flew in trail, one element directly behind the other, all elements aligned according to chalk numbers. This was necessary since the cargo in the gliders was arranged in landing order, according to its use by ground troops.

Close spacing between elements required we keep a semblance of forma-tion after dark. If a pilot dropped back more than 300 feet, he would lose the dim blue formation lights of the plane ahead. Once out of formation, he could never hope to get back in the dark. Moreover the gliders had to be kept close to each other. Without a concentration of firepower after landing, the glider troops would be doomed for their airborne weapons were woefully small.

After much maneuvering we finally headed out from the Kuriate Islands just off the Tunisian coast near Sousse. A beautiful sunset painted the lower sky. Stretched out in front eastward as far as eye could see from "Chalk 88" was a long, slow-moving line of C-47s, C-53s, and CG-4A gliders. It resembled a mammoth snake. At last light, the northwest wind whipped up huge waves on the Mediterranean Sea below.

The air, extremely bumpy at our 250-foot altitude made formation flying difficult. It must have been man-killing in the glider — bouncing at the end of an elastic tow rope stretched to 300 feet. To worsen our situation the interphone wire to the glider (it was taped to the tow rope) broke soon after takeoff. We would not be able to talk to Sgt. Evans for the rest of the mission.

Malta rose out of the Mediterranean 200 miles from the Kuriates, and our first checkpoint. Capt. Johnny Blalock, leading our four-ship echelon, had the navigator aboard and in his hands rested our destiny. As the night grew blacker, Grad and I became increas-

151

ingly concerned, for the most skilled navigator, we thought, could only make an educated guess at wind drift correction. The wind seemed nearer 40 m.p.h. than the forecasted 25. But we couldn't ask Johnny Blalock and his navigator up ahead because we had to keep strict radio silence. In a little while the air became so rough Grad and I spelled each other at 15-minute intervals on the controls, resting our leg and arm muscles in between turns. What it was like in the glider behind could only be imagined.

After dark, things changed. The air cooled off. Our cylinder-head and oil temperatures, which had been running in the red warning zone — even with the engines' cowl flaps partly opened — gradually ran down and the needles on the gauges dropped to within the safe limits marked by green lines. In the 100° temperature, the old C-53s just plainly balked at pulling the heavily-loaded gliders at slow speeds. After all, we were *cruising* at only 105-110 m.p.h., ten to fifteen miles an hour below the normal *climbing* speed.

Grad and I estimated Malta's promised beacons at an hour and forty-five minutes from the Kuriates. The time came and passed. No Malta. We never did see it. A few minutes later Johnny turned the formation to the left. As we straightened out, concerned about our four gliders colliding during the turn, either with each other or with us, Grad and I rechecked the new course on our gyro compass. Allowing for the probable wind drift the course looked about right. Johnny's navigator must have made a dead-reckoning turn. We hoped he knew what he was doing for it was only about 70 miles (45 minutes with our crossed head-wind) to Cape Passero and Sicily. Long since, we had lost sight of the other Group planes ahead of us. Our small echelon bored through the night sky alone.

The cockpit seemed to get warmer and quieter as we got closer to the target. Up ahead in the blackness somewhere was enemy territory. And on each side of us, invisible to our eyes, were Allied ships with quick-fingered gunners. At 250 feet, moving over the water far less than 100 miles an hour into the headwind, we felt almost helpless to do anything.

Grad said nothing. I said nothing. A few guttural grunts passed back and forth about time, speed, altitude, and other purely mechanical matters. They required no thought. Outside on the wings, the engines vibrated evenly. Every now and then the hydraulic system would "wheeze" to break the tomb-like silence in the cockpit.

Back in the crew compartment, Minnie and Herb were equally inarticulate. Herb busied himself with his radio. Minnie changed the "Colors of the Day" recognition flares in the Very pistol at 2000 hours, (8 P.M.) spending the rest of the time staring at the engine gauges in the cockpit — leaning on the arm rests between Gradwell and myself. Occasionally he would climb up into the astrodome, look back at the gliders; then back to the cockpit, bending low to peer out the windshield between us. His must have been the hardest sweat with nothing to occupy his mind. If we got in trouble, so would he. How helpless could one feel?

"Here's your helmets," Minnie said, thrusting two tin hats into the cockpit.

"Thanks," I said apologetically, embarrassed at putting on a ground-troop-type helmet in an airplane. Then I found I couldn't get my radio headset over or under it. I tried hanging the top piece around the back of my neck with the ear-cups jammed under the helmet. Every time I moved my head, the headset fell off.

"Throw the stupid thing away," I told Minnie, not meaning to hurt his feelings.

Closer, closer we inched through the sky toward Sicily. Still we saw nothing. Johnny Blalock led the way on a straight course as though he was flying down a civil airway at home. Ha-rum-rum-rum, ha-rum-rum-rum went the engines. Every now and then Herb turned up the volume on his radio and we could hear di-di-di, dah-da- di-dah-dah-dah or some other signal in code coming from his headsets. Minnie paced up and down the crew passage, throwing the plane out of trim with each walk. But no one said anything.

Red streaks! Dead ahead. Anti-aircraft fire! Maybe 15 miles ahead. And then the wandering finger of a lone searchlight.

All of a sudden I was cold. I felt a great shiver. I jerked. I looked at Gradwell staring ahead at the fireworks, then peered again through the windshield like a frightened little boy. Ice water suddenly poured through my arteries. Seconds before I had been burning up with heat. Now I was cold and could feel sweat beads gathering on my forehead. Then I sensed my heart thumping and could count each beat distinctively. So this is what it's like to be scared, I thought!

Out of the corner of my right eye sat Gradwell like a stone monument, looking ahead, silhouetted in the dim cockpit light. He showed no emotion at all — just a sort of fascination. I couldn't see Minnie without making it obvious, so I didn't try. I wondered about my own appearance. I felt they were watching me for some sign of fear. I broke the spell.

"There it is."

"Yeah. Flak."

"Right on schedule."

"Unh, hunh."

It was an hypnotic sensation to watch the stuff come up into the sky, but the danger of our diverted attention to it could be deadly: gliders, tow ships, tow ropes all tangled up and end-over-end. We had to hold in tight formation.

"Keep an eye on me and be ready to take over," I yelled at Grad.

"Yeah. I'll keep looking too," Minnie said from behind my shoulder.

Roman candles! That's what the flak looked like at first. A tremendous volley of tracers spraying up at us from dead ahead, slightly left, and almost below. We could easily make out the dim form of an angry ship right on our course in the cleared safety corridor! To make things worse it was flying a barrage balloon low over its stacks.

The good old trigger-happy navy was at it again.

Johnny Blalock's reaction came instantaneously. He turned right, into the echelon, to keep from angling the formation over the ship and into the balloon. But a right turn into a left echelon is pure murder, especially to number four ship on the slow inside of the turn.

Violently I wrenched 381 to the right, barely avoiding a collision with Lt. Jimmy Hayes who was flying number three directly in front and I chopped the throttles to keep from overruning him. There was nothing else left to do. At 250 feet we had no room for maneuver. The old plane shivered and shook but she held in.

"Mac," Minnie mumbled as we straightened up, "you got down to 85 miles an hour in a 60° bank!" His voice was low, broken and full of reproach. There had been no time to watch the instruments. It was either throttle, wheel, rudder and luck, or oblivion. With no power in a 60° bank, old 381 should have stalled out at 85 and spun in but she didn't. We all knew it had been a close call.

Now we were headed out on a new course. We could see the searchlights and tracer fire on the shore of Sicily. The whole coastline was beginning to light up with gunfire farther to the northeast just as it should. Checking the line of land-fire and searchlights against our compass, we guessed the first flak had come from Cape Granitola or Cape Passero — both on the southern tip of the island. We had to be on course! But why was there a ship in our cleared corridor? Something had gone wrong. Our confidence in the entire invasion plan was shaken.

My reflexes began to get less certain. Confusion and fear saturated my thickening head. We had flown on our new course to the northeast for about three minutes when, ka-flooey, up came those red lines of light again! Right up from the water and straight in front. We were so close this time, we couldn't even see the tracers curve.

Slam, bam, we went — up on our right wingtips again. This time it was just too sudden for us. I never knew where the others went, but Grad and I broke off violently. Jimmy's plane was about to come through my cockpit, and closing fast, when I dumped the nose with all my strength and skimmed under the other planes and gliders with full throttle. It was enough to make an atheist pray.

Coming out we were less than 100 feet above the water. How Sgt. Evans kept his glider behind us I'll never know. What prevented a tangled mess of four planes and four gliders is a mystery. I wouldn't give 1 chance in 10,000 to come out of that maneuver in wide open sunshine.

Grad and I were on our own. Where to we did not know. And where were the ships? Fortunately we had lost them, but we had also lost our formation. This meant we were minus a navigator. Now what?

Sensing we must be in the middle of the whole British-Greek invasion armada hauling Viscount Montgomery to Sicily, I turned to sea hoping to get outside of what would be a line of ships several miles deep — all flying those blasted balloons. After five minutes we headed northeast, parallel to the coast. I pulled up to 500 feet to clear our own aerial fleet in case other formations were cruising in the vicinity. One thing sure, we wouldn't surprise the Germans on Sicily — not tonight. The enemy obviously knew where we were, so hugging the water didn't seem so important as avoiding a mid-air collision.

I strained my eyes through the windshield to recognize something, anything, and constantly glanced back to my flight instruments in the cockpit. Suddenly it seemed we were in a right-hand steep turn. With a sharp pull on the wheel I leveled the wings, but the pattern of searchlights and flak-fire along the shore slanted strangely. I felt very heavy in my seat and my artificial horizon indicator in the cockpit showed a steep left turn, while the rate-of-climb needle began dumping. The altimeter was winding down.

Vertigo!

"Gradwell," I shouted. "Take it!"

Old ever-ready Grad seized the controls and deftly righted the plane. The instruments settled back to normal. The searchlights and anti-aircraft fire on the shore looked reasonable again, but I felt tilted even after everything else straightened up. I was tired and cold, and dripping with sweat.

I suppose all pilots have experienced vertigo occasionally. Once before, while flying in clouds, it had happened to me. This time the intense strain on my eyes in the dark, plus a liberal dose of fear, brought it on. My fuzziness was over in a minute, but I asked Grad to fly for another quarter of an hour until I was sure of myself and could become completely unhypnotized.* I was thankful for a sharp co-pilot. Without Grad we would have "bought the Mediterranean."

We were now completely lost. A quarter-moon lighted up the area and we were approaching the island from the east. If we eased in close to shore we might chance upon some prominent points along the coast — silhouetted against the dimly lighted western sky. We recalled on our maps how Augusta, to the north, and Syracuse to the south (just a few miles apart), hung down pendant-like on little peninsulas into the north side of the little

* In flying school we had been warned of the temporary loss of orientation which causes a pilot to believe momentarily that his senses are right and his flight instruments are wrong — that he is turning while flying straight or climbing when really diving. This is called "vertigo."

bays which made their harbors. So we headed toward land to hunt for them.

The panel clock read 10:45 P.M. when we spotted the lights of a city from four miles out. The little bay and pendant peninsula stood out clearly in the dark water, and the space between looked very still and quiet. We couldn't be sure which city we had blundered onto. Then we remembered that Syracuse was to be bombed by B-17s from 10,000 feet at 11 o'clock. So we simply circled outside the harbor until, promptly at 11 o'clock, the little city we were watching began to explode and searchlights and tracers fanned upward from every direction. Our navigation problem was settled. It was Syracuse. The glider landing zone was directly inland, just to the south.

Now our thoughts turned to Sgt. Evans in the glider. We concluded he must be thoroughly confused and it would only be right and fair to take him inland to his landing zone, even though we had been ordered to cast him loose offshore. We couldn't pass over Syracuse harbor at low altitude without getting shot down: we had seen the flak thrown at the B-17s. Besides billows of smoke from the burning city were blowing out to sea, cutting visibility in the harbor to zero. On the other hand, if we cut in farther south, we would risk running through C-47 formations still northbound. That left us one alternative.

A finger of land called Cape Murro di Porco jutted out into the sea below Syracuse. It was immediately south of this Cape that northbound C-47s were scheduled to pass after releasing their gliders. It followed that if we went inland directly over the Cape, we would avoid flak, smoke, and mid-air collision. We silently hoped Evans had studied his maps and would recognize the prominent landmarks on the way in. We had no way to communicate with him.

The decision was made. We headed toward the Cape at 500 feet. About half a mile out an enemy gun position opened up and curving red fingers arced gracefully into our flight path. I racked the old plane in a tight turn to the left and went back out to sea.

Grad and I conferred. We decided to try it again only this time at water level. We didn't think the enemy gunners could get much of a shot at us that way.

Down we went, picking up speed, throttles forward.

The sinking moon ahead silhouetted the shoreline making visibility good. We came in low, leaving propwash wakes in the water, aiming dead-center at the Point. Our tactic worked. The gunners heard us coming but could not determine from what exact direction. They opened up but not until we were on top of the gun position. We got by with no hits. (Later we learned the glider got by unscathed too.)

Over land, we used our extra speed to get back up to altitude. By the time we spotted Evans' landing zone several miles inland, we had reached 1500 feet and leveled off. Not a single searchlight or gun broke out, not one. We wagged our wings and blinked our formation lights. Evans cut off the tow line like a shot. That boy was on the ball! After all the wandering and roller coastering he took, he knew where he was.

We said a silent prayer for Sgt. Evans and his men, now loose without power in the black night over Sicily, and made a 180° diving turn toward Cape Murro di Porco, intending to buzz the unfriendly gun at about 200 miles an hour. Then I remembered that damned tow rope still dangling off our tail. I told Gradwell to release it.

"Mac," he said, "let's keep the rope and drop it on the gun! I'll aim it. You keep the speed down."

I throttled back a bit and set the nose right on the Point. We approached the gun from a shallow glide at about 100 feet; Gradwell glued his eyes down the nose while his fingers clutched the rope release lever. We got within 500 or 600 feet horizontal distance when the gun swung around shooting directly at us.

At about 300 feet Gradwell pulled the knob and I rammed the throttles all the way forward. The tracers swung close. I waited for the bullets.

"We got him!" Minnie shouted from behind me. I nearly jumped through the windshield.

Minnie had been standing up in the astrodome, looking aft.

"When we passed the gun," he shouted excitedly, "tracers started swinging around to follow us and all of a sudden they stopped dead — about halfway around the circle."

The spectacle of our tow rope wrapping the gun crew in its coils and heavy hooks was gratifying. We had been flying about four hours under tense and rugged conditions, and the rope bombing victory was the psychological lift we needed to get home*.

Old 381 leaped upward with the throttles forward, half-empty of fuel and with no load dragging behind. We reached 6000 feet in a very few minutes and headed south for Malta, passing over hundreds of ships driving in toward the island. From 6000 feet they looked like so many water bugs in the fading moonglow.

Turning west from Malta toward our base at Goubrine, we encountered a monstrous crosswind. Oddly it was from a direction opposite that on the way in. It took a full 30 minutes correcting our course south to get on the old-fashioned four-quadrant radio beam that would lead us back home. Either the beam was on the wrong bearing (our compass was out of order) or we were getting some sort of unknown magnetic interference.

We didn't worry much until we crossed the Tunisian coast and could not identify the port city of Sousse or,

---

* Tow pilots became quite skilled at spot-dropping their nylon tow ropes. With a heavy steel clamp on each end, the long rope could cause much damage hurtling down at more than 100 miles an hour.

157

for that matter, anything else that was supposed to be there. Puzzled, we continued on the beam, gradually losing altitude, until the dim runway lights of an airport popped on directly under us. We could see a plane landing. Low on gas, we turned sharply, followed it on in. To our amazement it was a British Bristol Beaufighter, one of our escorts. There were no night-fighters around on bases at Sousse or Goubrine!

A jeep came out to meet us. I pulled off the runway, throttled the left engine back and yelled from my cockpit window.

"What airport is this?"

"Sfax," came the G.I. answer.

Sfax! 80 miles south of Goubrine! How did we end up here?

It was some consolation to learn later that 40 crews from our 51st Wing were asking themselves the same question. We figured a German U-boat had set up a false beam to lose us. Luckily it took us right over another airfield instead of out into the barren, forbidden stretches of the Sahara Desert, from which we probably would never have returned.

Old 381's gas gauges showed 40 gallons when we landed and we were stuck until morning.

No hero tales to the ground crews tonight, I thought. No homecoming welcome that is so great a part of aerial combat. Worse yet, someone else was getting old Doc Bagley's post-mission issue of "combat crew" bourbon.

To crown our misery we found the ground crews of the fighter field rather sarcastic about transport pilots in general and lost ones in particular. To save face we got out flashlights and looked old 381 over from stem to stern. We were sure she had picked up holes — but no luck. There wasn't even a dent in her old aluminum hide; not a bit of evidence to show we had been anywhere near combat.

At that point, about 2:30 A.M., we were completely disgusted and deflated. We cursed radio beams, intelligence briefings, navy ships, trigger-happy sailors, and bad luck. When we had exhausted the subject, we rolled up on the ground under the wing and went to sleep. My last thought was about Sgt. Evans, whom we released to fate somewhere over Mussolini's hostile rock-strewn island of Sicily.

And then it all came back into perspective. Worse things could have happened to us this night than being stuck at a friendly but unhospitable fighter base in North Africa.

EDITOR'S NOTE

The fate of Sgt. Evans and his airborne troops was recounted in an intelligence debriefing report of one of the glider troopers: "On the way into our landing zone Sgt. Evans hit a telephone wire, and then a stone wall. The crash sheared off most of the glider's nose and broke both legs of Evans and his co-pilot and injuring a third man so badly he couldn't walk. The rest of us had a job to do on some pillboxes so we gave the injured men first aid and some rations and laid them under the wings of our crashed glider. We set off to do our job and promised the men we would be back during daylight.

"We got our pillboxes that night, and some more too, even though not many of us made it to the rally point. By the time I got back to the glider in the afternoon, Evans said that German fighter planes had strafed them twice during the day — but missed, fortunately.

"With the help of a medical team, I got the three men to a hospital ship in Syracuse harbor before dark. That night German JU-88s bombed the hospital ship and sank it. The next day I found out that our three men were rescued .and put on another ship bound for the hospital in Tunis."

The Strait of Messina. Sicily lies to the upper left while the mainland of Italy appears at lower right. Photo has caught Ninth Air Force B-24s blasting ferry docks which helped supply Sicily.

Across the slim peninsula of Italy, south of Rome, 18 German divisions dug in behind a string of fortifications called the Gustav Line. Various Allied ground force attempts to break through these fortifications in the winter and early spring of 1944 had failed, including the all-out drive sparked by the spectacular aerial destruction on March 15, 1944, of the center anchor, the town of Cassino and its historic monastery perched nearby on a mountaintop and occupied by German forces. Four days later air forces began a maximum effort to choke off supplies, ammunition, and reinforcements coming down to the Germans from the north via rail, highway, and coastal ship. It was called "Operation Strangle," and in six weeks it had reduced the southward flow of supplies from 5000 to 400 tons per day. On May 11, when the Allied ground forces hit the Gustav Line, it crumbled.

Here is the story of this tactical air tour de force, a new art for destroying land armies.

Working on the Railroads

Maj. Richard Thruelsen
and
Lt. Elliott Arnold

TAKE any railroad tunnel, unless it has a mountain on top of it. Then take two P-47 Thunderbolts, each carrying a 100-pound bomb under each wing. The two Thunderbolts ride fast and low down the railway line toward the tunnel, one about 50 feet above the other. Just before the mouth is reached the lower Thunderbolt pulls up sharply and releases his two bombs. If the pilot is good at this sort of business, the bombs will plunge into the tunnel at a speed of something over 300 miles an hour, bounce into its depths and explode when the time fuse goes off a split second later. Meanwhile the sec-

ond Thunderbolt has zoomed over the ground covering the tunnel and dropped its two bombs somewhere between the two entrances. With 2000 pounds of explosive blowing up and 2000 pounds blowing down, simultaneously, that tunnel takes a terrific beating.

Or take the P-39 Airacobra fighters, which found their cannon and machine guns could generally set fire to schooners carrying Germans supplies along the west Italian coast, but seldom sank same. One bright lad decided he'd fly low, drop his empty 75-gallon belly tank (which is releas-

B-24 Liberators fly over the Adriatic on their way to bomb targets in Italy.

able and always contains some gas when it's dropped) on the schooner deck and then strafe the tank and see what happened. The tank, filled with gas vapor, exploded with a mighty roar and the schooner foundered.

Both of these improvisations in the art of destruction were developed in Italy during a tactical *tour de force* called "Operation Strangle."

The Problem: On March 15, 1944, the Germans had some 18 divisions facing the Allied forces in central Italy. Approximately half of these were strung along a line across the peninsula roughly connecting Pescara, on the east coast, to Sulmona, Cassino, and Gaeta. Another 9 divisions were drawn up in a semi-circle facing the Allied bridgehead at Anzio. Both of these German lines of position made exemplary use of the terrain, being well dug in and heavily fortified on high ground, facing our only lines of approach. To cut the human cost of breaching these lines was the job given the Mediterranean Allied Air Forces.

The best way Air could do this job

was by cutting the enemy's lines of supply. To maintain themselves on the two fronts during normal conditions (that is, while no concerted Allied land offensive was being prosecuted) the 18 German divisions required an average of 4000 tons of supplies every day. During the winter and early March they were receiving just about what they needed.

It was estimated that in the event of an Allied ground offensive, the German requirement would rise from 4000 to 5500 tons a day. All these supplies had to come from Germany or northern Italy. On March 15, it was thought the Germans had about 10 days' reserve of ammunition and two days' supply of fuel in dumps immediately behind their lines.

Of the 4000 tons the Nazi forces were receiving, 700 tons reach the front lines by sea — 500 tons by the west coast and 200 by the east. The other 3300 tons reached the fighting sectors via the four railroad trunk lines which traverse Italy between the Rome area and the Pisa-Florence-Bologna-Rimini network to the north.

By the middle of March plans had been laid for a general Allied offensive later in the spring. To the Strategic and Tactical and Coastal Air Forces was given the task of throttling German communications during the several months preceding the ground operations and keeping them cut during the offensive. This program of interdiction was called "Operation Strangle."

The interdiction planned would have four consequences. (1) It would cut German supplies to a point where Nazi ground forces would be starved for war materials. (2) It could destroy some of the material actually in transport. (3) It would destroy rolling stock, already a cause for German concern. (4) It would force upon the enemy a vastly increased use of motor transport and motor fuel — not only straining his sources of supply but also burdening his already hard-pressed railroad facilities with the increased importation of these necessities.

The Method: Strategic's responsibility in the plan was the crippling of the marshaling yards of northern Italy and the installations in the Alpine passes. The half-a-dozen ports which served the German water-borne traffic were to be considered targets of opportunity. These communications attacks were to be made by the Fortresses, Liberators, and the night-flying Wellingtons whenever the force was not busy on targets of higher strategic priority.

The Coastal Air Force was given the task of pounding at harbors and the destruction of shipping off both coasts north of the battle zone.

The participation of the Tactical Air Force was more involved. Designers of the plan drew a line across Italy, connecting Pisa, Florence, and Rimini. Then they drew another line across the breadth of the peninsula just north of Rome. Between these two lines, they said, Tactical will squeeze and squeeze, until the main arteries are choked and

162

the flow of supplies is cut down to a trickle.

This is a simple directive. The job was in no wise so simple. Railroad lines and railroad installations are difficult targets to knock out. They are hard to hit, they are in most cases easily reparable and the enemy, of course, always has the alternative of bridging any gap in his line with motor transport — off-loading the freight on one side of the break and reloading it on the other. The answer was to concentrate on those spots which would be hard to repair and to effect so many breaks that German reconstruction could not keep pace with Allied destruction.

The most vulnerable portions of any railway line are its bridges and viaducts. Then come tunnels, marshaling yards and maintenance, and repair installations such as round houses and machine shops. Last on the list are stretches of tracks, which are easily reparable. Tactical picked its targets in that order.

Fighters, fighter bombers, dive bombers, light bombers and medium bombers were all used. First priority on all operations was given to the actual support of the ground army, both before and during the offensive, but the major portion of Tactical's effort was confined to the great squeeze play. Between March 15 and May 11, the opening of the land offensive, Tactical made 10,200 attacks — 5900 on bridges and tunnels, 1600 on marshaling yards, and 2700 on trackage.

During those two months 12,372 tons of bombs splattered the communication system of central Italy. Strategic dropped another 6650 tons of bombs on the communications targets in the north.

The skill Tactical's dive bombers and bombers acquired in destroying their tiny targets was impressive. While the dive-bombing Thunderbolts tossed bombs into tunnel mouths, one wing of medium bombers set an April record of one direct hit on a bridge for every 22 sorties. Six months before it had taken this same wing an average of 59 planes over the target to insure a direct hit on a bridge. Oddly, the mediums found that the law of probabilities was wrong — they could be more sure of hitting a span if they bombed across it and not along its longitudinal axis. The spread of the formation took care of any errors in range and bridges can be picked out much easier when approached from the side.

Luck helped skill sometimes. A formation of British Wellingtons went out one night to bomb an important bridge by the light of flares which they dropped. The first Wellington over dropped a 4000-pounder. It was seen to hit the bridge, from 7000 feet — but nothing happened. The bomb's fuse had failed to work. This was a sad moment, for a direct hit on a bridge at night is almost a miracle. The second Wellington over dropped several smaller bombs. One of them also hit the bridge — close enough to

B-25 Mitchells of the Tactical Air Force knocked out the rail junctions that fed German supplies down into the Rome area. Here, B-25s are bombing the railroad yards at Terni, north of Rome.

This B-24 received a direct hit by flak while bombing rail yards in northern Italy.

the first hit to explode the big bomb. The Wimpys' bombardiers were satisfied they had been living right.

The Results: The rail facilities and harbor installations in central and northern Italy had been under attack ever since the beginning of the Sicilian campaign and much destruction had been inflicted. Particularly, the attacks on the Rome yards had already deprived the enemy of a large amount of storage track and forced him to back his waiting cars up the lines far to the north.

"Operation Strangle" was set in motion on March 15. By March 29 the three lines leading to Rome from the north, and the east-coast line, were blocked. It was calculated there were nine effective blocks, which would require a matter of weeks to repair, eleven temporary blocks which could be repaired in several days, and eight doubtful blocks which were based on pilot's claims or bomb-strike photo interpretations. The enemy was working feverishly at all breaks and using motor transport to relieve the situation.

On April 6, all through lines remained blocked (though supplies were moving via the motor transport shuttle system) and the number of confirmed blocks had risen to 23. There were four additional, claimed. Repair efforts were everywhere in evidence. Photo reconnaissance and secret ground reports brought back information that trans-shipment was most energetic between Chiusi and Rome, where trains were being off-loaded to road transport at all possible points. At Stimigliano, where the railroad and the road run along the bank of the Tiber, the Germans had built a number of piers into the river. This suggested they might be planning to float supplies down the Tiber to their dumps around Rome — a desperate expedient.

On April 21, there were 31 confirmed and 12 claimed blocks. All through lines had remained cut in a number of places. Repair efforts continued, although it was noticeable that on some of the less important connecting lines the enemy repair activity was sporadic. Above Chiusi, station sidings everywhere were full of cars. Flak guns on railway cars began to appear, a testament of the enemy's concern. Group reports brought news of wholesale German impressment of Italian labor, carts, mules, and motor transport in both the repair and trans-shipment efforts.

On May 8 all through lines from the north and the front lines had been blocked for seven weeks. On this date 53 blocks existed: 21 of these were bridges which would require one to several weeks to repair.

Reconstruction at breaks — which appeared in new places almost hourly — was particularly noticeable in the Florence-Chiusi segment and the Rimini-Ancona stretch of trackage. Repair efforts in some areas continued to lag, but there was no tendency to abandon lines. On some by-pass tracks, badly cratered by our dive-bombers, the Germans neglected repairs for several days and then the multiple cuts would be quickly and simultaneously repaired. At Cecina, three spans of an important rail bridge had been demolished early in "Operation Strangle." The Germans worked six weeks and finally repaired the breaks; 18 hours later two spans were again demolished, and they gave it up as a bad job.

Ground reports indicated that the pressure of trans-shipping and long distance motor transport haulage had strained the German gasoline, tire and truck situation to the breaking point. Destruction of marshaling yards at Bologna, Verona, Bolzano, Treviso, Udine, Padua and other north Italian junctions had been continued by Strategic B-24s. There were stories of long, loaded truck convoys crossing the Alpine frontier from Germany to Italy.

By May 18, seven days after the land offensive had started, the lines were cut at 92 points. Although service had been restored temporarily on some isolated segments — such as between Empoli and Chiusi, and Fano and Foligno — no through railroad traffic was able to approach closer than 50 miles above Rome. A number of road bridges had been knocked out, complicating the motor transport system. For the first time during "Operation Strangle" the enemy showed a tendency to abandon considerable stretches of rail line north of Rome. Shuttling, due to the large number of cuts, had fallen off sharply and a high percentage of the German military transport on the peninsula was now on a through motor transport basis. This motor transport was hard hit during the general German withdrawal. Over two days, May 24 and 25, Tactical's fighters and fighter-bombers destroyed 1000 Nazi vehicles on the roads immediately behind the front. They damaged 1000 more.

On the east coast, reports indicated the Germans were depending for the most part on horse-drawn transportation along the mountainous roads 15 or 20 miles inland. In the central sector, an informant reported, "the Germans are forcing thousands of Italians to prepare trenches and foxholes along sides of main highways leading north from Rome. These to be used by truck drivers in case of air attack."

Strategic, during this period, continued its attacks on the Po Valley marshaling yards and blocked the Brenner Pass line in several places.

Did "Operation Strangle" succeed in the job it set out to do? An American airman who lived behind the enemy lines for some months returned with news that in the front line area the German army rations, during the spring, were cut by one-third. And most of this was drawn from the countryside. The offensive, on all parts of the line, progressed ahead of schedule. Twenty-five days after the opening of the ground action, Rome was taken and the German armies were withdrawing to the north along the whole of the Italian front.

Testimony to the destructive effects of "Operation Strangle" was found on all sides by the advancing Allied troops. Rail lines, bridges, and viaducts were blown to bits by bombing. Nazi attempts to move supplies and equipment by truck had also suffered severely; in one 25-mile stretch of road north of Frosinone, Eighth Army troops counted the hulks of 175 trucks and supply vehicles burned or blasted by bombing and strafing. Just south of Subiaco, on the German retreat route from the Cassino sector, there were 102 burned-out wrecks in one mile. Nazi prisoners reported that for the two weeks ending with the capture of Rome all branches of the Wehrmacht on the Italian front had been short of fuel, ammunition, and rations.

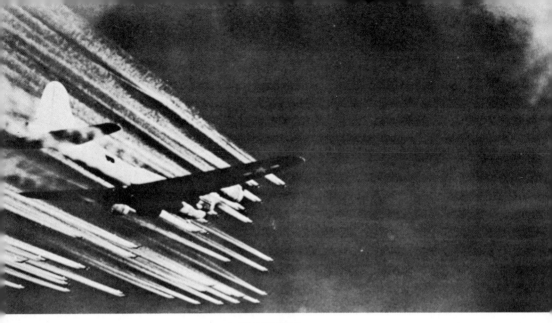

PART FIVE

THE STRATEGIC AIR
OFFENSIVE: A FLAMING YEAR

June, 1943–June, 1944

Introduction

WHILE THE ALLIES were enveloping Sicily and driving the Germans northward up the Italian boot, another kind of war — the strategic air war — unfolded in the skies over France and Germany.

By the spring of 1943, Eighth Air Force, operating with only two to six combat groups of B-17s, had doggedly wrung itself out in a variety of daylight strategic strikes over Germany in conjunction with the RAF night missions.

This Combined Bomber Offensive (set in motion by the January Casablanca Conference of top British-American leaders) awaited only the high priority of the Combined Chiefs of Staff, a nod that was given in May when the North African campaign ground to a stop.

Six heavy bomb groups were added to the Eighth by June, 1943. More were coming. With these the Eighth began to develop the muscle eventually needed to blanket targets with mass concentration and follow-up. Hitherto its strikes had been sporadic, follow-up raids impossible. The destructive effect of air bombardment had not been cumulative. The enemy's power to recoup was efficient and quick as in the case of the campaign against the German rubber industry in early 1943.

With reinforcements arriving, prospects now brightened and Eighth's objectives were three-fold: to destroy the German aircraft, ball-bearing and oil industries — three vital target systems. Loss of any one could be fatal to the Nazis.

To do this would require long, unescorted missions, deep into Germany. Complicating the problem was the doubling of German fighter strength in Western Europe from 500 to nearly 1000. Then, too, new Luftwaffe aerial armament included a mortar-type rocket with lethal radius of more than 100 yards and fused to explode at 1000 yards, far outranging the .50-caliber machine guns on the B-17s. The appearance, about this time, of the Republic P-47 Thunderbolt was heartening. Equipped with 100-gallon belly tanks the "Jug" pilots could accompany the formations all the way across France to the German borders. And well did this sturdy new fighter perform, driving the rocket-throwing Nazi fighters to desperate ends of flying fighter cover for fighters, much as they did during the Battle of Britain. Then, too, added range was given to the P-38 by external fuel tanks.

But the German border wasn't far enough. An "all-the-way" superior fighter was urgently needed. Unfortunately it would not be available until late 1943 and early 1944, when the P-51 Mustang would begin arriving in numbers. America's neglect of fighter development during the 1930s would exact a heavy price in the first months of the flaming year.

Defensively the B-17F was an improvement over the "E" of early days. New nose guns filled an open spot in its defensive armor and crew flak suits promised reduction of combat casualties. The tight 18-plane combat box and the stacking of two or three boxes vertically in a combat wing formation proved a defensive breakthrough against swarms of enemy fighters. The establishment of tight and strict aircrew discipline which permitted no evasive action enroute to target bordered on incredibility in the German mind. American formations became "Ramrods" that would not be deterred by flak or fighters. It took raw courage to hold formation position through dense fields of flak and hordes of rocket-throwing German fighters coming in from all quarters. It was a simple matter of hold together or be slaughtered individually.

First stage of Combined Bomber Offensive's flaming year got off with a series of shattering daylight aerial assaults on varied Nazi industry in July, 1943. The intensity of enemy fighter opposition soon had the Eighth hanging on the ropes. It was all too evident that the Luftwaffe had to be stopped before deep penetration missions could be undertaken. Two industries that would cause the greatest dislocation and damage to the Germans, it was felt, were oil and ball-bearing works. Oil was critical to Luftwaffe operations and shortage of ball-bearings promised to be the best bottleneck in aircraft production.

Thus were planned two of the most important and tragic missions of the early strategic offensive: Ploesti of August 1, 1943, and Regensburg Schweinfurt of August 17. Both were to be fairly successful but unbearably costly, and sadly, each had to be a one-shot effort for lack of reserves at this time to follow up.

The Rumanian oil fields of Ploesti produced one-half of all German oil and were within range of Allied bases in North Africa. The Ploesti force accumulated on airfields around Bengasi, Libya. It consisted of two Ninth Air Force B-24 Groups and three from Eighth Air Force. After comprehensive mission training, the 177 Liberators fought their way to Ploesti through flak and fighters in one of the fiercest, most dramatic air battles in all of history. Fifty-four of the big LIBS were lost. First results indicated 40 per cent of Ploesti's cracking and refining capacity were wiped out. Air leaders were jubilant, but the elation was short-lived. Within three months the Germans had the plant back into full production. Inability to mount a follow-on mission had made Ploesti a Pyrrhic victory.

The Regensburg-Schweinfurt mission followed in quick order. Schweinfurt produced half the ball-bearing output of Germany while the Messerschmitt factories at Regensburg and Wiener Neustadt built nearly half of the Luftwaffe's single-engine fighters. Destruction of these factories would appreciably reduce the Nazi's war-making effort.

To reach Schweinfurt the bombers had to penetrate 200 miles into Germany. Regensburg lay 100 miles farther on. Plans called for a twin-pronged mission with the Regensburg force leading the van, and upon completion of the bomb run fly on to bases in North Africa. Immediately following, the Schweinfurt force would strike the ball-bearing works and turn back for England. The bold mission got underway on the morning of August 17 with 146 B-17s in the Regensburg force and 230 in the Schweinfurt force. Battling through furious Nazi fighter attacks, the strike accomplished nominal results, but at high losses. Twenty-four of the Regensburg "Forts" were shot down, 36 of those bound for Schweinfurt, with more than 100 sustaining crippling damage.

The victories were empty ones, but the Eighth Air Force pressed on, hoping for better luck. Deep penetration missions followed to targets in Poland, East Prussia, and Germany and on October 14 a second try was made to Schweinfurt.

It was this mission which became one of the fiercest, most costly air battles of the entire war. Out of 291 heavy bombers, 60 were lost (1500 trained air crewmen), while the Germans lost only 35 fighters. New Luftwaffe fighter tactics had met the bomber box formations. In alternate waves FW-190 and ME-109 single engine fighters attacked the front and ME-110 twin-engine fighters in the rear with rockets. The Luftwaffe pilots succeeded in breaking open the tight boxes as the flaming Forts fell from the sky. Once the formation came apart, packs of fighters ruthlessly attacked individual planes. Despite the losses, the strike caused such destruction that the Germans immediately began dispersion of their ball-bearing industry and requisitioning large quantities from Sweden and Switzerland.

Through the early winter months the Eighth continued its strategic bombardment mainly with the use of Pathfinder planes equipped with H2X airborne radar. Rarely did the formations go beyond the radius of their belly-tank equipped P-38 and P-47 fighter escort.

Meanwhile, British Bomber Command Halifaxes and Lancasters following "Pathfinder" Mosquitoes and equipped with H2S radar, pressed their sustained offensive against the big industrial centers of the Ruhr Valley. Enormous damage was done to Essen and the great Krupp Works there. Other targets included Cologne, Aachen, Bochum, Duisburg, Wuppertal, Dusseldorf Dortmund, Kassel, Mannheim. Frankfurt and the port cities of Hamburg, Bremen, Wilhelmshaven and Kiel were pasted in massive area bomb strikes. Special missions included the highly successful 19-plane (Lancasters) night attack on the Moehne, Eder and Sorpe Dams. This skillful but costly mission breached the dams sending mountainous torrents of water through the Ruhr Valley, causing high damage and loss of German life.

Of special note were the massive night attacks on Hamburg on July 24-25 and August 2-3 during which 8623 tons of bombs turned the city into a roaring conflagration, producing a fire storm comparable to the Tokyo fire bomb raids and the A-bomb drop on Hiroshima and Nagasaki.

During the fall and winter, RAF night bombers continued their runs to German cities. It was in August that the Battle of Berlin began in earnest, and by March 25, 1944, the RAF had made 10,000 night sorties to Berlin in 20 missions which completely laid waste 6427 acres of the city: 50 per cent of Berlin's industrial plants were leveled, 60 per cent of commercial business wiped out. Heaviest attack was on the night of February 15-16, when 2643 tons of bombs tumbled onto the city. Throughout the city-busting campaign RAF bombers also planted thousands of tons of magnetic sea mines in the Baltic and German waters. In 1943 alone, RAF bombers dropped 25,225 of the deadly eggs.

By the end of 1943 the results of the American daylight air offensive were not too encouraging. German aircraft production had actually increased from 15,055 in 1942 to 17,490 in 1943, broken down as follows: 7440 single engine, 2555 twin engine fighters, and 6155 bombers. Despite mounting losses to Allied fighters, the Luftwaffe was stronger in December than it was in June, 1943.

But the Luftwaffe had problems, too. British-based American mediums in constant daylight raids had driven the German aircraft from their bases near England, farther and farther back toward their homeland. The Luftwaffe had tried every conceivable tactic, yet the Allied bomber formations were getting through and heaping terrible destruction on Germany. Irrevocable orders had gone out to German pilots to ignore escort fighters and attack the bombers. The attrition of elite, experienced pilots had been telling.

Dissatisfied with the results of the strategic air offensive, a reorganization of the entire effort took place in December with the creation of the United States Strategic Air Forces in Europe under Gen. Carl A. Spaatz. The new command took over direction of the Eighth and Fifteenth Air Forces, both of which were now up to full strength. The Eighth Air Force Commander, Gen. Ira Eaker, was replaced by Gen. Jimmy Doolittle, and transfered to Italy.

The new order issued by the AAF Chief, Gen. H. H. Arnold was simple: to destroy the Luftwaffe in the air and on the ground and in the factories. The invasion of Europe could not be undertaken until this had been done.

And so it was that 1944 began with a furious assault on German fighter factories. Fortunately, a new fighter, the long-range P-51 Mustang, began arriving in Europe in November. It had flown its first all-the-way escort in December and answered the critical problem of deep penetration strikes. From the start it proved superior to anything in European skies.

On January 11, 800 heavies, with escorting fighters, hit aircraft factories in Oschersleben, Brunswick, Halberstadt, and other cities. Although 53 bombers were shot down, along with five escort fighters, returning airmen claimed destruction of 292 Nazi fighters. The campaign now rose in crescendo with a massive blow at all German aircraft industry in February, 1944. A period of good weather over Europe at that time enabled Spaatz and his staff to launch this series of concentrated, rapid-fire attacks which became known as "Big Week."

Between February 20 and 25 more than 1000 heavies of the Eighth Air Force, aided by 500 B-24s from the Fifteenth Air Force, flew more than 3500 sorties. Flanking the formations on their deep penetration missions were strong fighter escort. In conjunction, the RAF mounted five massive night attacks while our fighters flew some 3500 individual sorties against the Luftwaffe in the air.

The results were highly encouraging. German aircraft production was set back two months.

The strategic air offensive now got into high gear. On March 4, P-51 escorts flew all the way to Berlin for the first time. It was an ominous sign to the Germans, the fulfillment of something the pompous Hermann Goering said would never happen. Two days later, on March 6 and again on the 8th, formations of more than 1000 heavy bombers struck the German capital. Throughout March every serviceable bomber was thrown into the offensive and American fighters, in a switch of tactics, began ranging far out ahead of the bombers to seek out and destroy the Luftwaffe defenders before they came near the formations. By the end of March the Luftwaffe had lost 800 of their first-line home air defense fighters and Allied air superiority had been achieved over Europe.

This period marked the beginning of the rapid decline of the Luftwaffe. "Big Week" and the follow-up strikes had broken the back of the Germans in the factories, the refineries, and in the air. From now on German fighters rose only to protect vitally important targets.

Meanwhile the Italian-based Fifteenth Air Force heavies and its strategic fighters (which had assisted in the climactic "Big Week" operation) were aiding the Russians by striking targets in German-occupied Balkans, denying the Luftwaffe use of Balkan bases for air strikes against the Eastern Front, and running "shuttle" missions to bases in the Soviet Union. Much of Fifteenth Air Force activities was also devoted to dropping supplies to anti-

German partisan movements in Yugoslavia, attacking Axis ports in France and Greece, and pounding the Brenner Pass through which German armies in Italy were supplied.

With the rapid decline of the Luftwaffe, the next big target system to come under the strategic attack was German oil.

The campaign got underway in April, 1944. Oil targets in northern, central, and eastern Germany were assigned to Eighth Air Force. The synthetic plants in the Ruhr were assigned to British Bomber Command, while those in southern Germany, Austria, Hungary, the Balkans, southern Poland, and Rumania—especially Ploesti — were given to the Fifteenth Air Force. By July, 1944, 66 major plants had been attacked with a loss of 400 million gallons, and Germany's production of oil products had been reduced to 20 per cent of minimum requirements of the German Wehrmacht. The attacks would continue through the spring, summer and fall, following the Normandy invasion, to the violent end that the German war machine became immobile for lack of fuel.

The destruction of the Nazi aircraft industrial base and its production capacity by the Combined Bomber Offensive went hand in hand with another equally important objective— the extermination of the Luftwaffe in the skies and on the airfields. This job went largely to the fighter wings of Eighth, Ninth and Fifteenth Air Forces and RAF Fighter Command, with an able assist from the airfield-busting mediums, the B-26s, A-20s, B-25s and their British counterparts.

As early as mid-1942, U.S. fighter pilots joined with the RAF Fighter Command in the gradual hacking away at the Luftwaffe in swirling aerial combat and low-level strafing of enemy airfields from the French Channel coast inland. British Spitfires, Beaufighters, Mosquitoes, Hurricanes, Typhoons, Tempests, and U.S. P-38 Lightnings and P-47 Thunderbolts fanned out over France and the Low Countries to the limit of their radius of action on armed reconnaissance patrol, combat sweeps, and strafing strikes. It was also the job of the Spitfire, Lightning, and Thunderbolt to provide escort to outgoing and incoming formations of heavy bombers and at this work they became known as the "Little Friends."

Because of the intense anti-aircraft defenses ringing German airfields it was considered as dangerous and demanding of flight skill to strafe an enemy airfield as to meet the enemy fighters in the air. And so in the European Theatre, fighter pilots were credited for aircraft destroyed on the ground as well as in the air. This was especially significant after February, 1944 when the Luftwaffe refused to send up its dwindling fighters except on vital missions—a move which forced Allied fighter pilots down on to the deck to pursue the Germans in their lair with a vengeance hitherto unknown.

Until the appearance of the high performance, long-range P-51 Mustang in November, 1943, Allied fighters were hampered by their short-range capability and restricted to areas this side of the German border. The Luftwaffe had wisely awaited the escort fighter "drop-off" point before attacking bomber formations. But all this changed when Mustangs showed up over Germany. Even Luftwaffe Fighter Chief himself would not, at first, believe reports of the P-51. Then one day four Mustangs bounced his ME-110 and chased him all the way back to Berlin. His alarming reports of this superior American fighter convinced the German High Command to undertake a priority jet fighter development program. For only the German jets could surpass the Mustang. But it was the eleventh hour and time would run out for the Luftwaffe before the jet could be available in numbers that would count.

Starring units of the European fighter air war were the three fighter wings of the Eighth Air Force, the 65th, 66th and 67th, each having 5 combat groups and each group 3 squadrons.

The magnificent story of these men lies deep within the statistical record they produced. In the last three years of the war the three wings were credited with nearly half (9275) of all German aircraft (20,419) destroyed by the entire U.S. Air Forces in Europe. Top Group was the 4th, with 1006½

enemy kills to its own losses of 241 planes. A close second was the 56th Group with 1006 destroyed, to 128 losses. Third was the 255th with 860 destroyed, 175 lost. All three top units belonged to the 65th Fighter Wing.

The three wings produced 568 air aces, 28 of whom knocked down 20 or more enemy aircraft, and 9 were credited with 30 and up.

The roster of the Eighth Air Force aces reads like a page from air war's hall of fame. Top man was Lt. Col. John C. Meyer (37 victories) following by Capt. John T. Godfrey with 36, Lt. Col. Elwyn G. Righetti with 34½, Lt. Col. Francis S. Gabreski with 33½ and Col. David Schilling with 33. Maj. George Preddy (30 kills) shot down 6 enemy aircraft in 6 minutes over Hamburg on August 6, 1944. Capt. Robert S. Johnson's 28 victories were all air-to-air and the second highest in this category in the Theatre. Col. Hubert "Hub" Zemke (28 kills) was leader of the famed 56th "Wolfpack." He teamed with Schilling and Gabreski to earn from Luftwaffe fighter pilots the title of the "Terrible Three."

Complementing the Eighth and strong right arm in the fighter air war was the tactical Ninth Air Force, reconstituted on British soil in the fall of 1943 after a brilliant record in Africa. By the end of the war, the Ninth Air Force aces numbered 71, led by Lt. Bruce W. Carr with 25½ victories and Lt. Glenn T. Eagleston with 23½. Fifteen of their aces shot

Metallic paper strips dropped from the air proved to be one of the most effective countermeasures against German radar. Called "window," it is here being dropped during a raid on Essen.

Three famous fighter pilots of the war against Germany. From left: Capt. Robert S. Johnson whose 28 victories made him the second-ranking ace in the European theater; Col. Hubert ("Hub") Zemke, the leader of the famed 56th Wolfpack who had 19½ kills; and Maj. Walker M. ("Bud") Mahurin who destroyed 19¾ enemy planes in aerial combat.

down 10 or more aircraft.

Luftwaffe killer in the south was the Italian-based Fifteenth Air Force whose P-38s and P-47s roamed the skies of the Balkans, Southern France, and Germany. 1st. Lt. John J. Voll (21 kills) and Maj. Herschel H. Green (18 victories) led their roster of 68 aces.

While statistics fail miserably in conveying the drama of fighter combat they do set apart the magnificent role played by the U.S. fighters. During "Big Week," for example, Hub Zemke's 56th Group shot down 43 Nazi aircraft without suffering a loss.

To the American destruction of the Luftwaffe must be added the enviable record set by RAF Fighter Command, and the Australians, Canadians, French, Poles, and other nationalities who flew with the RAF. It is equally impressive. Twice as long in combat (from 1939 on) British and Dominion pilots shot down more than 5000 Luftwaffe planes in air-to-air combat alone, with several thousand credited to them on the ground. Top British ace was Wing Commander J. E. Johnson, with 42 enemy aircraft to his credit.*

By early spring, 1944 the control of the air over Europe belonged to the Allies. The Luftwaffe was in steady decline. Great scars of destruction marked all major German industrial cities. Hitler's 1000 year Third Reich could no longer effectively produce oil, aircraft and ball bearings needed for its once-powerful armed forces. Oil, the key to modern war, was in short supply. The invasion of Europe was now possible and for the next three months the task of Allied air forces would be devoted to the destruction of German defenses and communications in preparation for the land invasion of northern France.

* Others include: Group Capt. Clive Robert Caldwell, Royal Australian Air Force — 28½; Flight Leader G. R. Beurling — 31 and Squadron Leader Henry W. McLeod — 21, both of the Royal Canadian Air Force; Group Commander "Sailor" Malan — 32 and Wing Commander Colin F. Gran — 27½, both of the Royal New Zealand Air Force; and Maj. Malcolm S. Osler — 12, of the South African Air Force. French ace Pierre Henri Clostermann had 33 victories; Flight Lt. Svein Heglund of Norway — 14; Col. Kaj Birksted of Denmark — 10; Flight Officer Vicky N. Ortmans of Belgium — 11.

Top Luftwaffe ace was Maj. Erich Hartmann with 352 victories. Leading aces of other countries include Maj. Ivan Kozhedub, Russian Air Force — 62 kills; Lt. Ilmari Juutilainen of the Finnish Air Force — 93; Capt. Count Constantin Cantacuzine, (Rumania) — 60; Maj. Adriano Visconti, Italian Air Force — 26; Lt. Dezso Szentgyorgyi (Hungary) — 29; Lt. Rotnik Reznak (Slovakia) — 32 plus; Lt. Cvitan Galic (Croatia) — 36 plus; Lt. Col. Wirold Urbanowica (Poland) — 19; Pilot Officer Josef Frantisek — 28, and Wing Commander Karel M. Kuttelwascher — (both Czech).

The aces from the Balkan countries flew with the Luftwaffe on the Eastern Front. There were no aces from the Netherlands or Greece although their squadrons flew with the RAF. Some Spanish flyers flew with the Luftwaffe.

"Operation Gomorrah" was the British Bomber Command's ominous code name for the destruction of Hamburg, the second largest city in Germany. There were many reasons why it had to be eliminated: its shipyards, the most extensive in Europe, were turning out submarines which preyed on British and American shipping; it was a vital port for Nazi Germany and the most heavily defended city in occupied Europe.

Many raids had been leveled against this luscious target, but all were sporadic and scattered. By early summer came the order for its complete obliteration as a "matter of absolute urgency." For Bomber Command, whose night missions had been wiping out German industrial areas for over a year, it was a maximum effort and never before had they made such careful plans.

On the night of July 24, 740 Lancasters and Halifaxes rose from British bases and nosed out across the North Sea, on a night mission to Germany, as they had done many times before. The one difference this time would be in results which Nazi Propaganda Minister Goebbels would call "a catastrophe the extent of which staggers the imagination . . ."

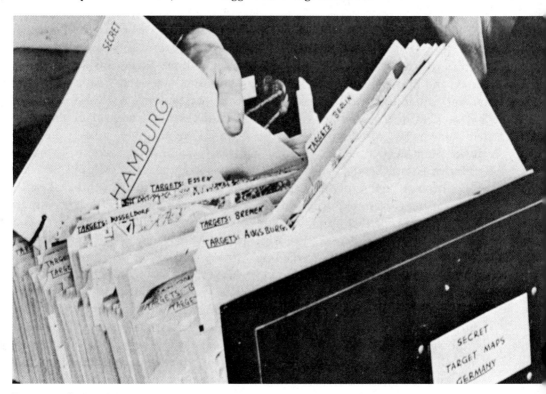

Target: Hamburg — Secret.

The Night Hamburg Died

Martin Caidin

As THE LAST HOURS of July 24, 1943 slip into the approaching darkness of the eastern horizon, the crews of nearly 800 four-engine heavy bombers walk to their planes. More than 5000 British airmen — pilots and co-pilots, bombardiers and navigators and radiomen and gunners — prepare to turn Gomorrah from a paper plan into flaming reality.

The weather this evening is crisp and clean, with excellent visibility. Within the capacious bays of the Lancasters and Halifaxes hang the bombs; fat and squat high-explosive missiles and land mines, incendiaries in clusters and singly, all destined for the city of Hamburg.

Merlin engines cough and rumble, shake through their innards, and then spit great blasts of smoke from the exhausts as the propellers spin faster and faster. The great bombers vibrate with their power. Across the darkening English countryside there reverberates the song of thunder; a satisfying sound to all the veterans of the German blitz who hear the bombers' cry and think of the hell that will be wrought in some German city tonight.

At dozens of airfields there comes the sound of squealing brakes as the Lancasters and Halifaxes taxi slowly on the perimeter tracks of their airfields. Nose to tail, the giants rumble along in elephantine fashion, a procession of death about to take wing. At each field two lines of heavy bombers meet at the head of the active runway; brakes squeal, and are locked. The pilots and co-pilots run the engines one by one to full power, checking magnetos, carburetor and cylinder head temperature, flaps and trim settings, oil pressures and amperes and hydraulic pressure reading. When they are satisfied as to the operation and the sound and feel of their machines, the engines subside in their great roar and fall back to a massed whispering of idling Merlins.

Then comes the signal for take-off — the rejection of the earth by 791 great bombers. Each take-off is a long moment of tension. The bomber stands firmly locked to the runway by her brakes. In the cockpit the pilot slowly and smoothly advances the throttles, adding power, spinning the great blades faster and faster. Then she quivers with the great might of the four motors, anxious to roll. The pilot and co-pilot snap glances at the instruments, and suddenly the brakes are released, the giant is free.

The bomber lunges forward, propellers chewing hungrily at the air, dragging the heavy weight forward. The speed picks up in a steady progression, accelerating as the indicator needle reached around to 40, 50, 60. The tail comes up, there is less drag, and the speed increases even more. 70, 80 . . . the wings grasp at the air, there is the tugging of lift. With deft touches on the rudder pedals the pilot holds her down the runway, rushing along the paved strip. Then the bomber reaches that instant when lift overcomes the ponderous weight of the machine and its drag through the air. With the gentlest of pressure the yoke comes back in the pilot's hand, the wheels lift slightly from the earth, and the machine of destruction is airborne. She is in her element now.

The wheels come up, lock into place with a dull thud that travels the length of the fuselage. The engine sound is tremendous as the roar smashes into the runway and then the earth, and reflects back again. Then there is even more speed, the wings bank slightly and the machine slides onto her predetermined course. Now the ship is moving fast enough to dismiss the additional lift of the flaps, and the surfaces slide back into the wings, lock into place, and the wing is again clean.

England falls away beneath the bomber, as it does beneath a dozen great bombers, and then several dozen, and soon the figure is more than 100 . . . 200, 400, 700, nearly 800 massive machines grimly marching toward Germany. The Channel beckons and the coast of England slides beneath the transparent noses of the bombers, falls away past the wings, and provides a murky view for the tail gunners in their steel and glass cages, surrounded by four .303 calibre machine guns.˙

It is a good night for flying, and they all hope, for bombing. There is majesty in the heavens tonight; the spectacle of 800 giants marching in a great river of wings and engines and booming thunder is overwhelming. But through all the feeling of this immense effort, the majesty of flight, there is the grim conviction that some of these men will die tonight, that the sleek lines of the Halifaxes and Lancasters will be punctured and holed and blasted by cannon shells and the crooked slash of flak fragments.

The phalanx of bombers seems almost overwhelming in its strength, indomitable in its sheer number. The opposition, however, is formidable as well; the Germans are skillful and courageous and their equipment is outstanding. They have struck before with terrifying results, and they hope to do the same tonight. But Gomorrah still holds hidden its surprises . . .

Far ahead of the main bomber force the Pathfinders streak through the skies of occupied Europe, then venture into the heartland of the Reich, rushing along the northern coastline. All told tonight there are 791 bombers in the heavens, but 51 of these will not attack Hamburg. Some are assigned diversionary missions, and as the Pathfinders race for the target of Hamburg, the other bombers fan out on their assigned routes.

Along the German defense lines are great Würzburg and Freya detection and warning stations, and tonight these are a special target for a weapon never used before in Europe. It is an innocuous little thing, the tiny strip of tinfoil, but dropped by the millions in unbelievable locust swarms, the tinfoil is a great monkey wrench jammed into the heart of the German defense effort.

Small British formations race over Holland and Belgium and strike into Western Germany. Along their path of flight the tiny strips of tinfoil flutter through the skies, drifting slowly toward the ground. The main bomber force that rushes toward Hamburg also begins to release its tinfoil cargo, and the result is unprecedented.

On the German radar screens it appears that all of Europe is under a mass invasion of thousands and thousands of bombers. The warning centers are in a state of agitation, and they report, one after the other, that enormous forces of enemy bombers are approaching. They call out cities in the Ruhr as targets, they flash alarms of "hostiles, many" along all points of the coast, the Low Countries, and into Germany itself.

Not only the tinfoil flutters to earth; the bombers split open the night sky with blinding flares, the famous Christmas tree clusters that shatter the darkness with savage brilliance, drifting in sputtering and blinding light. They also drop bombs that scream horribly as they rush toward the earth. All across Germany and in the occupied countries the air raid sirens shriek their warning. Factories shudder to a halt as workers rush for shelter. People clear the streets and hurry into the underground havens, for there is no doubt about it tonight — the radar screens are infallible — Germany is being struck almost everywhere by the greatest armada of bombers ever to leave the British Isles.

The main force of Lancasters and Halifaxes pushes across the North Sea, droning its way into the east, toward Hamburg. Already the "Window" is having its effect, for even as the bombers move out from England the German defenses are making their moves to smash the bombers. But they will not do so tonight ...

The Pathfinders are well ahead of the initial wave of bombers. Navigators bend to their scopes and instruments like priests at an altar, and with the same religious fervor they call out commands to the pilots. Using their complicated long-range electronic navigational system known as Gee, the navigators check at regular intervals the progress of their flight. Each new position is reported to the flight deck as the Lancasters rush toward the unsuspecting city of Hamburg, which for more than a full year has not felt a heavy assault.

A giant German Würzburg radar antenna on the French beach which sent out its waves 50 miles to detect approaching enemy planes.

Exactly 15 miles northeast of Heligoland, the Pathfinders—and later the main stream — ease from their established course of flight. The bombers are bracketed in the invisible electronic beams of their navigational systems, and the moment has come to take up a new compass heading. The pilots ease down on rudders and gently move the control yokes. Ailerons and rudders move ever so slightly, and the Lancasters rush directly toward Cuxhaven, 75 miles from the target city.

Cuxhaven tonight is especially important, for on the radar screens of the H2S equipment it is clear and sharp and absolutely identifiable, a marker pointing directly at the two million inhabitants of Hamburg. The navigators remain glued to their scopes, starting intently at the clocklike finger of the timebase as it rotates around and around, a perpetual circular movement across the face of the flickering cathode ray tube.

All bombers with H2S move toward their target on the guidepost of the flickering scopes. The navigators see along the very bottom of the cathode tube the first sparkling of green, the shimmering line of the enemy coastline. As the bombers draw nearer and nearer to their target the coastline climbs deliberately up the face of the glass. It is a sparkling electronic echo, a reflection of radiation probing to the earth and back to the bomber in much less than a hundred-thousandth of a second. The coastline slides upward until it stretches across the center of the cathode tube. As it continues to move there appears the first echo-sign of the communities on the land. These are the towns on the coastline and slightly inland, revealed nakedly to the navigators as a series of bright patches of light of varying sizes.

It is almost as if the sky were aligned with invisible guidelines attuned to the marvelous equipment within the bombers. Now the scopes show a serpentine ribbon, dark and seemingly shapeless—the river Elbe, pointing its crooked finger all the way to Hamburg. At first the finger itself lacks definition; it is a wavering blur and the distant city no more than a shapeless, flickering blob on the scopes. But the bombers chew up the distance at several miles every minute, and with each passing minute the blur loses its electronic mistiness and begins to resolve into a meaningful pattern.

Bright fingers begin to show clearly from the larger mass; these are the extensions of the docks. Soon all Hamburg can be seen on the scopes, and the river and canals, the major areas that reflect most clearly leap into prominence. This is the electronic introduction, unknown to any of the two million inhabitants below, to the ten days of hell of Gomorrah.

There are different impressions with different meanings as the Battle of Hamburg explodes into life. Along the Channel coast the German defense network is a center of wild activity. The command posts of the Freya warning apparatus have long before flashed their alert warnings to all the night fighter units assigned to duty, and the Germans are prepared to exact a disastrous toll of the British heavy bombers. There is no question, from the first sightings and alert flashes, that a very large-scale British raid is in the making tonight, and the moment the first definite course of the bombers is reported, the pilots signal their mechanics to close the canopies. The motors of the twin-engine fighters roar as the airplanes trundle down their runways, lift quickly into the dark skies, and disappear into the night.

Each pilot remains in contact with his ground control unit and receives specific vector control—fly to altitude, take up the ordered compass course, additional instructions will be transmitted en route as the planes approach the bombers. But neither the German ground controllers nor the fighter pilots and their radar operators in the Messerschmitts and Junkers know of the incredibly effective diversionary flights or of the millions and millions of tinfoil strips fluttering invisibly down through the black night.

Because of the ground tracking reports that a giant force of hostiles is moving into Holland and Belgium and Western Germany, the command centers order the majority of fighters airborne toward Amsterdam, where they will be directed into the armada of the Lancasters and Halifaxes. As the fighters drone through the night, they continue to receive reassuring reports of the progress of the bomber force—unaware that the fluttering tin-foil actually constitutes the bombers.

Then there appear the first cracks in the armor of the German defense. Several pilots call back to their command stations and complain bitterly that they cannot find the enemy; the bombers are assuredly heading in another direction. At one moment a heavy bomber force is reported en masse over Amsterdam and within a minute the ground stations call in excitedly that the bombers are actually somewhere else over the coastline. Hardly does this call finish when another station in great agitation breaks in to report "many hostiles!" west of Brussels, and a few moments later another excited voice shouts over the airwaves that the bombers are actually far out to sea.

With every passing minute the confusion mounts steadily, and before anyone realizes the true situation, Germany is undergoing a deadly crisis. No one knows for certain exactly where the bombers really are. Actually, every radar station on the ground is certain that the bomber force even at that moment is roaring through its defense area. And this, of course, is patently impossible. Yet the flash warnings and the demands for fighters still come over the radio channels in an unbroken stream.

What transfers normal confusion into absolute chaos is that the fighters too are reporting the bombers — in all parts of the Low Countries and over Western Germany! Virtually every fighter plane that has been vectored to the reported positions of the bombers is "encountering hostiles," but in a fashion perplexing to the pilots and their radar scope operators. Again this is impossible, but it is happening. From one part of the Continent to the other, the pilots report contacts by radar, and that they are closing in rapidly to attack.

In the command stations, the controllers look at one another in complete bewilderment. The pilot reports are consistent — but what they report is absolutely impossible!

The target is picked up on the scope, and the operator gives his orders to the pilot. Fly 10° left, climb 300 feet, bomber dead ahead. The pilots do as they are bid, straining their eyes for a glimpse of the giant four-engine shape they know is ahead of them. But the rate of closure is too swift! It is almost as if the bomber were rushing head-on at the fighter . . . the scope reports a target from 1 to 2000 yards out, closing rapidly. It comes down to 7, 6, and 500 yards, and the pilot is prepared to blast loose with heavy cannon and guns.

But at 500 yards, the target disappears! One instant it is there before the eyes of the operator, a sharp blip on his scope, and the next instant . . . it is gone. But there! Again, directly ahead — another Britisher! And again the target closes rapidly, and again it disappears suddenly at 500 yards!

In the skies this night there is more than one team of pilot and radar operator who argue mightily with each other. Confidence and determination in their maneuvers quickly fade into bewilderment, and all across Germany the ground stations hear the cries of: "I cannot follow any of the hostiles!" and "They are driving us crazy; they are very cunning!"

The precious minutes of bomber interception before the target — wherever it is tonight, the bewildered controllers and pilots have absolutely no idea—are rapidly disappearing. Whatever happens, before long it will be too late to interfere with the smashing of the target, and bombing is rarely so effective as when the raiders are free of the disturbing pursuit and the actual firing runs of the fighters.

Then, suddenly, during a momentary lull in the frenzied and contradictory reports from the ground stations, a voice wild with frustration and rage breaks into the command channel. It is a controller, unquestionably hysterical, who shouts in a shrill voice over and over that "There are a thousand bombers over Hamburg, a thousand of them. They are attacking Hamburg this very instant!" There is no question now of where the bombers are, no question that this is the enigmatic force that has driven the defense system crazy. For now the Germans can see the bombers, hear the overwhelm-

ing thunder of the massed motors. The Pathfinders have done their task well, and the marker flares and fires within the city are gleaming brightly, a burning candle beckoning to an immense swarm of lethal moths.

By the time most of the fighters respond to the frantic orders to fly to Hamburg at maximum speed, it is too late. The pilots from more than a hundred miles away notice with apprehension the pale flickering glow on the horizon which, as they close the distance to Hamburg, assumes an orange and then an unholy twisting red. When they arrive over the city they are shocked by the sight before their eyes. The earth has been ripped asunder and great crimson flames writhe in agony on the surface . . .

EDITOR'S NOTE

For bombing purposes, the city was divided in quarters.

In one-half hour the 740 bombers dropped 2396 tons of bombs on the 1st quarter. Again on the night of July 27-28, 739 British heavies dumped 2417 tons, and on July 29-30, 2382 tons on the 2nd and 3rd quarters. By August 2, thick palls of black smoke still hovered over the beleaguered metropolis when 1425 tons more fell from Bomber Command heavies. The strikes turned Hamburg into a living hell, with great fire storms that produced cyclonic winds. For six days a continuous blanket of heavy smoke prevented photo recon estimates of damage. When aerials were taken the results were terrifying, even to the British; 75 per cent of the city had been completely razed, 10 square miles eradicated. The remainder was uninhabitable. "Operation Gomorrah" had lived up to its name.

Next morning the smoke rising from the Hamburg refinery fires could be seen for 100 miles.

Oil was the Achilles heel of the German Wehrmacht and the big Ploesti refineries in Rumania produced one-third of all this precious liquid Hitler needed to run his "blitzkrieg." It was No. *1* target on Allied planning boards.

A stab at the Ploesti works had been made on June *11, 1942* by *12* B-24s, under Col. Harry A. Halverson, from bases in Egypt. All *12* returned but little damage had been accomplished.

Orders for a second powerful strike were approved at the Casablanca Conference in January, *1943*. Under a code name of "Tidal Wave," plans called for an unescorted treetop-level daylight strike. Most of the *2300*-mile round trip from bases in Africa would be over enemy territory. And since there were to be no fighter escorts, surprise was all important. The course ran from Africa across the Mediterranean, up over the *9500* foot Yugoslavian mountains then down the Danube Valley and onto the flats of Rumania for the final run. If it added up to near-suicide, there was no other way to sneak in under enemy defense warning system and achieve surprise.

During the summer five groups of B-24s from Eighth and Ninth Air Forces gathered on airfields in Tunisia and began intensive practice over models of the refining plants built on the desert sands. The B-24s were modified with addition of an extra fuel tank in the bomb bay and rear-rangement of the top-turret guns in the formation lead planes to fire forward allowed sweeping ahead of the armada. Extra guns were mounted in the noses of lead planes.

The bold mission got underway at *0710* hours on August *1, 1943*. The crews knew this one would be rough but little could they know that before the day was out nearly one-third would go down to German flak and fighters; that on this one mission heroism in the skies would remain forever unsurpassed and a grateful nation would award five Medals of Honor —the largest from any one single military operation in history.

Here is the grim story of "Liberty Lad," one of the *177* B-24s that hit Ploesti that day and barely made it back, as told by Maj. Kenton D. McFarland, its pilot.

188

The B-24s take off from their African base headed for the infamous Ploesti raid.

Ploesti: Hell at Fifty Feet

Maj. Kenton D. McFarland, USAF,

as told to Arturo F. Gonzalez, Jr.

IT IS ONLY four in the morning, and the sun hasn't even poked up over the desert's rim, but the men seem magnetized as they drift toward the long line of fat, full, dull green Liberators parked neatly along the northern edge of our Benghazi field which bears the ignominious label of Site Seven. When the 6 x 6 truck slows down in front of the "Liberty Lad," I hop off; the crew chief and a couple of ground-crew members slide out of the darkness to report that the plane is topped off with a full load of 3100 gallons and

189

ready to go. As I spread out the map in front of the ship and we squat in the red, gritty sand for a last look, I can't help but think of what led up to this mission—and what still lies ahead.

There'd been mystery. It all began in England when the mysterious Field Order 58 came through and sent us out flying low-level practice runs in between our Eighth Air Force missions over the Continent. Then, more low-level stuff in Africa when our unit was transferred.

Rumors had us slated for some dambusting, a low-level raid on Berlin, maybe even a strike at Berchtesgaden itself. When the target turned out to be Ploesti — a place most of us had never heard of — plenty of money changed hands.

There's been some laughs, too, because buzzing a fat, dumb, and happy B-24 with official approval is every bomber pilot's dream. Out on practice runs, our planes had knocked over an English church steeple, made dozens of tractor drivers dive for ditches, killed a couple of strolling camels and had even come back with desert sagebrush caught in the bomb-bay doors.

And practice — God, we'd never practiced for a mission quite so thoroughly. The RAF had rigged up sand-table models of the 40 square miles of refineries. And then the AAF had filmed the models to show us the target under low-level approach conditions. They'd even laid out 40 miles of whitewash and oil drums in the desert to give us a target to bomb in

our last two max-effort practice runs. It was touch and go whether we'd have something to bomb, I recall; the Arabs kept making off with the oil drums during the night.

We'd had briefings, and then briefings about briefings, to boot. Oil experts, photo recon men, the wheels from Bomber Command Headquarters — they had all told us about the Rumanian flak crews that weren't going to fire at us, the fighter fields where the interceptors would be caught napping, the Sunday timing designed to bring us on target when everyone else was off duty, about the radar stations facing the wrong way and how our low-level approach and radio silence would catch the Jerries with their pants down. Most of us discounted this pep talk from the wheels; we knew Ploesti was going to be a tough one.

For the majority of us, this is the last raid before Stateside, too: 25 missions completed and you are rotated home. All but us poor characters picked for the Ploesti raid; we're frozen until this one last little chore is completed. I have 31 missions myself; and even though they tell me I get to go home afterward, I'm not looking forward to my 32nd.

I check my watch. "Let's crank her up," I grunt. Cigarettes flick out, and laden down with chutes, tin hats, and ditching gear, we squirm under the bomb-pregnant ship through the hatches to our positions. There is that one last nervous check: covers ripped off the turrets, red sand wiped off the plexiglass, fuel caps checked and safetied, the new N-7 low-level bombsight examined, bomb load, electrical and hydraulic system checked, the controls tested. Item by item, we go over the list of hundreds of final checks, just as we have done on the 31 previous missions.

Our planes sit in column formation on the ground, parked for swift take-off time, the nervous bark of engines becomes a sustained roar and the planes — "Sad Sack," "Old Baldy," "Vulgar Virgin," then finally "Liberty Lad" — lumber down to the end of the taxi strip and rev up for a final check of the mags. Then there's a surge, a sagging forward, the long, long roll down the desert strip into the billowing clouds of blinding red sand, and finally we jockey our 65,000 pounds of plane, crew, and load into the blue Mediterranean skies.

177 planes and 500,000 pounds of bombs on a strike against Hitler's fuel tank. Ahead: 2100 miles and 14 hours of flying, balloon barrages, flak, fighters — and possible death.

We wheel at 2000 feet waiting for the other squadrons to burst through the clouds of swirling sand and sort themselves out into column formation. Our outfit, the 93rd—the "Flying Circus"—tightens up behind Col. Addison Baker. My eyes are already glued to the squadron leader whom I'll have to shadow for the next 14 hours if I'm going to hold formation the way I should. Compton's 376th sweeps up,

the "Killer" Kane's 98th, the 36 planes of Col. Johnson's 44th, the 30 ships in Col. Wood's 389th. Loose and ragged as yet, unafraid of fighters or flak, we shape up into a column of aircraft five miles long and drone out toward Corfu and the Albanian coast.

"Pilot to navigator."

"Pilot to tail gunner."

We check out our intercoms. All okay. There are tracers arching against the blue ahead of us and I pass the word to the gunners to join the other aircraft in checking their fifties. Bursts of fire from above me, in the waist and the tail, mark the rounds popped off into the sea. For a while anyway, it's easy going as we plod along at 160 m.p.h. I turn the controls over to Podgurski, my co-pilot, and play combat correspondent by snapping a few pictures. A nice souvenir for my grandchildren.

"I can't see anything wrong with those ships," one gunner cracks to another over the intercom. There's a trace of envy in these words as we watch a couple of planes wheel out of formation and head back home. The commanders have found something wrong with the planes and have decided that they cannot successfully complete the raid. We hate to lose a single plane on this one; we need every bomb we can possibly lug over Ploesti.

The hours wear on in a continuous roar, the plane sucking up her 202 gallons of fuel per hour without a hitch. The men chomp on their taste-

191

less combat rations with the normal amount of complaining about G.I. food. Ahead lies the German-held island of Corfu and we maneuver to pass well west, then north of it to avoid giving the German radar a look at the size and direction of our formation. Our gunners begin to search the sky for the Messerschmitt 109s or Focke-Wulfs, which just possibly might be lurking there.

We see a plane in the formation ahead swing out of formation. Is he in trouble? Strict radio silence freezes us all; no one dares even to ask who it is or if anything's wrong. It turns out to be death in the silence of pantomime. The Lib drops away from the formation, plunges seaward and explodes in a burst of greasy smoke and spray beneath us.

"Poor bastards," someone mutters as we stare, looking for the parachutes that never blossom. When it's all over, we shudder and yet think to ourselves, Thank God that this one didn't involve us.

As we cross the coastline, we come to grips with clouds and mountains. A flare pops out of Baker's Liberator to tell us he's applying power to climb over the cumulus that is settling down on the mountaintops ahead of us. I shove the throttles a couple of notches closer to the firewall and painfully, sluggishly, a weary "Liberty Lad" lugs its 30 tons up a couple of thousand feet. We clamp our oxygen masks over our mouths.

The mountains are topped finally

and, wingtip to wingtip, we begin to drop out of the miles of billowing clouds toward relatively clear skies over the plains of Rumania. Pod points excitedly to a large river ahead of us and laughs into the intercom: "That can't be the Danube, guys. It ain't blue." But it is the Danube, and we circle over the river twice at about 4000 feet, squeezing together into tight formational alignment.

Still, there's been no flak, no fighters, no foul-ups. And no news is good news, I figure, as we wheel into combat line and wait for the mission commander to lead his 177 planes toward the target.

We head for Pitesti, the town that's the group's first navigational checkpoint. We're to fly over Pitesti, then Targoviste, then turn right at Floresti — our IP — on a heading of 127 per cent, making our bomb run on Target White, the Concordia Vega lube oil cracking plant in the midst of the Ploesti industrial complex.

Streaming over Pitesti, we're right on schedule, radio silence is still intact and we're down to less than 500 feet, low to duck in under the German radar. It's like a Mack Sennett movie all the way. Farm couples down in the streets fall on their knees to pray. Kids toss rocks at us. Horses bolt, overturning wagons full of families. A gal bathing nude in a river almost pulls the entire outfit off course.

My men are now talking and joking nervously over the intercom. As we get closer to Ploesti, though, the idle chatter dies away.

Suddenly the 376th is turning right, following a railroad spur. We're boxed in, so we wing over gently and slide back into formation. Mordovancy, my new navigator (four former navigators had been mortally wounded by flak fragments over Italy), up front in the nose, clicks on his intercom and says simply, "I think we turned too soon."

Pod looks agitated, too, as he chimes in, "We were supposed to turn on the third town, not the second. I think that was Targoviste we just went over!"

The knot in my stomach's getting even tighter.

Polka dots of black burst in a row above us, and fragments platter like hail off the ship. I pull in my neck instinctively and drop the plane another 50 feet. The whole squadron seems to hug the ground just a little bit harder with every splatter of flak. In the waists, the guys are opening up at the flak pits. It's like a cow-town gun fight at close quarters now, instead of the impersonal combat at 20,000 feet that we're used to.

"Pick up that flak tower to the right!"

"There's another gun emplacement coming up on the left!"

"I think I can see fire from an eighty-eight battery ahead."

"Tail gunner, what did we do to those emplacements we just passed over?"

Now we're dropping lower, lower, flying faster. And a city is ahead of us at last!

"It's too big for Ploesti," Pod shouts. "God it's Bucharest! We did turn too soon!"

The whole group now swings to the left, wheeling away from Bucharest in search of the target which still is more than 14 minutes away. It's not a battle now, planned and precise, but more like a barroom brawl with every man for himself. Compton's planes sweep off to the right, but Baker leads our group right into the flak barrage.

We hit Ploesti from the strong side in — instead of the weak; haystacks open up to sprout machine guns; houses fold their roofs back to unveil belching flak emplacements. Ground crews are running up barrage balloons all around us.

I yell at Podgurski once again. "Keep your hands and feet on the controls in case I get my head blown off."

All guns are firing now and the ship shakes convulsively. Everybody up front calls out targets and the gunners pour fifty-calibre tracers in as we streak past. I don't see if we're scoring, but the gunners are yelling excitedly so I guess we're blasting our share of ground emplacements. I notice plenty of German camouflage, dummy tanks, and so on. Some of the installations have blast walls around them. They'll be tough to knock out.

Smoke pots bubble cloudily below us. We're getting into the heart of the target area and the Jerries are trying

193

to mask it, but the smoke is least effective at noon — one original reason for the timing of our attack. Flashes and black, oil columns of smoke reveal where preceding bombers have already come in and dropped their load. That knot in my stomach tightens another notch as I realize we'll be crossing at 50 feet over gasoline storage tanks that have already been hit with delayed-action bombs timed to go off at any moment.

We're over a target. It's a refining area, though, and I begin to look for a likely cracking plant to home in on.

A Liberator ahead is hit and streams scarlet flame from the waist window. Still the pilot presses home the attack. I see the bombs drop. Then he pulls the ship up sharply, trying desperately to give his men enough altitude to bail out. One . . . two . . . three rag dolls pop out, half-open white chutes flowing behind them. The Liberator shudders, and drops down in a ball of fire. The three parachutes drop right into the holocaust.

Tracers lace the air. A bomb explodes and a gas-storage tank rises 1000 feet into the air between two Liberators. I see another ship go into a black, oily cloud; it never comes out. Baker's plane is on fire; still he presses home his attack and drops his bombs. Then his ship somersaults to the ground in a flaming skid.

A ship from the 93rd hits something — a balloon cable, I suddenly realize. The ship slides up the cable, seems to break through, then suddenly its tail snaps completely off and the plane squirts into a fiery trail along the ground.

The turbulence is terrific. Prop wash and the hurricane-like gusts of hot air from the exploding oil tanks are tossing our Lib around like a leaf.

The next moments are a crescendo of light and noise. Nine rounds of anti-aircraft fire explode against the fuselage, starting just aft of the cockpit and lacing us from there to the tail — four rounds smashing us from the left, five from the right. We're seared by the odor of cordite, blinded by the smoke of the fires started in the nose section, deafened by the roar of the explosions. We've been chopped badly by twenty-millimeters, point-blank cross-fire. The ship sags, but miraculously maintains flying speed.

Pod yells at me, pointing to the instrument panel: "Number Three is running away. Shall I feather it?" he asks.

I need every ounce of power I can get. "Let the son of a bitch wind off," I yell.

A cracking plant looms up ahead of us. The leader is dropping his bombs, and I head for it, too. Slade the bombardier, also sees it, and the plane slows perceptibly as he rolls the bomb-bay doors open.

We pass directly over the plant, and our six 500-pounders and a scattering of incendiaries drop behind us.

We crank the bomb-bay doors closed. With them shut, the battered plane picks up speed and we maneu-

"A cracking plant looms up ahead of us. The leader is dropping his bombs, and I head for it, too."
The Astra Romana refinery, Ploesti.

ver better through the curtain flak and oil explosions.

I spot a river and hug it as we try to sneak out of Ploesti. We're so low that our props kick up a feathery spray. Splashes all around us reveal the lattice-work of small-arms cross-fire being poured down on us from the riverbanks. We're alone; I don't see a single other of the more than 150 planes that went to Ploesti.

I'm not thinking at all now about our prearranged escape route and rendezvous at Lake Balta-Potelel, 120 miles to the south. I just want to get the hell out of the flak and head for home. There's a hill ahead and we climb slowly toward it. It seems to be a hundred miles away and our plane seems to move only inches each minute. We finally roar across the crest and the flak slacks off. Ahead? Ahead there are Liberators — one . . . two . . . four . . . a half-dozen. Like sleepwalkers they're cruising aimlessly — no formation — shocked silly.

Somehow a formation evolves and we nestle into it. Dazedly, we make a feeble attempt to assess the damage the flak has done to the plane. Our radio is smashed, so we can't communicate. Our intercom and oxygen systems have been shredded with shell fragments. Our trim tabs are out, too, but somehow Podgurski and I are managing to fly the plane even with the control surfaces chopped up as they are. Engine 3 has me worried.

The formation climbs to 1000 feet, heading for the Danube, the mountains, and the coast.

Johnnie Brown, in the top turret, begins yelling, so I know that fighters are heading our way. I concentrate on keeping the plane low and tucked into formation.

The German guns wink at us for 15 minutes but we stick together and only one goes down. Finally, with a last snarling pass, they head for home base.

We're flying a shattered aircraft, nearly 1000 miles from safety. But suddenly we feel as if we have it made; the worst seems over.

Smathers, our radioman, sticks his head in the cockpit. "Go back and lie down," I order him. Flak fragments have made him a mass of blood from head to foot, his khakis blackened and wet. In back, they patch him up with their first-aid kits. Later, he pops his head in again, and insists he's all right and he thinks can get our radio receivers working.

The cumulus over the mountains has ballooned to 40,000 feet by this time and as we climb to breast the range, we find a comparatively clear path at about 15,000 — several thousand feet over the rugged peaks. Occasional cloud patches down on the deck gives us the willies but this seems trivial and pretty risk-free after Ploesti. Or at least we feel that way until we see two Liberators move side by side into billowing cumulus and then watch, horrified, as pieces of airplane — the deadly drizzle of a mid-air collision — rain out of the cloud.

196

Once over the mountains, I tell Johnnie Brown to begin pumping our reserve fuel from the two bomb-bay tanks to our wing tanks.

The odor of gas tells me the bad news even before Johnnie clambers back into the cockpit to give it to me himself. "We can't pump into 1 and 2," he reports. "The fuel lines are cut or collapsed."

Things don't look so rosy any more. With only two engines, we're going to have to baby the plane for more than 500 miles if we're to get home.

I make the first of several tough decisions. Do we turn back while we still have power and bail out to become POWs, or do we take a chance and continue heading out over the Med, where bailing out is usually fatal? I decide I don't want to be a POW.

There is mechanical sputtering and coughing; Number 1 has exhausted its fuel supply. Podgurski feathers the prop and both of us hit the right rudder pedal a little harder to keep the ship on course. The aircraft begins to sag slightly, dropping behind and below the squadron. I don't even dare tamper with our worthiness to the extent of waggling our wings in the age-old sign of distress. "I just hope those lucky stiffs remember to tell Rescue where they left us," someone mutters.

Below us is the coast of Greece; behind us, the enemy. Ahead of us is the Axis-controlled Mediterranean Sea, and with us, that gnawing question: Will the ship stay in the air when the Number 2 engine runs dry?

We don't have long to wait for an answer. In 15 minutes, Number 2 croaks its last. Both Pod and I give the plane full right rudder and sick Number 3 — and 4, take up the strain. Down we go, gradually, but down nevertheless. The slightest relaxing of pressure and the plane tends to lurch dangerously to the left. She still drops.

Drops too fast, in fact! I pass the word to toss out everything that we don't absolutely need. There are going to be a few surprised fish below. Oxygen bottles, fire extinguishers, the AAF's beautiful new aerial camera, ammunition boxes — these stream out of the hatches in a hurry.

Johnnie Brown comes forward and asks, "The guns, too?"

We're still within fighter range but we have to chance it. Ten well-used fifty-calibres and a couple of hundred pounds of ammunition go over the side, too. Back in the ship, the crew pick up fire-axes and start chopping away at any excess metal or insulation they think may be weighting "Liberty Lad" down. The chopped chunks of metal go out, then the fire-axes.

Smathers and Brown huddle over the shattered communication equipment. I pass word back to the rest of the men to get into ditching position, sitting on the floor, oarsman-style, with their backs to the forward bulkhead.

Down the ship continues to drop, the altimeter flicking off the footage as we are drawn slowly but continuously toward the sea: 6500 feet . . . 6000 . . .

5500 . . .

Brown, standing by, stuffs a couple of extra chutes behind our back to give us all the leverage we need to keep full rudder pressure for the fight to keep her up and on course. At 5000 feet the ship finally seems to level out. Denser air, jettisoning the equipment and the ever-lightening fuel load have resulted in equilibrium. Now all Podgurski and I have to do is fly this crate 700 miles home on the strength of our leg muscles.

The seconds become minutes. Our thighs and calves tighten and knot with cramps. The minutes become hours. Our legs go to sleep and Brown massages them, encouraging us all the time.

Then we get a break. Smathers sticks his banged up old head — bandages, blood and all — into the cockpit and tells me that he has the radio receiver and transmitter operating and can work 3460 KC, the squadron's operational frequency. We can now request and receive QDM's directional fixes from our AAF station 75X at Misuita, Libya. There's at least a chance that we'll now be able to find out what direction to fly toward home base. We shift course gingerly at each new fix and I shave 10° off every fix just to make sure we don't miss the point of land we're heading for and spend an extra hour of flying over the Gulf of Sirte.

"Land!"

Podgurski sees it first, a thin black line along the horizon. The sun is dropping rapidly as we strain ahead to see if indeed we have finally crossed the Med. But then we look again and realize the lowering sun has played a cruel trick on us. There is no land, only the unending gray of the sea into which we may have to plunge this ship at any moment. And ditching at night in the sea is almost certain suicide.

Land? This time I think I see it. But I dare not disappoint myself and the crew by announcing it. "Johnnie Brown, come up for a second," I ask. He pops up and I tell him to take a look for me. He stares intently at the horizon.

It is land. He passes the word and this time the cheer we get from behind must be audible all the way back to Ploesti.

As we cross the coastline in the gathering dusk, we breathe a collective sigh of relief. Here, at least, it will be comparatively safe to bail out should everything fail. But I'm determined now to bring the ship in. Our QDM tells me we're north of the base and I gingerly turn the plane to the right. In a short while, Benghasi is below us. Ahead I see an airstrip . . . it isn't our Site 7, but the 376th's field. Any port in a storm. Besides, they've got a hospital there and Smathers is still bleeding and in pretty bad shape.

Brown reaches above him and triggers the Very flare gun, arching a couple of red streaks against the pitch black, Tunisian sky. The base floodlights the landing strip in return and Brown pumps our wheels down by hand.

I make my turn into the final approach at 2000 feet using one-half flaps. Then everything in the ship cuts out, I lose all my instrument light and am sitting in darkness trying to bring this cripple in.

Brown flicks on his flashlight and focuses it on my airspeed indicator. I hold it at 120 m.p.h. If it increases, I know I'm diving the ship too much; if it decreases, I know I'm approaching stall angle. I hold it . . . hold it . . . hold it . . . hold it — and then with the screech of smoking rubber, we pile onto the runway and begin a roll that lasts for 6000 feet. No brakes.

As we stop, the ambulance, a jeep, and fire trucks surround us.

We sit at our positions with hardly a word. Slade comes up to me and shakes my hand. "If I'd known you were even thinking of landing this junk heap, Lieutenant, I would have bailed out twenty minutes ago," he says. He congratulates me, though, for so nimbly dodging the balloon cables over the target area. I don't dare tell him that I never saw a one of the cables he is talking about.

Our mission to Ploesti is over.

EDITOR'S NOTE

Shortly after takeoff, "aborts" began. Eleven dropped out as the formation crossed the Mediterranean, including the lead navigation ship. Its place was taken by Col. Keith Compton flying the mission commander Gen. Uzal Ent, and an inexperienced navigator. Once across the Mediterranean high cloud formations split the armada. Col. John R. "Killer" Kane led his 96th Group under while others climbed over the top. This split shattered the time factor, so important in surprise. Shrouded in radio silence, the formation elements quickly lost contact with each other and proceeded independently.

Well into Rumania, Compton, leading his 376th Group misidentified a checkpoint, turned his group for the run to Ploesti and ended up over the suburbs of Bucharest, the Rumanian capital. Blindly following was the 93rd Group. By the time both swung left toward Ploesti the cat was out of the bag and alerted German defenses all along the final flight path threw up a deadly barrage of flak. The same reception met the other formations farther north. Air battle organization and discipline vanished. Time over targets could not be met. Briefed approaches were impossible and bombardiers took pot luck. Squadrons off schedule caught the fury of delayed-action explosions. Dense, choking smoke from raging oil fires blacked-out target areas. German flak, small-arms fire, dangling balloon cables and towering smokestacks hidden in the pall that enveloped the target turned Ploesti into a valley of death. Bombers were seen to penetrate solid walls of fire, emerge white and scorched. A few, mortally wounded on the bomb run, deliberately dove their craft into the targets. Scores of German fighters craftily waited to jump the limping armada on its way home. Out of 194 B-24s which took off from Africa, 177 made it to the target and about one-third never made it back. Neither did

"Dense, choking smoke from raging oil fires blacked-out target areas." These captured German films record the intense damage caused by the bombing of Ploesti on August 1, 1943.

440 airmen, while 200 more wound up in German POW camps and 79 were interned in neutral Turkey where some of the bombers, short of return flight fuel, had landed.

While the Ploesti damage (40 per cent of production), was repaired and the plant returned to full capacity in a month, the threat of a repeat performance tied down large elements of the Luftwaffe for the next nine critical months. Renewed attacks on Ploesti began in the spring of 1944 by the Italian-based Fifteenth Air Force and by August, 1944 it was in ruins.

Two weeks following Ploesti, the second great epic in the strategic air campaign took place in the skies deep over Germany. It was a twin-pronged strike at industrial targets in the cities of Regensburg and Schweinfurt. The Messerschmitt factory at Regensburg produced nearly half of the Luftwaffe's single-engine fighters while Schweinfurt housed the Nazis' great ball-bearing works, producing about 50 per cent of Germany's total. Destruction of these industries would put a dent in Hitler's capacity to wage war, and appreciably reduce the industrial base of the Luftwaffe.

Schweinfurt lay 200 miles beyond Allied fighter escort range, while Regensburg was 100 miles farther on. The mission plan called for two waves, the first force of 146 bombers to strike Regensburg and the second of 230 heavies to hit the factories at Schweinfurt.

The bold mission got underway on the morning of August 17, with the Regensburg force in the van. Dropping their fighter escort near the German border, the B-17s were immediately set upon by hordes of Luftwaffe fighters who were called in by German controllers from as far away as the Baltic. The ferocious attack continued for an hour and a half — ten thousand eternities to the crews. But the formations rammed through despite the violent loss of 24 big craft and damaged every building in the Messerschmitt plant. While the Luftwaffe waited to bounce the force again on its way home, the formation blithely turned south and flew over the Alps to bases in Africa.

The Schweinfurt Force which was to follow immediately on the heels of the Regensburg bombers, was delayed by weather for 3½ hours. Had it been on time it would have slipped relatively easily into Schweinfurt while the Luftwaffe was hitting the Regensburg-bound formation. But being late, by the time the Schweinfurt B-17s dropped their escort and reached Germany, Luftwaffe fighters had refueled, rested, and rearmed; and they rose up for the second time in a day to press the attack on the huge formation during the entire mission to and from target. Out of 230 bombers dispatched, 36 were lost and nearly 100 were shot into crippling condition. Air crew casualties were atrocious. So ferocious and sustained was the Luftwaffe attack that crews fought until they were completely exhausted. Even so, the formation made 80 direct hits on the two ball-bearing works.

Lt. Col. Beirne Lay, Jr. (today a well-known movie, television, magazine, and book writer) vividly describes how it was in the skies over Germany that day from his co-pilot's seat on a Regensburg-bound B-17.

I Saw Regensburg Destroyed

Lt. Col. Beirne Lay, Jr.

IN THE BRIEFING ROOM, the intelligence officer of the bombardment group pulled a cloth screen away from a huge wall map. Each of the 240 sleepy-eyed combat-crew members in the crowded room leaned forward. There were low whistles. I felt a sting of anticipation as I stared at the red string on the map that stretched from our base in England to a pinpoint deep in Southern Germany, then south across the Alps, through the Brenner Pass to the coast of Italy, then past Corsica and Sardinia and south over the Mediterranean to a desert airdrome in North Africa. You could have heard an oxygen mask drop.

"Your primary," said the intelligence officer, "is Regensburg. Your aiming point is the center of the Messerschmitt One Hundred and Nine G aircraft-and-engine assembly shops. This is the most vital target we've ever gone after. If you destroy it, you destroy 30 per cent of the Luftwaffe's single-engine fighter production. You

fellows know what that means to you personally."

There were a few hollow laughs.

After the briefing, I climbed aboard a jeep bound for the operations office to check up on my Fortress assignment. The stars were dimly visible through the chilly mist that covered our blacked-out bomber station, but the weather forecast for a deep penetration over the Continent was good. In the office, I looked at the crew sheet, where the line-up of the lead, low, and high squadrons of the group is plotted for each mission. I was listed for a co-pilot's seat. While I stood there, and on the chance suggestion of one of the squadron commanders who was looking over the list, the operations officer erased my name and shifted me to the high squadron as co-pilot in the crew of a steady Irishman named Lt. Murphy, with whom I had flown before. Neither of us knew it, but that operations officer saved my life right there with a piece of rubber on the end of a pencil.

At 5:30 A.M., 15 minutes before taxi time, a jeep drove around the five-mile perimeter track in the semi-darkness, pausing at each dispersal point long enough to notify the waiting crews that poor local visibility would postpone the takeoff for an hour and a half. I was sitting with Murphy and the rest of our crew near the "Piccadilly Lily." She looked sinister and complacent, squatting on her fat tires with scarcely a hole in her skin to show for the 12 raids behind her. The postponement tightened, rather than relaxed, the tension. Once more I checked over my life vest, oxygen mask, and parachute, not perfunctorily, but the way you check something you're going to have to use. I made sure my escape kit was pinned securely in the knee pocket of my flying suit, where it couldn't fall out in a scramble to abandon ship. I slid a hunting knife between my shoe and my flying boot as I looked again through my extra equipment for this mission: water canteen, mess kit, blankets, and English pounds for use in the Algerian desert, where we would sleep on the ground and might be on our own from a forced landing.

Murphy restlessly gave the "Piccadilly Lily" another once-over, inspecting ammunition belts, bomb bay, tires, and oxygen pressure at each crew station. Especially the oxygen. It's human fuel, as important as gasoline, up where we operate. Gunners fieldstripped their .50 calibres again and

oiled the bolts. Our top-turret gunner lay in the grass with his head on his parachute, feigning sleep, sweating out his 13th start.

We shared a common knowledge which grimly enhanced the normal excitement before a mission. Of the approximately 150 Fortresses who were hitting Regensburg, our group was the last and lowest, at a base altitude of 17,000 feet. That's well within the range of accuracy for heavy flak. Our course would take us over plenty of it. It was a cinch also that our group would be the softest touch for the enemy fighters, being last man through the gantlet. Furthermore, the "Piccadilly Lily" was leading the last three ships of the high squadron — the tip of the tail end of the whole shebang. We didn't relish it much. Who wants a Purple Heart?

The minute hand of my wrist watch dragged. I caught myself thinking about the day, exactly one year ago, on August 17, 1942, when I watched a pitifully small force of 12 B-17s take off on the first raid of the Eighth Air Force to make a shallow penetration against Rouen, France. On that day it was our maximum effort. Today, on our first anniversary, we were putting 30 times that number of heavies into the air — half the force on Regensburg and half the force on Schweinfurt, both situated inside the interior of the German Reich. For a year and a half, as a staff officer, I had watched the Eighth Air Force grow under Maj. Gen. Ira C. Eaker. That's a long time to watch

Over Schweinfurt, an Me-110 goes down in flames before the guns of American Flying Fortresses.

from behind a desk. Only 10 days ago I had asked for and received orders to combat duty. Those 10 days had been full of the swift action of participating in four combat missions and checking out for the first time as a four-engine pilot.

Now I knew that it can be easier to be shot at than telephoned at. That staff officers at an air force headquarters are the unsung heroes of this war. And yet I found myself reminiscing just a little affectionately about that desk, wondering if there wasn't a touch of suicide in store for our group. One thing was sure: headquarters had dreamed up the biggest air operation to date to celebrate its birthday in the biggest league of aerial warfare.

At 7:30 we broke out of the cloud tops into the glare of the rising sun. Beneath our B-17 lay English fields, still blanketed in the thick mist from which we had just emerged. We continued to climb slowly, our broad wings shouldering a heavy load of incendiary bombs in the belly and a burden of fuel in the main and wing-tip! Tokyo tanks that would keep the Fortress afloat in the thin upper altitudes 11 hours.

From my co-pilot's seat on the right-hand side, I watched the white surface of the overcast, where B-17s in clusters of six to the squadron were puncturing the cloud deck all about us, rising clear of the mist with their glass noses slanted upward for the long climb to base altitude. We tacked on to one of these clutches of six. Now the sky over England was heavy with the weight of thousands of tons of bombs, fuel, and men being lifted four miles straight up on a giant aerial hoist to the western terminus of a 20,000-foot elevated highway that led east to Regensburg. At intervals I saw the arc of a sputtering red, green, or yellow flare being fired from the cabin roof of a group leader's airplane to identify the lead squadron to the high and low squadrons of each group. Assembly takes longer when you come up through an overcast.

For nearly an hour, still over Southern England, we climbed, nursing the straining Cyclone engines in a 300-foot-per-minute ascent, forming three squadrons gradually into compact group stagger formations — low squadron down to the left and high squadron up to the right of the lead squadron — groups assembling into looser combat wings of two to three groups each along the combat-wing assembly line, homing over predetermined points with radio compass, and finally cruising along the air-division assembly line to allow the combat wings to fall into place in trail behind Col. Curtis E. LeMay in the lead group of the air division.

Formed at last, each flanking group in position 1000 feet above or below its lead group, our 15-mile parade moved east toward Lowestoft, point of departure from the friendly coast, unwieldy, but dangerous to fool with. From my perch in the high squadron in the last element of the whole procession, the air division looked like huge anvil-shaped swarms of locusts — not on dress parade, like the bombers of the Luftwaffe that died like flies over Britain in 1940, but deployed to uncover every gun and permit maneuverability. Our formation was basically that worked out for the air corps by Brig. Gen. Hugh Knerr 20 years ago with 85-mile-an-hour bombers, plus refinements devised by Col. LeMay from experience in the European Theatre.

The English Channel and the North Sea glittered bright in the clear visibility as we left the bulge of East Anglia behind us. Up ahead we knew that we were already registering on the German RDF screen, and that the sector controllers of the Luftwaffe's fighter belt in Western Europe were busy altering their *Staffein* of Focke-Wulfs and Messerschmitts. I stole a last look back at cloud-covered England, where I could see a dozen spare B-17s, who had accompanied us to fill in for any abortives from mechanical failure in the hard climb, gliding disappointedly home to base.

I fastened my oxygen mask a little tighter and looked at the little ball in a glass tube on the instrument panel that indicates proper oxygen flow. It was moving up and down, like a visual heartbeat, as I breathed, registering normal.

Already the gunners were searching. Occasionally the ship shivered as guns were tested with short bursts. I could see puffs of blue smoke from the group close ahead and 1000 feet above us, as each gunner satisfied himself that he had lead poisoning at his trigger tips. The coast of Holland appeared in sharp black outline. I drew in a deep breath of oxygen.

A few miles in front of us were German boys in single-seaters who were probably going to react to us in the same way our boys would react, emotionally, if German bombers were heading for the Pratt & Whitney engine factory at Hartford or the Liberator plant at Willow Run. In the making was a death struggle between the unstoppable object and the immovable defense, every possible defense at the disposal of the Reich, for this was a deadly penetration to a hitherto inaccessible and critically important arsenal of the *Vaterland*.

At 10:00 we crossed the coast of Holland, south of The Hague, with our group of Fortresses tucked in tightly and within handy supporting distance of the group above us, at 18,000 feet. But our long, loose-linked column looked too long, and the gaps between combat wings too wide. As I squinted into the sun, gauging the distance to the barely visible specks of the lead group, I had a recurrence of that sinking feeling before the take-off — the lonesome foreboding that might come to the last man about to run a gantlet lined with spiked clubs. The premonition was well founded.

At 10:17, near Woensdrecht, I saw the first flak blossom out in our vicinity, light and inaccurate. A few minutes later, at approximately 10:25, a gunner called "Fighters at two o'clock low." I saw them, climbing above the horizon ahead of us to the right — a pair of them. For a moment I hoped they were P-47 Thunderbolts from the fighter escort that was supposed to be in our vicinity, but I didn't hope long. The two FW-190s turned and whizzed through the formation ahead of us in a frontal attack, nicking two B-17s in the wings and breaking away in half rolls right over our group. By craning my neck up and back, I glimpsed one of them through the roof glass in the cabin, flashing past at a 600-mile-an-hour rate of closure, his yellow nose smoking and small pieces flying off near the wing root. The guns of our group were in action. The pungent smell of burnt cordite filled the cockpit and the B-17 trembled to the recoil of nose and ball-turret guns. Smoke immediately trailed from the hit B-17s, but they held their stations.

Here was early fighter reaction. The members of the crew sensed trouble. There was something desperate about the way those two fighters came in fast right out of their climb, without any preliminaries. Apparently our own fighters were busy somewhere farther up the procession. The interphone was active for a few seconds with brief admonitions: "Lead 'em more." . . . "Short bursts." . . . "Don't throw rounds away." . . . "Bombardier to left waist gunner, don't yell. Talk slow."

Three minutes later the gunners reported fighters climbing up from all around the clock, singly and in pairs, both FW-190s and Me-109-Gs. The fighters I could see on my side looked like too many for sound health. No friendly Thunderbolts were visible. From now on we were in mortal danger. A co-ordinated attack began, with the head-on fighters coming in from slightly above, the nine and three o'clock attackers approaching from about level and the rear attackers from slightly below. The guns from every B-17 in our group and the group ahead were firing simultaneously, lashing the sky with ropes or orange tracers to match the chain-puff bursts squirting from the 20-mm cannon muzzles in the wings of the jerry single-seaters.

I noted with alarm that a lot of our fire was falling astern of the target — particularly from our hand-held nose and waist guns. Nevertheless, both sides got hurt in this clash, with the entire second element of three B-17s from our low squadron and one B-17 from the group ahead falling out of formation on fire, with crews bailing out, and several fighters heading for the deck in flames or with their pilots lingering behind under the dirty yellow canopies that distinguished some of their parachutes from ours. Our

twenty-four-year-old group leader, flying only his third combat mission, pulled us up even closer to the preceding group for mutual support.

As we swung slightly outside with our squadron, in mild evasive action, I got a good look at that gap in the low squadron where three B-17s had been. Suddenly I bit my lip hard. The lead ship of that element had pulled out on fire and exploded before anyone bailed out. It was the ship to which I had been originally assigned.

I glanced over at Murphy. It was cold in the cockpit, but sweat was running from his forehead and over his oxygen mask from the exertion of holding his element in tight formation and the strain of the warnings that hummed over the interphone and what he could see out of the corners of his eyes. He caught my glance and turned the controls over to me for a while. It was an enormous relief to concentrate on flying instead of sitting there watching fighters aiming between your eyes. Somehow, the attacks from the rear, although I could see them through my ears via the interphone, didn't bother me. I guess it was because there was a slab of armor plate behind my back and I couldn't watch them, anyway.

I knew that we were in a lively fight. Every alarm bell in my brain and heart was ringing a high-pitched warning. But my nerves were steady and my brain working. The fear was unpleasant, but it was bearable. I knew that I was going to die, and so were a lot of others. What I didn't know was that the real fight, the *Anschluss* of Luftwaffe 20-mm cannon shells, hadn't really begun. The largest and most savage fighter resistance of any war in history was rising to stop us at any cost, and our group was the most vulnerable target.

A few minutes later we absorbed the first wave of a hailstorm of individual fighter attacks that were to engulf us clear to the target in such a blizzard of bullets and shells that a chronological account is difficult. It was at 10:41, over Eupen, that I looked out the window after a minute's lull, and saw two whole squadrons, twelve Me-109s and eleven FW-190s climbing parallel to us as though they were on a steep escalator. The first squadron had reached our level and was pulling ahead to turn into us. The second was not far behind. Several thousand feet below us were many more fighters, their noses cocked up in a maximum climb. Over the interphone came reports of an equal number of enemy aircraft deploying on the other side of the formation.

For the first time I noticed an Me-110 sitting out of range on our level out to the right. He was to stay with us all the way to the target, apparently radioing our position and weak spots to fresh *Staffein* waiting farther down the road.

At the sight of all these fighters, I had the distinct feeling of being trapped — that the Hun had been tipped off or at least had guessed our destination and was set for us. We were already through the German fighter belt. Obviously, they had moved a lot of squadrons back in a fluid defense in depth, and they must have been saving up some outfits for the inner defense we didn't know about. The life expectancy of our group seemed definitely limited, since it had already appeared that the fighters, instead of wasting fuel trying to overhaul the preceding groups, were glad to take a cut at us.

Swinging their yellow noses around in a wide U-turn, the 12-ship squadron of Me-109s came in from twelve to two o'clock in pairs. The main event was on. I fought an impulse to close my eyes, and overcame it.

A shining silver rectangle of metal sailed past over our right wing. I recognized it as a main-exit door. Seconds later, a black lump came hurtling through the formation, barely missing several propellers. It was a man, clasping his knees to his head, revolving like a diver in a triple somersault, shooting by us so close that I saw a piece of paper blow out of his leather jacket. He was evidently making a delayed jump, for I didn't see his parachute open.

A B-17 turned gradually out of the formation to the right, maintaining altitude. In a split second it completely vanished in a brilliant explosion, from which the only remains were four balls of fire, the fuel tanks, which were quickly consumed as they fell earthward.

I saw blue, red, yellow, and aluminum-colored fighters. Their tactics were running fairly true to form, with frontal attacks hitting the low squadron and rear attackers going for the lead and high squadrons. Some of the jerries shot at us with rockets, and an attempt at air-to-air bombing was made with little black time-fuse sticks, dropped from above, which exploded in small gray puffs off to one side of the formation. Several of the FWs did some nice deflection shooting on side attacks from 500 yards at the high group, then raked the low group on the breakaway at closer range with their noses cocked in a side slip, to keep the formation in their sights longer in the turn. External fuel tanks were visible under the bellies or wings of at least two squadrons, shedding uncomfortable light on the mystery of their ability to tail us so far from their bases.

The manner of the assaults indicated that the pilots knew where we were going and were inspired with a fanatical determination to stop us before we got there. Many pressed attacks home to 250 yards or less, or bolted right through the formation wide out, firing long 20-second bursts, often presenting point-blank targets on the breakaway. Some committed the fatal error of pulling up instead of going down and out. More experienced pilots came in on frontal attacks with a noticeably slower rate of closure, apparently throttled back, obtaining greater accuracy. But no tactics could halt the close-knit juggernauts of our

Fortresses, nor save the single-seaters from paying a terrible price.

Our airplane was endangered by various debris. Emergency hatches, exit doors, prematurely opened parachutes, bodies and assorted fragments of B-17s and Hun fighters breezed past us in the slipstream.

I watched two fighters explode not far beneath, disappear in sheets of orange flame; B-17s dropping out in every stage of distress, from engines on fire to control shot away; friendly and enemy parachutes floating down, and, on the green carpet far below us, funeral pyres of smoke from fallen fighters, marking our trail.

On we flew through the cluttered wake of a desperate air battle, where disintegrating aircraft were commonplace and the white dots of 60 parachutes in the air at one time were hardly worth a second look. The spectacle registering on my eyes became so fantastic that my brain turned numb to the actuality of the death and destruction all around us. Had it not been for the squeezing in my stomach, which I was trying to purge, I might easily have been watching an animated cartoon in a movie theater.

The minutes dragged on into an hour. And still the fighters came. Our gunners called coolly and briefly to one another, dividing up their targets, fighting for their lives with every round of ammunition — and our lives, and the formation. The tail gunner called that he was out of ammunition. We sent another belt back to him.

Here was a new hazard. We might run out of .50-calibre slugs before we reached the target.

I looked to both sides of us. Our two wing men were gone. So was the element in front of us — all three ships. We moved up into position behind the lead element of the high squadron. I looked out again on my side and saw a cripple, with one prop feathered, struggle up behind our right wing with his bad engine funneling smoke into the slipstream. He dropped back. Now our tail gunner had a clear view. There were no more B-17s behind us. We were the last man.

I took the controls for a while. The first thing I saw when Murphy resumed flying was a B-17 turning slowly out to the right; its cockpit was a mass of flames. The co-pilot crawled out of his window, held on with one hand, reached back for his parachute, buckled it on, let go and was whisked back into the horizontal stabilizer of the tail. I believe the impact killed him. His parachute didn't open.

I looked forward and almost ducked as I watched the tail gunner of a B-17 ahead of us take a bead right on our windshield and cut loose with a stream of tracers that missed us by a few feet

The air battles between German fighters and American bombers were replete with tense moments. In this painting by C. E. Turner a Focke-Wulf FW-190 is making a head-on attack on a Boeing B-17.

as he fired on a fighter attacking us from six o'clock low. I almost ducked again when our own top-turret gunner's twin muzzles pounded away a foot above my head in the full forward position, giving a realistic imitation of cannon shells exploding in the cockpit, while I gave an even better imitation of a man jumping six inches out of his seat.

Still no letup. The fighters queued up like a breadline and let us have it. Each second of time had a cannon shell in it. The strain of being a clay duck in the wrong end of that aerial shooting gallery became almost intolerable. Our "Picadilly Lily" shook steadily with the fire of the .50s, and the air inside was wispy with smoke. I checked the engine instruments for the thousandth time. Normal. No injured crew members yet. Maybe we'd get to that target, even with our reduced fire power. Seven Fortresses from our group had already gone down and many of the rest of us were badly shot up and short-handed because of wounded crew members.

Almost disinterestedly I observed a B-17 pull out from the group preceding us and drop back to a position about 200 feet from our right wingtip. His right Tokyo tanks were on fire, and had been for a half-hour. Now the smoke was thicker. Flames were licking through the blackened skin of the wings. While the pilot held her steady, I saw four crew members drop out the bomb bay and execute delayed jumps. Another bailed from the nose, opened his parachute prematurely and nearly fouled the tail. Another went out the left-waist-gun opening, delaying his opening for a safe interval. The tail gunner dropped out of his hatch, apparently pulling the ripcord before he was clear of the ship. His parachute opened instantaneously, barely missing the tail, and jerked him so hard that both of his shoes came off. He hung limp in the harness, whereas the others had shown immediate signs of life, shifting around in their harness. The Fortress then dropped back in a medium spiral and I did not see the pilots leave. I saw the ship though, just before it trailed from view, belly to the sky, its wing a solid sheet of yellow flame.

Now that we had been under constant attack for more than an hour, it appeared certain that our group was faced with extinction. The sky was still mottled with rising fighters. Target time was 35 minutes away. I doubt if a man in the group visualized the possibility of our getting much farther without 100 per cent loss. Gunners were becoming exhausted and nerve-tortured from the nagging strain — the strain that sends gunners and pilots to the rest home. We had been aiming point for what looked like most of the Luftwaffe. It looked as though we might find the rest of it primed for us at the target.

At this hopeless point, a young squadron commander down in the low squadron was living through his finest hour. His squadron had lost its second element of three ships early in the fight, south of Antwerp, yet he had consistently maintained his vulnerable and exposed position in the formation rigidly in order to keep the guns of his three remaining ships well uncovered to protect the belly of the formation. Now, nearing the target, battle damage was catching up with him fast. A 20-mm cannon shell penetrated the right side of his airplane and exploded beneath him, damaging the electrical system and cutting the top-turret gunner in the leg. A second 20-mm entered the radio compartment, killing the radio operator, who bled to death with his legs severed above the knees. A third 20-mm shell entered the left side of the nose, tearing out a section about two feet square, tore away the right-hand-nose-gun installations and injured the bombardier in the head and shoulder. A fourth 20-mm shell penetrated the right wing into the fuselage system, releasing fluid all over the cockpit. A fifth 20-mm shell punctured the cabin roof and severed the rudder cables to one side of the rudder. A sixth 20-mm shell exploded in the Number 3 engine, destroying all controls to the engine. The engine caught fire and lost its power, but eventually I saw the fire go out.

Confronted with structural damage, partial loss of control, fire in the air and serious injuries to personnel, and faced with fresh waves of fighters still; rising to the attack, this commander was justified in abandoning ship. His crew, some of them compara-tively inexperienced youngsters, were preparing to bail out. The co-pilot pleaded repeatedly with him to bail out. His reply at this critical juncture was blunt. His words were heard over the interphone and had a magical effect on the crew. They stuck to their guns. The B-17 kept on.

Near the initial point, at 11:50, one hour and a half after the first of at least 200 individual fighter attacks, the pressure eased off, although hostiles were still in the vicinity. A curious sensation came over me. I was still alive. It was possible to think of the target. Of North Africa. Of returning to England. Almost idly, I watched a crippled B-17 pull over to the curb and drop its wheels and open its bomb bay, jettisoning its bombs. Three Me-109s circled it closely, but held their fire while the crew bailed out. I remembered now that a little while back I had seen other Hun fighters hold their fire, even when being shot at by a B-17 from which the crew were bailing. But I doubt if sportsmanship had anything to do with it. They hoped to get a B-17 down fairly intact.

And then our weary, battered col-umn, short 24 bombers, but still holding the close formation that had brought the remainder through by sheer air discipline and gunnery, turned in to the target. I knew that our bombardiers were grim as death while they synchronized their sights on the great Me-109 shops lying below us in a curve of the winding Blue Danube, close to the outskirts of Regensburg. Our B-17 gave a slight lift and a red light went out on the instrument panel. Our bombs were away. We turned from the target toward the snow-capped Alps. I looked back and saw a beautiful sight — a rectangular pillar of smoke rising from the Me-109 plant. Only one burst was over and into the town. Even from this great height I could see that we had smeared the objective. The price? Cheap. 200 airmen.

A few more fighters pecked at us on the way to the Alps and a couple of smoking B-17s glided down toward the safety of Switzerland, about 40 miles distant. A town in the Brenner Pass tossed up a lone burst of futile flak. Flak? There had been lots of flak in the past two hours, but only now did I recall having seen it, a sort of side issue to the fighters. Col. LeMay, who had taken excellent care of us all the way, circled the air division over a large lake to give the cripples, some flying on three engines and many trailing smoke, a chance to rejoin the family. We approached the Mediterranean in a gradual descent, conserving fuel. Out over the water we flew at low altitude, unmolested by fighters from Sardinia or Corsica, waiting through the long hot afternoon hours for the first sight of the North African coastline. The prospect of ditching, out of gasoline, and the sight of other B-17s falling into the drink seemed trivial matters after the vicious nightmare of the long trial across Southern Germany. We had walked through a high valley of the shadow of death, not expecting to see another sunset, and now I could fear no evil.

With red lights showing on all our fuel tanks, we landed at our designated base in the desert, after 11 hours in the air. I slept on the ground near the wing and, waking occasionally, stared up at the stars. My radio headset was back in the ship. And yet I could hear the deep chords of great music.

While the Combined Bomber Offensive hammered at German industry by day and by night from hedgerow level to the thin heights of the atmosphere, Allied fighter pilots challenged the Luftwaffe over Europe. Theirs was a world that could transform instantaneously from the grim realities of kill-or-be-killed to the majestic, almost hypnotic unrealities of the silent eternal universe.

This near phenomena of aerial combat is beautifully captured by Britain's leading ace of the war . . .

Hun in the Sun

Group Capt. J. E. Johnson, R.A.F.

EVERY FIGHTER PILOT has experienced the swift transformation from the confused mix-up of a dog-fight to the dangerous solitude of a seemingly empty world. For the sky is a big place. Its horizons are infinite and a man's capacity in its vastness is very limited. I was to learn from hard experience that one moment the air space can be saturated with a hundred twisting Spitfires and Messerschmitts. Two or three parachutes blossom open and drift toward the earth below. The wing of a Hurricane, or is it a 109, spins lazily down like an autumn leaf. A plume of dark smoke draws a parabolic curve against the backcloth of the sky whilst high above the impersonal sun glints on the perspex canopies of the 109s.

Throughout it all the radio is never silent — shouts, oaths, exhortations, and terse commands. You single out an opponent. Jockey for position. All clear behind! The bullets from your eight guns go pumping into his belly. He begins to smoke. But the wicked tracer sparkles and flashes over the top of your own cockpit and you break into a tight turn. Now you have two enemies. The 109 on your tail and your remorseless, ever-present opponent "g," the force of gravity. Over your shoulder, you can still see the ugly, questing snout of the 109. You tighten the turn. The Spit protests and shudders, and when the blood drains from your eyes you "gray-out," but you keep turning, for life itself is the stake. And now your blood feels like molten lead and runs from head to legs. You blackout! And you ease the turn to recover in a gray, unreal world of spinning horizons. Cautiously you climb into the sun. You have lost too much height and your opponent has gone — disappeared. You are completely alone in your own bit of sky, bounded by the blue vault above and the colored drapery of earth below.

It was the second mission to Schweinfurt, on October 14, 1943, which offered the shocking proof to the high cost of daylight long-range bomber missions without fighter escort. For on this autumn day 291 bombers, headed out across Europe from English bases for another deadly run on the German ball-bearing works. Spitfire, P-38, and P-47 fighter escort was able to reach only as far as Aachen and Duren near the German border. The Luftwaffe waited and the moment the Thunderbolts broke off nearly 400 German fighters headed into the formation and sustained their attack to and from Schweinfurt, except for a brief respite during the bomb run over the city where flak "became so thick it could be walked on."

Waves of single- and twin-engine rocket throwing fighters created deadly havoc. As the big Forts fell out of their positions and plunged to earth, the boxes loosened and broke, so determined, so vicious was the attack. It was on this mission we exchanged 60 Fortresses and nearly 1500 trained crewmen for 35 German fighters, but the big Schweinfurt works were seriously damaged to the extent the Nazis began re-gearing their ball-bearing industry.

The epic of Schweinfurt II goes down in air war history with Ploesti. In the skies to Schweinfurt, bravery was not unique to any one side. Here is an account of the battle by a Luftwaffe fighter pilot who rose up to turn back those who were intent on destroying his homeland.

Schweinfurt Skies:
Where Brave Men Met

Sr. Lt. Heinz Knoke, Luftwaffe

AT 1315 THE ALERT SOUNDS. Geiger waves as I taxi out to take off. Over Antwerp we establish contact with Fortresses accompanied by an escort of Spitfires. My stovepipes make an engagement with Spitfires impossible for me. I do not wish to jettison them, except in case of emergency. For the moment I shall have to wait for a chance to attack later.

I trail the Fortresses, which are divided into a number of groups, all heading southwest, keeping off to the side and waiting for the moment when

The result of one of the Eighth Air Force's fiercest, largest, and most sustained air battles was the destruction of approximately 75 per cent of the ball-bearing production in Schweinfurt. This is a picture taken during the October 14, 1943 raid.

the Spitfires turn about in order to reach England again.

Eventually I have an opportunity to attack in the Aachen area. Before I am able to open fire, however, my left wing is hit and the left stovepipe shot away. I can hardly hold the unbalanced aircraft on an even keel. A large hole gapes in my left wing. I am afraid that the main spar is damaged. It is possible that the wing will come off completely under too great strain. I must avoid sharp turns and shall try to fire my second rocket at the enemy.

My pilots have meanwhile discharged their rockets to good effect. Fuhrmann and Fest each score direct hits. Their bombers explode in mid-air. The remainder of the rockets do not have any effect, as far as we can tell. My own rocket also passes through the middle of the formation without hitting anything.

I break away and come down to land at Bonn (Hangelar). I immediately taxi up to the repair depot and call for a maintenance inspector. He confirms my fears that the main spar in my left wing is in fact broken. That puts my plane out of action from the point of view of any further operations. In the course of the night it will be fitted with an entire new wing.

Slowly I wander across the runway to the control tower. Aircraft from the battle, Messerschmitts and Focke-Wulfs, come in to land all the time. There are altogether nearly 30 aircraft being rearmed and refueled. They all belong to different Fighter Wings. It is a pity that most of the pilots are inexperienced. Not a single formation leader is among them.

The Americans apparently are again attacking the ball-bearing factories at Schweinfurt. They pass overhead at a great height heading southeast.

It makes me sick to think· of my plane being unserviceable. Suddenly I make up my mind that I am going to fly in my damaged plane, nevertheless. Despite the warning of the inspector, I have it refueled and rearmed.

I call together the pilots who have landed and tell them to consider themselves as being under my command. We all take off in a large, compact group at 1700 hours. The Americans by this time are homeward bound. I hope to cause them a lot of trouble.

I have to handle my plane like a basket of eggs. Soon we are at an altitude of 22,000 feet. Right ahead of us is a formation consisting of about 250 Fortresses. Gradually we close in on them. One by one I send my aircraft in to attack.

I myself remain behind the enemy formation and pick off as my target a lone Fortress flying off to the left and a little below the main body. At a range of 500 feet I open fire in short bursts. The American defenses reply: their tracers come whizzing all round me, uncomfortably near my head. The usual pearl necklaces become thicker and thicker. Once again there is altogether too much of this blasted metal in the air.

I am at a grave disadvantage in that

I have to fly behind the massed enemy group for several minutes without being able to take evasive action. I keep looking anxiously at my wing with the hole in it.

Suddenly my poor plane is literally caught in a hail of fire. There is a smell of burning cordite. The engine still seems to run smoothly, however. I bend double-up behind it. It offers good enough cover. Closing up to within 300 feet, I take aim calmly at my victim.

Woomf! My fuselage is hit. The sound is more hollow than that made by the engine or wings.

My own shooting takes effect. By this time the Yank plane is in flames, swerving off to the left as it drops away below the formation. Four parachutes mushroom open.

Suddenly my aircraft is hit several times in succession and badly shaken. It sounds like a sack of potatoes being emptied over a barrel in which I am sitting. Flames come belching out at me from the engine. The smoke is choking me, and my eyes water.

So they have got me now, after all. It is a shambles!

I slide back my side windows because of the fumes. The smoke grows denser. Hot oil from the engine flows like treacle down my left wing-root. In a wide swing to the left I break away from the enemy formation. I have the satisfaction of observing my Fortress crash in flames in the Eiffel Mountains. A huge column of smoke comes billowing up from the pine forest.

That is that!

I cut the ignition and fuel. The thermometer shows oil and radiator temperatures at boiling. Good God! what a mess my left wing looks. It will probably break off at any moment.

The flames subside. The fire is out. I pull the emergency release and jettison the canopy. The slipstream rush takes my breath away at first. The wind tugs at my helmet and whips the scarf from my neck.

Shall I bail out? My Gustav has been shot full of holes, but it still flies.

I feather the propeller and start gliding. Heading east, I begin to lose altitude. Listening to the whistle and moan of the wind over my wings and fuselage, I am drenched with sweat. Ahead, the River Rhine, a silver ribbon winding across the sun-baked countryside below. The broad Rhineland plain is shimmering in the heat.

12,000 feet: with a little luck I may still be able to make Hangelar Airfield, near Bonn.

10,000 feet: I seem to be losing altitude much too quickly. A Messerschmitt 109 is not like a glider.

Is there any life left in the engine? I turn on the fuel and ignition, adjust the pitch control, and put the nose down to gain forward speed. There is a clattering and banging, but the engine starts.

It has done it! Not daring to touch the throttle, I climb back gingerly up to 12,000 feet. Then it begins to smoke and smell of burning again.

Cut ignition switch and resume glide!

I cannot coax it to Hangelar. I dare not take a chance on that engine again.

6000 feet . . . 5000 . . . 3000. I pick out what looks like a large field, and spiral down toward it. The ground comes rushing up at a terrific speed.

I prepare for a belly landing, and once again switch on the ignition. The engine starts. I have to make tighter turns in order to reach the landing field. Suddenly the engine begins to grind and clatter to a standstill for the last time. Cut!

It has seized. The prop is rigid, held as if by a vise. My plane becomes heavy and unresponsive to the controls. It begins to stall, and the left wing drops.

Damn!

I push the nose down hard and regain control. Houses flash past below in a nearby village. My airspeed indicator registers 200 miles per hour. I almost scrape the tops of some tall trees below.

150 miles per hour: I must touch down.

120 miles per hour: my wingtips scrape the treetops.

The indicator registers 100 miles per hour. I smash through two or three wooden fences. The splintering posts and cross-bars fly in all directions. Dust and chunks of earth hurtle into the air. I hit the ground, bounce, bracing myself for the crash hard against the safety belt, with feet clamped on the rudder pedals. A dike looms ahead. Holy smoke!

C — r—— ash!!!

And then a deathly silence. I unfasten the safety belt and drag myself out of the seat. My Gustav looks like an old bucket which has been well kicked around and trampled underfoot. It is a total wreck. There is nothing left intact except the tail wheel.

Blood oozes from my right sleeve.

The early months of 1944 saw the Combined Bomber Offensive in high gear. The long-range, fast, maneuverable P-51 Mustang now gave massive bomber formations a fighter-escort superior to anything the Luftwaffe had in the sky.

A spell of good weather in late February kicked off a continuous sustained six-day aerial blitz of German industrial resources (mainly the aircraft industry) from which the Third Reich would not recover.

This week, February 20-25 became known as "Big Week" and Allied Air Chiefs, recalling the bitter lessons of the past one-shot missions, instituted a follow-up strike strategy that turned the German cities and industrial facilities into an orgy of destruction. Through March and into April the relentless pounding continued, converting German production capacity into rubble and Luftwaffe into a "blinded boxer with one arm gone."

By the end of March the long-sought air superiority had been achieved. Here is the story of the great aerial offensive of early 1944 and the climactic follow-up that broke the back of the Luftwaffe.

"Big Week": Beginning of the End

Maj. Arthur Gordon

THE DATE WAS February 25. That morning heavy bombers from the fifteenth Air Force, based in Italy, roared across the Alps to attack the Prufening Messerschmitt factory in Regensburg. One hour later the same target was hit by British-based heavies escorted by fighters making the longest round trip of the war. Other Eighth Air Force formations attacked Augsburg, Stuttgart, and Furth. The day was a landmark in the air war over Europe. More than 2000 American planes, operating from bases 1000 miles apart, were launched against Germany.

The six days between February 20 and February 25 were most significant in the history of strategic bombing. In some 3800 bomber and 4300 fighter sorties, the Eighth and Fifteenth Air Forces attacked factories whose estimated production was more than two-thirds of Germany's single-engined and more than three-quarters of her twin-engined fighters. The cost was high. On February 24 the Eighth Air Force alone lost 49 heavies over Schweinfurt, Gotha, and Rostock. The

The long-range P-51 Mustang came into the picture in great strength in early 1944 and escorted the bombers to their farthest targets. The result — greatly' reduced bomber losses from air attack.

next day, when two American spearheads met at Regensburg, the Eighth and Fifteenth expended a total of 65 heavies over this and other targets. Altogether, in the cyclonic month of February, 250 four-engined bombers failed to return to their bases. But at the end of the month, looking at their PRU (Photo Reconnaissance Unit) pictures and damage assessments, the chiefs of the Strategic Air Forces knew that the price was not too high.

They knew without question that during February the wastage of the Luftwaffe's fighter strength exceeded its replacement capacity by a substantial margin. They estimated that the productive capacity of the Nazi aircraft industry as planned for March was down by at least 50 per cent for an undetermined period. Just how

long a period depended on the recuperative capacity of the Germans and the ability of precision bombers to return to the targets when factory repairs had advanced sufficiently to make it necessary. Even pessimists conceded that without further bombing the crippling effects of "Blitz Week" would last between one and two months.

This was not long but it might be long enough. If the strain on the Americans had been great, the pressure on the Luftwaffe had been almost unbearable. During February the American heavies claimed 540 enemy fighters destroyed in combat. American fighters, whose camera guns made reliable checking easy, shot down 365. There was little doubt that the German Air Force was taking a beating

221

which it could not stand indefinitely.

This did not mean that the Luftwaffe could be discounted as a formidable fighting force. Its front line strength was being maintained intact, partially at least from stored reserves. Its pilots were still good, still brave. Those who read only newspaper headlines and expected the skies over Germany suddenly to be clear were bound to be disappointed.

On February 29, Fortresses and Liberators made the third attack on Brunswick in ten days. They bombed through the overcast and enemy air opposition was practically nil. Only one bomber and six fighters were lost.

There were various possible conclusions to be drawn from this. The most probable was that the Germans were unwilling to expend their dwindling forces when bad visibility hampered the American effort. Instrument bombing had made great strides but was still no substitute for pinpoint visual bombing. Bombs dropped through the overcast could hurt Jerry but not enough to make him risk his precious aircraft. Another possible reason for the Germans' reluctance to fight was weather conditions on the ground. Sending up fighter formations through overcast, under severe icing conditions, was too expensive a pastime for the once prodigal Luftwaffe.

There was, however, a way to force the Germans' hand. Every indication was they would fight desperately to defend their capital. So the Americans went to Berlin. They went in daylight and they went four times within six days. On at least some of the missions they hardly bothered to conceal their intentions. A fight was what they were looking for.

Luring the Luftwaffe into combat was only one of several valid reasons for daylight blows at the heart of Germany. The great ball-bearing works at Erkner, in the suburbs of Berlin, was high on the list of priority targets. The ferocity with which the Germans usually defended Schweinfurt indicated the dependence of their war economy on ball-bearing production. The attacks on these plants, coordinated with blows at aircraft industry, were designed to make the replacement of aircraft factories more and more difficult.

Then, too, there was the psychological effect to be considered. Berliners were reeling under night attacks by the British Bomber Command. If they lost their fancied daylight invulnerability the effect on their morale could hardly fail to be shattering. In any case, Berlin attacks would reveal whether the Luftwaffe would prefer to accept daylight bombing unopposed by anything except flak or conduct combat on a grand scale.

The first attack on March 4 was not a fair test. Appalling weather, with condensation trails that made formation flying virtually impossible, forced the recall of the bulk of the force. One formation slipped through escorted by fighters whose round-trip penetration of 1200 miles exceeded even their Regensburg performance and set a new distance record for the war. Very few enemy aircraft were seen over the cloud-shrouded city. Of American heavies, 15 were lost but only one as a direct result of enemy fighter action. The cold was intense. One gunner, whose oxygen equipment froze, died of anoxia. The first assault on "Big B," as combat crews called it, was at best a glancing blow.

Still, it gave jittery Berliners a fore-taste of what was coming. Two days later, driving straight across northern France and Germany, a great aerial armada fought its way through oppo-sition of unparalleled ferocity. Amer-ican fighters guarding bomber boxes reported close to 600 enemy aircraft in the skies over Germany. Living on borrowed time, the Luftwaffe seemed willing to live — and die — boldly. Individually its planes were no match for our fighters. One Mustang group over Berlin claimed 20 enemy aircraft destroyed, 1 probable, and 7 damaged, for no loss. Altogether that day escort-ing fighters knocked down 83 oppos-ing Germans, losing 11 of their own. The score was somewhat equalized by the fact that a certain percentage of Nazi pilots could, and undoubtedly did, parachute to safety. Still, if any American fighter pilot wanted to claim that bombing Berlin without long-range fighter support would be pro-hibitively expensive, no bomber man would disagree with him.

Losses were heavy enough as it was. Some combat wings got through easily but others sustained fierce attacks from fighters and rocket-carrying fight-er-bombers: 69 American bombers failed to return to England, the sever-est loss yet suffered by the Eighth Air Force. A few cripples landed in Swe-den. These losses were reported promptly with the grim honesty that had characterized Allied air communi-ques from the beginning. It was an-nounced the next day that gaps in the ranks were already filled with replace-ments.

Proof of this was given on March 8 when another very strong force re-newed the assault on the German capital. Again the Luftwaffe rose to defend it, but this time its claws were somewhat blunted and air opposition was somewhat weaker. Our fighter es-cort had another field day, destroying 83 against a loss of 15. Our bomber losses dropped to 38.

Visibility was considerably better than expected. All crews had been briefed to hit the ball-bearing plant at Erkner if they could see it. They all saw it. The factory and the surround-ing area were literally smothered un-der 350,000 incendiaries and 10,000 small HE bombs. A lone American photo-reconnaissance pilot who flew over the capital a few hours later, brought back pictures that confirmed the story told by strike photographs. He nearly failed to bring them back. In the 60°-below-zero cold his gas gauge froze. As he landed and tried to taxi to the dispersal point, his en-gine coughed and stopped — out of gas.

When released to the press, the figures on the number of bombs dropped caused various British newspapers to go into an arithmetical dither and come out with headlines announcing 1100 American heavy bombers over Berlin, a very considerable exaggeration although over 1000 had been used in the great attack of February 20. Still, the actual number represented a tremendous striking power, especially when concentrated on a single target. Veteran crews flew beside newcomers to the United Kingdom who found themselves, to their astonishment, getting a good look at Berlin before they had even had a glimpse of London.

On March 9, when another force approximately the same size attacked Berlin for the fourth time, bombing through overcast, enemy opposition was practically nil. Only 7 bombers and 1 fighter were lost. On the 11th, a relatively small force attacked Munster which was also cloud-covered. No bombers were lost at all. On March 15, only 3 failed to return from an attack on Brunswick. The British press began to speculate rather wildly on the whereabouts of the vanishing Luftwaffe.

Meanwhile, USSTAF chiefs warned that weather was the main factor in curtailing German fighter activity. Events of the following week were to prove them right.

On other air fronts the crescendo was still rising. Ninth Air Force Ma-

rauders, supplemented occasionally by the heavies, were consistently hammering airdromes, railroad yards, and rocket sites on the invasion coast. In Italy, heavies of the Fifteenth were giving a beautiful illustration of the flexibility of air power with alternating attacks on long-range strategic targets such as Vienna and tactical blows such as the classic pulverization of Cassino on March 15. Nor was the RAF idle. It turned in some perfect examples of night precision bombing, dropping its new 12,000-pounders on munitions factories in Southern France. On the night of March 15, more than 1000 British heavies carrying more than 3000 tons, dropped the heaviest single bomb load of the war, with Stuttgart as the main target.

In the middle of the month, the dormant Luftwaffe woke up. On March 16, attacking Ulm and Augsburg, USSTAF bombers met resistance: 22 were lost. On the 18th, a multiple attack on aircraft factories in southern Germany cost us 43 bombers, 16 of which made forced landings in Switzerland. The Luftwaffe was suffering, too: 207 were claimed as destroyed in these two attacks but there were no signs of imminent collapse.

From this confusing pattern of enemy fighter reaction no clear-cut conclusions could be drawn except that the Germans were reluctant to risk their squadrons in bad weather. That the Luftwaffe was being steadily weakened was certain. Just how far from collapse it was, no one this side of the

Rhine could say. For the Allies, the future held forth the promise of increasingly better weather and the opportunity to raise the tempo of the war still higher. To the Germans it offered the bleak prospect of constantly waning strength and the constant necessity for concealing that progressive weakness, either by sulking on the ground or by sending into the air every plane that could be scraped together by stripping trainer and reconnaissance units, converting bombers to twin-engined fighters and reconverting fighter-bombers back to fighters.

In the weeks ahead, visual strategic bombing would remain the prime objective of the USSTAF, with tactical bombing available when necessary. Overcast bombing would continue to be carried out whenever bad flying conditions did not outweigh its effectiveness.

For the Luftwaffe, the defense of key industrial targets would remain priority number one, with an apprehensive reserve always alert to meet the forthcoming invasion. There seemed little doubt that no matter to what extent he might rely on radio-controlled glider bombs or other devices to repel landings, Jerry would almost certainly try to maintain an anti-invasion air force.

To what extent he would succeed, time and the course of the war would tell.

B-17 Flying Fortresses unloading their bomb loads on Berlin targets.

The pompous, arrogant Luftwaffe Chief was often asked by his military associates what would happen to Germany when American fighters could fly all the way to Berlin with the bombers. He boastfully derided those who raised this question, guaranteeing such a fanciful thing could never happen. The day American fighters appear over Berlin, he chided, "my name will be Meyer."

On March 4, 1944 the hefty Luftwaffe leader's hand was called, for it was on this day the 4th Fighter Group, operating out of Debden Airbase in England appeared over the German capital for the first time in their Mustangs.

For the Germans it was the most ominous sign of the entire war, for it signaled the moment Allied bomber formations got free rein to any spot in Germany. The historic first fighter mission to Big B was led by the combat veteran, Col. Donald J. Blakeslee, 4th Group Commander. For Blakeslee, a brilliant, daring ace, this long-sought moment of triumph over the Luftwaffe would turn to bitter gall. Here is that story.

First Fighter to Big "B"

Grover C. Hall, Jr.

THE CHATTER STOPPED suddenly, the same as the shrill cacophony of sparrows in a magnolia tree suddenly subsides at the sound of a BB shot perforating a leaf. It was Blakeslee. The pilots popped to.

Blakeslee strode up the aisle as if it wasn't long till press time. He turned around to face the pilots.

He said: "Okay." At Debden that meant at ease.

You couldn't rightly tell whether Blakeslee had a glint or twinkle in those pale blue eyes, and whether it was excitement or the March bluster that flushed his face.

As always, he wore the beaten-up, clay-colored leather jacket he had drawn when he first came to Debden and the one in which he said he would finish the war. He was champing gum. He held a cigarette in his right hand. The cigarette was a reliable herald of what was known as a shaky do.

"Well," Blakeslee began in his vibrant, baritone voice, "you've seen what the show is. We're going to Berlin."

He paused. That sentence had a lot of punch. He continued:

"We're going to Berlin. The weather is not too good. Swope will give you

226

the gen on that in a minute. We'll be with the bombers over the target on the bomb run. And we've been chosen to lead the first box in over Berlin. Any questions?"

The mechanics, shivering in their greasy green overalls and leather jackets, stood atop the revetment to see their motors off on the historic mission. The wind was so icy it was hard to remember that the mechanics had been burned brown there in the summer before. Each speculated whether his plane would make it back.

Blakeslee taxied out on the east-west runway and made a radio check with the tower. The other 47 planes taxied up behind, weaving left and right in order to see ahead. In a way it made you think of the taxi fleets at Pennsylvania Station. Bundled in heavy flying-clothes, their faces obscured by helmets and oxygen masks, the pilots appeared stripped of their individuality and personality. Through the glass canopies they looked like shapeless brown sacks. When they moved you couldn't recognize them, save for the plane numbers.

Locking the wheels, Blakeslee gunned his motor and the plane pranced. He released the brakes and the craft moved forward, somewhat sluggishly at first because of the heavy babies under each wing. He and his Number 2 were clocking 100 m.p.h. by the time they reached the hump in the runway. The flagman beside the runway, a pilot thus disciplined for breaking R/T silence on a previous

mission, waved the next two off.

They circled about the field where the blue ribbon beets once grew until the group was in combat array. All 48 Mustangs, plus two spares, were airborne in eight minutes. The ones and twos were joined by the threes and fours, making a section of four. A flight of eight joined another flight to make the squadron. Then the squadrons, led by Blakeslee with 336th, joined and the group was formed. Blakeslee got over the control tower and set his compass for Berlin. They pointed their noses up for the climb across the Channel. At the French coast they reached an altitude of about four miles and leveled off.

The Forts were already far ahead, escorted by Thunderbolts whose range at that time was not sufficient to take them all the way to Berlin. They would turn back when the 4th arrived at the rendezvous.

"Shirtblue Red 2 to Horseback," said Lt. Woodrow Sooman, of Republic, Wash., just after they passed over Dummer Lake. "Oxygen failing. Over."

"Horseback to Shirtblue Red 2," Blakeslee came back. "Let down and return to base. Off."

Sooman banked out of the formation and started back for Debden at 10,000 feet, below which oxygen is not needed. "Red Dog" Norley moved on up to take Sooman's place on Blakeslee's wing.

Others called up for permission to abort on account of this kind of engine trouble and that. Soon Blakeslee and "Red Dog" were the only ones left of Shirtblue (336th) Squadron. Lt. Charles Anderson, a sallow, black-haired ace from Gary, Ind., flying with 335th Squadron, called Blakeslee:

"Greenbelt Blue 4 to Horseback. Rough engine. Don't think I can make it to target. Over."

"Horseback here," responded Blakeslee. "Okay, Blue 4, return to base."

The rest continued on toward the rendezvous with the bombers. They were tense and uneasy, but even so, flying in the rarified atmosphere five miles up left them drowsy and listless. But flak bursts prevented any from nodding.

Sooman felt lonesome as he scooted back alone over the heart of Germany. He sighted a JU 52 (transport) at 1500 feet. Sooman worked himself up-sun and attacked the transport from the side. As he was about to break off, pieces from the splintered transport flew off and bounded off the metal side of his Mustang. The transport spiraled down in such fashion as to suggest that Sooman's burst had killed the pilot.

Meanwhile, Anderson was fretfully cruising toward Debden. The show of shows, the first attack on Berlin, story enough for a hundred grandchildren — and he was going in the opposite direction. His hankering to see Berlin was keen, especially where the RAF had plastered it. His motor sounded a little better now. Why not try it? Anderson kicked the rudder, completed a port turn and resumed the vector leading to Berlin.

Shortly after noon, at the appointed time, Blakeslee caught sight of the five combat wings of B-17s. He took his place some distance in front of the first bomber box to sweep way any Huns in the path of the bombing run. Weaving back and forth with high speed skids, Blakeslee scanned the dirty billows for specks that would grow into 190s and 109s.

The specks were spotted just before the Forts discharged their bombs, single and double contrails appearing in all directions. Fifteen-plus 109s and 190s came in for a frontal attack on the bombers. Green flares, fired two at a time, rainbowed out of the Forts to signal for fighter intervention.

"Horseback here. There they are. Stick together and clear your tails . . . Here we go!"

The pilots caught the eagerness and zest in Blakeslee's voice. For a moment he rammed the throttle forward and spurted ahead of his squadrons, kinking his craft from side to side to clear himself. Blakeslee always did that before attacking. Millikan used to say: "That's why he's been here so long."

Blakeslee whipped his plane over to initiate the split-ess diving down on the Huns in a violent bounce. All Blakeslee's bounces were violent. He was heavy with the reins and spurs in racking his Mustang about. The air speed needle popped the whip toward the red line, which line was the factory's means of saying that the wings might not stay on beyond this speed.

Blakeslee positioned himself astern one of the 109s and flew right up his slipstream for some of his garden hose shooting. The 109 racked it this way and that, but he couldn't shake Blakeslee. "Red Dog" was following on his right wing, rigid and excited. "Red Dog" fidgeted in his cockpit and shouted, "Let'im have it, Colonel, let'im have it!"

Blakeslee flipped the gun switch on and trimmed his kite up to get set for the kill. He pressed the red button on the stick to water the flowers. Nothing happened. He got the 109 in the ring again and pressed down. "Red Dog" kept watching the leading edge of Blakeslee's wing to see the orange power puffs. But Blakeslee's guns wouldn't fire. He was a hornet without a stinger.

"Goddamn sad sack!" roared Blakeslee. The Hun was flat out, wondering why the American hadn't fired. In angry frustration, Blakeslee pushed the throttle to the firewall and pulled up abreast of the 109. He looked over the Hun. He waved with mocking sweetness. The Hun didn't remember anything in the book about this, but what did he have to lose? He acknowledged Blakeslee's wave with a waggle of his wings.

Later Blakeslee came in with the others. Each crew chief sprinted out to the hardstand where his kite parked and turned his back as the pilot gunned it. Tired and aching, the pilots signed Form 1 and got out of their ships stiffly. Their knees were too stiff to bend. They just sat on the wings and smoked, so numb the icy wind went unnoticed. They looked like football players on the way to the showers, or miners emerging from the shafts at the end of the day.

Blakeslee was a little different. He whammed the canopy back and there was a sulphurous cascade of four-lettered words, followed by:

"Can you beat it?"

As if the mechanics crowded about his ship could know what he meant.

"Beat what, sir?"

"I'll be a sad sack — my goddamn guns wouldn't fire. Not one of them. There we were — I had him right in my sights and my guns jammed!"

"Jesus, that's tough."

"I pulled right up beside him," Blakeslee went on, "and looked at the dumb sap. He must have thought I was crazy!"

Blakeslee signed Form 1 with a right hook, got out and flailed his legs with his gauntlets as he entered the 335th interrogation room. He unloaded his chute pack and let it crumple on the concrete floor. He slumped in a chair and bit a chocolate bar in two as if it were the Jerry's head.

Nothing could plunge a "gung ho" aircrew into the psychological abyss of gloom quicker than having to turn back home from a combat mission because of a mechanical failure. When it happened it was called "abortion," and it brought with it a sense of personal guilt, of let-down to yourself, your buddies, your outfit. If it didn't, there was no place for you in the air war.

Lt. Bert Stiles, B-17 co-pilot, whose pen created some of the classic prose to come out of the air war, puts it this way.

Abortion

Bert Stiles

WE WERE SO TIRED we didn't get up for breakfast, just stayed in the sack until the last possible minute.

In the rush to get to briefing I forgot to wear my G.I. shoes. Sam forgot his dog tags. When we got to the ship, Beach couldn't get his guns installed in the turret.

"Call the turret man," Sam yelled. "Doesn't anyone ever get anything done around here?"

There was a little oil dripping off Number 1 engine, but the crew chief guessed it would be all right.

We were flying an old ship, one that had 24 missions with no engine changes. For three days we'd been flying a new airplane with big bulletproof windows. It was supposed to be our own.

"So we get this crate today," Sam said. "Look at those goddamn windows." They weren't bulletproof and they weren't clean.

I almost wrenched my shoulder out of joint on the primer and started to rave slowly under my breath. There wasn't any armor plate.

We took off into a blue mist. When Benson called up to give me the heading, I had to ask for a repeat. The interphone was fuzzy. We were flying the high squadron for another group, forming over another field. We climbed out through the heavy haze. The cylinder head temperature on Number 1 engine was way high. I opened the cowl flaps. The prop was throwing a wash of oil back on the cowling. "Number 1 is smoking a little," Crone called up. "We ain't on fire, are we?"

"We might be soon," I said. "Keep an eye on it."

There was no horizon, no sky, no England, just the soft gray mist. The group leader shot his red-green flares, and called his airplanes. The squadron leaders fired their flares and called their wing men and second-element leaders.

"My goddamned heated suit is shorted out," Sharpe said.

"Something's wrong with this oxygen in the ball," Beach said. "The indicator doesn't indicate."

The formation was lost all over that part of England, wandering around in the haze.

The fuel pressure was slowly rising. The oil temperature on Number 1 was on the climb. Nobody salted off over interphone. The tension in the ship was growing into a threat.

"This is a sad goddamn crate," Sam said. "Why did we have to draw it?"

The wing started out across the Channel. Eight hours till chow time; 45 minutes till flak time at the Dutch coast. We were headed for Leipzig.

Number 1 nacelle was covered with oil now, the oil pressure had dropped five pounds, the fuel pressure was still rising slowly. The air-speed indicator froze up, and we stalled out, hanging in the blue mist. Sam punched the nose down and we came out 500 feet below the rest of the formation.

"That was close," was all he said.

It isn't a very bright play to stall out with a maximum load.

Crone was having oxygen troubles, too. "I think I got a leak," he called up. "The gauge is falling off."

The throttles wouldn't slide easy. I couldn't keep in position and stay in. Neither could Sam. There was no horizon to go by, nothing at all to go by, just mist. The oil pressure kept on falling off, and the cylinder-head temperature kept on rising.

"You tired old bastard," I said softly. I could see Number 1 engine giving up after we got across the Zuider Zee, and Number 2 and 3 throwing in the towel on the bomb run in the Leipzig flak area. I could feel the whole ship slowly coming apart. Combat fatigue.

The formation was climbing. I jacked up the rpm and turned the superchargers on full. She wasn't in the mood. We were about a mile behind and 200 feet low, and getting more behind and further below.

Sam shoved the nose down, jerked off his oxygen mask, and swore all the way around the 180°.

"We're not taking this airplane anywhere," he said.

The relief washed through the ship in a cool wave.

Maybe we'd get it today, I thought. Maybe the 190s would be waiting there. I could see the flak puffing up there, reaching for us.

None of that for us.

We never aborted before, I thought. The taste of the word was bad. Maybe we could have made it. Maybe that wagon would have held together. I was glad I wasn't Sam. I was glad I didn't have to decide.

Maybe Doolittle would be sore. Maybe Spaatz would call up and give us ten extra missions. They wanted those bombs delivered, those boys.

231

They wanted to hear about black towers of smoke, and plumes of flame, and flattened cities.

It was just a trucking job, but that airplane didn't feel like trucking.

Grant found the field.

We could have feathered Number 1 to make it look good, but we didn't.

The ground crew was all out there when we taxied in. The crew chief was looking at something on the ground. The squadron jeep was out there. Maj. McPartlin had on his squadron CO look, ready to start chewing.

I knew what they were all thinking. No guts. A rough one, so they come home.

Nobody looked at anyone else while we unloaded our stuff. Nobody made much noise. The sun shone wanly through the mist.

"She wouldn't have took you there." The crew chief came over after he'd looked at the engines. "Number 1 is all through."

The crew brightened up a little then, and there was some chatter on the truck going back.

"It ain't natural, us being here this time of day," Crone said.

"Why did they give us that crate?" Sharpe said. "I thought we owned that other one, that new one."

"We will, after today," Sam said. "I'm going to tell those guys a thing or two."

He had to report up to headquarters with his story.

I felt as beat-up as if we'd gone all the way.

Disregarding tremendous danger, an Eighth Air Force Republic P-47 fighter is shown here swooping down on a flak tower located on a German airfield in occupied France. Picture was taken from a motion picture gun camera.

Pilots of many nations, defeated by Germany, flocked to the Allies for another chance to fight the Nazis. Where they came from, how they came, was of small concern. Most important, they held a burning desire for revenge.

They were taken in, retrained in Allied equipment and assigned to combat units, either individually integrated or as a national unit. The role they played in the destruction of the Luftwaffe was tremendous.

None were more vicious, more determined, more fearless of the Germans than the Poles. They fought with a cunning, revenge, and vindictiveness that was without measure.

One such was Michael Gladych, former Polish Air Force fighter pilot and here is that story.

The Amazing Michael Gladych

Robert S. Johnson with Martin Caidin

EARLY IN 1944 the operations of the 56th Fighter Group were "imperiled" by a single fighter pilot. The amazing thing was that he flew in a Thunderbolt instead of fighting against them. So fiercely desperate was Flight Lt. Michael Gladych to kill Germans that often we feared for his life as he tore after enemy aircraft. Prior to his "temporary visit" with the 56th Group, Mike Gladych had flown in combat with the Polish, French, and British air forces.

We did not envy Gladych his past experience. When Mike joined our ranks for temporary flight duty, he had just completed five years of close brushes with death. When German troops assaulted Poland, Mike flew like a madman in an obsolete PZL-11 fighter and managed to shoot at least five German planes out of the air before his country collapsed. With several other pilots Mike then fled to Rumania where he was thrown into jail by pro-Nazi police. The Polish flyers escaped and, barely one step ahead of the Gestapo, reached France. But the Gestapo never gave up its quarry that easily, and one night in a dark Lyons alley a trained German killer went after Mike. In a savage hand-to-hand struggle Gladych killed the German, but paid heavily for his victory. He fell unconscious — blind.

He came to in darkness, bound hand and foot, a captive in an insane asylum. For five days and nights the horror-stricken Gladych endured the tormented shrieks of the inmates. He felt he, too, was going mad. Five days after his capture a French doctor explained that his commitment to the asylum had been in error. In his towering anger Mike felt pain stabbing his blinded eyes.

"Go ahead!" the doctor shouted. "Open them; *open them!*" and Mike Gladych, miraculously, could see. He owes a tremendous debt to that doctor, who had wisely diagnosed Mike's blindness as acute strain on the optic nerves, which could be cured only by a sudden and great shock.

After his recovery Mike flew obsolete French fighters in a courageous but lost battle against the Luftwaffe. He fled to England and with other Polish exiles joined the Royal Air Force. He was obsessed with the urge to kill Germans, and his fellow pilots predicted that his frenzy for battle to the death with anything of German origin would soon cause Mike's own demise. Over France in a British fighter, Mike lost his squadron and single-handed ripped into three German fighters. In a furious battle he shot down two and then ran out of ammunition. Blazing with anger he rammed the third plane. Pieces of wreckage burst into the canopy, slashing Mike's head and eyes. He set course for home, and fainted.

He returned to consciousness two days later, swathed in bandages in a British hospital. Luck not only rode with Gladych, it hugged him tightly.

In a fantastic flight his fighter droned in a gentle glide to England. With Mike unconscious at the controls the airplane touched ground at high speed, in almost level altitude. It tore itself to pieces as it skidded out of control and came to a stop — two hundred yards from the hospital! After repairing his skull, which was laid open to the bone, the doctors told Gladych he'd never fly again. Mike just didn't believe them; several months later he was in a Thunderbolt over Berlin.

On February 26, the boys went to Happy Valley, our name for that charming area known as the Ruhr, where it seemed possible to step out of your airplane and walk on the flak bursts. I stayed at home and sweated them out, and I mean sweated. Mike Gladych had my airplane, and I was convinced that I'd never see it again, or that Gladych would drag himself home in a wrecked Thunderbolt. Unbelievably, the airplane came home in flyable condition. Mudge and Barnum had flown off Mike's wing; somewhat dazed about the entire event, they related the proceedings.

Mike flew Number 3 to Barnum, and they noticed early in the flight that Gladych maintained a perfect position. No one ever worried when they had The Killer with them. Mike could see enemy planes, it seemed, when they were still out of sight. Suddenly, they noticed that Gladych was no longer in formation. Dismayed, they circled, trying to locate the missing Thunderbolt. They were at 18,000 feet, and just east of the Ruhr Valley. And down below, 18,000 feet below, in fact, was a Thunderbolt hell-bent for leather after a Messerschmitt ME-109. Mudge and Barny dove after the two planes; sure enough, it was my fighter, the HV-P lettering standing out clear and sharp.

The book says a Thunderbolt can't hold a turn at low altitude with the ME-109, but Mike never read the book. He clung to the tail of the German fighter, moving in closer and closer. They were right on the deck, actually flying beneath the tops of trees. Mudge and Barny couldn't understand why Gladych didn't cut down the Messerschmitt; he had plenty of lead but refused to fire. When the German pilot saw the other two Thunderbolts, he ran for safety, skimming the trees as he fled down a valley. He had good reason to run, with the three big fighters on his tail. Halfway down the valley was an opening to the right, and several miles farther a gap on the left. Mudge took the first turn, and as the Messerschmitt burst out of the valley, snapping to the left, he stared almost into the guns of Mudge's Thunderbolt. He and Barny cut loose at the same time; the Messerschmitt splattered along the ground for several hundred yards in a shower of flame.

Mike throttled back and circled the burning fighter, he wanted to be sure that the pilot was dead. Had that German survived the crash and run from his plane, Mike was prepared to cut him down with his propeller or wingtip. When Mike returned, and I'd heard the tale, I asked him why he didn't fire. He couldn't; the gun switch was broken. Not being able to shoot down the ME-109 so infuriated him that he tried to spin the German in, or run him out of gas. He was actually trying to run the Kraut out of gas over his own home, 350 miles from our base!

Mike Gladych helped to keep things from getting *too* boring. Mike never quit; he always stayed in the middle of a fight until he figured he had just enough gas to get him home. But not until his fuel reached the critical point would he even think of ending his one-man war with the Luftwaffe. And sure enough, we had regrouped and were on the way home and ... no Mike. Gabreski yelled for him, "Hello Keyworth White Three, what is your position?" After three calls and no reply we began to worry. That was a foolish thing to do with Gladych.

The radio crackled and Mike's voice came back in a monotone, "Hello Gabby, hello Gabby, this is Mike. I'm okay. I am being escorted out by three Focke-Wulfs over Dummer Lake." Gabby muttered something unintelligible as he racked his fighter around to try and reach Mike in time to help. He might as well have saved the fuel. Gladych turned into the three German fighters, and exploded the leader. And at that moment his fuel reached the critical stage; if he fought a minute longer he'd never get back to England.

There's always one way to get home in the Thunderbolt, and Mike took it, gunning for the deck in a screaming power dive, the two Focke-Wulfs hot on his tail. Mike dropped below tree-top level, engine howling, trying to shake his pursuers. As he flashed over a clump of trees, an air base loomed before him. No one could ever accuse Gladych of being a slow thinker; he poured a long burst of bullets into the German planes and crewmen as he thundered overhead. The first man in a surprise strafing attack rarely ever gets hit; the ones that follow usually catch all kinds of hell. Later, a grinning Mike told us, "You know, it's funny thing, they no bother me after I cross the field." The Germans had blasted both of them out the sky.

Mike didn't have the fuel to get back to England. In a solid overcast above the Channel the engine sputtered and died. At the last possible moment Mike bailed out. and jerked open the chute. Two hundred yards off shore, he dropped into the water, shucked his harness, and swam to the beach. That same day he was back at the field.

Col. Francis S. Gabreski with his foot on the tire of his P-47 Thunderbolt poses with his ground-crew. Twenty-eight German kills can be seen stenciled on the side of the P-47.

Even to this day little has been told of the secret special air missions which took place throughout the war in all theatres of the world. Tied in with intelligence and counter-espionage activities, these hush-hush missions played a large role in final victory. British and American aircraft involved varied from light, single-engine fabric covered "grasshoppers" to converted B-24 Liberators. Workhorse was the faithful C-47, but B-17s, British Lysanders, Wellingtons, Mosquitoes, and others were used.

The work involved parachuting agents, radios, ammunition, weapons, food, medicine, and money, to partisan groups in enemy territory, air-landing on secret camouflaged dirt airstrips or open pasture lands behind enemy lines to deliver supplies to resistance movements and evacuate wounded and downed American flyers who had made their way into underground channels. Another major activity was leaflet dropping, (called "nickeling" by the British) urging civilians to resist and the German soldiers to give up. Billions were dropped during the war.

A large share of this super-secret activity took place in the Balkans. In September, 1944 nearly 1150 Americans were evacuated from Rumania (most were Fifteenth Air Force air crews down over the Ploesti oilfields), while 300 air crewmen were rescued from Bulgaria. In the last four months of 1944, 830 clandestine landings were made in Greece and Yugoslavia evacuating nearly 8000 individuals, 900 of whom were Allied air crews. The first four months of 1945 saw nearly 400 secret night landings in Yugoslavia and Albania with over 3500 individuals brought out.

Some of the most dramatic chapters of the war, yet untold, took place during these operations. Try as they may, the Germans could not stop them, imposing the most vicious penalties upon those partisans who were caught, including such types of death as burning alive. Despite the penalties of the German occupation forces, this type of Allied-partisan teamwork prospered and the enemy at best shadow-boxed it.

Similar activities mounted out of bases in Britain took place in Occupied France and Poland. Perhaps the best known to the enemy were our activities in Scandinavia, especially those conducted in broad daylight in and out of neutral Sweden and led by the famed Norwegian-born Arctic air explorer Bernt Balchen, a colonel in the American Air Force.

Here is that story.

Scandinavian Carpetbagger

Capt. Eric Friedheim

BERLIN-BOUND PASSENGERS at Bromma Airport near Stockholm were just boarding their JU-52 transport when a B-24 sailed down through the early morning fog and rolled to a stop at the far corner of the field. Swedish officials did not seem to pay much attention but the air and press attachés from the German Embassy who happened to be at the airport watched suspiciously. Obviously, this was not another American combat plane making an emergency landing on neutral soil. The Liberator was painted green and there were no identifying markings on its fuselage. The two Nazis also thought it odd that no one stepped from the plane until the JU-52 had roared down the runway and headed off in the direction of Germany. And when nine men finally emerged attired in civilian clothes the Germans were convinced this was a case for investigation by the Gestapo.

The date was March 31, 1944, and in neutral Stockholm the arrival of a mysterious airplane could mean many things. In this atmosphere of espionage and intrigue, jittery Nazis were on the alert for any portent of the coming Allied invasion of the West and there was little doubt in their minds that the nine men from the Liberator were linked to events of magnitude.

Enemy suspicion reached fever pitch when one of the civilian passengers was identified as Bernt Balchen, a Norwegian by birth and now a colonel in the American Air Forces. Balchen, the Germans well knew, was one of the world's foremost authorities on Scandinavia and the Arctic. It was Balchen who had been chosen by Gen. Arnold early in the war to establish vitally important outposts in Greenland and along the polar regions so that the AAF could open a new aerial highway to Great Britain. To the Germans, his sudden appearance in Sweden was a matter of great significance.

Nazi undercover agents had no difficulty in trailing the Liberator's crew to a suite at the Grand Hotel in Stockholm. By assiduous surveillance, the Germans learned that Balchen and his men held several meetings with American diplomats and representatives of the Swedish and Norwegian governments. After a week, during which the Gestapo seldom let them out of sight, the Germans deduced generally what was afoot.

Balchen was in Stockholm to evacuate 2000 Norwegian military trainees from Sweden to Great Britain where they would be absorbed by the great Allied armies that were massing for D-day. He was also canvassing the possibility of repatriating some 1500 American pilots and crew members who had been interned after making emergency landings in Sweden. Plans for these undertakings had been discussed at the American Embassy in London a month before and Balchen, as an officer of the Air Transport Command, was to establish a secret airline running between the British Isles and Sweden.

Gen. Spaatz already had agreed to turn over a handful of war-weary B-24s and seven bomber crews who had finished their combat tours with the Eight Air Force. Balchen insisted that the Liberators carry civilian airline markings and that their crews comply with Sweden's commercial air regulations. The Swedes, in turn, promised their AA batteries would not fire on the American planes provided they flew over certain areas reserved for commercial traffic. This would call for exacting navigation since these areas were only 20 miles wide.

For his British terminus, Balchen selected a remote airdrome at Leuchars, near the eastern coast of Scotland. The next problem was to plot the safest route across enemy-occupied Norway.

Allied intelligence knew the Germans had at least 250 night fighters based in Southern Norway near Bergen, Stavanger, Oslo, Gossen, and Trondheim. The enemy's coastal emplacements were formidable. And it was necessary to assume the Gestapo's intensive sleuthing in Stockholm had given the Nazi defenses ample warning of the impending operations.

Operations got underway in April, 1944, and during this month, Maj. David Schreiner made seven flights between Scotland and Stockholm. First passengers were the Norwegian trainees and Schreiner packed nearly 40 of them into his Liberator on each trip.

"It was anything but a luxury ride for those boys," Schreiner recalled. "I just packed them in like sardines. But nobody complained. They had been waiting for two years to get out."

The Germans, of course, increased their vigilance over Norway and sent up numerous patrols in an effort to intercept the B-24s. On several occasions, British detectors picked up enemy aircraft circling the route but each time the Liberators escaped by taking refuge over the Shetland Islands. The British also provided night fighter escort on some of the runs and during the entire evacuation operation the Germans failed to bag a single American plane.

Word spread to other Allied governments that the Air Transport Command's secret airline was operating into Sweden. Applications for passenger space poured into the American Embassy in London from all parts of Europe. Somehow space was found to fill part of these requests and by the end of June a large assortment of

American, British, and Russian officials were ferried over the route. Once the airline even transported the entire refugee government of Norway.

One day in July, Balchen received an urgent summons from U. S. officials in London. A desperate plea for help had come from the underground in Norway: unless supplies were furnished immediately the resistance movement in that country would collapse.

Officials explained the situation to Balchen. They told him that for the moment not a single plane could be spared to help the Norwegian patriots. They also hoped to drop Allied spies into Norway because our intelligence about German military movements in the area was far from complete. They asked Balchen if his organization would be willing to use its transports for these operations.

Balchen quickly calculated the risks. It was one thing to parachute men and equipment onto the comparatively rolling terrain of France and the Low Countries during hours of darkness. Norway, however, was something else again. Here there were mountains and rough weather and the missions would have to be carried out in daylight. Moreover, Norway was well patrolled by the Luftwaffe and there would be few spots available for forced landings if anything went wrong.

After a brief consultation with Lt. Col. Keith M. Allen, one of his aides, Schreiner, and Capt. Robert C. Durham, another of his veteran pilots,

Balchen gave his decision.

"We'll do it," he said.

Work started immediately to prepare one of the Liberators for the new job. In the air forces these sorties to aid the underground were known as "carpetbagger missions" and some modification in the aircraft was necessary. Into the bomb bays went 12 350-pound containers packed full with machine guns, ammunition, explosives, and other material necessary for sabotage. Packages of food and clothing were stowed in the waist. The aperture normally covered by the belly turret, and known as the Joe Hole, would be used to release the packages and any individuals parachuting down to join the underground.

The first mission to supply the Norwegian patriots was flown on July 17, 1944. In the Liberator were Balchen, Schreiner, Durham and other veterans of the secret airline, including 1st Lt. Robert Withrow and Sgts. Albert Sage, William Jesperson, Joel Williamson, Wilford Bollinger, and Neil Richards. Briefing for the mission had been exacting. Courses had been planned painstakingly to avoid interception and flak positions. The route selected was believed the safest one possible and if the Liberator remained on course the chance for success was good.

The run from Scotland to the rendezvous point was negotiated with clocklike precision. The Liberator skirted every ground battery and lookout post. The signal was received from the ground party and supplies fell squarely on the target. Quickly the Liberator circled and pointed its nose for home. The navigator was just giving the plot when Balchen shouted to Schreiner:

"Go north!"

There was a loud chorus of protests.

"Go north!" Balchen insisted.

Reluctantly, Schreiner swung the Liberator about and headed deeper into Norway.

Ten minutes later, Balchen pointed excitedly at a towering mountain peak.

"There it is!" he yelled. "The highest mountain in Norway. I wanted all of you to see it."

Encouraged by the success of the first mission, Balchen's airline strove to fly carpetbagger operations whenever weather conditions were favorable. Increasing quantities of supplies went down to the patriots and word came back that the resistance forces were using them to good advantage. Balchen's men had great admiration for the patriots and they took to writing them notes of encouragement. They also enclosed cigarettes and copies of American magazines in the packages. The patriots delighted in taunting the Gestapo by leaving the magazines in the lobbies of Norway's principal hotels.

During the course of these missions, the Liberators also dropped Allied secret agents and soon a highly efficient intelligence network was established. Liberator crews also brought back considerable information about the enemy's northern defenses. On one occasion they spotted a hidden airfield harboring new types of jet planes. Another crew discovered installations that were identified as V-bomb sites.

Late in the summer of 1944, the British were informed that one of Germany's highly secret V-2 rockets had fallen into Swedish territory. The rocket failed to explode and was almost intact when the Swedes found it. The Swedish government was willing to give it to British scientists but the problem was how to transport it to military laboratories in the south of England.

Inevitably, the British called on Balchen. Would be bring back the rocket? Balchen said he would. A message was sent to Stockholm. Load the rocket on a Liberator and bring it down at once. A reply came back in a few hours. The rocket weighed 8000 pounds. It was dismantled and crated and the crates wouldn't fit into the Liberator.

Balchen went into a huddle with Allen. They decided the only way to bring that rocket back to England was in a C-47. Allen agreed to try it.

He flew over to Prestwick immediately to borrow a C-47 but the only one available was a battered airliner known around the base as "The Bug." Its magnetic compass was faulty and the radio compass didn't work at all. Operations refused to take responsibility when Allen told them what he intended to do.

Quickly the blue and black invasion

stripes were painted over and commercial airline markings stenciled on the wings. Allen took off for Stockholm with Durham, Withrow, and a Norwegian radio operator named Engeland. When they landed in Sweden, "The Bug" did not have enough gas left in its tanks to taxi to the hangar. After the crates were loaded aboard, Allen was told that all flights over Norway had been canceled because of the lack of cloud cover. He decided to risk it and "The Bug" took off with its heavy load, barely clearing a pile of rocks at the end of the runway. In the bright daylight over Norway, the transport would have had little chance if spotted by enemy fighters but luck was with it and it reached the North Sea without detection. German shore batteries took some shots at "The Bug" as it roared across the coastline but their aim was poor. At seven the following morning the rocket was in the hands of the British.

Having demonstrated that nothing was too difficult for it to handle, Balchen's secret airline soon was asked to undertake another seemingly impossible job.

For a long time, Allied air forces had been trying to sink the German battleship *Tirpitz*, but as of September, 1944, the vessel was still afloat at her anchorage at Altenfjord, Norway. Except for photo reconnaissance pictures, intelligence had little information regarding the condition of the warship or about the anti-aircraft defenses protecting the harbor approaches. The only way to find out was to drop spies in the area with the hope that they could send out reports by portable transmitters.

Allen and Schreiner agreed to fly two Allied secret agents as close to Altenfjord as possible and a B-24 quickly was modified to permit installation of additional gasoline tanks in the bomb bay.

The flight from Britain to the drop zone and return covered more than 2600 miles and took 16½ hours. It was probably the longest combat mission ever flown in the ETO. The two agents parachuted down close to the harbor and within a day had established contact with England.

On September 21, 1944, Allen and the old reliables — Schreiner, Durham, Jesperson, Sage, Bollinger, Krasevac, Schick, Neil, and Richards — took off to drop several spies in a heavily-defended region of Norway. The secret agents came down successfully but one of the Liberator's engines suddenly went out. Allen decided to head northeast to Murmansk for an emergency landing rather than risk the long return flight to Britain. The plane was just passing over the outskirts of Murmansk when it was coned in the searchlights of the Russian harbor defenses. Anti-aircraft let loose a heavy barrage.

The Liberator shuddered under the impact of a direct hit and Allen ordered his men to bail out. He kept flying level until all had gone over the side and then prepared to follow. But another shell tore through the wounded bomber. The Liberator faltered and then plunged into the water, a flaming mass of wreckage.

The Russians deeply regretted the tragedy which nevertheless was excusable, for there had been no opportunity to alert the warships and harbor defenses that a friendly airplane was approaching.

Allen was buried with military honors at Murmansk and to the small wooden cross over his grave was affixed the simple inscription:

"In performance of duty."

It was a grievous loss to Balchen and the others who had performed so valiantly in all the Scandinavian operations. But their work continued. And it was not until victory came that the exploits of these men could at last be heralded to the world.

With the coming of spring, 1944 the days lengthened over Europe. Long-range fighters continued their incessant search for the disappearing Luftwaffe in the sky and on the ground and protecting the heavies of Eighth and Fifteenth Air Forces now beginning the strategic campaign against German oil. With the industrial heart of Germany largely converted to ruins, all air forces now turned to the forthcoming invasion — "Operation Overlord."

The months of April and May provided fitting climax to a flaming year over Europe, for during this time the full weight of Allied airpower was given to paving the way for the landings in Normandy.

Air Preparation for "Operation Overlord"

Maj. James F. Sunderman

"THE ALLIES owe the success of the invasion to the air forces. They prepared the invasion; they made it possible; they carried it through." This lamentful statement came from Luftwaffe Chief *Reichsmarschall* Hermann Goering.

The air preparation for the invasion of Western Europe began many months before the ground forces were even committed to battle. The Ninth Air Force was set up in England in

October, 1943. The organization was composed of A-20, B-26, B-25 medium bombers, P-38, P-47 fighter bombers, and C-47 troop carriers. It eventually grew into the largest single tactical air force in the world.

In addition, the British 2nd Tactical Air Force was established to concentrate maximum firepower against German attempts to reinforce the possible invasion areas of Western Europe.

Allied air strikes for "Overlord" had three primary objectives: isolation of assault area from German ground reserves, and from enemy air reinforcements, and destruction of coastal defenses and radar that might endanger the attack.

In a tremendous campaign to paralyze the French railroads, Allied bombers in two months of pre-invasion attacks dropped 76,000 tons of bombs on rail centers and bridges. By D-Day every bridge over the Seine below Paris had been destroyed, leaving the Germans virtually cut off from reinforcements. "The whole railway system was in such a mess," wrote a historian, "that most of the German reserves had to walk into Normandy after D-Day."

The Wehrmacht desperately tried. One combat group of the German 265th Infantry Division took a week to cover 100 miles by rail. The 3rd Parachute Division tried to move east from Brest by confiscating bicycles and carts, but had to split up. One regiment was welcomed by Gen. Rommel

at St. Lo on June 16, 10 days after D-Day. The 17th S.S. Panzer Grenadier Division tried to move up from Thouars (in Central France) on June 6. Elements were forced to detrain by cuts in the rail system. They had to march by secondary roads at night and took five full days to cover 200 miles to Periers. The 9th and 10th S.S. Panzer Divisions took about two weeks to reach the front from Metz.

The campaign against the Luftwaffe airfields within 130 miles of the proposed beachhead was mounted in the three weeks preceding the assault, so as to preclude reconstruction. 67,000 tons of bombs devastated the airfields allowing the Germans to mount only a few attacks against the invasion armadas. Churchill had this to say: "So great was our superiority in the air that all the enemy could put up during daylight over the invasion beaches was a mere hundred sorties." Against this pitiful response, the allies flew 14,600 sorties within the 24-hour period of D-Day.

A third type of air support which helped the invasion to succeed was the neutralization of V-1 launch sites in France. Their presence had become known and their menace hovered over the invasion. In the six months before D-Day, allied aircraft flew 25,000 sorties and dropped 36,000 tons of bombs on the V-1 sites. This campaign, coupled with the attack on the French railways, set the V-1 program back by three months at least. The first V-1 was not launched until a week after

"The whole railway system was in such a mess that most of the German reserves had to walk into Normandy after D-Day."

The V-1 flying "Buzz Bomb" shortly after launch from a German site.

D-Day, a delay which may have sealed the fate of the German resistance. Gen. Eisenhower later declared that if the Germans had been able to use V-1 a few months sooner, "Overlord" would have been "exceedingly difficult, perhaps impossible."

To support pre-"Overlord" operations in April, 1944, the AAF mustered in the ETO a total of 99 combat groups including 39 heavy bomber, 11 medium and light bomber, 32 fighter, 14 troop carrier, and 3 reconnaissance. This level of activity was sustained and expanded as air operations reached a climax. By June, 1944, AAF strength was increased by 2 heavy bomber and 1 fighter group to 102 combat groups.

U.S. aircraft on hand in the ETO in June, 1944 numbered 10,343 including 7505 *first line* combat planes, broken down by 2929 heavy bombers, 804 medium bombers, 387 light bombers, 3046 fighters, 339 reconnaissance.

During the three months, April through June, 1944, the AAF flew an average of 57,400 *effective* sorties a month, with June the peak month. In support of D-Day operations that month, the AAF flew 82,369 *effective* sorties, including 27,713 heavy bomber; 8908 medium and light bomber; and 50,748 fighter.

The AAF dropped 262,516 tons of bombs in France on all forms of every communication and transportation, on airfields, on Hitler's Atlantic Wall defenses. Heavy bombers accounted for 119,460 tons, and the medium, light and fighter bombers 143,056 tons.

The RAF contribution more than doubled these figures and its last minute neutralization of German radar kept the enemy from detecting the direction of the main landings and gave Eisenhower's forces advantage of tactical surprise on D-Day.

Before dawn of D-Day, 1136 heavy bombers of the RAF Bomber Command had dropped 5853 tons of bombs on selected coastal batteries lining the Bay of the Seine between Cherbourg and Le Havre. At dawn, the AAF took up the air attacks, and in the half-hour (from 0600 to 0630) before the touchdown of the assault forces, 1365 heavy bombers dropped 2746 tons of high explosives on the shore defenses while landing craft with their troops waited 1000 yards off shore from the beaches. This was followed by attacks by medium bombers, light bombers, and fighter bombers on enemy defense emplacements. During the first eight hours of June 6 alone, Allied aircraft dropped 10,000 tons of bombs on German defenses and communications. While the pre-invasion tactical air campaign rolled at high crest, Eighth Air Force bombers continued attacking industrial targets deep in Germany. The object was to draw off Luftwaffe fighters from Allied air operations in France. The ruse worked. During the entire pre-invasion air softening of the beachhead area and surrounding territory, our flyers encountered little German fighter opposition.

A variety of other air preparations

took place such as photo mapping of every inch of German coastal defenses which gave our air intelligence the detailed information needed to target bombers and fighter bombers and pinpoint, for the Supreme Commander, the most feasible areas to pour his troops ashore. Weather planes ranged far and wide in practice missions for their all-important D-Day forecasting duties. One thing made it all possible — the defeat of the Luftwaffe. "The lack of German air superiority," said Hitler's Gen. Guderian "led to our complete breakdown . . . "

The flaming year had driven from the skies the mighty Luftwaffe which had been the keystone to every German military conquest on the ground.

The price had been high. U.S. air crew casualties alone for June, 1943 to May, 1944 numbered 27,576, including 8690 killed and 15,862 missing or captured, while total British and American casualties in all European theatres during this period were over 140,000. They were far greater than those killed and wounded in the entire massive invasion of Normandy itself.

Air power's role in "Operation Overlord" was a decisive one, said Gen. George C. Marshall, U.S. Army Chief of Staff. Without it, he stated, "it would have required at least 15 weeks for the Allies to land as many divisions as the Germans had available in Belgium and Northern France.

Ninth Air Force A-20s bomb German defenses on northern French coast in an attack to soften up installations on the D-Day invasion coast.

PART SIX

D-DAY TO V-E DAY:

June, 1944 – May, 1945

The Tactical Air Sweep

Lockheed P-38 Lightnings with zebra-stripe invasion markings flying low-level sweeps over Normandy.

Three factors defeated us in the West where I was in command. First, the unheard-of-superiority of your air force, which made all movement in day-time impossible. Second, the lack of motor fuel — oil and gas — so that the Panzers and even the remaining Luftwaffe were unable to move. Third, the systematic destruction of all railway communications so that it was impossible to bring one single railroad train across the Rhine. This made impossible the reshuffling of troops and robbed us of all mobility.
—General Von Rundstedt, Commander-in-Chief
German Armed Forces in Western Europe

Introduction

By Spring, 1944 a crippled Luftwaffe hung tenaciously to its bases in Western Europe, the victim of declining aircraft and fuel production and staggered by losses in air battles with Allied fighters. Across France and Belgium disrupted rail and road communications paralyzed movements of troops and supplies. Debris-scarred German cities and industrial areas marked the pathway of a violent, incessant year of strategic bombardment. Aerial destruction of German radar warning stations left the German High Command with grossly inadequate intelligence about Allied invasion plans.

The stage was set for the final campaign of the war — invasion of Europe — and this event got underway in the early hours of June 6, 1944, between midnight and 6:00 A.M.

At 0145 hours, 813 transports of IX Troop Carrier Command preceded by 20 Pathfinder aircraft (each with 13 member drop teams scheduled to flare-mark landing areas) began dis-

gorging paratroopers of U.S. 101st and 82nd Airborne Divisions on the Cherbourg Peninsula, inland from the beaches of Normandy. Simultaneously, 237 transports of two RAF Groups dropped 4130 paratroopers of the British 6th Airborne Division into the same area but to the east of the U.S. landings.

On the heels of this aerial envelopment, 104 CG-4A and 98 British Horsa and Hamilcar gliders cut loose over small fields of Normandy, bringing in additional men, anti-tank guns, howitzers, and other heavy battle equipment.

At daylight, following heavy air and sea bombardment of the Normandy coastal defenses, five Allied divisions, under an air cover of 171 fighter squadrons, assaulted the beaches of Normandy between Caen and Montebourg and seized a foothold in France.

While the massive night airborne landings had gotten somewhat scattered, they served to screen German

251

reinforcements in the immediate area from reaching the beach landings. And in the air overhead, only a few German planes succeeded in penetrating the Allied air patrols to attack ships in the convoy.

Follow-up airborne activites on D-Day consisted mainly of glider resupply missions and paradrops. Some 208 CG-4As brought reinforcements to the U.S. airborne troops while a large British 256-glider operation in the evening was highly successful. By mid-afternoon the British forces had linked up with the beach forces.

The array of air power supporting the whole invasion effort was staggering. The U.S. Eighth and Ninth Air Forces comprised some 3000 combat aircraft. Of near equal strength were the British 2nd Tactical and their Air Defense Forces (formerly Fighter Command). On D-Day alone U.S. airmen flew more than 8722 combat sorties while the RAF added another 5676. Compared to this the Luftwaffe put up less than 50 sorties — full proof of the decisiveness of the pre-invasion air battle.

Facing the massive Allied ground assault were some 58 German divisions scattered throughout the Low Countries and France. Battered by continuous aerial attack in the weeks prior to D-Day, their immediate deployment to the Normandy area was impossible. By D plus five, the Allies had 16 divisions ashore while the Germans had succeeded in moving only 14 divisions into the Cherbourg area.

Two weeks later, the Allied forces had increased to one million men, and on June 27 the big port of Cherbourg fell, giving a major access-way into France, through which troops, supplies, and heavy armor could pour ashore.

Tactical air forces began moving into quickly built airfields in Normandy within one week after the landings. By July 31, 17 out of Ninth AF's 18 fighter-bomber groups were operating from Normandy airstrips supporting the 19 American and 16 British-Canadian divisions poised for the drive across France.

Despite overwhelming numerical superiority on the ground, the initial Allied break-out from the landing area was stopped by strong German defense positions around Caen and St. Lo. U.S. and British airpower was called in to break the deadlock. On July 18, British heavies struck Caen, followed by a maximum U.S. effort at St. Lo on July 25, when 1500 Eighth Air Force heavies and 900 Ninth Air Force mediums carpet-bombed five miles of the front. Fixed enemy positions were saturated with neary 3500 tons of bombs, gouging a gigantic hole in German defenses. Through this break Lt. Gen. George S. Patton poured his Third Army tank columns south into Brittany, preceded by waves of hard-striking fighters and bombers wreaking destruction on the retreating Nazi ground forces.

Rebounding to the St. Lo breakthrough the Germans counter-attacked

Headed for France, an American C-47 pulls a British Horsa glider loaded with airborne troops into the air on the morning of D-Day.

Having completed its part in a raid on the Nazi supply system, this Ninth Air Force B-26 Marauder bomber is seen over the Channel headed back for its base in England. These hard-hitting medium bombers shuttled back and forth across the Channel helping to clear the way for the invasion ground forces. Far below can be seen a portion of the invasion fleet.

at Avranches, with the hope of driving a wedge through Allied lines to the sea. When it failed, the invasion armies (the British from the North and the American from the south) began closing a giant pincer around all German forces in Normandy. Desperately the Nazi Panzers slipped backward, to avoid the trap, through a small opening called the Falaise-Argentan pocket. It was in this narrow corridor that Allied tactical air struck the Panzers with terrible force, turning the columns of armor, trucks, and mobile weapons into twisted junk. The scene was compared by Gen. Eisenhower to a page from Dante's *Inferno*.

The Nazi rout became a pell-mell flight across France as the Germans headed for the safety of the Siegfried Line.

The exploits of tactical air now became full and dramatic. As Gen. Patton raced his Third Army toward Germany, his unguarded southern flank along the Loire River was protected solely by the fighters, fighter bombers, and mediums of Brig. Gen. O. P. Weyland's 19th Tactical Air Command. So effective was this sweeping air flank, that a German force of 20,000, moving up from southern France, surrendered, without any ground action, to the air commander. It was an event without precedent in history.

As the Germans retreated toward their homeland, the tactical air offensive increased in intensity and scope. Co-ordination between ground and air forces reached a near perfect level. Leap-frogging from base to base behind the racing Allied armies, Ninth AF's tactical units put on a show of mobility astounding even Allied air leaders. Luftwaffe airfields were flown into almost before the last German plane left. Reconnaissance aircraft watched every German move, called in fighter bombers to eliminate German troop concentrations, traffic jams, artillery fire. Strafing Thunderbolts turned the highways into nightmares for the fleeing enemy.

Meanwhile, Allied forces landed in Southern France west of the French Riviera in an equally spectacular operation. More than 5000 paratroopers and glider-borne forces preluded the initial beach assault. Meeting light resistance these forces raced up the Rhone Valley, brilliantly supported by Twelfth Air Force tactical aircraft. They linked up with the main Eisenhower drive out of Normandy in less than a month.

As the Allied armies struck out across France, a second thrust northward through the Low Countries was designed to outflank the Siegfried Line, cross the Rhine, and enter the northern plains of Germany. In conjunction with this advance, commanded by British Gen. Bernard Montgomery (of Alamein), the Allies launched "Operation Market" — the largest airborne operation of the war. The aim of "Market" was to secure both sides of the Rhine River and permit Montgomery to drive his two land

Part of the airborne invasion of southern France, these parachutists fill the sky over the coastal area somewhere between Nice and Marseilles.

Members of the 1st Airborne Task Force attend mass at their glider just before taking off for invasion of southern France.

armies into Germany. Beginning on September 17, Pathfinder teams were dropped to mark paratroop and glider landing zones. The initial phases were a success, but inclement weather prevented airborne reinforcements from arriving on time. Between September 17 and 30, 4934 British and U.S. Troop Carrier planes and 2239 gliders dropped and landed nearly 35,000 U.S. and English troops, 20,000 on the first day — September 18 — and 2856 tons of cargo. Allied tactical air flew some 5200 sorties in support of the giant maneuver. While the operation itself was successful, its objective was not. The Germans drove the airborne troops back across the Rhine and proceeded to dig into strong positions from the North Sea to Switzerland blocking that route into the homeland.

Failure to turn this northern end of the Siegfried Line bogged the ground war down as winter weather set in.

Meanwhile, the strategic campaign of U.S. and RAF Bomber Command heavies against the German oil industry proceeded at high pace. Main target for the 1000 heavies of the Fifteenth Air Force was Ploesti and other Balkan oil plants. The 2000 four-engine bombers of Eighth Air Force turned onto the synthetic oil industry at Merseburg-Leuna and plants in Czechoslovakia and Western Poland. RAF Bomber Command's 1100 heavies continued hammering synthetic oil plants in the Ruhr. By September of 1944 German oil production was down to one-quarter of normal. This great campaign which left the Luft-waffe and the Panzer divisions stranded for lack of fuel was achieved at high cost. The Germans had ringed their oil industry with the war's heaviest concentration of flak guns and skilled crews. In the month of July alone Eighteenth and Fifteenth AF lost 642 heavies, but the campaign was a brilliant success. The production curve of gasoline dipped rapidly and by spring, 1945 it was down to 7 per cent of normal capacity.

The impact reverberated throughout the German nation and its war effort. Lack of fuel completely negated the rising production of German jet fighters, cut down Luftwaffe pilot training to almost zero, forced German ground forces to hoard precious gasoline for weeks in order to make one movement of any kind. Coupled with the Allied tactical air disruption of railroad and highway facilities, the strategic strike on oil strangled the German economy and the mobility of its armed forces.

At the same time heavies continued their concentration on submarine pens in German port cities and on V-1 and V-2 weapon sites.

By December, 1944 the German back was to the wall. Hitler personally directed his forces to launch a counter-offensive through the Ardennes Forest in a move to buy time at all costs and capture large stocks of Allied fuel. Using their last available gasoline and gathering up what remained of the Luftwaffe, the German Wehrmacht crushed through Allied lines, pushing some 50 miles before it ground to a stop. Unfortunately a spell of extremely bad weather at this time of year prevented Allied counter-air attack. But on December 23, the weather cleared and during the next week mediums, heavies and fighter bombers pasted the narrow German salient with more than 100,000 tons of bombs. The historic stand of Allied ground forces at Bastogne and St. Vith held the Germans to their narrow wedge from which they began to withdraw on December 27. During the next month the "Bulge" was eliminated.

It was during this time the Luftwaffe made its farewell appearance. On New Year's Day, 1945, it launched an offensive against Allied airfields on the Continent, flying some 800 sorties, destroying 127 Allied aircraft, mainly on the ground, damaging nearly 140. In exchange, the Germans lost nearly 200 of their own precious combat aircraft. This hopeless effort marked the end of the Luftwaffe in Western Europe. A few of the battered units were soon after transferred to the Russian Front where the Soviets were pushing westward toward Germany.

At the beginning of 1945, Germany was no longer an industrial nation. Its transportation facilities were at near collapse. Its airfields were packed with aircraft which had no fuel. The entire structure of the Third Reich was crumbling from within and without.

In January and February the Allied armies pushed through the Rhineland with little opposition. On March 24 a massive airborne invasion, "Operation Varsity," leaped across the Rhine, de-positing 17,000 troops into an area less than 23 miles square in four hours.

"Varsity" was preceded by a three-day tactical air interdiction sweep that directed 3471 sorties against rail and road communications in Germany, making 215 rail cuts, destroying 80 locomotives, 2383 railroad cars and 318 trucks. Simultaneously, heavy bombers dumped 6600 tons of explosives on military installations. "Varsity" was the most successful of all airborne missions of the war, involving 1783 British and U.S. troop carrier planes, 1275 gliders. Less than 20 Luftwaffe planes came even within sight of the Troop Carrier Formations. The breach of the Rhine sealed the final fate of Germany.

For the big bombers the strategic air offensive was finished by April 1, 1945. There were no more targets left.

Allied troops, with complete air superiority overhead, surrounded the industrially rich Ruhr and 400,000 of Germany's crack troops. Tactical air's mediums and fighter bombers swept over the Reich like locusts striking targets of opportunity and catching nearly 3000 fuel-less Luftwaffe planes jam-packed on German airdromes.

German defenses collapsed as American tank columns swiftly rolled through the country and into Austria and Czechoslovakia. On April 25, Allied ground forces met the Russians driving in from the East at the Elbe River and two weeks later, on May 7, the Nazi government of Adolph Hitler surrendered unconditionally.

By D-Day all of the rail bridges in eastern France between Paris and the sea had been destroyed. This photograph shows a locomotive caught during the bombing of a bridge.

D-Day. U. S. paratroopers coming down over a field on which glider troops have already landed.

"You needn't worry about the air. If you see a plane it will be ours."
*- Gen. Dwight D. Eisenhower, Supreme Allied Commander, to his troops
on the eve of D-Day, June 6, 1944.*

General Eisenhower's high tribute to Allied air power had been made
possible by months of unending work on the ground and unceasing
heroism in the air.

Looking back over the months that preceded D-Day, a certain orderly
and logical sequence of achievements can be discerned. First of all, the
Luftwaffe was forced back into Germany by the heavy bombers of the
Eighth Air Force and their fighter escorts who dealt such terrible blows
to the war-making capacity of the Reich that Hitler was forced to husband
his dwindling air strength to protect the homeland. Medium bombers and
fighters of the Ninth Air Force and the RAF's 2nd Tactical Air Force
also helped by making the coastal airdromes too hot for the Luftwaffe to
use with any comfort. But it was primarily strategic pressure on "Das
Vaterland" and the steadily dwindling aircraft reserves that cost Jerry all
hope of contesting the air over the beaches.

Once this forced withdrawal of the enemy air force was accomplished,
Allied airmen were able to turn their attention to the network of communications on which the Germans relied to supply the armies of the
Atlantic Wall. Heavies, mediums, light bombers and fighters of both the
RAF and AAF hammered marshaling yards, junctions, tunnels, and
bridges into a state of chaos. By D-Day 14 road bridges across the Seine
between Paris and the sea were knocked out. By D-Day plus one, the remaining six were destroyed. The effect on Rommel's ability to shift troops
into the Normandy area quickly can easily be imagined. And the onslaught against rolling stock and road traffic never ceased.

Another pre-invasion function of air power was to observe enemy preparations while denying him the benefits of photo reconnaissance. In endless sorties, Allied photo planes obtained coverage of the entire enemy-held
coastline. At low tide they photographed the steel obstructions planted by
the Germans to repel landing craft. Inland they kept a watchful photographic eye on the progress of the anti-glider and anti-paratroop installations. Our fighters sweeps were unable completely to prevent German
photo reconnaissance, especially at night, but restricted it to a point where
the Germans obviously were kept guessing.

The fourth tactical contribution of Allied air power was the blitz on
German coastal defenses themselves for weeks before D-Day. Bombers
poured an endless stream of high explosives on naval guns — 155mm and
170mm — housed in steel and concrete emplacements. On the night before
D-Day, the RAF dropped 5000 tons on ten of these crucial batteries in
the area between LeHavre and Cherbourg — more tonnage per battery

than London ever received at one time during the night blitz of 1940.
Allied air power had paved the way. Now, on June 6, 1944, it would
spearhead the final assault. As darkness gathered around the air bases on
the English countryside on June 5, the supreme moment drew nigh for
the air assault forces.

Air Power in the Invasion

from "Air Force" Magazine

INSIDE THE METAL SKINS of hundreds of C-47s, soot-faced paratroopers knelt in final prayer. Standing beside their fragile craft, glider pilots checked their watches as the minutes ticked away toward midnight. On the Channel coast, civilians felt their beds rock and houses shudder as the RAF hurled down on ten Nazi gun emplacements the heaviest night bomb load of the war. All day long, Lightnings had patrolled the Straits, guarding ship movements from hostile eyes. Now the great armada was well underway, a thousand phosphorescent wakes gleaming under clouded skies. At bomber and fighter stations all over England, lights burned behind guarded doors as the last secret orders came in. Weeks of tension were building to a final climax. This was it; this was D-Day.

Shortly before midnight, three airborne divisions were on their way — the American 82nd and 101st and the British 6th. At six minutes past mid-

night, one great sky serpent, nine planes wide and 200 miles long, thrust its head across the enemy-held coast. Ten minutes later the lead plane of the 9th Troop Carrier Command's Pathfinder group was over the designated drop zone. Lights by the open door of the Skytrain winked red and then green. Carrying radio equipment that would greatly facilitate navigation for succeeding aircraft, the first stick of paratroopers tumbled into the flak-streaked darkness. The time was 0016 June 6, 1944. The liberation of Europe from the West had begun.

Almost unchallenged the great procession swung back toward its base. As the head recrossed the English coast, the tail was still going out, roaring across the choppy Channel at 300 feet. As each section of the body passed over Cherbourg Peninsula at a slightly increased attitude, hundreds of parachutes blossomed in the gusty air. Some came down through clouds that hung as low as 500 feet. As fast as they hit the ground, the paratroopers seized key position and began clearing the landing areas of obstructions left by the Germans. Gliders came spiraling down — British Hamilcars and Horsas and the smaller American CG-4As — carrying fighting troops, ammunition, land mines, field artillery, jeeps, medical supplies, and even complete radio stations in some cases. The heavy Horsas actually mowed down German obstacles. The giant Hamilcars, with greater wingspread than a Lancaster, disgorged tanks. Some cracked up but still delivered cargoes. Later the Germans complained bitterly about the Allied use of dummy paratroopers. One American glider landed by mistake on a roof, spilling out a combat team who promptly captured the village. Others were briefed to land directly on top of gun positions, silence the gun crews, and get away before the Allied bombers returned to the job. They did.

The losses among the Skytrains, flying unarmed and unescorted at less than 1000 feet were astonishingly light. The Americans lost only 26 aircraft out of almost 1000 dispatched, a bargain price to pay for the achievement of landing two crack divisions behind the Atlantic Wall. All the lessons learned in the dangerous night exercises during the past weeks in Britain were brilliantly applied. The Ninth Air Force's Troop Carrier Command could well be proud of the night's work.

By the time the Skytrains were back at base, preparing to fly reinforcements to the men they had dropped, the daylight forces were being briefed for the greatest air effort in history. Everything was going to be thrown in, from heavies to fighters.

Probably the first four-engine American aircraft to participate in the invasion plan were six Fortresses that dropped leaflets warning the French of the storm about to break. Long before any daylight, hundreds of heavies and mediums were airborne, some taking off by moonlight. D-Day had been postponed 24 hours to let the weather improve but it was still far from perfect. Through breaks in the clouds, crews of the heavies caught glimpses of the sea armada far below. Some claimed that their bombers were rocked even at that altitude by the concussion of naval broadsides being fired across the beaches.

At dawn 1300 American heavies took over where the RAF left off. As a result, the gunfire greeting the seaborne forces was much weaker than expected. The great guns on our battleships could and did silence the shore guns still able to fire, and early reports indicated only two destroyers and one LST sunk out of an armada of 4000 ships. This shows how thoroughly the way had been prepared by air power.

Marauders, flying lower than on any occasion since their disastrous debut in the ETO, had a better view than anybody. They saw tanks crawling ashore to engage the enemy, fields filled with the wreckage of gliders, bomb-pocked ground littered with parachutes. Fighters, never less than 200 feet over the beachheads, prowled restlessly up and down looking for the Luftwaffe. On the whole they were disappointed. Goering had issued a statement to the effect that the invasion had to be repulsed even if the Luftwaffe perished in the effort, but apparently the Luftwaffe was not ready for a showdown. Barely 50 enemy planes were seen in the battle area all day. Four of the 12 JU-88s that made a pass at one of the beachheads were destroyed. With approximately 10,000 Allied sorties being flown, the odds against the Luftwaffe were 200 to 1. The Supreme Commander was right; the assault troops did not have to worry about the air.

All through D-Day endless air processions went on. The Eighth Air Force flew over 4300 sorties; this was as many battle flights in one day as the Eighth Air Force had completed in its first seven months of operations over Europe. The Ninth chalked up better than 4800 and the RAF's 2nd Tactical Air Force recorded some 2000. It is probable that in the first 24 hours more than 13,000 battle flights were flown. When the late summer darkness descended, the Allied night fighters took up patrols and shot down 12 enemy aircraft that attempted to attack the beaches.

Air opposition stiffened slightly the next day. Air losses were even — both sides losing 23. For the Allies, however, this represented only a tiny frac-tion of the total forces engaged. By noon of D-Day plus two, only 289 aircraft were missing of some 27,000 sorties flown — an overall loss ratio of barely 1 per cent. Meanwhile, the Luftwaffe lost 176.

The close support afforded by the tactical air forces during the first three days was magnificent. The Marauders, sometimes flying three missions a day at whatever altitude the weather permitted, added their bomb weight to the naval bombardment of the stubborn German stronghold of Caen. Bomb-carrying P-47s pinpointed the troublesome gun positions and silenced them. Meanwhile 1000 American heavies blasted airfields in a wide arc around the battle zone. Gen. Eisenhower referred to the "long and brilliant campaign conducted in the past months by the combined air forces." It had been, he said, an essential preliminary to invasion and he congratulated the airmen on keeping up the good work. Other Allied leaders agreed that the air support was all that could be desired.

On Friday, June 9, the uncertain weather became so bad that all Allied air activity ceased. This respite gave the Germans a chance to bring up badly needed supplies and hindered the landing of our own. The communications of both sides, to a large extent, were at the mercy of the weather, but what was favorable to one handicapped the other. Bad weather tended to bottleneck Allied air superiority around Rommel's throat.

On Saturday, when the skies cleared somewhat, our planes found the roads behind the enemy lines choked with reinforcements. They took up strafing where they had left off on Thursday. Marauders flew in as low as 200 feet. One came back with a fragment of its own bombs lodged in the wing: 28 enemy aircraft were destroyed that day; 26 of ours were lost. Sunday was the same story except that our losses were even lighter and the Luftwaffe more elusive than ever.

By Saturday, emergency landing strips were being used by Allied planes running short of fuel or suffering battle damage. Sites for these landing strips were chosen before the invasion troops left England. Engineers had landed on D-Day and bulldozers followed that night. The first strip had been carved out of a cornfield under sniper fire and was ready for action by Friday afternoon.

By Monday, a Spitfire wing was in full operation and air evacuation of the wounded by transport plane had begun. With the Troop Carrier Command's great fleet of Skytrains virtually intact, supply by air assumed great importance as airdromes were captured farther inland.

As these words are written, on the morning of June 12, D-Day plus six, the German Air Force had yet to put in an appearance. Rommel seems to be committing his reverses piecemeal but they are battling without benefit of air power. Germany certainly has enough front line air strength left to make a fight of it for a limited time at least, but so far she is either unable or unwilling to do so. Probably both. Airfields near the battle zone are likely to prove death traps for grounded aircraft. Besides, if the Luftwaffe moves its limited fighter strength forward, American heavies will smash targets left unprotected in the Reich. Already since D-Day Italian-based Fortresses in great strength have attacked factories in Austria. The Nazis are in the unhappy position of a boxer with only one hand to guard himself. If he tries to protect his face, he risks a knockout blow in the solar plexus.

A Spitfire Mark XI with invasion markings.

While the gigantic preparations for the Allied invasion of France could not be hidden, even from the Germans, the specific time and place was one of the best kept secrets of the war. And there were some interesting and awkward situations as the final moments rolled by.

Invasion Alert

To THOUSANDS of American airmen in Britain, the first warning that H-hour was at hand came when iron security regulations were clamped down on stations, guards were doubled, briefing room doors were locked and no one was allowed to leave. Post visitors were not told of the alert until after they were admitted and then found that they could not leave. In some cases, this sequestration led to awkward situations. At one fighter station, presumably unadorned by any WACS, the harassed supply officer was pestered by indignant female hostages to provide certain items which he never before in all his Army career had been called upon to produce. At an-

other base, the local vicar arrived in high dudgeon to demand the release of several young women of his parish who, he said, were not adequately chaperoned. They were not released. A farmer, finding the village veterinarian was among those interned, wistfully drove a sick cow up to the gate. The sentry informed him that the cow could be treated only inside the fence and that it would have to stay there. At another station, two innocent passersby, who displayed mild curiosity at the blue and white zebra stripes with which all invasion aircraft were feverishly being painted, were enticed inside and held.

When massive formations of B-17s and B-24s were diverted from their strategic campaign against the heartland of Germany to lend support to ground forces, the versatility and flexibility of air power reached a high peak. Frequently in the early days of the invasion the combined power of strategic and tactical air forces were thrown at German field defenses, laying down a carpet of death and destruction no army could withstand. "Carpet or pattern bombing" was a new technique devised to relieve critical situations such as uncorking the bottleneck at St. Lo and breaking up the German counter-attack at Avranches. Through the five-mile breach in the St. Lo lines, Gen. Patton poured his Third Army in his epic dash across France.

Pacing the Attack

Maj. Arthur Gordon

THE STORY GOES that a GI from Georgia in a foxhole near St. Lo raised his head from the shuddering ground and screamed in his buddy's ear: "You know, Ah'm beginn' to think that dam-yankee Sherman was a right easy-goin', friendly sorta fella aftuh all!"

A few hundred yards ahead of this particular dogface, 1500 heavy bombers of the Eighth Air Force, flying at medium altitude, were unloading more than 3000 tons of general-purpose and fragmentation bombs on an area five miles long and two wide. Thousands of other doughboys watched the bomb-carrying fighters comb the area, saw hundreds of mediums add their bomb-weight to this cauldron of steel and flame. The date was July 25. The terrific aerial smash was the one that en-abled the Americans to break out of the Normandy peninsula and drive headlong toward Paris.

The resulting devastation, as described by observers who covered the area afterward, was appalling. The neat orchards and hedgerows and farmhouses looked as if they had been beaten with a giant flail. Dead cows and dead Germans lay sprawled in the craters. The craters themselves were not too large to interfere with tank movements, but roads were pitted, railroads were twisted into fantastic shapes, telephone poles were sheared off like matchsticks.

It seemed impossible that human beings could survive such a barrage, but some did. Those who expected the Germans to be completely "anaesthetized" were too optimistic. The Jerries suffered far more than they did at Cassino, where they had deep cellars in which to hide, but plenty of them survived. The important question was whether they had enough fight left in them to stem the advance that followed. Results proved that they did not.

The weather was cloudy, as usual, but not so bad as that of the day before when the same armada had been forced to return to base without dropping more than a third of its bombs. On both days some bombs fell short. These errors could have been the result either of malfunctions or of poor visibility caused by the dust and smoke of the bombs. The casualties among Allied personnel were regrettable, but they were not unforeseen. The margin for error had been made purposely small. No one doubted for a moment that among the assault troops the lives saved by the air blow far exceeded those lost by it.

The basic reason for this use of heavy bombers as tactical support was simply the desire on the part of Allied commanders to bring maximum pressure to bear on strong German defenses. There was no intention to divert the Forts and Libs more often than was necessary from their primary mission: the destruction of strategic targets. But it was significant that when they were diverted, as on July 18, July 25, and July 30, important ground gains followed.

What the high command thought of the value of all-out bombing of field defenses in open country was best indicated by their continued use of it. The Canadian breakthrough southeast of Caen on August 8, an attack which began at night, was paced by about 1000 RAF heavies some of which brought their bombs back, because again dust and smoke made dead-accurate bombing impossible. The air support was continued the next day when 600 American heavies hurled down 20,000 fragmentation bombs. This was considerably fewer heavies than the number employed at St. Lo two weeks earlier. The reason probably was the air chiefs' conclusion that after bombing by a certain number of combat wings, the target was so obscured as to make additional bombing unprofitable and dangerous. On that same day, the remainder of Eighth Air Force B-17s and B-24s attacked other targets, including launching sites for robot bombs. The Canadian drive, plowing through a defense belt at least ten miles wide, threatened to unhinge the whole German position.

In most of these cases where the heavies were employed, the Allies were facing German defenses in depth, with Jerry solidly dug in and awaiting attack. When the enemy was on the move, however, either forward or backward, the main burden of air support reverted to the mediums and fighters of the tactical air forces.

One of the most valuable contributions made by Allied air power in the entire campaign was the assistance it rendered in breaking up the German counter attack aimed at Avranches, a thrust designed to pinch off the American spearheads driving south into Brittany. This was a full-scale effort by four German divisions, and the work of the fighter-bombers — especially RAF rocket-firing Typhoons — in blasting enemy armor played a large part in saving the Allied armies from what would have been an awkward position had the Panzer thrust succeeded.

This protective role, however, was a rare one. When Gen. Bradley said that air-ground co-operation in Normandy was "away beyond anything we believed possible," he probably had in mind day-to-day performance — a day, for example, like July 28, when 70 tanks and 884 other vehicles were reported destroyed by Normandy-based planes alone. The effect on German communications was catastrophic.

There were innumerable reports of direct appeals from Allied tank commanders for air support to bomb a stubborn gun emplacement or knock out a defiant Tiger tank. As a rule, the requests were answered promptly, and although pinpoint accuracy was not always obtained, sooner or later the obstruction was cleared. In one case of complete reciprocity, a P-47 pilot reported to Allied artillery that the Germans seemed to be using a certain house as a headquarters. The artillery commander obliged by putting a couple of shells into the building. The Thunderbolt, swooping down, picked off the Jerries as they fled from doors and windows.

From the start, the tactical air forces showed a willingness to experiment boldly and profit by experience. A fairly typical day was June 20 — D-plus-14. At that stage of the game the Germans, fighting hard, were being pushed back toward Cherbourg. They had reached a fairly strong defensive position west and southwest of the city and, although somewhat disorganized, were in a position to inflict heavy losses on the attacking forces.

It was decided by the high command not to use the heavies but to let the tactical air forces make an all-out effort to harass and demoralize the Germans before the VII Corps moved forward. Although little if any opposition from the Luftwaffe was expected, the airmen knew that the operation might prove expensive; low-level attack against disciplined ground troops usually is. Still, one reason for the attack was to balance losses against objectives achieved and to be guided accordingly in the future. An advantage of this particular operation was that Cherbourg was doomed, the terrain was certain to be captured eventually, and results could be judged by first-hand inspection on the ground and by subsequent interrogation of captured enemy ground forces.

There was little time to plan the operation — about six hours, to be exact; six hours in which to organize an air effort calling for about 1000 sorties against an area three miles wide and seven miles long; six hours in

General H. H. Arnold, left, Commanding General, U.S. Army Air Forces and Lt. Gen. Omar N. Bradley, Commanding General U.S. Ground Forces in the European Theatre of Operations walk along a French beachhead shortly after D-Day. They appear very jubilant with the results of their joint efforts in the invasion.

which to get the field orders down to the groups; six hours in which to let the ground forces know exactly what was going to happen. It took some tall hustling on the part of headquarters and all the way down the line, but they did it.

H-hour was 1400. The plan called for ten squadrons of RAF fighter-bombers from the 2d Tactical Air Force to bomb and strafe the target area for 20 minutes from H-minus-80 to H-minus-60. Then 12 Ninth Air Force fighterbomber groups were to take over for an hour, from H-minus-60 to H. Then eight groups of Ninth Air Force Marauders bombing from medium altitude, were to pinpoint gun positions from H to H-plus-60. Finally three groups of A-20s were to give the Germans a last-minute shellacking. Weather prediction was 1000-2000 feet overcast, which might call for pathfinder technique. Actually the weather was somewhat better than this, and visual as well as pathfinder methods were used.

The troops were withdrawn 1200 yards. The air attack began dead on schedule and proceeded like clockwork. The fighter bombers — 25 of which were lost out of about 550 attacking — claimed good results from strafing, glide- and dive-bombing of trains, flak-guns, machine-gun positions, troops, and motor transport. The bombers, only one of which failed to return, reported excellent to unobserved results. The ground forces were of the opinion that no great material

damage had been done but that the enemy had been scattered and disorganized and that the advance had been made considerably easier.

While tactical support held the center of the stage, the strategic blows continued. Fighter factories that the Germans had laboriously repaired by combining crippled plants were hammered again. The blitz on oil production continued, aided by the RAF's night blows. Most of the fighter opposition was encountered in Southern Germany, where Jerry seemed to be concentrating the bulk of his remaining fighters in an effort to meet attacks either from England or Italy. Striking from Italy on July 18, heavies of the Fifteenth Air Force and their escort attacked Friedrichshafen and met about 250 enemy fighters, 66 of which were claimed destroyed. On July 25, bombing the Hermann Goering tank works at Linz, Austria, they again encountered stiff opposition and shot down 65, losing 19 bombers and two fighters. On both days, British-based heavies were employed on tactical targets, allowing Jerry to concentrate his full strength, such as it was, on the invaders from Italy.

There was considerable discussion as to the wisdom of pulling the big bombers off strategic targets, even occasionally, to give close support to ground troops. But the question was beginning to seem academic. The truth was that the Allied air forces could now dispose sufficient strength to meet all tactical requirements and maintain strategic bombing too.

This was the happy state of affairs that prevailed as the second anniversary of American participation in the European air war drew near. In August, 1942, 12 Fortresses had made the first stab at the Nazis, bombing the marshaling yards at Rouen. In August, 1944, after two years of bitter fighting and heartbreaking effort, the U.S. Air Force and their British allies were dominating the skies and were pacing the ground assault upon crumbling Fortress Europe.

The greatest tactical air feat of the war unfolded when the colorful Gen. George S. Patton led his Third Army from the Normandy breakout in a wild dash across France, relying completely on the fighters and the bombers of Gen. O. P. Weyland's 19th Tactical Air Command as the sole protecting force on his exposed southern flank.

It was a bold, imaginative operation directed by Weyland with skill and energy. Here is the story of its conception and successful execution.

Patton's Air Cavalry

S/Sgt. Mark Murphy

FROM THE TIME of Philip of Macedon, army commanders have worried about flanks, simply because most of the time an army is much longer than it is wide. To the rear of an army's front line are reserve troops and supply depots and communications. A standard method of winning a campaign is to strike the enemy's flanks, destroy his supply routes, and cut off his front line troops from support and materiel.

In past wars, cavalry often was used to protect the flanks of an army. In the present conflict, the Germans frequently have employed armored patrols for the purpose. The roving cavalry or armor would cover its own flanks, spot any enemy strength and engage the opposition until support arrived.

Patton, however, had another idea. He was in one hell of a hurry, so he called in Weyland and gave him the task of protecting an exposed flank — not the flank of an army moving methodically across known terrain, but that of a mechanized army moving with incredible speed, now in one direction, now in another, destroying the enemy, heading relentlessly toward the German homeland.

And so for the first time in history, air, in addition to its duties of column support, reconnaissance and all the odd work of a tactical force, was given a task which until recent months in this war had been a ground job. This was no mere reconnaissance assignment. Weyland's forces were expected to cover the exposed area and handle anything that developed. Previously, armies had moved so far, stopped, regrouped and moved on again. Patton, confident that his air support would protect him, kept on going for weeks after it was expected he would stop. He and Weyland took on a job requiring nerve and skill as well as imagination.

The 19th Tactical Air Command and the Third Army were kept under wraps until August 1, although both had been activated for some time, and the 19th had done a lot in the softening up of the French coast prior to D-Day. Late in July, there was the business at St. Lo, the breakthrough and some feints which caught the Germans neatly. The British were left to hold the pivot at Caen, their troops engaging the bulk of German units in the area, while the Americans cut loose on a wild jaunt through France.

Although takeoff of the 19th on August 1 was delayed until later afternoon because of bad weather, the Third Army had launched operations bright and early, and, in the hours remaining before dusk, the airmen were able to knock out both German armor and German trucks.

After the ground forces broke through in a drive past Avranches, the 19th really had its work cut out for it. Groups were assigned to hang over the armored columns of the Third Army, to prevent attack by enemy planes and to knock out stuff holding up the columns. Armed reconnaissance squadrons had the long range jobs of isolating battlefields, which is a military way of saying they had to kill any troops coming to the support of the enemy, to spot and break up any concentrations, and to keep the enemy constantly off balance.

AAF pilots were told not to bust any bridges because that might hold up the progress of the American armies who were definitely on their way. If there were no targets for the column-supporting groups, they were left free to wander 30 miles ahead in search of objectives to bomb or strafe. Fighter Control stations kept track of what was going on and often sent squadrons out to hit targets noticed only minutes before by recon outfits.

Patton moved his headquarters, and the 19th TAC headquarters moved, too. The command's tasks grew daily. In addition to giving the Third Army armed support by conducting reconnaissance missions, there was the job of protecting a bottleneck at Avranches, through which the Third Army's men and materiel were pouring, and some work to be done on ships in the harbor of St. Malo. American pilots were going on three and sometimes five missions a day.

Almost daily new groups were being added to the 19th as its functions were broadened. In the first five days of the Third Army's drive, the airmen flew 1088 sorties and lost only three planes. They knocked out 250 motor vehicles, 12 tanks, 9 horsedrawn vehicles, 4 locomotives, 9 railroad cars, and 2 naval vessels; cut 5 railroad lines; destroyed 17 gun positions, 7 fuel and supply dumps, 2 marshaling yards, a gas tank and an enemy head-quarters, and attacked 21 troop concentrations. All this was in addition to ceaseless patrol and reconnaissance.

The enemy withdrew to concentration points at Brest, St. Malo, Lorient, and on the Painpol Peninsula, and the Third Army, finished with Normandy, had overrun Brittany where the fields and weather were better for air operations. The enemy tried to cut our traffic through Avranches, and Patton started east in a move threatening the Germans facing the U.S. First Army

An American fighter pilot leans on the wing of his P-51 Mustang. On the fuselage are stenciled symbols for his interdiction work — two Messerschmitts, a locomotive, and two ammunition carriers. The five goose-steppers stand for five German soldiers who tried to defend their ammunition carrier.

and the British in the area of Mortain and Vire.

Meanwhile, continuing the Brittany campaign, Patton set out to get the river Loire for his right flank. The 19th TAC was assigned to guard this flank, and dispatches of those days read something like the description of a character of Stephen Leacock's who jumped on his horse and rode off in all directions. Word from the Third was received at the 19th's headquarters that "movement east, south and west by ground troops was greatly facilitated."

By the end of the first week of the campaign, the 19th was in full strength, and some of the Luftwaffe got up to be knocked down, 33 enemy planes being destroyed on August 7. Patton kept moving his headquarters close to the head of his columns. But 19th TAC headquarters had communications troubles. The farther it moved inland, the farther it was from its airbases.

Gen. Weyland, however, flew up to confer with Gen. Patton nearly every day, and operations continued unceasingly. Planes blasted enemy armor and gun positions, flew over areas that the Third Army might move into, bombed and strafed targets they found there and watched over the supply routes.

When the Germans used our color recognition panels on their tanks, the TAC pilots would fly low and look over the vehicles as carefully as a six-mile-a-minute speed would permit.

Then they'd zoom upward, circle and come back down to pelt the enemy with bombs and bullets. The Germans had to use horsedrawn equipment much of the time (for lack of gas and oil for their motorized equipment), and our flyers killed a lot of horses, something which bothered them considerably more than killing Germans, who needed it.

During the action which closed the Argentan trap, some of the 19th's Thunderbolts pounced upon a concentration of nearly 1000 enemy vehicles and destroyed at least half of them.

At this stage of the campaign, enemy ground troops began surrendering to the TAC flyers. One unit of about 400 Germans waved white flags at a fighter squadron which was lining up for a strafing attack. The squadron reported the location of the troops to Fighter Control and waited around until some ground soldiers rounded up the Boches. An 18-year-old boy among the prisoners said the field kitchen of his outfit had been bombed and that he hadn't had anything to eat for four days. Our planes then dropped leaflets outlining the advantages of yielding and thousands of German troops capitulated voluntarily.

German concentrations were falling one by one, and on August 18 there was a harvest of 7000 jammed vehicles. Because most of the enemy equipment was in the British sector, the 19th was denied the jackpot. While the American flyers were credited with

General George Patton consults with Air Force generals at an advance headquarters in Europe. Left to right: General Carl A. Spaatz, General Patton, Lt. Gen. Jimmy Doolittle, Maj. Gen. Hoyt S. Vandenberg and Maj. Gen. O. P. Weyland.

a few hundred trucks, some tanks and railroad rolling stock, the score of the RAF's 2nd Tactical Command was 1159 motor transports destroyed and 1725 damaged; 124 tanks destroyed and 96 damaged.

Meanwhile, the Allies had landed in Southern France and were 30 miles inland. The Germans were very unhappy.

Late in the month a cold front cut down flying time, and on several days the Third Army sent its own armored patrols along its right flank on the line of the Loire. There was little danger, though, because the 19th TAC had taken care of the enemy all along that 400-mile stretch. When the planes were flying, there was either no air opposition or plenty of it, the enemy preferring to jump our P-38s, P-47s, and P-51s when it had an eight or ten-to-one advantage.

Our scores usually ran about four enemy craft destroyed to one of ours lost. On one occasion, 8 P-51s dispersed more than 80 German planes. Another day 8 P-47s, jumped by 12 ME-109s and 20 FW-190s, got 6 and damaged 1 for an American loss of 2 planes and pilots. In a broadcast to its troops, the German High Command declared that the Luftwaffe while outnumbered, really was doing something, even though German soldiers "tied to a single front" might not realize it.

As the enemy tried to cross the Seine

before the fall of Paris, the Thunderbolts made things miserable for him. There were practically no bridges left standing, and some of the Germans were trying to swim across the river. Most of them were using ferries, and the 19th, making things worse, put delayed action bombs in the ferry slips.

Pressing ever onward, the Americans skirted Paris on two sides, leaving the 2nd French Armored Division to occupy the encircled city after the French Forces of the Interior had a field day routing Germans out of their fine billets.

On August 25, the Luftwaffe took a terrific beating. Mustangs and Thunderbolts of the 19th and of the 9th Tactical Air Command of the Ninth Air Force destroyed 77 enemy planes in the air and 50 on the ground, got 11 probables and damaged 33. The total American loss was 27 aircraft. Over Germany, Eighth Air Force fighters and bombers accounted for 11 in the air and 40 on the ground. The Germans launched a few jet-propelled craft which traveled like hell but never got anywhere near our planes.

The 19th's assignment after the fall of Paris was a tough one, calling for widely diffused action. Patton was far across France and the TAC was supporting him. At the same time it was bombing Brest and other enemy targets in Western France. When these coastal installations finally capitulated, Weyland was able to devote his full strength to the campaign in the East.

In September things began to slow down, although in the middle of the month the 19th herded in 20,000 Germans to surrender in one of the oddest actions of the war. These troops yielded to what amounted to a couple of platoons of infantry and a battalion of MPs brought up for the purpose. A young infantry officer arranged the surrender after days of negotiations when he threatened, among other things, to have some circling P-47s come in and bomb the Germans. The Thunderbolts had been attacking them for weeks and they didn't want another minute of it.

Ground-air co-operation between the 19th TAC and the Third Army reached an all-time high if you can go for the fantastic story they tell at TAC headquarters. It's about a young airman, a lieutenant colonel, who was forced to bail out behind the German lines. According to the tale, he hid in a town for two days, waiting for Patton's columns to approach the area. After a Frenchman had sneaked him across the lines, the colonel reached Third Army Headquarters, where he described the enemy-held town and its defenses and suggested that it be taken immediately.

"Give me a forty-five and I'll take it myself," the flyer is said to have volunteered.

The colonel's enthusiasm is supposed to have so pleased the two-gun man (Patton) to whom he was reporting, that half an hour later, American tanks rolled into town on information an AAF officer had obtained on flying-boot reconnaissance.

Aerial resupply of the surging Allied armies was a feat of gigantic proportions. The job went to the Troop Carrier boys with their slow, unarmed C-47 cargo planes. Theirs was the unenviable task of going into front line strips. It took a lot of guts and skill and there was little glory to be earned.

When 35,000 paratroops and glider infantry were delivered deep behind enemy lines in northern Holland in September, 1944 to secure both sides of the Rhine River, there was only one lifeline of supply — by air. Troop Carrier pilots rose to the occasion. Here is the story of a typical day.

Special Delivery to No Man's Land

1st Lt. Joseph D. Guess

TODAY, at last, the fog was lifting and the sun was showing.

At 0800, it was decided to run the mission. Soon the motors of more than 200 C-47s would be making the ground throb beneath them at the Wing's bases. Gen. Clark looked at his overall plan. One of his officers pointed out that the plan called for landing at three bases in Holland. They looked at their map of the day.

"The enemy isn't cleared from three fields in this area," this officer said. "The situation is confusing there. At this moment we have no fields to land on." With his finger he indicated a point on the map two miles north of Grave and eight miles southwest of Nijmegen. "There's a small German fighter field there that may be cleared by this afternoon. But that's only one field."

"Give us three hours," said Gen. Clark, "and one field and we'll land and unload all planes."

The C-47s were loaded.

By 1100 the German fighter field — 1000 yards by 1400 yards — had been cleared. The Germans had been pushed from one to two miles away. Whether they could be held there was an open question.

At 1115 the first of the C-47s, its seams bulging with tightly-packed cargo, lumbered down the runway and took off for a field in Holland that might — and then again might not — be cleared of the enemy when it came time to land.

Meanwhile, a force of Eighth Air Force and RAF fighters was readying for take-off to the same area. Obviously the Luftwaffe would challenge fiercely

The first of the C-47s with their "seams bulging with tightly-packed cargo" on their way to a first landing in Holland.

such a mass landing of supplies as this.

Probably the longest aerial supply train that ever headed for a front line nosed its way over the enemy coast before 1300. The sky wasn't too clear, and the sky train went in at low altitude.

Beneath it, a furiously speeding fighter escort plane occasionally would turn sharply upon a Dutch haystack or a lone farmhouse, spraying lead into a hidden flak gun that was trying to get the range.

Some of the fighter escorts went ahead to set up a ring of protection around the small field at Grave.

At 1350 the first C-47 set its wheels on the dirt landing strip. Three hours — 180 minutes — to land, unload, and dispatch more than 200 large planes.

It was a task that might have unnerved the traffic control officers at the largest and best equipped airfield in England — or the U. S.

But there was no control tower at this field. There were no traffic control officers. There was sharp, vicious fighting a mile and a half away. There were squadrons of desperate Luftwaffe fighter pilots trying to penetrate the Allied fighter ring. In the offing, the Eighth Air Force and RAF fighters were mixed with the Germans in a great, swirling dogfight.

The first C-47s to land carried English anti-aircraft personnel and equipment, including big Bofors guns. The ordinary unloading time for this cargo was three to four hours. They did it in 45 minutes.

At one time there were more than 100 C-47s on the field — 100 closely parked, defenseless sky freight wagons. The men who were hurrying with the unloading knew they would be duck soup if even a half-dozen enemy planes could get close enough to strafe them.

Above the field, the traffic pattern was jammed with a long orderly line of cargo planes ready to land. One dirt landing strip was cluttered with those that had landed. Another strip was jammed with aircraft ready to takeoff. And all traffic directions were coming by radio from one parked C-47 on the ground.

Yet there was not one moment of confusion.

The supplies rolled out on the field: 132 jeeps; 73 jeep quarter-ton trailers; 31 motorcycles; 3375 gallons of gas for vehicles; 38,700 pounds of ammu-nition; 60,730 pounds of rations. In all, 657,995 pounds of combat equipment and 882 fighting men were unloaded on a field 1000 by 1400 yards.

While the Wing was making this great supply delivery — without which the unprecedented airborne operation would have failed — it also was loading many of the glider personnel that had been stranded in no-man's land, and taking them back to England so they could fly again against the Hun.

Planes that were loading these essential men dropped out of the line that was squirming from the unloading area down a dirt strip to the take-off line; then, when ready, they edged their way back into the procession.

The Luftwaffe was going crazy trying to get in close enough to shoot up the C-47s. One force of 50 Luftwaffe fighters headed toward the field. Within a few blazing minutes, the Eighth Air Force had shot down 32 of the Germans, probably shot down another and damaged 8. The remaining Huns scattered.

At 1650 — three hours to the minute — the last of the C-47s took off. The job had been done.

Back to England they went, and landed. Not a single cargo plane had been lost in the most dangerous re-supply mission ever undertaken by air to the front battle lines.

While Allied ground armies pushed across France, fighter pilots relentlessly hunted down the fast-disappearing Luftwaffe in the air and on the ground. Here in dramatic prose, 38-victor ace John T. Godfrey of the famous 4th Fighter Group, recounts these waning days of the Luftwaffe. Twice during his combat career the ingenious Godfrey was shot down over enemy territory, and twice he escaped from the Germans to make his way back to England.

Last Encounter with the Luftwaffe

John T. Godfrey

ON AUGUST 6, I flew as leader of Free Lance Section. This to me was the best job in the 4th Group. Not being tied down to any squadron or group commander, I was free to roam anywhere in Germany. Flying at 30,000 feet or down to zero, north, south, east or west, the skies were mine, and I relished every minute of it.

Five months ago, flying over Berlin, there were only a few fighters protecting the Forts; now Allied fighters were everywhere. I didn't waste time around Berlin, but flew eastward for 30 miles, hoping to pick up stray German planes. My plan worked. I saw a single ME-410 flying at 2000 feet. After asking the boys to give me cover, I dove down. Approaching from the stern was suicide against this type of plane, for they had rear gunners. So, swinging to the right, I quartered into the plane and shot with a 30° deflection. I aimed for the tail first, and then eased right rudder as the bullets traveled along the fuselage to the starboard engine. This caught on fire immediately. Throttling back I jockeyed my plane to the stern of the 410 and blanketed the port with fire. It was out of control and in flames when I pulled up over it. One of the boys called on the RT, "Look at that poor bastard."

I looked down and saw a man plummeting to earth, his defective parachute streaming unfurled above him. It was a sickening sight, and I could imagine the frantic efforts he must have made pulling on his shroud lines before the earth crushed him. What a horrible way to die.

I flicked on my camera switch and followed the 410 down to earth. It struck the ground and a huge column of fire shot a hundred feet into the air.

279

It wasn't every day I had the time and protection to record on film the positive proof of a destroyed plane.

I rejoined my three comrades; we flew at 1000 feet searching for more targets. Glover saw the airdrome first and reported it to me. I opened my throttle for as much speed as possible as we went down to strafe. I picked out a DO-17 partly concealed at the far end of the field. Sighting was done by guess, for the windshield in front of my gun sights was covered with oil picked up from the riddled 410. I held my head way over to the right and watched my bullets flick up the earth in front of the Dornier. Pulling back on the stick raised the nose of the plane slightly, and the four machine guns hit home. The DO-17 exploded. I felt my plane tremble as machine-gun fire from the ground hammered into it. I yanked back on the stick and climbed to free myself from this hotbed of blazing shells. Crash! The windshield in front of the gun sight looked like a cobweb with a small hole in the center. I felt a sharp tug on my left temple as the bullet creased me before it splat into the armor plate by my head. For a second the concussion of the bullet knocked me senseless, but I came to with my plane climbing. I could feel blood dripping down my forehead. Quickly I adjusted my goggles. They were close-fitting and I hoped they would keep the blood from running into my eyes. But I knew I was lucky. If it hadn't been for the oil on the windshield I would have been peering into the ring sight — and would have caught the bullet squarely between my eyes.

The other three planes were now striving to catch me. Then the cracking of a voice over the RT sent me numb with fright, "Johnny, you're streaming glycol."

I looked at my instruments and saw with horror that my engine temperature registered in the dangerous red area. One of two things would happen very shortly — either my engine would freeze, or it would blow up. All reasoning left me and I panicked. Still keeping the plane in a climbing position, I worked frantically to pull the emergency release which would send my canopy free from its sliding racks. My hand fumbled desperately but shook so much I had to use the other hand to steady it. Whoosh! A blast of air rushed into the cockpit as the canopy tore free. Now all I had to do was unbuckle my harness straps and step over the side. Ten minutes ago I had watched a man bail out of a plane, and his parachute hadn't opened; I tried to erase the picture of the plummeting man from my mind. I wanted to say something calm and dramatic to the boys before I bailed out, but when I did speak it was in a high-pitched voice, screaming with despair.

"I'm bailing out, boys. Tell Charlotte I'll see her when I get back!" The words rushed out in my urgency to leave this death-trap of a thousand exploding horses.

Reaching up to yank the helmet

and earphones off my head, I hesitated as I heard the calm voice of Freddie Glover: "Don't jump, Johnny, there's still a chance."

I tried to collect my wits, to think of what Freddie was saying. "Now sit back and relax for a second. You're still flying and the plane won't blow up. Look at your instruments and tell me how your oil pressure is." I looked at the blur of needles swimming before my eyes. I have to concentrate, I kept telling myself over and over again.

"Normal, Freddie."

"Good, that's a good sign. Now unscrew your wobble pump and start priming your engines. That'll force raw gas into your cylinders and have the same effect as the glycol. No bull, Johnny, — I've heard of somebody else doing it and it works."

The wobble pump was on my dashboard; it had a small handle similar to an outboard motor's starting handle, and when pulled out would spring back. With my right hand I pulled out the handle and then thrust it back in to feed the gas into the cylinders. It didn't work easily. Freddie was flying close to me now and continued his encouragement as I worked the pump in and out.

"Freddie, it's working. My engine temperature is away from the danger zone."

"Good, Johnny — now throttle back and don't push your engine. Try to keep climbing; the higher we go the cooler the air will be — every little bit helps."

I throttled back and began climbing at only 50 feet a minute, continually pushing my wobble pump in and out, in and out.

Freddie and his wingman left me when I reached 18,000 feet. He had done his job well, and now my safe return would rest on the strength of my arm and the fuel supply. Patteau, my wingman, was flying in a zigzag manner, first on one side, then on the other — protecting my tail. My plane had been hit near Berlin, 675 miles from Debden. The chances of getting back seemed very remote, but desperately I pumped and pumped, injecting life into my dying engine. Gone were the thoughts of the two enemy aircraft I had destroyed. Flak and enemy fighters no longer seemed threats to me.

By the second hand of my plane's clock I counted one, two, three, four . . . 16 times a minute I worked the plunger. Three hours more to Debden equaled almost 3000 injections; and if I subtracted the time I had started, it would make . . . but I couldn't think. This type of calculation was too much for me at the moment. The wind whistling through the cockpit was cold and penetrating. I could feel it biting into my very soul. Regrettably I lost height in an attempt to find a warmer layer of air. How much can a body endure before the breaking point?

The agonies of the flesh were forgotten when my engine spit and died. A frantic search of my instrument panel made me hastily switch on the reserve gas tank. The motor caught, but the instruments had made me aware of a greater threat. Thirty-nine gallons of gas left, and I had no idea of my exact position.

Then I saw it. Thank God, just ahead of me was the Channel. I had lost the battle for height as my cold body demanded warmer and warmer air. I was at 4000 feet when the plane left the shores of Holland. The glove on my right hand had frayed open from the continual friction of the hot handle of the plunger. What had been blisters under the glove were now red welts of bleeding, slippery flesh, and the plunger kept slipping from my grasp. Blasts of air continued to blow into the cockpit with tornado force. I didn't think I could stand it much longer. Panic-stricken, I called my wingman.

"Patty, I don't think I have enough gas to make it. Call Air Sea Rescue for a fix. I'm switching over now." My left hand flicked the button which would set my radio on the Air Sea Rescue frequency. I listened in a daze at Patty informed them of my plight, and they gave him a vector onto the nearest field. If I could last 21 more minutes I could make it.

The ground control officer seemed calm and confident, as if there were nothing to worry about. They knew my exact position at all times, and if I did bail out, a seaplane would be sent in minutes.

How long is 21 minutes? To me it was measured by the times my weary arm worked the plunger in and out.

If ... if ... a small word but it meant so much to me. If my gas holds out, I can make it. If I can press this plunger several hundred more times, England will be under my wing. I did not count ... I dared not.

My wheels touched down at Beccles. No circling of the field for me; I landed on the nearest runway — with no regard for wind or traffic. I didn't even taxi to the control tower; I pulled off on a grassy plot near the end of the runway and shut off the engine. I climbed out of the cockpit and lit a much needed cigarette.

Did I have any premonition of my fate on that last mission of August 24? No. There was no dream to forewarn me. Even the wobble pump which I now used to prime my engine before starting was just another instrument on the panel. That mission of August 6, when it had played such an important part of my life, was pushed far into the back of my mind. Everything was the same — the takeoff, the joining of squadron and group, the climb over the Channel, the constant whine of the Germans trying to jam our RT. The flak, which always plagued us when we entered over the enemy coast, still had its terrifying effect, and we dodged in and out of the black explosions.

So many things could have happened to make me turn back. My radio could have gone dead; the motor could easily have started spitting; my belly tanks could not have dropped; my oxygen could have run low — all or any of these mishaps had forced me back on previous missions.

I had no reason to ask the squadron leader to break formation, since there were no enemy fighters in sight; but I wanted to leave the many fighters who were protecting the bombers, to see if there was more action near the ground.

Two boys in my section found a marshaling yard with trains in abundance — not good enough targets for me. I wanted bigger game, and left them with their little set of trains. Up ahead I suddenly saw an enemy airfield. And there they were — eight juicy fat JU-52s, sitting peacefully at the edge of the field. One pass, I promised myself; there's no harm in that. Down I went, building up speed, in my dive to the ground. One JU-52 loomed bigger and bigger in my ring sight. Now, I said, and pressed the button to watch the fat JU-52 wither in a shroud of machine-gun fire. Pulling up I waited; no flak. Then — down again, this time joined by my wingman. Another JU-52 melted into the ground.

Again, again, again — five passes and each time my bullets hit home. But now the flak was all around us. And the ground was alive with gunners of every kind, all of whom were firing at us.

Why didn't I leave now? What was I trying to prove?

I heard the crunch of a shell as it exploded near my wing. But down again I flew, to assure the destruction of the last two planes on the field. The light tattoo of a machine-gun fire raked my plane from the hub of the propeller 'to the tail assembly. Not one struck the cockpit. My motor was suddenly sluggish, but there was that one last plane — and I dove once more for my final kill.

But there was no fast pull up now. As I flew over the burning wreck, my engine began to falter badly, but my momentum carried me up to 1500 feet before the 1200 horses gave their last gasp. I aimed the nose of the plane at a small clearing I could see ahead. And as my plane started its downward plunge, I felt a strange sense of relief — there were no flashbacks of my life, no self-pity for what was happening. For I was tired, dead tired of the struggle. As I pulled back on the stick to ease the crash, I felt the plane slide into the soft earth. My head shot forward and hit the gun sight as the plane crunched to a stop.

Dogsbody

Group Capt. J. E. Johnson, RAF

It is fascinating to watch the reactions of the various pilots. They fall into two broad categories: those who are going out to shoot and those who secretly and desperately know they will be shot at, the hunters and the hunted. The majority of the pilots, once they have seen their names on the board, walk out to their Spitfires for a pre-flight check and for a word or two with their ground crews. They tie on their mae-wests, check their maps, study the weather forecast and have a last-minute chat with their leaders or wingmen. These are the hunters.

The hunted, that very small minority (although every squadron usually possessed at least one), turned to their escape kits and made quite sure that they were wearing the tunic with the silk maps sewn into a secret hiding-place; that they had at least one oil-skin-covered packet of French francs, and two if possible; that they had a compass and a revolver and sometimes specially-made clothes to assist their activities once they were shot down. When they went through these agonized preparations they reminded me of aged countrywomen meticulously checking their shopping-lists before catching the bus for the market town.

Except for brief diversions to lend a hand in the tactical air war, the strategic heavy bombers of Eighth and Fifteenth Air Forces and the RAF Bomber Command continued their incessant day-night pounding of German cities and industry.

For over a year they had dealt crippling blows at various segments of the German economy and war-making potential — rubber, ball-bearing, aircraft, shipyards, submarine pens, V-sites and other key targets — turning factories and installations into rubble. But always the resilient Germans, through dispersion, underground facilities, and regimentation of civilian population, managed to resume a degree of production. During the last year of the war, for example, underground factory output of fighter aircraft actually increased, though the planes were of little use to a prostrate Luftwaffe.

284

It was not until the final year of the war that strategic air power found the Achilles heel of the German nation — oil. The obliteration of this vital segment of national and military life, more than any other factor, brought on the final quick collapse of the Third Reich by depriving it of its mobility. Lack of oil strangled the economy and paralyzed the once powerful Wehrmacht. It eliminated Germany as an industrial nation.

Here is the story of this decisive strategic air campaign, by reporters covering the missions during the latter part of the war.

Striking Oil

Air Force Overseas Correspondents

ON NOVEMBER 2, 1944, the biggest air battle of the war took place over Germany when half of a force of more than 1000 Eighth Air Force heavy bombers, escorted by 900 fighters, attacked the giant Leuna synthetic oil refinery at Merseburg. For the first time in many weeks, the Luftwaffe, which had remained in hiding while Allied bombers were laying waste whole cities, rose to defend a target. And its fierce resistance and the recklessness with which its carefully husbanded fighters were expended — 208 Nazi planes were destroyed — testified to the desperation of the Reich with regard to its gasoline situation.

It is more than just a play on words, therefore, to say that the picture of a badly mauled Germany driven behind the defensive bastions of its homeland is a portrait in oil. Fuel and lubricants, the lifeblood of machine warfare, had been systematically drained from its veins. Blow by blow, the sledgehammers of strategic bombing had pounded away until Hitler's oil production of more than a million metric tons per month had dwindled to a thin, sluggish trickle.

Beyond the welter of dates and figures that detail the story of our campaign to strike oil is the simple fact of its overwhelming importance to the enemy and the prime necessity, from our point of view, for its destruction. This was recognized early in the war. As far back as 1940, the RAF went after specific oil targets in the Ruhr and elsewhere. However, it was not until the turning point in Africa and the culmination of the slow growth of Allied air superiority, that the smashing of Nazi refineries and synthetic plants could assume its rightful priority.

The target was large and sprawling. There is very little oil in Germany itself. The principal producers are the synthetic plants in the three main coal regions of Silesia, the Ruhr, and around Leipzig. Various coke oven plants, gas works, and L. T. Carbonization units add their volume to the total of Hitler's refined products, but by far the greater percentage of natural petroleum sources are scattered through the occupied countries. The great Ploesti refining district in Rumania, for example, was able to furnish 28 per cent of greater Germany's demands for oil.

It was realized at the beginning of the oil offensive that an effective reduction of Nazi output called for neutralization of the Luftwaffe to permit a concentrated assault. Long-range precision bombardment was required before the industry could be gravely hurt. There had been successful missions against oil before 1944 — notably the attack on the Ploesti fields in August, 1943 — but as long as the enemy's air force maintained and expanded its fighter strength, all strategic bombing efforts were threatened with prohibitive losses. The first objective, therefore, of the U.S. Eighth and Fifteenth Air Forces and the RAF Bomber Command, became the demolition of aircraft plants, ball-bearing factories, and related industrial installations. By May of this year the Luftwaffe was limping badly. Single-engine fighter production had been cut by more than 60 per cent, twin-engine manufacture

by about 80 per cent. Thousands of planes had been destroyed in combat and on the ground. The capacity of German airmen to interfere seriously with Allied operations was limited.

The field was now cleared for the kickoff, and goals were assigned as follows: the RAF was to attack petroleum plants in the Ruhr; the Eighth Air Force was to operate in central, northern, and eastern Germany, eastern Czechoslovakia, and western Poland; the Fifteenth Air Force was to strike at southern and southeastern Germany, southern Poland, Austria, Hungary, Italy, southern France, and the important Balkan countries, including Rumania. It was a master plan to dovetail three powerful air armadas in a campaign against Hitler's oil refineries, synthetic fuel manufacturing plants, and stored reserves.

The ensuing air campaign was consistent and effective. Between the middle of May and October 19, the Eighth made 112 assaults on more than 30 individual refineries and synthetic plants in some of the biggest daylight attacks of the war. In July, the Fifteenth aimed its bombs at oil targets on 17 days of the month while during the short nights the RAF was also diligent. And pacing the drive was a week-in, week-out demolition of storage tanks, depots, railway tankers, and other supplies by all Allied air forces in Europe, both strategic and tactical. The list of important places hit included Ploesti, Almasfuzito, Trzebinia, Lobau, Zeit, Politz, Brux, Blechhammer, Merseburg, Magdeburg, Bohlen, Lutzkendorf, Ruhland, Hamburg, and many others. Total Nazi production of oil products declined steadily and inexorably. By October, the quantity available was less than one-fourth of what it had been, and the Wehrmacht was forced to dip heavily into its reserves.

By its very nature, an oil refinery is a good target. The process of refining petroleum requires installations that are rambling and well spread out, offering bombardiers wide areas upon which to sight. Smokestacks, often more than 100 feet tall, and distillation equipment situated well above ground, make camouflage extremely difficult. And ideal landmarks were provided by the clusters of tank farms which are used to accumulate crude oil to supply the refineries and to store the finished products until shipment can be made.

Synthetic plants, too, need complicated facilities. The manufacture of oil from coal shale by either the Bergins method, which provides the greatest percentage of aviation gas, or the Fischer Tropsch system, requires plants for distillation, carbonization, compression, conversion, catalysis, and purification, as well as oven houses, gas generators, large gas tanks, injector plants, water gas works, and other specialized equipment. Authorities say that it takes two years to build a synthetic plant from the ground up.

In addition, the number of direct hits necessary to incapacitate a refinery is smaller than for most targets. To render a plant unproductive, only one of its components has to be seriously impeded. Destruction of either the cracking plant, the distillation unit, or the boiler house will suspend normal operation of the refinery until it is repaired or rebuilt. And the high volatility of the product itself, which may ignite from other causes when even a near-miss occurs, greatly increases the probability of damage.

The Germans have made frantic efforts to reduce this vulnerability, and their methods have been partially successful. One of the great proving grounds for this epic race between offense and defense was Ploesti. That facet of the campaign is worth considering in some detail, not only because it was the greatest single source of Nazi oil, but also because the fields have since fallen into Allied hands, thus making complete evaluation possible.

At Ploesti, the oil region covers an area of 19 square miles, densely crowded with refineries and pumping stations interconnected with a railway network. The plants are in three principal groups — at Ploesti, Campina, and Brazil — and were potentially capable of a crude oil output of 709,000 tons per month. The largest of these units, Astra Romana, served as the central receiving station for oil from most of the other plants, and pumped it to the Giurgiu terminal of the pipeline on the Danube, over which it was transported to the Reich. The proximity of Rumania to the Nazi forces on the Russian Front enabled the Germans to supply them with ease, while some of the fuel requirements of the hard-pressed divisions in Italy could also be met with Rumanian lubricants and gasoline.

When the first attacking party of 177 B-24s came over without fighter escort in the now historic low-level attack of August 1, 1943, a tremendous amount of damage was accomplished in spite of the loss of 54 planes. Astra Romana's powerhouse was put out of operation, and its cracking installation was demolished, as well as half of its functioning capacity. Greditul Minier, Colombia Acquila, and Steaua Romana — three of Ploesti's most modern plants — were hit hard. Half of the Phoenix Orion refinery was obliterated, and the Lumina works had a large proportion of its vital parts reduced to rubble.

At the time of the opening salvo against German oil in early 1944, Ploesti's estimated production was 458,000 tons of crude output per month, of which 177,000 tons represented maximum gasoline production. During April the Fifteenth Air Force — this time flying at 20,000 feet with fighter escort — softened up the target for its Sunday punch by pounding the railroad marshaling yards which lie to the north and south of the oil fields themselves.

From May, 1944 on, the heavies concentrated on the refineries. The enemy reacted with strong countermeasures of active and passive defense, exploiting every old trick and a couple of new ones. Their fighters were up in force, with the Rumanian and Nazi pilots flying ME-109s. Anti-aircraft guns, including four-barreled 20-mm, 88-mm, 105-mm, and 128-mm guns, threw up a curtain of flak that at all times was heavy, intense, and accurate.

But fighter interception and ack-ack were not the sole extent of Hitler's defense preparations. Beginning with the last strike in May, the whole Ploesti area was screened by a thick, swirling artificial fog. Approximately 2000 smoke generators were employed in this capacity and functioned in the same manner every time Allied airmen came over. On the last battle, however, there was but little smoke. Continued hammering of communication lines had paid off, and the defenders could not get in supplies of the necessary chemicals.

Another defensive feature at Ploesti was the construction of huge blast walls — requiring enough brick to build a sizable modern town—around every single installation at each refinery. Nothing quite like them had ever been seen. Some were 6 feet thick at the bottom and tapered upward to a height of 20 feet, where they were 2 feet wide. Even a series of three pumps had a complete square of blast walls around it, and from the air the whole arrangement had the weird, dazzle-painted appearance of a gigantic, one-story, multi-roomed, roofless house.

There were three large-scale raids

in the month of May, at the end of which the Steaua Romana refinery, the third most productive, had been definitely knocked out, and the overall output at Ploesti had been trimmed down to 217,000 tons monthly.

June brought another three attacks and an innovation in the Fifteenth Air Force's tactics. On the 10th, P-38s made a low-level bombing-strafing run on Romana Americana Refinery. They dropped between 40 and 50 bombs weighing 500 pounds each and set fire to the Crutzell crude oil distillery plant. When they left, 10 oil storage tanks were blazing and the mechanical work shops were almost completely demolished.

Five stabs in July caused important material damaged to the Romana Americana and Concordia refineries. Storage facilities of the Unirea Refinery were severely rocked, and the giant Astra Romana plant was once again subjected to an aerial pummeling.

In August, up to the time of the capture of the Ploesti fields by the Soviet Army, several heavy strikes were carried out by the Fifteenth Air Force with one night bombing foray by RAF Wellingtons and Halifaxes. In addition, there was a straight fighter sweep by P-51s and P-38s on August 6. By the end of the last mission, the capacity of the main Rumanian refineries was reduced from its rated 709,000 tons of crude output per month to a mere 77,000 tons — a drop of 90 per cent. No wonder, then, that the following recommendations appeared in the withdrawal orders issued by the command of the Nazi 26th Panzer Division in Italy:

"Armored units which are not completely ready for action and those which cannot be taken along on account of the fuel position must be blown up. Commanders will have to decide which motor transport will have to be taken along and which left behind, basing their decision on the fuel position . . ." Eloquent testimony to the leak which air power had created in the German gas tank.

On the less cloudy side of the enemy's ledger with respect to his "fuel position" are several important considerations. First is the fact that the word "destroy" must be used cautiously when applied to the oil industry. A refinery is a vulnerable mechanism, it is true, but it can be repaired if spare parts are readily available. A plant may be struck with the greatest possible accuracy, with the right number, type, and size of bombs. Most of the surface structure may be demolished, most of the machinery smashed. But the foundations will probably be left standing, the bulk of underground pipes and other works will be little harmed, and some of the machines will no doubt be available for repair or salvage. Hitler's men are well aware of this, and in June a special commissioner was appointed to direct such renovation activities. He was given preference for labor and material even over armament manufacturers, and the result has been the creation of a well trained corps of skilled workmen who are specialists in just this type of emergency work.

Moreover, extravagant pains have been taken to have spare parts within reach. Just as in the Reich substitute bridges are ready to replace existing spans which the Nazis think may be demolished, so extra machinery and building materials have been deposited in the vicinity of many essential oil plants. By this means, it is possible for a refinery to be in production again remarkably soon after it has been saturated with bombs.

The speed of German restoration is best illustrated by recent figures. Whereas in September it was known that oil capacity had fallen to its low point of approximately 25 per cent of the pre-attack level, the belief among experts was that volume might rise during the winter months because bad weather would probably interfere with our operations.

To soften the effects of such assaults, the enemy has been surrounding his oil targets with some extremely strong batteries of anti-aircraft guns. At Brux, for example, photo reconnaissance shows that the number of AA weapons had been increased from 84 heavy guns in July to about 200 in late October. Politz is now guarded by more heavy guns than are used to protect entire cities such as Bremen, Hanover, Frankfurt, or Munich.

Another advantage for Jerry lies in the fact that bombing of refineries and synthetic plants is rarely a visual pinpoint operation. Because of smoke screens and other reasons, it frequently has to be performed by instruments. And as the weather grows worse, the problem becomes more difficult for the Allies and easier for the Nazis.

Nevertheless, the persistent bombing of her oil industry has been very costly to the Reich—may, in fact, have been the substance with which her skids were greased on the Western Front. Outward indications of a serious pinch are everywhere in evidence. Commanders of Panzer divisions are now required to submit daily reports on consumption and have been ordered to utilize horse-drawn vehicles wherever possible. The German Air Force training program, which always received a top priority on gas, has been drastically limited. Training periods have been shortened, and new pilots do much less flying. Needless to say, civilian use of vital gas and oil has been virtually eliminated.

Obviously, the enemy is desperate. The bombardment of his oil industry has been and continues to be his worst headache. And when the wheels of the Wehrmacht grate and grind to their last stop, Germany's defeat may well be ascribed in part to too many troubled waters — and not enough oil.

A peculiar characteristic of aerial warfare was the sense of respect and admiration between combatants over Europe. This trait of airmanship transcended national and political boundaries and found its expression in many ways.

French Ace Pierre Clostermann, who flew with the RAF, puts it this way.

Walter Nowotny

Pierre Clostermann

ON MARCH 15 last I was leading a section of four Tempests in a rat scramble over Rheine/Hopsten at 8000 feet. Suddenly we saw at ground level a Messerschmitt 262 without any camouflage, its polished wings glittering in the sun. It was already in the flak corridor and about to put down. The barrage of tracers was already up to cover its approach. In accordance with the new orders I decided not to attack in these conditions, when, without warning, my Number 4 dived vertically toward the small bright dot which was nearing the long cement runway. Hurtling through the air like a bullet Bob Clark miraculously went through the wall of flak without being hit and fired a long burst at the silvery Me-262, which was in the final phase of its approach. The Messerschmitt crashed in flames just on the edge of the airfield.

A fortnight later we learnt by cross-checking captured documents and prisoners' reports that the Me-262 had been piloted by Nowotny*. Everyone had gone to bed. Bruce Cole, Clark, Brooker, and I had stayed up and we were glancing at an illustrated article on Nowotny in a review called *Der Adler* which we had found at Goch. There was his picture, taken on the day he received the Iron Cross with swords, diamonds, and oak leaves — the highest German military distinction. A face like that of a tired child, with a trace of sadness and a determined mouth and chin.

"All right now," suddenly said Brooker, "time to go to bed. What a pity that type wasn't wearing our uniform."

Walter Nowotny was dead. Our adversary in Normandy and in the Ger-

* Maj. Walter Nowotny commanded the Luftwaffe's ME-262 jet fighter unit stationed near Osnabrück.

man skies had died two days before in the hospital at Osnabrück as a result of burns. The Luftwaffe, whose hero he was, would not long survive his death, which was as it were the turning point of the aerial war. That evening in the mess his name was often on our lips. We spoke of him without hatred and without rancor. Each one of us recalled his memories of him, with respect, almost with affection. It was the first time I had heard this note in a conversation in the RAF, and it was also the first time that I heard, openly expressed, that curious solidarity among fighter pilots which is above all tragedies and all prejudices. This war had witnessed appalling massacres, towns crushed by bombs, the butchery of Oradour, the ruins of Hamburg. We ourselves had been sickened when our shells exploded in a peaceful village street, mowing down women and children round the German tank we were attacking. In comparison, our tussles with Nowotny and his Messerschmitts were something clean, above the fighting on the ground, in the mud and the blood, in the deafening din of the crawling, stinking tanks.

Dog-fights in the sky; silvery midges dancing in graceful arabesques — the diaphanous tracery of milky condensation trails — Focke-Wulfs skimming like toys in the infinite sky. We too, of course, were involved in less noble fighting; that strafing of trains in the gray dawn of winter mornings when you tried not to think of the shrieks of terror, not to see your shells smashing through the wood, the windows shivering in fragments, the engine-drivers writhing in the burning jets of steam, all those human beings trapped in the coaches, panic-stricken by the roar of our engines and the barking of the flak; all those inhuman, immoral jobs we had to do because we were soldiers and because war is war. We could rise above all this today by saluting a brave enemy who had just died, by saying that Nowotny belonged to us, that he was part of our world, where there were no ideologies, no hatreds, no frontiers. This sense of comradeship had nothing to do with patriotism, democracy, Nazism, or humanity. All those chaps that evening felt this instinctively, and as for those who shrug their shoulders, they just can't know — they aren't fighter pilots. The conversation had ceased, the beer mugs were empty, the wireless was silent as it was past midnight. Bruce Cole, who was neither poet nor philosopher, let fall these words:

"Whoever first dared paint markings on a plane's wing was a swine!"

The decline of the Luftwaffe on the Western Front paralleled a compara-
ble situation in Russia. From the fall of Stalingrad (February 2, 1943)
onward, the Russian air and ground offensive rolled toward the borders
of Germany. A completely revitalized Russian Air Force, backed up by
U.S. lend-lease and an annual production of their own of between 30,000
and 40,000 combat aircraft per year (including YAK-9s, LA-9s,
MIG-5s, LA-7s, and TU-2s) was averaging some 2000 sorties per day
against the retreating Nazi air and ground forces. By April, 1945 Russian
air power was supreme, mounting in that month alone almost 216,000
sorties. (Russian estimates of Luftwaffe losses on the Eastern Front during
the entire war is 60,000 aircraft.) As the Soviet air and ground armies ap-
proached Germany, Luftwaffe pilots flew hopelessly to stem the Red flood-
tide. Here one of Germany's top dive-bomber pilots describes his last
mission in a JU-87.

The Closing Ring

Hans Ulrich Rudel, Luftwaffe

EARLY on the morning of February 9 a telephone call from H.Q.: Frankfurt has just reported that last night the Russians bridged the Oder at Lebus, slightly north of Frankfurt and with some tanks have already gained a footing on the west bank. The situation is more than critical; at this point there is no opposition on the ground and there is no possibility of bringing up heavy artillery there in time to stop them. So there is nothing to prevent the Soviet tanks from rolling on toward the capital, or at least straddling the railway and the autobahn from Frankfurt to Berlin, both vital supply lines for the establishment of the Oder front.

We fly there to find out what truth there is in this report. From afar I can already make out the pontoon bridge, we encounter intense flak a long way before we reach it. The Russians certainly have a rod in pickle for us! One of my squadrons attacks the bridge across the ice. We have no great illusions about the results we shall achieve, knowing as we do that Ivan has such quantities of bridge-building material that he can repair the damage in less than no time. I myself fly lower with the anti-tank flight on the look-out for tanks on the west bank of the river. I can discern their tracks but not the

293

monsters themselves. Or are these the tracks of AA tractors? I come down lower to make sure and see, well camouflaged in the folds of the river valley, some tanks on the northern edge of the village of Lebus. There are perhaps a dozen or 15. Then something smacks against my wing, a hit by light flak. I keep low, guns are flashing all over the place, at a guess six or eight batteries are protecting the river crossing. The flak gunners appear to be old hands at the game with long Stuka experience behind them. They are not using tracers, one sees no string of beads snaking up at one, but one only realizes that they have opened up when the aircraft shudders harshly under the impact of a hit. They stop firing as soon as we climb and so our bombers cannot attack them. Only when one is flying very low above our objective can one see the spurt of flame from the muzzle of a gun like the flash of a pocket torch. I consider what to do; there is no chance of coming in cunningly behind cover as the flat river valley offers no opportunities for such tactics. There are no tall trees or buildings. Sober reflection tells me that experience and tactical skill go by the board if one breaks all the fundamental rules derived from them. The answer: a stubborn attack and trust to luck. If I had always been so foolhardy I should have been in my grave a dozen times. There are no troops here on the ground and we are 50 miles from the capital of the Reich, a perilously short

distance when the enemy's armor is already pushing toward it. There is no time for ripe consideration. This time you will have to trust to luck, I tell myself, and in I go. I tell the other pilots to stay up; there are several new crews among them and while they cannot be expected to do much damage with this defense we are likely to suffer heavier losses than are worth the candle. When I come in low and as soon as they see the flash of the AA guns they are to concentrate their cannon fire on the flak. There is always the chance that this will get Ivan rattled and affect his accuracy. There are several Stalin tanks there, the rest are T-34s. After four have been set on fire and I have run out of ammunition we fly back. I report my observations and stress the fact that I have only attacked because we are fighting 50 miles from Berlin, otherwise it would be inexcusable. If we are holding a line further east I should have waited for a more favorable situation, or at least until the tanks had been driven out of range of their flak screen round the bridge. I change aircraft after two sorties because they have been hit by flak. Back a fourth time and a total of 12 tanks are ablaze. I am buzzing a Stalin tank which is emitting smoke but refuses to catch fire.

Each time before coming in to the attack I climb to 2400 feet as the flak cannot follow me to this altitude. From 2400 feet I scream down in a steep dive, weaving violently. When I am close to the tank I straighten up for an instant to fire, and then streak away low above the tank with the same evasive tactics until I reach a point where I can begin to climb again — out of range of the flak. I really ought to come in slowly and with my aircraft better controlled, but this would be suicide. I am only able to straighten up for the fraction of a second and hit the tank accurately in its vulnerable parts thanks to my manifold experience and somnabulistic assurance. Such attacks are, of course, out of the question for my colleagues for the simple reason that they have not the experience.

The pulses throb in my temples. I know that I am playing cat and mouse with fate, but this Stalin tank has got to be set alight. Up to 2400 feet once more and on to the 60-ton leviathan. It still refuses to burn! Rage seizes me; it must and shall catch fire!

The red light indicator on my cannon winks. That too! On one side the breech has jammed, the other cannon has therefore only one round left. I climb again. Is it not madness to risk everything again for the sake of a single shot? Don't argue; how often have you put paid to a tank with a single shot?

It takes a long time to gain 2400 feet with a Ju-87; far too long, for now I begin to weigh the pros and cons. My one ego says: if the 13th tank has not yet caught fire you needn't imagine you can do the trick with one more shot. Fly home and remunition, you will find it again all right. To this my other ego heatedly replies:

"Perhaps it requires just this one shot to stop the tank from rolling on through Germany."

"Rolling on through Germany sounds much too melodramatic! A lot more Russian tanks are going to roll on through Germany if you bungle it now, and you will bungle it, you may depend upon that. It is madness to go down again to that level for the sake of a single shot. Sheer lunacy!"

"You will say next that I shall bungle it because it is the 13th. Superstitious nonsense! You have one round left, so stop shilly-shallying and get cracking!"

And already I zoom down from 2400 feet. Keep your mind on your flying, twist and turn; again a score of guns spit fire at me. Now I straighten up ... fire ... the tank bursts into a blaze! With jubilation in my heart, I streak away low above the burning tank. I go into a climbing spiral ... a crack in the engine and something sears through my leg like a strip of red hot steel. Everything goes black before my eyes, I gasp for breath. But I must keep flying ... flying ... I must not pass out. Grit your teeth, you have to master your weakness. A spasm of pain shoots through my whole body.

"Ernst, my right leg is gone."

"No, your leg won't be gone. If it were you wouldn't be able to speak. But the left wing is on fire. You'll have to come down, we've been hit twice by 4cm flak."

An appalling darkness veils my

eyes, I can no longer make out anything.

"Tell me where I can crash-land. Then get me out quickly so that I am not burnt alive."

I cannot see a thing any more, I pilot by instinct. I remember vaguely that I came in to each attack from south to north and banked left as I flew out. I must therefore be headed west and in the right direction for home. So I fly on for several minutes. Why the wing is not already gone I do not know. Actually I am moving northwest almost parallel to the Russian Front.

"Pull!" shouts Gadermann through the intercom, and now I feel that I am slowly dozing off into a kind of fog . . . a pleasant coma.

"Pull! yells Gadermann again—were those trees or telephone wires? I have lost all sensation in my mind and pull the stick only when Gadermann yells at me. If this searing pain in my leg would only stop . . . and this flying . . . if I could let myself sink at last into this queer, gray peace and remoteness which invites me.

"Pull!" Once again I wrench automatically at the joystick, but now for an instant Gadermann has "shouted me awake." In a flash I realize that I must do something here.

"What's the terrain like?" I ask into the microphone.

"Bad — hummocky."

But I have to come down, otherwise the dangerous apathy brought on from my wounded body will again steal over me. I kick the rudder-bar with my left foot and howl with agony. But surely it was my right leg that was hit? Pull to the right, I bring the nose of the aircraft up and slide her gently into her belly, in this way perhaps the release gear of the undercarriage will not function and I can make it after all. If not we shall pancake. The aircraft is on fire . . . she bumps and skids for a second.

Now I can rest, now I can slip away into the gray distance — wonderful! Maddening pains jerk me back into consciousness. Is someone pulling me about? Are we jolting over rough ground? Now it is over. At last I sink utterly into the arms of silence.

I wake up, everything around me is white . . . intent faces . . . a pungent smell . . . I am lying on an operating table. A sudden, violent panic convulses me: where is my leg?

"Is it gone?"

The surgeon nods. Spinning downhill on brand new skis . . . diving . . . athletics . . . pole jumping . . . what do these things matter? How many comrades have been far more seriously wounded? Do you remember? That one in the hospital at Dnjepropetrovsk whose whole face and both hands had been torn off by a mine? The loss of a leg, an arm, a head are all of no importance if only the sacrifice could save the Fatherland from its mortal peril. This is no catastrophe, the only catastrophe is that I cannot fly for weeks . . . and in the present crisis! These thoughts flash through my brain in a second, and now the surgeon says to me gently:

"I couldn't do anything else."

The revolutionary twin-jet ME-262 had been under development in Germany since 1938 but the priority given it was low and only in spring, 1944 did the first prototypes appear for flight test and combat evaluation. Even then, Hitler's dogged insistence that it be used as a bomber instead of fighter delayed the combat use of this potent weapon against the Allied strategic offensive.

The ME-262 was the one German aircraft which might have stopped the Allied strategic formations, had it been ready in 1943. Ironically, it could have been ready but for unwise and short-sighted air planning by the German Dictator himself and his High Command.

Companions of the ME-262 were the ME-163B Komet, liquid rocket motor, which appeared in autumn of 1944 to the consternation of the Allies; and the twin-jet reconnaissance bomber the Arado 234. Only small proportions of all these jets reached operational units, and then most were stood down for lack of fuel.

Of all three jet models, the ME-262 became the rising star and upon it were pinned the last hopes of German leaders. At the 11th hour Hitler ordered all ME-262s into operational status as fighters. The cream of the Luftwaffe fighter pilots gathered from all parts to fly the jets and German underground production facilities were tooled-up to produce 1000 per month.

But it was too late. The Allied strategic air campaign against synthetic fuel had nearly exhausted the Luftwaffe's remaining stocks by March, and in April the Luftwaffe was grounded entirely by empty gas tanks — sitting ducks for Allied flyers.

Here, by Luftwaffe fighter chief, is the pathetic story of "too little, too late."

ME-262 Jet Fighter: The Luftwaffe's Last Stand

Adolf Galland

IN JANUARY, 1945, we started on the formation of my unit that Hitler had ordered. It spread quickly through the fighter arm that our 44th Squadron was taking shape at Brandenburg-Briest. Our official nomination was a

The German ME-163B Komet.

JV-44.

Steinhoff was in charge of retraining the pilots. Lutzow came to us from Italy. Barkhorn, who had scored more than 300 kills in the East, Hohagen, Schnell, and Krupinski were coaxed out of hospital. Many reported without consent or transfer orders. Most of them had been in action since the first day of the war, and all of them had been wounded. All of them bore the scars of war and displayed the highest medals. The Knight's Cross was, so to speak, the badge of our unit. Now, after a long period of technical and numerical inferiority, they wanted once more to experience the feeling of air superiority. They wanted to be known as the first jet boys of the last fighter pilots of the Luftwaffe. For this they were ready once more to chance sacrificing their lives.

Soon after receiving the first planes we were stationed at Munich-Riem. In the early hours of the morning of March 31, 1945, the JV-44 took off in close formation, and 42 minutes later the planes landed in Munich. They had covered the distance of about 300 miles in record time.

Here in Munich the unit took on its final shape. The Squadron of Experts, as we were called, had as pilots one lieutenant general, two colonels, one lieutenant colonel, three majors, five captains, eight lieutenants, and about the same number of second lieutenants. None of us imagined that we were able to give the war the much-quoted "turn." The magic word "jet" had brought us together to experience once more *die grosse Fliegerei.*" Our last operation was anything but a fresh and gay hunting. We not only battled against technical, tactical, and supply difficulties, we also lacked a clear picture of the air situation of the floods coming from the West — a picture absolutely necessary for the success of an operation. Every day the fronts moved in closer from three sides. But worst

of all our field was under continuous observation by an overwhelming majority of American fighters. During one raid we were hit three times very heavily. Thousands of workers had to be mobilized to keep open a landing strip between the bomb craters.

Operation orders for the ME-262s now changed daily. Conditions in the armament industry were also turbulent. The time of commissioners, special commissioners, ambassadors of the Fuehrer, commissars, and special commissariats had started. All who were to increase production of the industry or to co-ordinate operations were appointed subordinate to each

A German Messerschmitt ME-262. This model was equipped with radar and was employed as a night fighter aircraft.

other, equal to each other, and over each other. From February until March the jet-fighter command went partly over to the SA. From their ranks came the so-called Commissariat of the Fuehrer for Jet Aircraft. A general of the Waffen SS., Hitler had appointed him although Goering in his turn had appointed a Special Commissioner for Jet Aircraft.

Surprisingly I was called by Goering to the Obersalzberg: it must have been somewhere around April 10. To my amazement he received me with the greatest civility, inquired after the progress of our initial actions, and gave me a restricted confirmation that my prediction concerning the use of bombers with the ME-262 in the defense of the Reich had been correct. This indicated that the *Reichsmarschall* had begun to realize that after all I had been right throughout all those sharp clashes of opinions of the last months. This was the last time I saw Goering.

Four weeks before the collapse of the armed forces the fighter arm was still in a position to represent a factor that could not be overlooked. Operations from Riem started despite all resistance and difficulties. Naturally we were able to send up only small units. On landing, the aircraft had to be towed immediately off the field. They were dispersed over the countryside and had to be completely camouflaged. Bringing the aircraft onto the field and taking off became more and more difficult: eventually it was a mat-

ter of luck. One raid followed another.

In this situation, the safety of the personnel was paramount and came before any orders to clear the airfield. Each pilot was responsible for his own cover on the airfield and had to dig his own foxhole. When it came to physical work you cannot imagine anything more lazy than a fighter pilot in his sixth year of service. My pilots moaned terribly about the stony ground at Riem. Returning from a mission, I was standing with them on our western airstrip, watching the bombers attacking railway stations in Munich in single waves. Suddenly somebody called, *"Achtung! Bombenangriff!"* Already the ugly finger of death, as we called the markers of the daylight raiders, were groping for our aerodrome. I chased after one of my pilots, who slithered into a nearby hole he had dug for himself. Hellishly narrow, I thought . . . oh, a single foxhole. It was very shallow. Then the first carpet of bombs roared down, passed over our heads. Nauseating — the whistle, the explosion, the blast, the tremor of the ground. A brief pause occurred after the attack of the first formation. I was lying on top of a sergeant. It was Knier. He was shaking, but in answer to my question he insisted that he was no more afraid than I was.

Our hole had a cover. A few splinters had struck this lid with a loud metallic clang. My back was pressed against it. "Knier, what's this on my back?" "100-pound bombs, Herr General," was the prompt reply. I certainly began to shake. Another five salvos followed at short intervals. Outside there was smoke, debris, craters, fire, and destruction. All the Germans had experienced this during the last years of the war: in the cities, in the factories, on the battlefield, on ships and U-boats; bombs, bombs, bombs? But it was an awkward feeling to be in the middle of a raid and, what is more, to be sheltered by one's own bombs.

During these last weeks of the war we were able to fit out some aircraft with additional weapons, which gave a greater firing power to the ME-262: R4M rockets of 3-cm caliber, and 500-g. explosives. A single hit from these was enough to bring down a multi-engined bomber. They were fixed beneath the wing in two racks that carried 24 rockets. In a feverish hurry our mechanics and servicing crew loaded up a few jet fighters. I took off in one of them.

In the district of Landsberg on the Lech I met a formation of about 16 Marauders. We called these twin-engined bombers Halbstarke. I opened from a distance of about 600 yards, firing in half a second a salvo of 24 rockets into the close flying formation. I observed two certain hits. One bomber immediately caught fire and exploded; a second lost large parts of its right tail unit and wing and began to spiral earthward. In the meantime the three other planes that had taken off with me had also attacked successfully. My accompanying pilot, Edward

Schallnoser, who once over Riem had rammed a Lightning because in his excitement he could not fire, waded into the Marauders with all his rockets. That evening he reported back to his quarters, parachute under his arm and a twisted leg.

Our impression of the efficiency of this new weapon was indescribable. The rockets could be fired outside the effective range of the defensive fire of the bombers. A well-aimed salvo would probably hit several bombers simultaneously. That was the way to break up formations. But this was the end of April, 1945! In the middle of our breakup, at the beginning of our collapse! It does not bear thinking about what we could have done had we had those jet fighters, 3-cm quick-firing cannons, and 5-cm rockets years ago — before our war potential had been smashed, before indescribable misery had come over Germany through the raids. We dared not think about it. Now we could do nothing but fly and fight and do our duty as fighter pilots to the last.

Service in action still demanded heavy and grievous losses. On April 18, Steinhoff crashed on a takeoff but managed to free himself from the burning wreckage of his jet plane with very severe burns. A few days later Gunther Lutzow did not return from his mission. Long after the end of the war, we were still hoping that this splendid officer might not have left us forever. In the same spirit and with the same devotion many more young pilots of our unit fell.

But the fate of Germany was sealed. On April 25 the American and the Soviet soldiers shook hands at Torgau on the Elbe. The last defensive ring of Berlin was soon penetrated. The Red flag was flying over the *Ballhausplatz* in Vienna. The German Front in Italy collapsed. On Pilsen fell the last bomb of the 2,755,000 tons which the Western Allies had dropped on Europe during five years of war.

At that moment I called my pilots together and said to them, "Militarily speaking the war is lost. Even our action cannot change anything . . . I shall continue to fight, because operating with the ME-262 has got hold of me, because I am proud to belong to the last fighter pilots of the German Luftwaffe . . . Only those who feel the same are to go on flying with me . . ."

In the meantime the harsh reality of the war finally decided the question: "Bomber or fighter action by ME-262?" in our favor. The leaders were completely occupied with themselves in Berlin and at other places. Numerous departments, which up to now had interfered with allocation and the operation of jet fighters, ceased to function or did not come through any more. Commanders of the bombers, reconnaissance, combat fighters, night fighters, and sundry testing units that had been fitted out with the coveted ME-262 passed their aircraft on to us. From all sides we were presented with jet fighters. Finally we had 70 aircraft.

On April 26, I set out on my last mission of the war. I led six jet fighters of the JV-44 against a formation of Marauders. Our own little directing post brought us well into contact with the enemy. The weather: varying clouds at different altitudes, with gaps, ground visible in about only three-tenths of the operational area.

I sighted the enemy formation in the district of Neuburg on the Danube. Once again I noticed how difficult it was, with such great difference of speed and with clouds over the landmarks, to find the relative flying direction between one's own plane and that of the enemy, and how difficult it was to judge the approach. This difficulty had already driven Lutzow to despair. He had discussed it repeatedly with me, and every time he missed his run-in, this most successful fighter commodore blamed his own inefficiency as a fighter pilot. Had there been any need for more confirmation as to the hopelessness of operations with the ME-262 by bomber pilots, our experiences would have sufficed.

But now there was no time for such considerations. We were flying in an almost opposite direction to the Marauder formation. Each second meant that we were 300 yards nearer. I will not say that I fought this action ideally, but I led my formation to a fairly favorable firing position. Safety catch off the gun and rocket switch! As usual in a dogfight, I was tense and excited: I forgot to release the second safety catch for the rockets. They did

302

not go off. I was in the best firing position, I had aimed accurately and pressed my thumb flat on the release button — with no result. Maddening for any fighter pilot! Anyhow my four 3-cm cannons were working. They had much more firing power than we had been used to so far. At that moment, close below me, Schallnoser, the jet-rammer, whizzed past. In ramming he made no distinction between friend or foe.

This engagement had lasted only a fraction of a second — a very important second to be sure. One Marauder of the last string was on fire and exploded. Now I attacked another bomber in the van of the formation. It was heavily hit as I passed very close above it. During this breakthrough I got a few minor hits from the defensive fire. But now I wanted to know definitely what was happening to the second bomber I had hit. I was not quite clear if it had crashed. So far I had not noticed any fighter escort.

Above the formation I had attacked last, I banked steeply to the left, and at this moment it happened: a hail of fire enveloped me. A Mustang had caught me napping. A sharp rap hit my right knee. The instrument panel with its indispensable instruments was shattered. The right engine was also hit. Its metal covering worked loose in the wind and was partly carried away. Now the left engine was hit too. I could hardly hold her in the air.

In this embarrassing situation I had only one wish: to get out of this crate, which now apparently was only good for dying in. But then I was paralyzed by the terror of being shot while parachuting down. Experience had taught us that we jet-fighter pilots had to reckon on this. I soon discovered that my battered ME-262 could be steered again after some adjustments. After a dive through the layer of cloud I saw the *Autobahn* below me; ahead of me lay Munich and to the left Riem. In a few seconds I was over the airfield. It was remarkably quiet and dead below. Having regained my self-confidence, I gave the customary wing wobble and started banking to come in. One engine did not react at all to the throttle. I could not reduce it. Just before the edge of the airfield I therefore had to cut out both engines. A long trail of smoke drifted behind me. Only at this moment I noticed that Thunderbolts in a low-level attack were giving our airfield the works. Now I had no choice. I had not heard the warnings of our ground post because my wireless had faded out when I was hit. There remained only one thing to do: straight down into the fireworks! Touching down, I realized that the tire of my nosewheel was flat. It rattled horribly as the earth again received me at a speed of 150 m.p.h. on the small landing strip.

Brake! Brake! The kite would not stop! But at last I was out of the kite and into the nearest bomb crater. There were plenty of them on our runways. Bombs and rockets exploded all around; bursts of shells from the

American and British prisoners released from Stalag Villa at Landshut, Germany, wait to board planes that will ferry them on the first leg of their trip back home.

An ME-262 jet-propelled aircraft at rest on a German airfield. The first German jet captured intact, it was flown over allied lines and surrendered by its pilot.

Thunderbolts whistled and banged. A new low-level attack. Out of the fastest fighter in the world into a bomb crater, that was an unutterably wretched feeling. Through all the fireworks an armored tractor came rushing across to me. It pulled up sharply close by. One of our mechanics. Quickly I got in behind him. He turned and raced off on the shortest route away from the airfield. In silence I slapped him on the shoulder. He understood better what I wanted to say than any words about the unity between flying and ground personnel could have expressed.

The other pilots who took part in this operation were directed to neighboring airfields or came into Riem after the attack. We reported five certain kills without loss to ourselves.

I had to go to Munich to a hospital for treatment of my scratched knee. The X-ray showed two splinters in the kneecap. It was put in plaster. A fine business!

The enemy, advancing from the north, had already crossed the Danube at several places. The JV-44 prepared its last transfer. Bar, who had come to us with the remnants of his Volksfighter test commando, took over the command in my place. About 60 jet fighters flew to Salzburg. Orders came from the *Reichskanzlei* and from the Luftwaffe Staff in Berchtesgaden for an immediate transfer to Prague in order to pursue from there the completely hopeless fight for Berlin. The execution of this order was delayed until it became purposeless.

On May 3, the aircraft of the JV-44 were standing on the aerodrome of Salzburg without any camouflage. American fighters circled overhead. They did not shoot, they did not drop any bombs; they obviously hoped soon to be flying the German jet fighters that had given them so much trouble. Salzburg prepared for the capitulation. The advanced units of Devers' army approached the town. As the rattle of the first tank was heard on the airfield, there was no other possibility left: our jet fighters went up in flames.

While German technology was developing the jet fighter in the late 1930s, Hitler's rocket and missile scientists at Peenemunde were experimenting with jet-propelled pilotless aircraft and supersonic rockets — the V-weapons — that could be ready as a military weapon in numbers by 1942.

In 1939, however, Adolph Hitler canceled the Peenemunde priority, relegating it to a low status of weapon development. Preoccupied with building his Panzer divisions and a Luftwaffe geared solely to support of those divisions for quick success in the field, Hitler would hear none of the pleas of his rocket experts.

It was four years later, as the Allied Combined Bomber Offensive got underway in May, 1943, that the German Dictator reversed his decision and gave the missile scientists the go-ahead to build the weapons. But again it was the story of too late. Great technical difficulties still had to be solved. When the V-weapons were finally ready, Allied air power had built up sufficiently to meet the threat and successfully cope with it.

Here is the story of the air campaign against the weapon that could have reversed the course of the war.

Guided Missiles Could
Have Won

Joseph Warner Angell

ALARMING underground reports of long-range "secret weapons," designed by the Germans to bombard England from Continental areas, reached the British with increasing frequency throughout the spring of 1943. Responding to the threat of new weapons, that might, if used in time, turn the course of the war, British Intelligence discovered that the disturbing rumors were founded on fact. In a vast and hitherto secret experimental station at Peenemunde, on the Baltic coast, the Germans were perfecting revolutionary weapons: the V-1, a jet-propelled pilotless aircraft, and the V-2, a gigantic supersonic rocket against which there could be no defenses, once it was airborne. And on the Channel coast of France huge labor forces were feverishly constructing a great chain of V-weapon launching sites.

Knowing that the new weapons must be stopped, the British decided to make the first attack on the more likely target — Peenemunde. The raid was planned with utmost care and secrecy, with Air Chief Marshal Sir Arthur Harris of the RAF Bomber Command in personal charge of preparations.

Late in the evening of August 17, 1943 — a day already made memorable by the Regensburg-Schweinfurt mission of the American Eighth Air Force — and in the brilliant light of a full moon, a great fleet of RAF heavy bombers began the long run to the Baltic coast. The thousands of airmen aloft over Germany were unaware of the actual nature of the Peenemunde installation. Fearful that revelation of the truth about Peenemunde would reach the public and arouse alarm and despondency in the homeland, Harris had briefed his men that they must be prepared to accept 50 per cent losses.

The attack against Peenemunde began shortly after midnight, and at the time appeared to be enormously successful. There is, however, wide and perhaps irreconcilable variance in final estimates of the success of the attack. The British and Germans at first regarded Peenemunde as "completely gone." Col. Walter Dornberger, who headed the German V-2 installation and who was talking with his brilliant rocket technician, Wernher von Braun, in the Officers Club when the first alarm sounded, now takes credit for having seen, after the first shock of the raid, that damage to key installations was negligible; and for ordering, therefore, a hasty setting of fires and a blowing up of roads and unimportant buildings so that British strike-photos,

taken on the following day, would give evidence of greater destruction than was actually accomplished.

In any case, there were two important consequences of the August raid. The Germans were given full warning that massive efforts would be made to prevent or disrupt the use of their new weapons, and they proceeded to disperse V-weapon production activity from Peenemunde.

Ten days after the raid on Peenemunde the Eighth Air Force sent out its first "Crossbow" (the Allied code name for all matters, particularly air counter-measures operations, pertaining to the German V weapons) mission — an attack by B-17s on the German construction at Watten on the French coast. The extreme ends of the secret weapons axis, in so far as it was visible to the Allies, had thus been hammered by Allied air power in the opening blows of the "Crossbow" campaign. But continued aerial reconnaissance revealed new constructions of colossal size, seven in all, four in the Pas-de-Calais and three on the tip of the Cherbourg peninsula.

Discovery of a second type of German construction on the French coast was made late in October. In response to reports from ground agents in the Pas-de-Calais, a close photographic cover of the area around a heavily wooded hamlet revealed a series of concrete structures, the largest of which were two curiously shaped buildings, each nearly 300 feet in length, resembling gigantic skis laid on edge. By

An air reconnaissance photograph of a German V-1 "Buzz Bomb" site under construction in France.

A drawing of a typical V-1 flying bomb ski launching site.

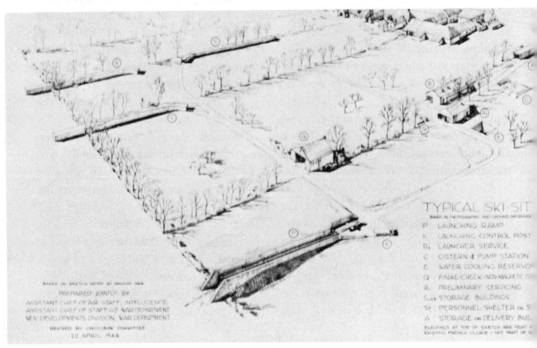

TYPICAL SKI SIT[E]

BASED ON PHOTOGRAPHIC AND GROUND INFORMATION

P   LAUNCHING RAMP
K   LAUNCHING CONTROL POST
D₁   LAUNCHER SERVICE
C   CISTERN & PUMP STATION
E   WATER COOLING RESERVOI[R]
Q   FINAL CHECK (NON-MAGNETIC CO[...])
R   PRELIMINARY SERVICING
S₁₀ STORAGE BUILDINGS
SH   PERSONNEL SHELTER or S[...]
A   STORAGE or DELIVERY BUIL[DING]

BUILDINGS AT TOP OF SKETCH ARE PART O[F]
EXISTING FRENCH VILLAGE - NOT PART OF S[...]

BASED ON SKETCH DATED 30 JANUARY 1944
PREPARED JOINTLY BY
ASSISTANT CHIEF OF AIR STAFF, INTELLIGENCE
ASSISTANT CHIEF OF STAFF G2 WAR DEPARTMENT
NEW DEVELOPMENTS DIVISION, WAR DEPARTMENT
REVISED BY CROSSBOW COMMITTEE
22 APRIL 1944

the middle of November, 21 "ski sites" had been identified.

As Allied reconnaissance of the French coast continued with unremitting effort, a significant relationship between the ski sites became apparent: the alignment of all the ski sites in the Pas-de-Calais indicated an orientation directly on London. It was impossible for British Intelligence to escape the conclusion that the closely integrated and rapidly growing network of installations, including the seven large sites, was to be used for some type of concentrated long-range attack against the world's most populous city — and the heart of the staging area for the forthcoming invasion of the Continent. It was not until Christmas Eve, 1943, that the Eighth Air Force struck its first great blow against the vast chain of ski sites.

Operation 164, the largest Eighth Air Force operation to date, put more than 1300 American aircraft over the ski site network. The crews were told only that they were attacking "special military installations" of critical importance, but the outside world learned for the first time of the new German threat. Bold headlines in American newspapers announced that U.S. and British fliers had hit the "Rocket Gun Coast," and editorial writers spoke of the possibility that the Germans had at last created their long-sought and "ultimate" diversion of Allied plans. Allied authorites continued to be silent on the significance of the Christmas Eve mission, but in London and Washington there were prolonged and intense discussions on the importance of the "Crossbow" threat and on the scale and type of effort necessary to preserve the safety of England and ensure that the forthcoming invasion of Europe would not have to be postponed or disrupted.

In February, ground agents had reported the appearance of a new type of site, apparently designed to launch the "Peenemunde projectiles." Designated "Modified Sites," these were very simple constructions as compared with the ski sites. They could be quickly built, easily camouflaged, and because of their small size were very poor targets. For the third time, the entire French coast was subjected to a "total" reconnaissance, which revealed an alarming number of the new type of sites. The Germans, meanwhile, continued to employ thousands of workers repairing bombed large sites and ski sites — whether in a desperate attempt to prepare them for use or as a means of drawing Allied bombs from targets in Germany, the Allies did not know.

A few weeks before D-Day, Eisenhower ruled that for such time as it would require the heavy bombers to strike a final blow against the large sites and ski sites, "Crossbow" would have priority over all other air operations.

The modified sites would, for the time being, be left alone. And whatever Hitler might, or might not, have up his sleeve, "Overlord" would begin on the day appointed.

In May, the big bombers pounded "Crossbow" sites for the last time before D-Day, and returned to their primary task of giving the final pre-invasion punch. On the morning of June 6, "Overlord" began. At the end of the first day's operations, Allied Forces had crossed the Channel and were holding the beachhead they had won that morning. And as the long last minute of D-Day passed into history, the great network of "Crossbow" sites — strung out along the French coast for hundreds of miles — remained shrouded in silence.

For six days after the launching of "Overlord," the "Crossbow" areas in the Pas-de-Calais and on the tip of the Cherbourg peninsula were quiet. No Allied aircraft bombed "Crossbow" targets, for the vast network of ski sites lay in ruins and the seven large sites were visibly shattered.

The tense days of anxiety and alarm over the "Crossbow" threat to the safety of England and the execution of "Overlord" appeared to be over. But on the night of June 12, 1944, the silence of the Pas-de-Calais was broken. Cataputed from the steel rails of a modified site launching ramp, hidden near a farmhouse on the French coast, the first German secret weapon fired in combat began it noisy, fiery journey to London. Four V-1s, or "flying bombs," struck London that night. During the next few days, German "Crossbow" batteries remained inoperative.

And then, on the night of June 15, there began an entirely new phase of the war in Europe — the Battle of the Flying Bomb. In little more than 24 hours the Germans fired nearly 300 V-1s against England. Clearly "Crossbow" was not a hoax.

Early in the morning of the 16th, as V-1s continued to strike London, Churchill assembled his entire War Cabinet, together with Air Chief Marshal Tedder, Field Marshal Brooke, chief of the British Imperial Staff, and others who were to have a voice in one of the war's fateful decisions. Though little was known about the number and capabilities of the modified sites, it was agreed that London would have to withstand whatever was in store for it — the Battle of France was to remain the primary concern of the Allies. Nevertheless, Gen. Eisenhower would be asked to take all possible measures to neutralize "Crossbow" sites, and long-standing plans for the deployment of balloons, fighter aircraft, and radar-controlled anti-aircraft against the flying bombs would be put into effect at once by the Air Defense of Great Britain.

Gen. Eisenhower's response was swift. On his orders, a comprehensive plan was drafted for the bombing of "Crossbow" sites by units of the American Eighth and Ninth Air Forces and by the RAF Bomber Command.

At once fleets of RAF heavies struck against the "Crossbow" network, principally the large sites, from which, it was presumed, the giant rockets would be launched. Having withstood the best efforts of "conventional" 2-ton bombs, the huge installations were soon being pounded by the British with their monstrous new "Tallboy" bombs, 12,000-pounders. The American Eighth struck repeatedly at the supposedly "neutralized" ski sites and other targets presumably related to the firing of V-1s. But for all the combined efforts of Allied air power — efforts that in July and August cost the Allies one-fourth of all their combat sorties and one-fifth of all their tonnage — the flying bombs still continued to rise in only slightly diminished numbers from their launching ramps' hidden along the coast of France. (The number of flying bombs that actually reached their targets in England was, toward the end of the summer, greatly reduced by new techniques of defense against air-borne V-1s.)

Meanwhile, it had been absolutely verified that the V-2 was in mass production. And against this weapon, which traveled far in advance of the speed of sound, there could be no defense, once it was airborne. Only by stopping the rockets at their firing sites or at production and transportation centers could the Allies prevent Hitler from using his now actual wonder weapon. The Eighth, therefore, struck Peenemunde repeatedly and with outstanding success. The RAF sent fleets of bombers to V-2 production centers deep in Germany, and from its bases in the Mediterranean the Fifteenth Air Force joined in the attack.

While pursuing their effort to prevent, or diminish, Hitler's use of the V-2, the Allies learned two facts about the highly-touted weapon that gave a kind of negative hope. For one thing, several of the large sites had been captured when Allied troops drove the Germans from the Cherbourg peninsula. The American air commander, Lt. Gen. Louis H. Brereton, toured these monstrous enemy installations late in June. Though he estimated the Cherbourg sites to be only half-finished — a reassuring finding — Gen. Brereton described them as "more extensive than any concrete construction we have in the United States, with the possible exception of Boulder Dam or similar waterway projects." The second negative reassurance came from the examination of a V-2 that had misfired at Peenemunde and landed, virtually intact, in Sweden. It was regarded by Allied scientists and technicians as a marvelous mechanism technically, but it was apparent that the V-2's warhead — barring use of a revolutionary explosive — was no greater than that of the simpler and less costly V-1.

However, if Hitler had vast quantities of V-2s, he could, the experts said, blow London off the map. The Allies therefore prepared a bombing plan, to be used when rocket firings commenced, that would require their entire bombing forces, in order to demolish in one great blow more than 250 V-2 targets in Germany, Holland,

The Eighth Air Force in its early days was under the brilliant leadership of Maj. Gen. Ira Eaker. He is seen here in a casual moment discussing air strategy while strolling on the lawn of RAF Air Chief Marshal Sir Arthur Harris' estate. Left to right are General H. H. Arnold, the Commanding General of the U.S. Army Air Forces, Chief Marshal Harris and General Eaker.

Belgium, and France. Simultaneously, plans were drawn for a mass evacuation of London.

The last V-1 fired from a launching site in France struck England on the afternoon of September 1, 1944. Allied ground troops, advancing rapidly up the French coast, had forced the flying bomb firing units to withdraw northward into Holland. Thereafter, the greatly reduced numbers of flying bombs that hit England were fired from Heinkel IIIs equipped to air-launch V-1s or from ground sites in Holland.

On the day the last V-1 was fired from France, British civil defense authorities halted their planning of precautionary measures against V-2 attack. On September 3, all operational air commands in the European Theatre were ordered to suspend every type of "Crossbow" operation pending further notice. Three days later, on the assumption that there would shortly be no further danger from either ground-launched V-1s or the still silent V-2, all Allied bombing attacks against "Crossbow" targets were canceled, except for occasional strikes against airfields that might be used for the air-launchings of V-1s. On September 7, a member of the British War Cabinet announced to the press that the "Battle of London" was over, except "possibly . . . a few last shots." As had been the case during the week following D-Day, the "Crossbow" danger appeared to be over.

But the cycle was to repeat itself, for at the dinner hour on the evening of September 8, the first of more than 1000 12-ton V-2 rockets that were to strike England fell soundlessly and exploded in a London suburb. Six seconds later a second V-2 struck another suburb. That same day the Germans fired several of their giant rockets against Paris.

But spectacular as was the scientific achievement apparent in the V-2, the weapon had been committed to battle too late, its military effectiveness was more limited than had been anticipated, and reliable intelligence reports indicated that the Germans had not produced sufficient quantities of the weapon to make it a long-continuing danger of great significance. Moreover, the steadily advancing Allied ground troops would, in time, deny Hitler the use of both V-2 factories and firing sites. This combination of evidence, all quickly evaluated in the Allied deliberations on the morning of September 9, led to the decision, and it proved to be a sound one, that only limited measures should be taken to meet the "Crossbow" threat in its third and penultimate phase.

The final phase of the Allied "Crossbow" campaign involved a series of discussions in December, 1944, and January, 1945, regarding the policy to be adopted following intelligence reports that the Germans were preparing to use a third V-weapon, variously designated the V-3, V-4, and the "final weapon." Early in December, American agents in Argentina and Turkey reported that "reliable sources" had revealed the Germans would, within 30 days, begin bombardment of American cities on the Atlantic seaboard with stratospheric rockets capable of demolishing 40 square kilometers around the point of impact. After painstaking investigations, the War Department and AAF Headquarters in Washington concluded that while such rockets and warheads might be in the experimental stage in Germany, it could be assumed that they were not ready for use in combat. In Europe, Gen. Spaatz came to a similar conclusion. And thus ended the Allied discussion of policy concerning the German V-weapons.

After September 8, 1944, the Germans fired some 1100 V-2s against England, as well as some 8000 V-1s fired between June and September of 1944. Against Continental targets, principally Antwerp, they concentrated a heavy fire of V-1s and V-2s. Belgium suffered far greater damage, proportionately, than did England. In both countries, the loss of life and destruction of property was appalling, considering the essentially limited numbers of V-weapons fired by the Germans.

Although only about 2500 V-1s and fewer than 100 V-2s exploded in England, nearly 10,000 British civilians were killed and some 25,000 were seriously injured. More than 200,000 buildings (principally dwellings) were totally destroyed or damaged beyond repair; 1,339,000 buildings, less seriously damaged, required some type of repair. At least 4,500,000 British civilians were rendered homeless or to some degree inconvenienced. In the second week of September, following the cessation of the major V-1 offensive, a labor force of more than 60,000 — many of them drawn from the armed services — was engaged on repairs to buildings capable of reconstruction.

It is impossible to do more than speculate on what Germany might have done with its long-range weapons, notably the V-2, had they been produced in far greater numbers and been committed to combat in the earlier years of the war. Dornberger and von Braun had stated that the V-2 would have been ready for combat as early as 1942 if Hitler had not canceled Peenemunde's first priority in 1939. The A-10, or transatlantic rocket, could have been operational by 1946, Dornberger suggests, if work on it had continued after the outbreak of war. As to Germany's capacity to manufacture great quantities of the V-2, Willy Messerschmitt, Germany's outstanding aviation authority, is known to have informed Hitler that with an all-out effort at the proper time, German industry could have produced 100,000 V-2s per month.

Though the major responsibility for the German failure to use the V-2 must rest with Hitler, and to some extent with his advisers in the High Command, it cannot be denied that once Hitler decided — in May, 1943 — to use the weapon, there remained unforeseen technical difficulties that

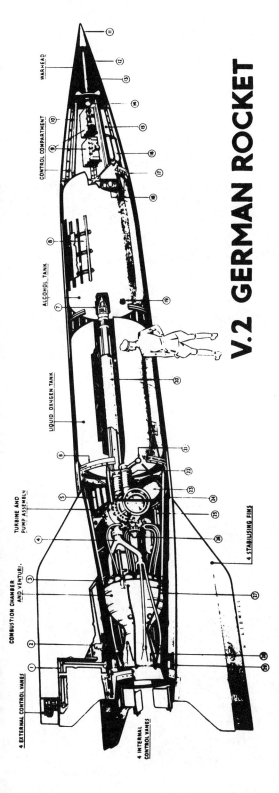

V.2 GERMAN ROCKET

1 CHAIN DRIVE TO EXTERNAL CONTROL VALVES.

2 ELECTRIC MOTOR.

3 BURNER CUPS.

4 ALCOHOL SUPPLY FROM PUMP.

5 AIR BOTTLES.

6 REAR JOINT RING AND STRONG POINT FOR TRANSPORT.

7 SERVO-OPERATE ALCOHOL OUTLET VALVE.

8 ROCKET SHELL CONSTRUCTION.

9 RADIO EQUIPMENT.

10 PIPE LEADING FROM ALCOHOL TANK TO WARHEAD.

11 NOSE PROBABLY FITTED WITH NOSE SWITCH OR OTHER DEVICE FOR OPERATING WARHEAD FUZE.

12 CONDUIT CARRYING WIRES TO NOSE OR WARHEAD.

13 CENTRAL EXPLORER TUBE.

14 ELECTRIC FUZE FOR WARHEAD.

15 PLYWOOD FRAME.

16 NITROGEN BOTTLES.

17 FRONT JOINT RING AND STRONG POINT FOR TRANSPORT.

18 PITCH AND AZIMUTH GYROS.

19 ALCOHOL FILLING POINT

20 DOUBLE WALLED ALCOHOL DELIVERY PIPE TO PUMP.

21 OXYGEN FILLING POINT.

22 CONCERTINA CONNECTIONS.

23 HYDROGEN PEROXIDE TANK.

24 TUBULAR FRAME HOLDING TURBINE AND PUMP ASSEMBLY.

25 PERMANGANATE TANK (GAS GENERATOR UNIT BEHIND THIS TANK).

26 OXYGEN DISTRIBUTOR FROM PUMP

27 ALCOHOL PIPES FOR SUBSIDIARY COOLING.

28 ALCOHOL INLET TO DOUBLE WALL.

29 ELECTRO HYDRAULIC SERVO MOTORS.

A schematic drawing of the German V-2 rocket.

Opposite, a German V-2 rocket being carried to its launching pad, then erected into position;
above, ready for firing, then on its way to a target.

317

had something to do with the failure to use the V-2 before D-Day, when it would have been more effective. Von Braun would have it that Hitler's belated decision was doubly wrong, in that he demanded the use of the weapon before it was technically ready.

In his last gigantic moments in the underground bunker in Berlin, with the thunder of Russian guns and British and American heavy bombs penetrating the buried recesses of steel and concrete, and with final knowledge that Allied tanks and foot soldiers were closing in from the East and West, it is not impossible that Adolf Hitler remembered certain words he had spoken to a German colonel of artillery two years earlier:

On that day in 1943, ten years after his first visit to the little rocket station at Kummersdorf, Hitler had summoned Dornberger and von Braun to his personal headquarters, to tell them that he might use the V-2 against England . . . in a moment of quiet, Hitler stared searchingly into Dornberger's eyes, and said:

If only I had had faith in you earlier! In all my life I have owed apologies to two people only — General Field Marshal von Brauchitsch, who repeatedly drew my attention to the importance of (the V-2) . . . for the future, and yourself. If we had had this rocket in 1939, we would never have had this war. Now and in the future, Europe and the world is too small for war . . . War will become unbearable for the human race.

UNITED STATES — BOMBERS

TYPE	DIMENSIONS	SPEED
Boeing B-17F Flying Fortress	Span: 103' 9" Length: 74' 9" Height: 19' 1"	Max: 299 mph at 25,000 ft. Cruise: 162 mph Svc. Ceiling: 35,000 ft.
Douglas A-20G Havoc	Span: 61' 4" Length: 48' Height: 17' 7"	Max: 339 mph at 12,000 ft. Cruise: 272 mph Svc. Ceiling: 25,800 ft.
Consolidated B-24H Liberator	Span: 110' Length: 67' 2" Height: 18'	Max. 313 mph at 25,000 ft. Cruise: 215 mph Svc. Ceiling: 28,000 ft.
North American B-25G Mitchell	Span: 67' 7" Length: 51' Height: 15' 9"	Max: 281 mph at 15,000 ft. Cruise: 200 mph Svc. Ceiling: 25,000 ft.
Martin B-26G Marauder	Span: 71' Length: 56' 1" Height: 20' 4"	Max: 277 mph at 10,000 ft. Cruise: 225 mph Svc. Ceiling: 20,000 ft.
Lockheed A-29 Hudson	Span: 65' 6" Length: 44' 4" Height: 11' 10½"	Max. 250 mph at 12,500 ft. Cruise: 190 mph Svc. Ceiling: 24,500 ft.
Douglas A-26 Invader	Span: 70' Length: 50' Height: 18' 6"	Max. 373 mph at 10,000 ft. Cruise: 280 mph Svc. Ceiling: 22,100 ft.

UNITED STATES — FIGHTERS, FIGHTER-BOMBERS

TYPE	DIMENSIONS	SPEED
Lockheed P-38H Lightning	Span: 52' Length: 37' 10" Height: 9' 10"	Max: 402 mph at 25,000 ft. Cruise: 300 mph Rate of Climb: 20,000 ft. in 8.5 mins.
Bell P-39Q Airacobra	Span: 34' Length: 30' 2" Height: 12' 5"	Max: 399 mph at 9,700 ft. Cruise: 213 mph Rate of Climb: 15,000 ft. in 3.8 min.
Curtiss P-40K Kittyhawk III	Span: 37' 4" Length: 33' 4" Height: 12' 4"	Max: 362 mph at 15,000 ft. Cruise: 290 mph Rate of Climb: 15,000 ft. in 7.5 min.

BOMB LOAD	POWERPLANT	ARMAMENT	RANGE
17,600 lbs. — Short Range 4,000 lbs. — normal	Four Wright Cyclone R-1820, 1,200 h.p. each, radial	Thirteen .50 cal. machine guns	Max: 3,600 mi. Combat: 2,100 mi. with 4,000 lbs.
2,000 lbs. internal 2,000 external	Two Wright Dble. Cyclone R-2600, 1,600 h.p. each, radial	Nine .50 cal. machine guns	Max: 1,090 mi. Combat: 525 mi. with 2,400 lbs.
12,800 lbs. max. 5,000 lbs. normal	Four Pratt and Whitney, R-1830, 1,200 h.p. each, radial	Ten .50 cal. machine guns	Max: 3,700 mi. Combat: 2,100 mi. with 5,000 lbs.
4,000 lbs. max. 3,000 lbs. normal	Two Wright Cyclone R-2600, 1,700 h.p. each, radial	Thirteen—Eighteen .50 cal. machine guns One 75 mm (Attack model)	Max: 2,400 mi. Combat: 1,560 mi. with 3,000 lbs.
4,000 lbs. normal	Two Pratt and Whitney R-2800, 2,000 h.p. each, radial	Eleven .50 cal. machine guns	Max: 2,400 mi. Combat: 1,300 mi. with 3,000 lbs.
1,400 lbs.	Two Wright Cyclone R-1820, 1,200 h.p. each, radial	Six .50 cal. machine guns	Max: 2,160 mi. Combat: 700 mi. with 1,400 lbs.
4,000 lbs.	Two Pratt and Whitney R-2800, 2,000 h.p. each, radial	Eight .50 cal. machine guns Fourteen 5″ Rockets	Max: 3,200 mi. Combat: 1,400 mi. with 4,000 lbs.

BOMB LOAD	POWERPLANT	ARMAMENT	RANGE
4,000 lbs. or Ten-5″ rockets	Two Allison V-1710, 1,425 h.p. each, inline	One 20 mm, four .50 cal.	2,400 mi. with Ext. tanks Combat: 350 mi.
500 lbs.	One Allison V-1710, 1,150 h.p., inline	One 37 mm (prop hub), two .50 cal., four .30 cal.	1,595 mi. ferry 750 mi. with 500 lb. bomb
Three-500 lb.	One Allison V-1710, 1,325 h.p., inline	Six .50 cal. wing guns	1,600 mi. or 350 mi. with 500 lb. bomb

TYPE	DIMENSIONS	SPEED
Republic P-47N Thunderbolt	Span: 42' 7" Length: 36' 1" Height: 14' 8"	Max: 467 mph at 32,500 ft. Cruise: 300 mph Rate of Climb: 25,000 ft. in 14.2 min.
North American P-51H Mustang	Span: 37' Length: 33' 4" Height: 13' 8"	Max: 487 mph at 25,000 ft. Cruise: 380 mph Rate of Climb: 30,000 ft. in 12.5 min.
Northrop P-61B Black Widow	Span: 66' Length: 49' 7" Height: 14' 8"	Max: 366 mph at 20,000 ft. Cruise: 235 mph Rate of Climb: 25,000 ft. in 14.8 min.

UNITED STATES — TRANSPORTS

TYPE	DIMENSIONS	SPEED
Douglas C-47 Skytrain Goony Bird	Span: 95' Length: 64' 5½" Height: 16' 11"	Max: 230 mph at 9,000 ft. Cruise: 155 mph Svc. Ceiling: 29,000 ft.
Curtiss-Wright C-46 Commando	Span: 108' 1" Length: 76' 4" Height: 21' 9"	Max: 265 mph at 13,000 ft. Cruise: 160 mph Svc. Ceiling: 25,000 ft.
Douglas C-54 Skymaster	Span: 117' 6" Length: 93' 10" Height: 27' 6"	Max: 275 mph at 14,000 ft. Cruise: 185 mph Svc. Ceiling: 30,000 ft.
Lockheed C-56 Lodestar	Span: 65' 6" Length: 49' 10" Height: 11' 10½"	Max: 251 mph at 7,500 ft. Cruise: 180 mph Svc. Ceiling: 23,400 ft.
Lockheed C-69 Constellation	Span: 123' Length: 94' 11" Height: 23' 8"	Max: 340 mph at 16,000 ft. Cruise: 255 mph Svc. Ceiling: 30,000 ft.
Boeing C-75 Stratoliner	Span: 107' 3" Length: 74' 4" Height: 20' 9½"	Max: 250 mph at 16,400 ft. Cruise: 190 mph Svc. Ceiling: 24,000 ft.
Consolidated C-87 Liberator	Span: 110' Length: 67' 2" Height: 18'	Max: 300 mph at 25,000 ft. Cruise: 191 mph Svc. Ceiling: 30,000 ft.

UNITED STATES — GLIDERS

TYPE	DIMENSIONS	SPEED
Waco CG-4A	Span: 83' 8" Length: 48' 8"	Max: 180 mph Norm: 150 mph Min: 38 mph
Waco CG-13A	Span: 85' 7"	Max: 190 mph

BOMB LOAD	POWERPLANT	ARMAMENT	RANGE
Three-1000 lb. or Ten-5″ rockets	One Pratt and Whitney R-2800, 2,800 h.p., radial	Eight .50 cal. wing guns	2,200 mi. or 800 mi. with 2,000 lb.
Two-1,000 lb. or Ten-5″ rockets	One Packard V-1650, 1,380 h.p., inline	Six .50 cal. wing guns	2,400 mi. or 850 mi. with 1,000 lb.
4,000 lbs.	Two Pratt and Whitney R-2800, 2,000 h.p. each, radial	Four 20 mm cannon	3,000 mi.—ferry 1,050 mi.—combat

CAPACITY	POWERPLANT	RANGE	CREW
Max: 10,000 lb. Norm: 7,500 lb. 21 troops	Two Pratt and Whitney R-1830, 1,200 h.p. each, radial	Max: 2,125 mi. Normal: 1,350 mi.	4-5
15,000 lbs. or 50 troops	Two Pratt and Whitney R-2800, 2,000 h.p. each, radial	Normal: 1,600 mi.	5
Max: 32,000 lbs. Norm: 14,000 lbs. or 50 troops	Four Pratt and Whitney R-2000, 1,450 h.p. each, radial	Max: 3,500 mi. Normal: 2,540 mi.	5-6
5,000 lbs. or 18 troops	Two Wright Cyclone R-1820, 1,200 h.p. each, radial	1,600 mi.	3-4
32,000 lbs. or 60 troops	Four Wright Cyclone R-3350, 2,200 t.o. h.p. each, radial	2,000 mi. with 20,000 lbs.	7-9
33 troops	Four Wright Cyclone R-1820, 1,100 h.p. each, radial	2,340 mi.	5-6
10,000 lbs. or 38 troops	Four Pratt and Whitney R-1830, 1,200 h.p. each, radial	Max: 3,300 mi. Normal: 1,400 mi.	4-5

CAPACITY	CREW
4,000 lbs. or 15 troops	2
8,000 lbs. or 42 troops	2

GREAT BRITAIN — BOMBERS

TYPE	DIMENSIONS	SPEED
DeHavilland Mosquito XVI	Span: 54' 2" Length: 40' 6" Height: 12' 6"	Max: 408 mph at 26,000 ft. Cruise: 300 mph Svc. Ceiling: 37,000 ft.
Vickers Wellington III	Span: 86' 2" Length: 64' 7" Height: 17' 5"	Max: 260 mph at 10,500 ft. Cruise: 180 mph Svc. Ceiling: 19,000 ft.
Handley Page Hampden	Span: 69' 2" Length: 53' 7" Height: 14' 11"	Max: 265 mph at 15,500 ft. Cruise: 215 mph Svc. Ceiling: 22,700 ft.
Armstrong Whitley V	Span: 84' Length: 72' 6" Height: 15'	Max: 230 mph at 18,000 ft. Cruise: 185 mph Svc. Ceiling: 24,000 ft.
Handley Page Halifax III	Span: 104' Length: 71' 7" Height: 21' 7"	Max: 282 mph at 13,500 ft. Cruise: 215 mph Svc. Ceiling: 24,000 ft.
Short Stirling III	Span: 99' 1" Length: 87' 3" Height: 22' 9"	Max: 260 mph at 10,500 ft. Cruise: 200 mph Svc. Ceiling: 20,500 ft.
Avro Lancaster III	Span: 102' Length: 69' 4" Height: 20'	Max: 270 mph at 19,000 ft. Cruise: 210 mph Svc. Ceiling: 21,500 ft.
Avro Lincoln II	Span: 120' Length: 78' 3½" Height: 17' 3½"	Max: 300 mph
Bristol Blenheim I	Span: 56' 4" Length: 39' 9" Height: 9' 10"	Max: 285 mph at 15,000 ft. Cruise: 220 mph Svc. Ceiling: 27,280 ft.

GREAT BRITAIN — FIGHTERS

TYPE	DIMENSIONS	SPEED
Blackburn B-37 Firebrand	Span: 51' 3½" Length: 39' 1" Height: 15' 2"	Max: 350 mph at 13,000 ft. Cruise: 256 mph Rate of Climb: 2,600 fpm (i)
Boulton Paul Defiant II	Span: 39' 4" Length: 35' 4" Height: 11' 4"	Max: 313 mph at 19,000 ft. Cruise: 259 mph Rate of Climb: 15,750 ft. in 8.5 min.

BOMB LOAD	POWERPLANT	ARMAMENT	RANGE
4,000 lbs.	Two Rolls Royce Merlin 73, 1,290 h.p. each, inline	Four 20 mm, four .303 some models	1,870 mi. with 1,000 lbs. 1,370 mi. with 4,000 lbs.
6,000 lbs.	Two Bristol Hercules XI, 1,370 h.p. each, radial	Six .303	Max: 2,120 mi. 1,325 mi. with 4,500 lbs.
4,000 lbs.	Two Bristol Pegasus, 1,000 h.p. each, radial	Four .303	Max: 1,990 mi. 870 mi. with 4,000 lbs.
7,000 lbs.	Two Rolls Royce Merlin X, 1,130 h.p. each, inline	Five .303	Max: 2,400 mi. 1,650 mi. with 7,000 lbs.
14,500 lbs.	Four Bristol Hercules XVI, 1,650 h.p. each, radial	Nine .303	3,000 mi.
14,000 lbs.	Four Bristol Hercules XI, 1,585 h.p. each, radial	Eight .303	Max: 2,330 mi. 740 mi. with 14,000 lbs.
22,000 lbs.- special modification 14,000 lbs.- normal max.	Four Packard Merlin 28, 1,390 h.p. each, inline	Eight .303	Max: 2,230 mi. with 7,000 lbs. 1,160 mi. with 14,000 lbs.
18,000 lbs. w/o modification	Four Packard Merlin 100, 1,650 h.p. each, inline	Two 20 mm, four .50 cal.	3,600 mi.
2,000 lbs.	Two Bristol Mercury, 905 h.p. each, radial	Five .303	1,460 mi.

BOMB LOAD	POWERPLANT	ARMAMENT	RANGE
Two-1,000 lb. or One-1,850 lb. torpedo	Bristol Centaurus IX, 2,500 h.p., radial	Four 20 mm	1,250 mi. with torpedo and aux. tanks 745 mi. with torpedo
	Rolls Royce Merlin XX, 1,260 h.p., inline	Four .303 in power turret	750 mi.

TYPE	DIMENSIONS	SPEED
Bristol Beaufighter X	Span: 57' 10" Length: 41' 4" Height: 15' 10"	Max: 330 mph at 14,000 ft. Cruise: 249 mph Rate of Climb: 1,850 fpm (i)
DeHavilland Mosquito XIX	Span: 54' 2" Length: 41' 2" Height: 15' 3"	Max: 378 mph at 13,200 ft. Cruise: 300 mph Rate of Climb: 2,700 fpm (i)

(i) initial rate

Gloster Gladiator Biplane	Span: 32' 3" Length: 27' 5" Height: 10' 4"	Max: 253 mph at 14,500 ft. Cruise: 212 mph at 15,500 ft. Rate of Climb: 20,000 ft. in 9 min.
Hawker Hurricane IIB	Span: 40' Length: 32' 3" Height: 13' 1½"	Max: 340 mph at 21,000 ft. Cruise: 307 mph Rate of Climb: 20,000 ft. in 7.5 min.
Hawker Typhoon	Span: 41' 7" Length: 31' 11" Height: 15' 3½"	Max: 405 mph at 18,000 ft. Cruise: 254 mph Rate of Climb: 15,000 ft. in 6.2 min.
Hawker Tempest V	Span: 41' Length: 33' 8" Height: 16' 1"	Max: 435 mph at 17,000 ft. Cruise: 351 mph Rate of Climb: 20,000 ft. in 6.1 min.
Vickers-Supermarine Spitfire IXE	Span: 36' 10" Length: 31' 4" Height: 12' 7¼"	Max: 416 mph at 27,500 ft. Cruise: 322 mph Rate of Climb: 20,000 ft. in 6.4 min.

GREAT BRITAIN — TRANSPORTS

TYPE	DIMENSIONS	SPEED
Armstrong-Whitworth Albemarle IV	Span: 77' Length: 59' 11" Height: 15' 7"	Max: 250 mph at 10,500 ft. Cruise: 180 mph Svc. Ceiling: 22,500 ft.
Avro York	Span: 102' Length: 78' Height: 20'	Max: 290 mph
Short Stirling	Development of the bomber for Troop Carrier Operations	
Vickers-Armstrong Warwick	Development of the bomber for Transport Operations	

BOMB LOAD	POWERPLANT	ARMAMENT	RANGE
2,200 lbs.	Two Bristol Hercules XVII, 1,725 h.p. each, t.o., radial	Four 20 mm, six .303, one .303 flexible	Max: 1,750 mi. Nor: 1,400 mi.
2,000 lbs.	Two Rolls Royce Merlin 25, 1,620 h.p. each t.o., inline	Four 20 mm	1,905 mi. with external tank 1,400 mi. w/o tanks
	Bristol Mercury IX, 840 h.p., radial	Four .303	410 mi.
1,000 lbs. or Eight rockets	Rolls Royce Merlin XX, 1,280 h.p. t.o., inline	Twelve .303	985 mi. with external tanks 480 mi. w/o tanks
Two-1,000 lb. bombs, or Eight-60 lb. rockets	Napier-Sabre, 2,200 h.p., inline	Four 20 mm or twelve .303	1,000 mi. with ext. tanks 610 mi. w/o tanks
2,000 lb. bombs or Eight-60 lb. rockets	Napier Sabre IIB, 2,420 h.p., inline	Four 20 mm	1,300 mi. or 820 mi.
750 lbs.	Rolls Royce Merlin 70, 1,710 h.p., inline	Two 20 mm, two .50 cal.	980 mi. with ext. tanks 430 mi. w/o tanks

CAPACITY	POWERPLANT	ARMAMENT	RANGE
4,000 lbs. or 10 troops	Two Bristol Hercules XI, 1,590 h.p. each, radial	none	1,350 mi.
50-56 troops	Four Rolls Royce Merlin 24, 1,620 h.p. each, inline	none	Max: 3,100 mi. 1,000 mi. with 50-56 troops

GREAT BRITAIN — GLIDERS

TYPE	DIMENSIONS	SPEED
Airspeed Horsa	Span: 88' Length: 67' Height: 21'	150 mph
G.A.L. Hamilcar	Span: 110' Length: 68' Height: 20' 3"	Diving: 187 mph Max. Tow: 150 mph Stall: 65 mph

FRANCE — FIGHTERS

TYPE	DIMENSIONS	SPEED
Bloch MB-152	Span: 34' 7" Length: 29' 10" Height: 13'	Max: 320 mph at 13,000 ft. Cruise: 220 mph Rate of Climb: 16,000 ft. in 6 min.
Dewoitine 520	Span: 33' 6" Length: 28' 9" Height: 8' 5"	Max: 330 mph at 22,000 ft. Cruise: 248 mph Rate of Climb: 13,000 ft. in 4 min.
Morane-Saulnier M.S. 406	Span: 34' 10" Length: 26' 9" Height: 9' 4"	Max: 305 mph at 16,000 ft. Cruise: 218 mph Rate of Climb: 16,400 ft. in 6 min.
Potez 631	Span: 52' 6" Length: 36' 4" Height: 11' 10"	Max: 280 mph at 13,000 ft. Cruise: 198 mph Rate of Climb: 13,100 ft. in 9 min.

SOVIET UNION — BOMBERS

TYPE	DIMENSIONS	SPEED
Iliuchin (Ilyushin) D.B. 3-F Med. Bmr.	Span: 70' 2" Length: 47' 6"	Max: 265 mph Cruise: 175 mph Svc. Ceiling: 28,000 ft.
Ilyushin IL-4 Med. Bmr.	Span: 70' 2" Length: 47' 6"	Max: 265 mph at 20,000 ft. Cruise: 185 mph Svc. Ceiling: 29,520 ft.
Tupolev SB-2bis Med. Bmr.	Span: 70' 6" Length: 41' 6"	Max: 279 mph Cruise: 217 mph Svc. Ceiling: 27,890 ft.
Tupolev Tu-2 Attack Bmr.	Span: 69' 10" Length: 45' 4"	Max: 357 mph at 12,000 ft. Cruise: 260 mph Svc. Ceiling: 36,000 ft.

30 troops

17,500 lbs.

BOMB LOAD	POWERPLANT	ARMAMENT	RANGE
	Gnome-Rhone, 1,100 h.p., radial	Two 20 mm, two 7.5 mm	400 mi.
	Hispano-Suiza, 1,000 h.p., inline	One 20 mm, four 7.5 mm.	950 mi.
	Hispano-Suiza, 860 h.p., inline	One 20 mm, two 7.5 mm	500 mi.
	Two Gnome-Rhone, 660 h.p. each, radial	Two 20 mm, six 7.5 mm, two 7.5 mm flexible mount	650 mi.

BOMB LOAD	POWERPLANT	ARMAMENT	RANGE
4,400 lbs.	Two M-88, 1,100 h.p. each, radial	Four 7.62 mm	2,500 mi.
5,950 lbs.	Two M-82, 1,600 h.p. each, radial	Four 12.7 mm	2,550 mi. 1,025 mi. with 5,950 lbs.
1,320 lbs.	Two M-103, 990 h.p. each, inline	Four 7.62 mm	1,430 mi. 500 mi. with 1,320 lbs.
5,000 lbs.	Two Shvetsov-ASh-82, 1,850 h.p. each, radial	Two 23 mm, five 12.7 mm	1,500 mi.

SOVIET UNION — BOMBERS (Continued)

TYPE	DIMENSIONS	SPEED
Tupolev TB-7 or PE-8 Hvy. Bmr.	Span: 131' 3" Length: 80' 6"	Max: 274 mph at 25,000 ft. Cruise: 165 mph Svc. Ceiling: 33,000 ft.

SOVIET UNION — FIGHTERS

TYPE	DIMENSIONS	SPEED
Ilyushin IL-2 Stormovik Ftr. Bomber	Span: 47' 10" Length: 38' Height: 10' 9"	Max: 280 mph at 13,120 ft. Cruise: 185 mph
Lavochin (Lavochkin) La-5	Span: 32' 2" Length: 27' 11" Height: 9' 3"	Max: 370 mph at 16,400 ft. Cruise: 250 mph Rate of Climb: 16,400 ft. in 5 min.
Petlyakov Pe-2 Ftr., attack, recon.	Span: 56' 3" Length: 41' 6"	Max: 335 mph at 16,400 ft. Cruise: 226 mph Svc. Ceiling: 29,520 ft.
Yakovlev 9P	Span: 32' 10" Length: 28' ½" Height: 8'	Max: 358 mph at 13,000 ft. Cruise: 245 mph Rate of Climb: 16,400 ft. in 4 min.

SOVIET UNION — TRANSPORTS

TYPE	DIMENSIONS	SPEED
Lisunov Li-2 (also P-84) DC-3 prewar license	Span: 95' Length: 64' 5½" Height: 16' 11"	Max: 225 mph Cruise: 155 mph Svc. Ceiling: 29,000 ft.
Tupolev ANT-6	Span: 132' 10½"	Max: 155 mph Cruise: 115 mph

SOVIET UNION — GLIDERS

TYPE	DIMENSIONS
Antonov A-7	Span: 62' 3" Length: 37' 9"

BOMB LOAD	POWERPLANT	ARMAMENT	RANGE
8,800 lbs.	Four AM-38, 1,300 h.p. each, inline	Two 20 mm, two 12.7 mm, two 7.62 mm	2,500 mi. with 4,400 lbs.

BOMB LOAD	POWERPLANT	ARMAMENT	RANGE
880 lbs. or Eight-56 lb. rockets	One AM-38F, 1,600 h.p., inline	Two 23 mm, two 12.7 mm, one 12.7 mm flexible	750 mi.
440 lbs.	One Shvetsov M-82FN, 1,640 h.p., radial	Two 20 mm	510 mi.
2,200 lbs.	Two Klimov VK-105R, 1,100 h.p. each, inline	One 12.7 mm, four 7.62 mm	1,200 mi.
500 lbs.	One Klimov M-105 PF, 1,260 h.p., inline	One 37 mm, one 12.7 mm	516 mi.

CAPACITY	POWERPLANT	ARMAMENT	RANGE
10,000 lbs. max. or 7,500 lbs. norm. or 21 troops	Two Schvetsov ASh-621, 1,000 h.p. each, radial	Four 7.62 mm	Max: 2,000 mi. Normal: 1,300 mi.
4,400 lbs. or 30 paratroops	Four AM-34, 830 h.p. each, inline		

GERMANY — BOMBERS

TYPE	DIMENSIONS	SPEED
Focke-Wulf Fw 200c Kurier	Span: 76' 11½" Length: 107' 9½" Height: 20' 8"	Max: 224 mph at 15,750 ft. Cruise: 172 mph Svc. Ceiling: 19,000 ft.
Dornier Do 217	Span: 62' 4" Length: 55' 9" Height: 16' 4"	Max: 348 mph at 18,700 ft. Cruise: 254 mph Svc. Ceiling: 30,000 ft.
Heinkel He 111	Span: 74' 1½" Length: 54' 5½" Height: 13' 9"	Max: 258 mph at 16,400 ft. Cruise: 212 mph Svc. Ceiling: 25,500 ft.
Heinkel He 177	Span: 103' 4" Length: 67' 3" Height: 21'	Max: 303 mph at 20,000 ft. Cruise: 215 mph Svc. Ceiling: 26,500 ft.
Junkers Ju-87 Stuka	Span: 45' 4" Length: 36' 6" Height: 12' 9"	Max: 210 mph at 16,000 ft. Cruise: 175 mph Svc. Ceiling: 24,500 ft.

GERMANY — FIGHTERS

TYPE	DIMENSIONS	SPEED
Focke-Wulf Fw-190	Span: 34' 6" Length: 29' 7" Height: 13'	Max: 408 mph at 20,600 ft. Cruise: 296 mph Rate of Climb: 20,000 ft. in 9.1 min.
Messerschmitt Bf-109	Span: 32' 6½" Length: 29' 4" Height: 8' 6"	Max: 452 mph at 19,685 ft. Cruise: 310 mph Rate of Climb: 16,400 ft. in 3 min.
Messerschmitt Bf 110	Span: 53' 5" Length: 41' 7" Height: 13' 1"	Max: 342 mph at 22,900 ft. Cruise: 200 mph Rate of Climb: 18,000 ft. in 7.9 min.
Messerschmitt Me 163B Komet	Span: 30' 7" Length: 18' 8" Height: 9'	Max: 596 mph at 30,000 ft. Rate of Climb: 30,000 ft. in 2.6 min.
Messerschmitt Me 262 Sturmvogel	Span: 40' 11½" Length: 34' 9½" Height: 12' 7"	Max: 540 mph at 19,700 ft. Rate of Climb: 3,937 fpm (initial)
Messerschmitt Me 410	Span: 53' 9" Length: 41' 1" Height: 14'	Max: 390 mph at 22,000 ft. Cruise: 310 mph Rate of Climb: 22,000 ft. in 10.8 min.

BOMB LOAD	POWERPLANT	ARMAMENT	RANGE
4,620 lbs.	Four BMW Bramo, 1,200 h.p. each, radial	One 20 mm, three 13 mm, two 7.9 mm	2,210 mi.
5,500 lbs.-internal 1,000 lbs.-external	Two BMW, 1,600 h.p. each, radial	One 20 mm, one 15 mm, two 7.92 mm	1,500 mi. with 5,500 lbs.
5,600 lbs.	Two Junkers Jumo, 1,340 h.p. each, inline	Two 20 mm, one 13 mm, four 7.92 mm	2,640 mi. 760 mi. with 4,400 lbs.
14,000 lbs.	Two DB 610 (2 engines each), 3,000 h.p. each pr., inline	Two 20 mm, three 13 mm, three 7.92 mm	3,417 mi. 1,100 mi. with 4,500 lbs.
3,960 lbs.-short range 2,200 lbs.-normal	One Junkers Jumo, 1,300 h.p., inline	Two 7.92 mm wings, two 7.92 mm flexible	1,200 mi. 620 mi. with 3,960 lbs.

BOMB LOAD	POWERPLANT	ARMAMENT	RANGE
1,100 lbs.	BMW 801, 1,700 t.o. h.p., radial	Four 20 mm, two 13 mm	525 mi.
1,200 lbs.	Daimler Benz 605, 1,500 h.p., inline	One 30 mm, two 15 mm	440 mi.
2,000 lbs.	Two Daimler Benz, 1,475 h.p. each, inline	Two 30 mm, two 20 mm, two 7.92 mm flexible	1,305 mi. 735 mi. with 2,000 lbs.
None	One Walter HWK rocket motor, 3,750 lbs. thrust	Two 30 mm cannon	
1,100 lbs.	Two Junkers Jumo, 1,980 lbs. thrust each	Four 30 mm cannon, twenty-four 50 mm rockets	652 mi. at 30,000 ft. 230 mi. at sea level
2,200 lbs. internal	Two Daimler Benz 603A, 1,750 h.p. each, inline	Four 20 mm, two 13 mm rear firing, two 7.9 mm	1,405 mi.

333

GERMANY — TRANSPORTS

TYPE	DIMENSIONS	SPEED
Focke-Wulf Fw200b Condor	Span: 108′ 3″ Length: 78′ 3″ Height: 20′	Max: 252 mph Cruise: 226 mph Svc. Ceiling: 23,600 ft.
Junkers Ju-52	Span: 95′ 11″ Length: 62′ Height: 14′ 10″	Max: 165 mph at sea level Cruise: 132 mph Svc. Ceiling: 20,000 ft.
Junkers Ju-290	Span: 138′ Length: 92′ 6″	Max: 243 mph at 18,000 ft. Cruise: 185 mph Svc. Ceiling: 19,700 ft.
Messerschmitt Me 323	Span: 181′ Length: 93′ 4″ Height: 23′ 3″	Max: 136 mph at sea level Cruise: 110 mph

GERMANY — GLIDERS

TYPE	DIMENSIONS	SPEED
DFS-230A		
Gotha Go 242	Span: 79′ Length: 52′ 6″	
Messerschmitt Me 321	Span: 181′	

ITALY — BOMBERS

TYPE	DIMENSIONS	SPEED
Breda 88 "Lince" (Lynx)	Span: 50′ 10″ Length: 37′ 9″	Max: 310 mph at 13,120 ft. Cruise: 185 mph Svc. Ceiling: 28,500 ft.
Cant Z 1007 "Alcione" (Kingfisher)	Span: 81′ 4″ Length: 60′ 4″ Height: 17′	Max: 280 mph at 15,000 ft. Cruise: 175 mph Svc. Ceiling: 26,500 ft.
Fiat B.R. 20 "Cigogna" (Stork)	Span: 70′ 6″ Length: 52′ 10″ Height: 14′ 1″	Max: 268 mph at 16,400 ft. Cruise: 180 mph Svc. Ceiling: 25,000 ft.
Piaggio P. 108B	Span: 108′ 3″ Length: 81′ 6″	Max: 250 mph at 13,120 ft. Cruise: 165 mph Svc. Ceiling: 26,000 ft.
Savoia-Marchetti SM. 79 ˙ Sparviero (Hawk)	Span: 66′ 3″ Length: 53′ 2″ Height: 13′ 6″	Max: 230 mph at 13,120 ft. Cruise: 165 mph Svc. Ceiling: 24,600 ft.

CAPACITY	POWERPLANT	ARMAMENT	RANGE
30 troops	Four BMW 132, 870 h.p. each, radial	Two 20 mm, two 13 mm	930 mi.
18 troops	Three BMW, 660 h.p. each, radial	Four 7.9 mm	800 mi.
18,700 lbs. or 40 troops	Four BMW, 1,600 h.p. each, radial	Three 20 mm, six 7.9 mm	Max: 3,785 mi. 2,490 mi. with 17,600 lbs.
18 tons or 130 troops	Six Gnome-Rhone, 990 h.p. each, radial	Eighteen 7.9 mm	500 mi.

CAPACITY
10 troops
5,300 lbs. or 25 troops
40,000 lbs. or 120 troops

BOMB LOAD	POWERPLANT	ARMAMENT	RANGE
2,200 lbs.	Two Piaggio XI, 1,000 h.p. each, radial	Three 12.7 mm, two 7.7 mm, one 7.7 mm flexible	Max: 1,450 mi. Norm: 900 mi.
2,600 lbs.	Three Piaggio XI, 1,000 h.p. each, radial	Two 12.7 mm, two 7.7 mm	800 mi.
2,600 lbs.	Two Fiat A.80, 1,000 h.p. each, radial	One 12.7 mm, two 7.7 mm	1,150 mi.
4,100 lbs.	Four Piaggio P.XII, 1,000 h.p. each, radial	Four 12.7 mm	2,500 mi.
7,770 lbs.	Three Alfa-Romeo 126, 750 h.p. each, radial	Four 7.7 mm	Max: 1,860 mi. 1,000 mi. with 2,640 lbs.

ITALY — FIGHTERS

TYPE	DIMENSIONS	SPEED
Breda 65	Span: 39' 8" Length: 31' 6" Height: 10' 11"	Max: 267 mph at 16,400 ft. Cruise: 195 mph Rate of Climb: 19,700 ft. in 11.5 min.
Capronia CA. 331B Raffica (Squall)	Span: 53' 10" Length: 38' 6½"	Max: 315 mph at 17,000 ft. Cruise: 200 mph Rate of Climb: 13,120 ft. in 9.3 min.
Fiat C.R. 42 Falco Biplane	Span: 31' 10" Length: 27' 3" Height: 10' 10"	Max: 265 mph at 13,000 ft. Cruise: 185 mph Rate of Climb: 16,400 ft. in 7 min.
Fiat G. 50	Span: 36' 1" Length: 27' 2" Height: 9' 2"	Max: 295 mph at 16,400 ft. Cruise: 178 mph Rate of Climb: 16,400 ft. in 8 min.
Fiat G. 55 Centauro	Span: 38' 10½" Length: 30' 9" Height: 10' 3"	Max: 385 mph at 23,000 ft. Cruise: 300 mph Rate of Climb: 26,250 ft. in 10.1 min.
Macchi C. 200 Saetta	Span: 34' 8½" Length: 26' 10" Height: 11' 6"	Max: 310 mph at 15,000 ft. Cruise: 250 mph Rate of Climb: 16,400 ft. in 6 min.
Machhi C. 202 Folgore	Span: 34' 8½" Length: 29' Height: 10'	Max: 370 mph at 16,400 ft. Cruise: 300 mph Rate of Climb: 19,685 ft. in 6 min.

ITALY — TRANSPORT

TYPE	DIMENSIONS	SPEED
Savoia-Marchetti S.M. 75 Marsupiale	Span: 97' 5" Length: 73' 10" Height: 17' 8"	Max: 230 mph at 13,120 ft. Cruise: 160 mph Svc. Ceiling: 24,600 ft.

BOMB LOAD	POWERPLANT	ARMAMENT	RANGE
1,800 lbs.	One Fiat A.80, 1,000 h.p., radial	Four 7.7 mm	682 mi.
2,640 lbs.	Two Isotta-Fraschini, 840 h.p. each, radial	Six 20 mm, two 12.7 mm flexible	1,125 mi.
440 lbs.	One Fiat A.74, 840 h.p., radial	Two 12.7 mm	630 mi.
300 lbs. internal	One Fiat A.74, 840 h.p., radial	Two 12.7 mm, two 7.7 mm	420 mi.
2,000 lbs.	One Fiat, 1,475 h.p., inline	Three 20 mm, two 12.7 mm	1,025 mi.
700 lbs.	One Alfa-Romeo R.A., 1,000, 1,175 h.p., inline	Two 12.7 mm, two 7.7 mm	475 mi.
700 lbs.	One Fiat A.74, 870 h.p., radial	Two 12.7 mm	540 mi.

CAPACITY	POWERPLANT	ARMAMENT	RANGE
7,700 lbs.	Three Alfa-Romeo 126, 750 h.p. each, radial		1,860 mi.

Index